We'd like to tell you that these movies aren't really terrible—but they are, Blanche, they are! Turn on your VCR and fasten your seatbelts for such cinematic gems as these:

The Adventurers (1970)

This smorgasbord—based on the Harold Robbins bestseller—offers kinks for everyone: Orgies! Drugs! Miscarriages! Lesbianism! High fashion! Thinly disguised characters based on real celebrities! A private torture chamber! And starring Jaclyn Smith as the overly bright *Teen* magazine reporter!

The Arrangement (1969)

"She's got a built-in crap detector," quips an ad man of screwed-up sex bomb Faye Dunaway in this whopper from Elia Kazan. No one perusing Dunaway's screen credits would make that claim, or what would she be doing here *and* in *Mommie Dearest*?

Queen Bee (1955)

From the moment Joan Crawford makes her grand entrance wearing just the gown a female impersonator would have chosen, it's clear why this is the movie most beloved by the star's fans as well as her detractors. And when she destroys a guest room with her riding crop while screaming, "You don't know the things they've made me do . . . and how ashamed I've been for it"—we understand exactly what she means.

BAD MOVIES WE Love

Movieline Magazine's Deliciously Trashy Tour Through More than 200 of Hollywood's Film Fiascos

EDWARD MARGULIES is an executive editor for the national film magazine *Movieline*. His entertainment articles have appeared in such publications as *Interview* and *L.A. Style*.

STEPHEN REBELLO reports on the entertainment business for *GQ*, *L.A. Style*, and *Movieline*, among others, and is the author of two other books. Both authors live in Los Angeles.

BAD MOVIES WE Love

■■■■■■■■■■■■■■■■■■■■■■■■

EDWARD MARGULIES **AND** STEPHEN REBELLO

With a Foreword by
Sharon Stone

A PLUME BOOK

PLUME
Published by the Penguin Group
Penguin Books USA Inc., 375 Hudson Street,
New York, New York 10014, U.S.A.
Penguin Books Ltd, 27 Wrights Lane,
London W8 5TZ, England
Penguin Books Australia Ltd, Ringwood,
Victoria, Australia
Penguin Books Canada Ltd, 10 Alcorn Avenue,
Toronto, Ontario, Canada M4V 3B2
Penguin Books (N.Z.) Ltd, 182–190 Wairau Road,
Auckland 10, New Zealand

Penguin Books Ltd, Registered Offices:
Harmondsworth, Middlesex, England

First published by Plume, an imprint of New American
Library, a division of Penguin Books USA Inc.

First Printing, August, 1993
10 9 8 7 6 5 4 3 2

LIBRARY OF CONGRESS CATALOGING IN PUBLICATION DATA
Margulies, Edward.
    Bad movies we love / Edward Margulies and Stephen Rebello ; with a
    foreword by Sharon Stone.
        p.   cm.
    Includes indexes.
    ISBN 0-452-27005-7
    1. Motion pictures—Reviews.   I. Rebello, Stephen.   II. Title.
PN1995.M2764   1993
791.43'75—dc20   92–42086
                                                           CIP

Printed in the United States of America
Set in Century Expanded
Designed by Leonard Telesca

Stephen Rebello dedicates this book to Lou, for the laughter.

Edward Margulies dedicates this book to Lillian, who gave him her sense of humor, and to Stan, who gave him his love of movies.

Acknowledgments

We were always secretly miffed when one of our role models, Frankie Fane (Stephen Boyd's ungrateful wretch of a character in *The Oscar*), didn't win the coveted gold statuette in the movie's finale. At least then we could have copped a few choice digs from his acceptance speech. Anyway, that only leaves us with an even more dubious role model, Neely O'Hara (the Show Biz Diva from Hell played to perfection by Patty Duke in *Valley of the Dolls*), to emulate, and she's too sincere for words when she wins her honorary Grammy. So, in her style—breathtakingly lifelike sincerity—we'd like to thank the many good souls who kept us in research materials, photographs, tapes, and spectacular dinners all the while we prepared this treatise.

First, for producing soul-shaking, life-changing movies that we so love—fabulous stills from which we were graciously permitted to sprinkle throughout the book—we salute Allied Artists, American-International, Columbia, David O. Selznick, the DeLaurentiis Entertainment Group, Disney, Hollywood Pictures, Howard Hughes, the Ladd Company, MCA, MGM, New Line, Paramount, Republic, RKO, Sony Pictures, Touchstone, Turner Entertainment, 20th Century-Fox, United Artists, Universal, and Warner Bros.

Our gratitude to Alfred P. Lowman for so enthusiastically and skillfully agenting us to Arnold Dolin, our ace editor and publisher, who actually paid us to have such a grand time.

For locating photographs and posters, we proffer sincere thanks to the staffs of the Margaret Herrick Library of the Academy of Motion Picture Arts and Sciences, the Allpoints Archive, the Edward Baer Collection, and to Collector's Book Store's own Mark Willoughby and Jake "Strider" Hughes.

A deep bow to Marvin Eisenman (known as "Marvin of the Movies"), who constantly warned us how impossible it would be to track down copies of the movies we wanted (no, *needed*) to see—then, found them for us anyway. Thanks, too, to Howard E. Green for his cheerful, first-class liaising.

For dinners, drinks, laughs, jibes, guidance, and constant reminders about how famous we were going to become, we could hardly ask for more from Lisa Margulies Chadwick, Millicent Craven, Roger Deakins and James Ellis, Howard and Amy Green, Lawrence Grobel, Andrew Harris, Todd Harris, Ferne Kadish, Kate Mantilini, Brandon Margulies, Lee and Linda Margulies, Stan Margulies, Melinda and Michael Miller, Joe Queenan, Arthur and Dorothy Rebello, Albert Sanchez, Emily Sears, Gary A. Smith, Venetia Stevenson, Sharon Stone, Janet Thomas, and Melissa Volpert. Hugs, kisses, and a wave to each and every one of you from that stretch limousine we're expecting to pick us up any second now. You've all helped to turn us into the impossibly spoiled despots we are today.

You'd be surprised (well, anyway, *we* were) just how many people "got it" and promptly suggested Bad Movies that made the final cut! Thanks for those, and oh so many other things, to Sue Cameron, Dick Clayton, David Elzer, Eve Golden, Doug Kelley, H. Lee Levine, Ellen Prague, Netta Shannon, Doug Taylor, Anne Thompson. Thanks, too, to John Cogswell. A nod, also, to Richard Natale for offering the observation—a very long time ago, indeed—that perhaps a column like the one that served as the springboard for this book might be, well, not a bad idea.

Many of the swell folks at *Movieline* magazine gave us a helping hand for which we're grateful, and while you know who you are, we thought we'd let everyone else know, too: Deborah Bauer, Lisa Bradley, Tom Cooney, Kevin Hennessey, The Hollywood Kids, Nancy Hopkins, Terry Loose, Joshua Mooney, Charles Oakley, Heidi Parker, and the gone-but-not-forgotten Christopher Hunt. Also, thanks to Siobhan Stofka. Of course, we couldn't have written one word without the assistance of Jasmine and Minerva Allpoints, as well as two more pals who'd prefer to be known here as Sport and Ace.

A very special thanks to Virginia Campbell who, as one of the executive editors at *Movieline*, kept us going with laughter, enthusiasm, and droll wisecracks, not to mention those out-there suggestions of a few films we might have otherwise overlooked.

Lastly, a very deep bow to Anne Volokh who, as publisher of *Movieline*, fosters our folie à deux and unfailingly encourages us to edge farther out on the precipice. She also, by the way, owns a knockout hat collection and knows how to throw one hell of a party.

Contents

Foreword by Sharon Stone   xv

Introduction   xvii

CHAPTER 1: The Breaking Point   1

Fatal Attraction ❤ The Fury ❤ The Hand That Rocks the Cradle ❤ Julie ❤ Looker ❤ Love Crimes ❤ Masquerade ❤ Midnight Lace ❤ Play Misty for Me ❤ Point Break ❤ Sleeping With the Enemy ❤ Tattoo

CHAPTER 2: Trash Yourself Cinema   18

Bad Influence ❤ Butterfield 8 ❤ The Fan ❤ Imitation of Life ❤ Love Has Many Faces ❤ Madame X ❤ Portrait in Black ❤ The Sandpiper ❤ The Star ❤ Too Much, Too Soon ❤ The V.I.P.s

CHAPTER 3: Slip Us a Mickey   33

Desperate Hours ❤ Harley Davidson and the Marlboro Man ❤ 9½ Weeks ❤ Wild Orchid

CHAPTER 4: What Will the Neighbors Say?   40

By Love Possessed ❤ The Chapman Report ❤ Desire Under the Elms ❤ The Long, Hot Summer ❤ Lucy Gallant ❤ No Down Payment ❤

Peyton Place ❤ Return to Peyton Place ❤ Ruby Gentry ❤ Strangers When We Meet ❤ The Stripper ❤ Two-Moon Junction

CHAPTER 5: Vanity, Thy Name Is Lucy   57

And God Created Woman ❤ Butterfly ❤ Communion ❤ The Game Is Over ❤ The Jazz Singer ❤ Mame ❤ Revenge ❤ Stella

CHAPTER 6: Viva las Divas   69

Another Man's Poison ❤ Autumn Leaves ❤ The Dark Mirror ❤ Dead Ringer ❤ Flamingo Road ❤ Female on the Beach ❤ Johnny Guitar ❤ Lady in a Cage ❤ Queen Bee

CHAPTER 7: A Gaggle of Starlets   82

The Best of Everything ❤ Change of Habit ❤ The Pleasure Seekers ❤ The Stepford Wives ❤ Three Coins in the Fountain ❤ Where the Boys Are ❤ Where the Boys Are '84

CHAPTER 8: All This, and Troy Donahue Too   92

Palm Springs Weekend ❤ Parrish ❤ Rome Adventure ❤ A Summer Place ❤ Susan Slade

CHAPTER 9: Bad Girls   100

Baby Face ❤ Back Street ❤ The Bitch ❤ Caged ❤ Duel in the Sun ❤ From the Terrace ❤ Go Naked in the World ❤ Half Moon Street ❤ Poison Ivy ❤ The Shanghai Gesture ❤ The Stud ❤ Sylvia ❤ Two Mules for Sister Sara ❤ Wild Orchid 2: Two Shades of Blue

CHAPTER 10: The Price of Fame   119

Beloved Infidel ❤ Harlow ❤ The Legend of Lylah Clare ❤ The Lonely Lady ❤ The Love Machine ❤ Mahogany ❤ Marjorie Morningstar ❤ Myra Breckinridge ❤ Slander ❤ Torch Song ❤ Trapeze

CHAPTER 11: The Stone Age   135

Action Jackson ❤ King Solomon's Mines ❤ Scissors ❤ Year of the Gun

CHAPTER 12: No, But I Saw the Book   141

Another Time, Another Place ❤ *Chanel Solitaire* ❤ *Claudelle Inglish*
❤ *Cocktail* ❤ *The Driver's Seat* ❤ *In the Cool of the Day* ❤ *Mandingo*
❤ *The Mephisto Waltz* ❤ *Walk on the Wide Side* ❤ *Youngblood
Hawke*

CHAPTER 13: Guess Who's Who   155

The Adventurers ❤ *The Arrangement* ❤ *The Carpetbaggers* ❤ *Eureka*
❤ *The Goddess* ❤ *The Greek Tycoon* ❤ *Once Is Not Enough* ❤
Where Love Has Gone ❤ *Written on the Wind*

CHAPTER 14: Bring On the Bimbos!   168

Bolero ❤ *Endless Love* ❤ *Flashdance* ❤ *Lipstick* ❤ *A Night in Heaven* ❤
Summer Lovers ❤ *Where Danger Lives*

CHAPTER 15: Overacting in Sensurround   178

Airport ❤ *Airport 1975* ❤ *Airport '77* ❤ *Avalanche* ❤ *The Cassandra
Crossing* ❤ *The Concorde—Airport '79* ❤ *Delta Force* ❤ *Earthquake* ❤
The Poseidon Adventure ❤ *The Swarm* ❤ *The Towering Inferno* ❤
When Time Ran Out . . .

CHAPTER 16: The Other Kind of "Disaster Movies"   196

Bluebeard ❤ *The Bride* ❤ *The Chase* ❤ *Exorcist II: The Heretic* ❤
Eyes of Laura Mars ❤ *Fear City* ❤ *52 Pick-Up* ❤ *Hanover Street* ❤ *Jet
Pilot* ❤ *King Kong Lives* ❤ *The Liberation of L. B. Jones* ❤ *No Mercy*
❤ *Orca* ❤ *Perfect* ❤ *Players* ❤ *Reflections in a Golden Eye* ❤
Revolution ❤ *Road House* ❤ *Siesta*

CHAPTER 17: Just What the Doctor Ordered   222

The Bramble Bush ❤ *The Caretakers* ❤ *Doctors' Wives*
❤ *Flatliners* ❤ *The Harrad Experiment* ❤ *The Interns* ❤ *Magnificent
Obsession* ❤ *Not as a Stranger* ❤ *Possessed*

CHAPTER 18: Bad Movies à Go-Go 235

The Grasshopper ❤ *The Happening* ❤ *R.P.M.* ❤ *Secret Ceremony* ❤
Skidoo ❤ *The Swinger* ❤ *The Thomas Crown Affair* ❤ *Wild in the
Streets* ❤ *X, Y, and Zee*

CHAPTER 19: Soap Gets in Your Eyes 248

Ada ❤ *All That Heaven Allows* ❤ *Ash Wednesday* ❤ *The Betsy* ❤
Diamond Head ❤ *Dying Young* ❤ *Last Rites* ❤ *The Last Time I Saw
Paris* ❤ *Love Story* ❤ *Monsignor* ❤ *The Other Side of Midnight* ❤ *The
Tarnished Angels*

CHAPTER 20: Slay It With Music 265

Great Balls of Fire! ❤ *Lost Horizon* ❤ *Purple Rain* ❤ *Satisfaction* ❤
Shout ❤ *Staying Alive* ❤ *Stepping Out* ❤ *Xanadu*

CHAPTER 21: The Hall of Shame 277

Beyond the Forest ❤ *Can't Stop the Music* ❤ *The Cobweb* ❤ *The
Fountainhead* ❤ *The Greatest Show on Earth* ❤ *Kitten With a Whip* ❤
Moment by Moment ❤ *Mommie Dearest* ❤ *The Oscar* ❤ *Sudden
Fear* ❤ *Valley of the Dolls* ❤ *Zandalee*

Selected Bibliography 295

Index 299

Index of Movie Titles 325

Foreword
by Sharon Stone

When these bad, bad men asked me if I'd write something about their book—in which I'd heard they had slammed me (along with practically everyone else in Hollywood, the big bad town we all love)—I said, "You're *not* kidding, are you, bad men?" and they said, "Oh no, my pretty, in fact you have your own *chapter!*"

Well, my big bad ego just couldn't resist looking into it. And look and laugh and titter and guffaw I did. Even at my own chapter—though not as much as some of the other chapters.

These guys really do love these "bad" movies, and I'm darn glad that they do. Because we try just as hard when we make a "bad" movie as when we make a "good" movie. After all, what makes a movie "good"? I'll tell you. It's "good" because you enjoy it, because it made you laugh (at it or with it) or scream or cry or howl or remember or forget or just simply to escape within it.

That's why I make them anyway, "good" or "bad."

So have some fun. Look inside these pages, rent a video, pop some popcorn, and laugh and love. And thanks for going to the movies.

Sharon Stone

Introduction

When people asked (and they did, they did) why we were writing a book-length celebration of Bad Movies, we gave it to them straight: "Because somebody was actually willing to pay us to watch, again, hundreds of movies we actually love and because no one before has ever done a book quite like it." Sure, gallons of ink have been spilled on celebrating such endearing Grade-Z horror and sci-fi stuff as *Plan 9 From Outer Space* and *Cat Women of the Moon*. However, as both of us are inveterate pop culture snobs, we weren't interested in writing about such low-budget stuff. And sure, other writers have assigned special places in the Bad Movie annals to such megabudget debacles as *Hudson Hawk* and *Ishtar*. Again, though, since both of us have years—years! —of experience in the journalistic and managerial areas of the entertainment business, we weren't interested in writing about those same old tired turkeys that are about as much fun for an audience as root canal. (More to the point, we weren't even willing to sit through those films again. We're crazy but not that crazy.)

Ask anyone who's been to their plex anytime recently and they'll tell you we live in a world polluted by Bad Movies. Occasionally, though, there are Bad Movies that separate themselves from the pack, special Bad Movies: those big-budget, big-star, big-director, aggressively publicized fiascos that have gone wonderfully, irredeemably, lovably haywire. We call them Bad Movies We Love. To rate a special place in our hearts and in this, our tome, not only did the movies have to be jaw-droppingly, astoundingly bad, they had to be fun bad—the kind of fun that means that, when you're wandering the aisles at the video store looking for a good time, if you're hip to these movies, you can't stop yourself from yanking them off the shelves; the kind of fun that means you guffaw when you see one of these movies even if (it happens all too often) you're surrounded by dolts who are actually sitting in polite silence, wondering whether or not Julia Roberts will be killed by her co-star; the kind of fun that means you've got friends who love 'em too—cool friends who will tell you about *another* one you mustn't miss. So, if you're curious why such notorious clunkers as *Days of Thunder, Heaven's Gate* and *Howard the Duck* aren't here, it's this simple: they're unlovable.

In fact, if there's one single factor that distinguishes the two hundred or so Bad Movies We Love splashed across these pages (and, believe us, experts with big hypodermics and restraints had to be called in to keep us from writing about hundreds more), it's that—despite the very best intentions of moviemakers who in the past have shown more than mere traces of talent—these flicks go way, way out there, to dementedly inspired places that few movies ever go.

To those die-hard, breathless movie buffs who would argue (we know they will) that, say, *Duel in the Sun* or *The Greatest Show on Earth* are great movies, we ask, "Have you seen them anytime lately?" To those moviemakers who offer proof that *The Hand That Rocks the Cradle, Fatal Attraction, Flatliners, The Sandpiper, Imitation of Life, Sleeping With the Enemy, Cocktail,* and their kin have earned profits in the zillions, insisting that zillions of moviegoers can't be wrong, we say, "Congratulations, you fooled 'em again."

In the life-altering process of actually watching all these movies again, we noticed that various Bad Movies present themes and motifs that surfaced repeatedly. That's why we've grouped the titles into chapters, rather than simply presenting them in A-to-Z order from start to finish. But don't worry, there are both title and general indexes at the back for reference purposes, and for purists, we haven't skimped on such can't-live-without-it nuggets of information as date of release, running time, availability on video and laserdisc, and producer/director/screenwriter credits. If you're anything like us, you'll already know how deeply important it is to seek out anything directed by, say, Delmer Daves, but we also hope to turn you on to the unsung charms of Ranald MacDougall, among many others. In fact, any time the clearly crazed handiwork of a master hairstylist, a gifted composer, or a mad costume designer has dazzled us with their worse-than-usual contributions, we note those credits too.

Alas, you won't find every Bad Movie We Love at your corner video and laserdisc store, but many of them are there, and these are noted at the end of each review with a "V" for video or an "L" for laserdisc. All films not so marked will turn up, sooner or later, on your own TV set, so don't overlook your local listings as a guideline to locate hard-to-find gems which you can tape for posterity. (This book couldn't have been written without the invaluable assistance of *TV Guide*.) Also, cable channels like TBS, TNT, and American Movie Classics are a treasure trove for Bad Movies We Love. Many of our favorites are available for rental by mail, and if that sort of thing interests you we suggest you contact a store like Eddie Brandt's Saturday Matinee for their yearly catalogue: 6310 Colfax Avenue, North Hollywood, CA 91606; (818) 506-4242. If all else fails—well, write your congressperson. What else have they got to do?

Where, you may wonder, did we ever get the idea for this mad book? Well, it all began with a mad column—also called "Bad Movies We Love" and also penned by us—in the mad monthly magazine *Movieline*. Over the past three years, the column has been growing steadily more popular. People send it flowers, priceless bijoux, and even the occasional indecent proposal—so we weren't surprised when the column itself suggested that it become a book. Who were we to stand in its way? More than 160 Bad Movies We Love were written expressly for this book. But a handful (well . . . okay, a *heaping* handful) of the films you'll find here first cropped up in the column:

Airport '75	*Kitten With a Whip*
And God Created Woman	*Mahogany*
The Best of Everything	*Mame*
Beyond the Forest	*Orca*

Butterfield 8
By Love Possessed
The Chapman Report
Can't Stop the Music
The Caretakers
Change of Habit
Claudelle Inglish
The Cobweb
Dead Ringer
Duel in the Sun
Female on the Beach
Go Naked in the World
The Goddess
The Happening
Harlow
The Jazz Singer

Parrish
The Pleasure Seekers
Portrait in Black
Rome Adventure
R.P.M.
The Sandpiper
Satisfaction
Skidoo
A Summer Place
The Swinger
Three Coins in the Fountain
Valley of the Dolls
Walk on the Wild Side
Wild in the Streets
Wild Orchid
Zandalee

Since writing those original pieces, we've viewed many of these forty titles yet again, and their charms have prompted us to embellish further on our first declarations of love.

So welcome, dear readers, to Bad Movies We Love Land, a place where no excess is too wretched. We've devised a system of rating these films: ❤ ❤ ❤ ❤ indicates that a film is so wretched and so lovable, you should get your hands on it right now; ❤ ❤ ❤ means you can't go wrong; ❤ ❤ indicates "proceed at your own risk"; ❤ means simply, you're on your own! If you love these movies as we do, we'd love to hear from you, especially with your suggestions for the Bad Movies *You* Love that you think belong in our next volume. We are easily swayed, and if you'll lend us —not give us, mind you—your copy of the Carol Lynley version of *Harlow*, the Lana Turner LSD epic *The Big Cube*, or the Sonny-directed Cher flick *Chastity*, we'll send you our autographed photo. Write us at *Movieline*, "Bad Movies We Love Suite," 1141 S. Beverly Drive, Los Angeles, CA 90035.

The Breaking Point

Terrific suspense movies like *Silence of the Lambs*, *Klute*, *The Conversation*, *Rear Window*, *Psycho*, and *North by Northwest* get us so worked up that—while our palms moisten, knuckles tighten, or we shudderingly watch through fingers clamped over our eyes—they practically tear questions from our throats. Like, for instance, Whodunit? When will they do it again? Why is she going up to the attic? Can't he see that guy hiding in the shadows? Why don't they call the cops? Don't they know there's a killer on the loose?

We're certain that the suspense movies in this chapter—all of them terrifically awful—will tear other kinds of questions from your throat. Like, for instance, How did these people think they'd get away with this? When does the suspense start? Where's Alfred Hitchcock when you need him? and, the most frequently asked question of all, Why am I watching this? We'll tell you why: because these flicks are simply too hilariously horrible for you to turn away.

Fatal Attraction (1987) ♥ ♥

For this unaccountable box office smash—call it "Play Misty for Me Again"—scores of actresses reportedly turned down the role of the hot-to-trot Manhattan psycho book editor who purrs at cheatin' married lawyer Michael Douglas, "Ever done it in an elevator?" Naturally, the part went to innately ladylike, highly controlled Glenn Close. Get past *that* casting implausibility—not to mention why anyone would find Douglas so ravishing or why

anyone talented would ever want to work for *9½ Weeks* director
Adrian Lyne—and you'll have no trouble buying Close madly
humping Douglas in her stainless steel sink as she smears her
breasts and his face with water. Douglas's missus, Anne Archer,
everyone's favorite studiedly sensual screen wife, conveniently
leaves town with their kid, allowing Close to romp with Douglas
in Central Park and act fascinated by his snooze-inducing monologue about how his cold father once comforted him at the opera
when *Madama Butterfly* terrified him.

Douglas must finally return to Archer, so Close slits her wrists.
Alas, he saves her life and, to thank him, she turns up at his office
in a full-length black leather coat, stammering, "This is terribly
embarrassing"—we heartily agree—and proffers tickets to *Madama Butterfly*. He declines, so Close stays home listening to
Puccini while switching a table lamp on and off (certainly our
favorite way of listening to operas) before telling Douglas that
she's preggers. "We're going to live with this for the rest of our
lives," Douglas counsels (meaning their baby, not the movie),
prompting Close to get wackier, blowing up his car (don't ask)
and making him tapes in which she confesses, "I feel you. I taste
you. I think you. I touch you."

Too bad she can't act him while she's at it, because, once
Douglas figures out that she's stealing the movie, he clenches his
teeth and pulls the hammiest faces this side of Mickey Rourke
when he tries killing her in retaliation for kidnapping his daughter
and hijacking her to—what a fiend!—an amusement park. Douglas, who gets no help from the cops but doesn't even bother to
lock the front door, gets sidelined when Close and Archer duke
it out, *Psycho*-style, in the bathroom. Though Close goes cross-
eyed when Douglas finally drowns her in the tub, she then leaps
out, to overact *even more* in the style that actually won her, along
with Archer, Lyne, *and the movie itself*, an Oscar nomination.
After this and the earlier *Jagged Edge*, Close looked in danger
of becoming the A-budget Jamie Lee Curtis of slasher flicks, but
she got out, well, almost in time.

The "director's cut" on home video offers an even sillier original
finale and a Norma Desmondesque Lyne sharing with his public
such riveting goodies as an *endless* audio tape he made of audi-

ences laughing and screaming while viewing his magnum opus. Talk about scary.

Produced by Stanley R. Jaffe and Sherry Lansing, directed by Lyne. Screenplay by James Dearden, based on his original screenplay for his earlier short film. C, 119 m., V, L

The Fury (1978) ❤ ❤

Listen up, now, for although this seems like an utterly incoherent, parapsychological thriller, in fact every plot point is carefully explained. Kirk Douglas and John Cassavetes both work for a government agency so secret that no one's ever heard of it, see, which is why Cassavetes has to kidnap Douglas's psychic son, Andrew Stevens, leaving Douglas for dead (only he's not) and— well, as Douglas says, "*Somebody's* gotta stop 'em." Got that? Stevens sends brain waves (but not acting lessons) to his psychic twin, Amy Irving, who's watching Carrie Snodgress demonstrate that when she's "in alpha" she can make model trains run, thereby making it clear that the potential for harnessing psychic powers is as limitless, say, as a filmmaker's imagination. Got that?

Why does classmate Hilary Thompson bleed when Irving touches her? Well, Irving's "power to psychometrize is spontaneous. Almost everyone exposed to it will bleed. Some will bleed a little, some will bleed a lot." Got that? (Too bad, then, that Irving didn't touch classmate Daryl Hannah, making her film debut, in order to save us all from prolonged exposure to Hannah's thespian efforts.) The "gifted" Irving transfers to the Paragon Institute, where Charles Durning blathers about "the bioplasmic universe. Occasionally, you make a connection between the timeless world and the physical world—you have what clairvoyants call a vision." Got that? (This might explain why other, more "gifted" actors had the "vision" to steer clear of this movie.)

Snodgress, who works at Paragon, is Douglas's girlfriend. When she tells him that the records indicate that Stevens is dead, Douglas explains that that means he's alive. Got that? He asks her to assist Irving's escape so she can lead him to Stevens. Irving is, in fact, having visions of Stevens being terrorized in unspeakable, inhuman ways—she sees that he's being made to watch, against his will, earlier scenes from this film—at the country estate of Fiona Lewis, who works for Cassavetes. Ah, it begins to make sense now, right? No?

"How's our boy wonder?" Cassavetes inquires, sporting a black glove, black arm sling, and matching black eyepatch. Some expert replies, "He's developing the power of an atomic reactor," but Lewis is much closer to the mark when she adds, "Or an atomic *bomb*." It all ends when Douglas and Irving race to the hideaway, but by then Stevens has levitated and whirled Lewis to death! Stevens dies, too, but not before transferring his evil soul into Irving. Cassavetes remarks to Irving—really Stevens, see?—"I hope you don't judge me too harshly. I don't say what I did was right or wrong. I only know that I acted"—*overacted* is the word we'd use—and she/he/they give the movie a big finish by, literally, exploding Cassavetes. If only someone had done the same to Brian DePalma before the movie was made.

Produced by Frank Yablans, directed by DePalma. Screenplay by John Ferris, from his novel. C, 118 m., V, L

The Hand That Rocks the Cradle (1992) ❤❤

"Don't fuck with me, retard," nasty psycho nanny Rebecca De Mornay hisses at slow-witted handyman Ernie Hudson who, like her, toils for Seattle's dullest yuppie couple in this crackpot hybrid of *The Nanny*, *Rebecca*, and *Fatal Attraction*. Ferret-featured De Mornay leaves no prop, no dialogue, no co-star unchewed while playing the widow of a gynecologist who committed suicide when accused of sexual impropriety.

Hired without a single reference to care for the tykes of Matt McCoy and Anabella Sciorra—the very couple whose testimony helped condemn De Mornay's husband—De Mornay wreaks ridiculous revenge. Acting demurely homey and selfless, she totally undercuts Sciorra by making a play for hubby and, worse, rewallpapering the nursery without asking permission. By contrast, whiny Sciorra's brittle bitch of a girlfriend complains that guys these days judge modern women to be failures unless they haul in "$50,000 a year and still make time for blowjobs and homemade lasagna." (A *woman* screenwriter penned those destined-to-be-immortal lines and, in the process, created a virulent new strain of Bad Movie: the feminist backlash schlocker.)

Happily for us, De Mornay grows tired of underplaying, and in a public bathroom stall, she bashes the restroom walls with a toilet plunger, overacting like fury. When the simpleton handyman accidentally spies her giving suck to the family infant, De Mornay in retaliation stashes a pair of Sciorra's daughter's panties in the handyman's repair wagon for horrified mommy to find. The shocked parents, natch, ship the poor guy back to the Home for Stock Disabled Characters. Sciorra's pal tries to warn her of De Mornay's true motives, and gets hers when the glass ceiling of a greenhouse slices her to ribbons. (Don't you just hate it when that happens?) Anyway, the cops in this movie don't bother to ask how it possibly could, so why should we?

While Sciorra's in the hospital with a bad case of jitters (and, certainly, a severe attack of career anxiety), De Mornay wears her clingiest nightie whenever the shirtless, rain-drenched McCoy's pecs need toweling off. Thrusting out her lips and breasts, De Mornay purrs, "That's all you need," but McCoy—unmistakably the invention of a woman writer—isn't having any, insisting "There's only one woman for me." Sciorra figures out De Mornay's game, and sends her packing. "Fine," De Mornay huffs, "I'll just go get my baby—I mean, my things—and be on my way."

But you know it ain't over yet. At one point, De Mornay declares, "I firmly believe what goes around, comes around." If that's true, whatever could De Mornay possibly have done to justify this bad a case of career karma? (The only real mystery here is: why did huge audiences swallow it whole?)

Produced by David Madden, directed by Curtis Hanson (who is to Hitchcock what Mountain Dew is to Moët). Screenplay by Amanda Silver. C, 105 m., V, L

Julie (1956) ❤ ❤

From the opening strains of its Academy Award–nominated (!) title tune to the finale when stewardess Doris Day is forced to land a pilotless passenger plane, *Julie* hits, and sustains, a pitch of all-out nuttiness.

After having found her first hubby dangling from a noose, Day weds Louis Jourdan, a raving lunatic of a concert pianist who—in the opening scene—jams down Day's foot on the accelerator pedal, sending their car careening around picturesque Monterey coast highway curves. After nearly killing them both, Jourdan murmurs, "Oh, Julie, I'm *so* sorry. So *desperately* sorry. Help me fight this thing." Is this "thing" a lack of talent? A decent script? No, jealousy that drives him batty if his wife so much as talks to other guys. Near her wit's end—Jourdan's piano compositions begin to sound suspiciously like the "Funeral March"—Day begins to catch on that the crackpot Frenchman killed her first husband and plans to do her in next. (Why must he drive Doris crazy before killing her, you wonder? So she can shred the scenery in an array of fabulous frocks, of course.)

"I know it was crazy," says Doris, in voice-over that suggests that her character moonlights writing Harlequin romances, "but I had the chilling sensation of being watched by Lyle. I could feel his presence. It was ominous. It was strangely disturbing." Apparently wising up ("All at once, I had the chilling urge to get out of the house—*fast!*"), she nevertheless takes her sweet time packing nice, tailored suits and toiletries while hubby skulks back toward the house looking wild-eyed. She escapes to San Francisco to begin anew, but Jourdan, getting nuttier by the second, torments her with phone calls: "Julie, you're going to die. You can't get away from me!" "Let's face it, honey," counsels Day's perky stewardess roommate, "you've been jittery as all get-out. What gives?" Understandably, Bad Movie aficionados thrill to the set piece when Jourdan runs amok on the plane, leaving Day alone at the controls to madly overact as she is guided from the ground by her macho flight crew: "Be casual. Everything depends upon it" and "Don't let that meter go lower than 120—you'll crash if you do!"

Eighteen years later, Karen Black in *Airport 1975* also found herself behind the joystick—and she lands the damned plane with an astigmatism. But *Julie* got there first and funniest. Trivia buffs, take note: *Julie* may hold the record for the number of times the microphone boom bobs into frame or casts a shadow.

(An accident? or part of Louis Jourdan's plan to drive us all crazy?)

With Barry Sullivan, Frank Lovejoy, Jack Kelly, Mae Marsh, Ann Robinson. Produced by Martin Melcher (then the real-life Mr. Day), directed and written by Andrew Stone, who later gave the world the 1972 remake of *The Great Waltz*. B&W, 97 m., TV

Looker (1981) ❤

Poor Albert Finney, many pounds and Bad Movies beyond his *Tom Jones* glory, got stranded playing the richest plastic surgeon in Beverly Hills, whose TV commercial model patients start becoming murder victims (disguised as suicides). His practice is booming, for women adore him—perhaps because he very noticeably omits jockey shorts from his wardrobe. Into his palatial offices for a post-surgical checkup comes flirty model Susan Dey, chirping, "You've made me perfect," and wondering aloud why he won't give her a tumble. But police investigator Dorian Harewood ruins Finney's day by probing the odd coincidence of two of his patients dying so violently. "Most L.A. girls OD on drugs," Harewood says offhandedly, "but those girls were destroyed beyond recognition." When another of Finney's gorgeous patients demands to be changed back—"I'm too perfect! They're killing all the girls that are perfect!"—the good doc drives to her apartment just in time to see her hurtle off a balcony, pursued by burly bruiser Tim Rossovich.

With Finney as the prime suspect and Dey the obvious next victim, the pair teams up and their trail leads to James Coburn and Leigh Taylor-Young, the very rich, very evil duo behind a company experimenting with replacing live actors with computer-generated images. Although the performances in this movie suggest the technology has long since been perfected, we watch with numbed disbelief as Finney and Dey penetrate Coburn's high-tech inner sanctum where mass audience mind control is being engineered through hidden messages conveyed in—oh, no!—TV commercials. "Fifteen years in prison is punishment," Coburn tells a group of well-heeled potential investors, "but fifteen years sitting in front of a television set is entertainment," forgetting to mention that fifteen *seconds* of this movie is living hell.

While the movie raves on and on about the evils of TV, we begin to notice that it's packed with "product placements"—which are, of course, just TV commercials worked into feature films—for everything from Shakey's Pizza to Fruit-of-the-Loom underwear. We watch one of Coburn's specially designed TV ads, to which someone responds, "Oh, those poor actors having to say lines like that." But Dey's zomboid performance elicits no pity, just mirth, as she falls under the sway of the commercials, droning, "I want it, I want it." Along the way, enjoy such other endearing absurdities as the rotund Finney shooting a slim security guard and slipping easily into his uniform, as well as an early appearance by computer-generated Vanna White playing one of Coburn's models. If *Looker* could kill, these careers would be dead.

Produced by Howard Jeffrey, directed by Michael Crichton. Screenplay by Crichton. Music by Barry DeVorzon. C, 94 m., V, L

Love Crimes (1992) ❤

You gotta hand it to Sean Young, who puts her offscreen notoriety—James Woods publicly accused her of a *Fatal Attraction*-type obsession with him—front and center by merely starring in a movie called *Love Crimes*. Investigators wondering why D.A. Young's been obsessed with Patrick Bergin—who, as a photographer, cons women into hilariously unspeakable depravities—offer two possibilities: "She's very irresponsible" or "She's out of her mind." Exactly.

With a haircut that makes her resemble Robert Downey Jr., Young is frustrated but fascinated by Bergin's women who, though he's made them get down on all fours and spew obscenities while he shoots Polaroids, won't press charges. "I know I'm an inconsiderate bitch," Young tells her pal Arnetia Walker in their gym's locker-room, "but I do it to make you look good." But, unlike earlier Young flicks, there's no one on hand to make her look good, especially in an unflattering bubble hairdo she wears to pick up Bergin. As he ties her to her bed, Bergin whispers, "You can always tell what a woman's like by her shoes."

She follows him to his cabin, where he locks her in a closet and says, through the door, "Does this give you a thrill? Did you wet your panties just a little?" Later, Bergin springs Young, handcuffs her to a couch and asks, "What were you afraid I'd do? What were you afraid I *wouldn't* do?" Some of the hootiest dialogue ever occurs when Bergin, cutting fish, asks his hostage, "Do you know there are fish in the North Atlantic, a species of ray, that have genitals just like that of a woman's? It's a well-known fact that sailors and fishermen often have sex with them." Young's response? She exposes her breasts, and screeches, "You want me to perform for you? You want me to act free and wild? You want me to dance naked? You want me to be scared of you? You want me to freak out?" Then, smearing fish blood and guts on her face, she bellows, "Am I fucked-up enough for you?" (We'll say! but there's more.) She confesses, "I hate the feeling of a man inside me. Do I have orgasms? Never." Then she tries to kill him with a butcher knife, so Bergin spanks her, bathes her, and takes Polaroids of her in the nude.

All this psychosexual game-playing unleashes Young's fantasies—about her childhood, about sex with Bergin, about other people we've never seen before in this movie having sex—then (eventually) she tries to run Bergin in and he sings her a song which, the credits point out, is called "Yodelling in the Valley," written and performed by Bergin. The credits suggest there's *no end* to his talents: "Polaroids by Patrick Bergin."

Produced by Rudy Langlais and Lizzie Borden. Directed by Borden. Screenplay by Allan Moyle and Laurie Frank. C, 97 m., V, L

Masquerade (1988) ❤ ❤

Some perverse soul cast Rob Lowe as a shady, studly yachtsman who beds rich babes—in particular, the Hamptons' richest, simpiest heiress, Meg Tilly. Basted in bronzer, lit like a *GQ* model, and smiling insipidly when described as a "two-dollar gigolo," Rob teaches poor little rich Meg about the perils of sex, murder, and lavishing red Ferraris on scuzzballs. She soon quits playing with her hair and staring at her Ferragamos to spout such sparklers as "Champagne . . . makes girls dance and drop their pants."

Rob's love is so addictive, it not only loosens Meg up but also toughens her. After she accidentally kills her obnoxious step-father, John Glover (who, in fact, deserves it for swallowing the scenery whole), Meggers whines, "This is going to ruin *every-thing*, isn't it?" But naturally, it doesn't. She and her stud puppet Lowe marry and share their Guilty Secret. Witchy Kim Cattrall plays another of Lowe's bedmates—his rich boss's wife—and, when he commemorates her birthday with Frederick's of Hollywood–style black lace panties, she coos: "You must want me to put these on?" He replies, "I can't bite them off if you don't!"—reading the line as if it were "Pass the Brie, Muffy."

There's a priceless Bad Movie moment when Cattrall hisses at Tilly in the powder room at a swank dinner party, "While you were plugging your stepfather, your husband was plugging me —and he was great!" The producers obviously found it easier to get Lowe to change his candy-colored pullovers and Topsiders than his expressions. Now, Tilly is supposed to be wan ("We have too much money," one character commiserates), but really, this gal never snapped back after *Agnes of God*. She's still acting as if she were hearing spectral voices, probably Audrey Hepburn's.

Watchably silly for much of its 91 minutes, the movie has a finale involving a rodent, a chewed wire, and a boat explosion. Movies like *Masquerade* killed MGM. If you're in the right mood, it'll slay you, too.

With Doug Savant, Dana Delaney, Erik Holland. Produced by Michael I. Levy, directed by Bob Swaim. Screenplay by Dick Wolf. C, 91 m., V, L

Midnight Lace (1960) ♥♥♥

Poor Doris Day: charming in comedies, winning in musicals, she was utterly ill equipped to play lady-in-distress parts. Poor us: that didn't stop her from trying, again and again. Here, as a moneybags matron being terrorized in London by a madman who telephones to say he's going to kill her "before the month is out" (you'll be praying for a montage of pages flying off a calendar), Day alternates between two modes—perky and ear-shattering— making this one sunny screamfest.

John Williams, bone-weary from again playing *Dial M for Murder*'s Scotland Yard inspector, thinks that Day's simply hysterical, and so do we: "Dial H for Hilarity." Myrna Loy, wearing perhaps the funniest hat in movie history, waves her cigarette holder about as she pooh-poohs Day's fear of the killer's phone calls. "Oh, they have them here, too?" asks Loy. "I was once in Dublin, and I got a call from a man who wanted to dress me in black underwear—*personally*, mind you. It was the most stimulating minute and a half I spent in Ireland." Rex Harrison, as Day's workaholic newlywed hubby, *suspiciously* postpones their vacation plans, then *suspiciously* mutters, "It's no picnic being married to an heiress."

Day doesn't know where to turn, since no one else hears the calls, or is around when she's trapped—alone!—inside the elevator of her own building. This last scene's a corker: Listening, in mounting panic to the *thump, thump, thump* of footsteps on the stairs outside the elevator growing closer, *closer, CLOSER*, Day works herself up into a frenzy of noisy hyperventilation. (Close your eyes, and listen to Day's "Uh, uhh, *uhhhh!*" on the soundtrack: It would double nicely as convincing aural evidence of a Day orgasm—that is, if she had ever played a character who'd had one.) Turns out that it's just John Gavin coming to the rescue, but someone should have rescued him from being miscast—his English accent is so laughably off, he's actually unintelligible (which suits us fine).

Finally, the death threats, faces at the window, strangers at the door all finally drive Day over the edge, and way, way over the top. "Oh God, somebody help me, help me!" Day blubbers, wails, and screeches as she descends her staircase into madness (and Bad Movie history, we might add) while, below, Loy and Harrison—polished purveyors of underplaying—look on, genuinely aghast. It all ends when Day dons her new lounging pajamas (the "midnight lace" of the title) and scampers out the second story window, in heels, onto the girders of the building being built next door. "What have I done?" she demands to know when facing the killer. Screen the picture sometime, Doris, and see for yourself.

With Roddy McDowall, Herbert Marshall, Natasha Parry, Hermione Baddeley. Produced by Ross Hunter and Martin

Melcher, directed by David Miller. Screenplay by Ivan Goff and
Ben Roberts, based on Janet Green's play *Matilda Shouted Fire*.
C, 108 m., V

Play Misty for Me (1971) ❤

Actor-director Clint Eastwood merrily miscast himself as a late
night radio deejay famed for such pearls as "Men have destroyed
the roads of wonder and their cities squat like black toads; in the
orchards of life, nothing is clean or real as a girl, naked to love
or be a man with." Women go wild for Eastwood's brand of bull,
particularly one caller who requests, "Play 'Misty' for me."

One night at a bar—while playing a self-indulgent scene with
regular Eastwood director Don Siegel—our hero comes on to
twitchy Jessica Walter. No sooner can you say *"Fatal Attraction"*
than Walter's acting possessive, schizy, and volatile, complicating
Clint's shaky relationship with Donna Mills, a sculptor with Jane
Fonda's *Klute* hairdo and an intriguing succession of female roommates. Mills, given to saying things like "I was trying to join the
revolt against the representational. Didn't quite make that,
though. So, now I'm just trying to play it cool. Not quite making
that, either," is supposed to be Eastwood's "grounded" gal.
(Mills's lisping landlord seems to exist solely so Eastwood can
prove what a real man he is by saying, "Why don't you go cruise
some sailors, huh?")

Walter won't leave Eastwood alone, calling to ask why he broke
their "date," purring, "It's just that I feel kind of silly sitting
here in my brand new lounging pajamas" (though not, we might
add, as silly as she looks). When he spurns her, Walter growls,
"You're nothing! You're not even good in bed! I just felt sorry
for you!" Then he finds her in his bathroom with her wrists
slashed—say, is this one of Glenn Close's most famous films, or
what? Eastwood keeps an appointment with media exec Irene
Hervey, the likeable B-movie actress of the '40s, who gets to
psychedelicize her image by asking Eastwood, straightfaced,
"What do you think of the concept? The unstructured, the loosey-
goosey, Monterey Pop, Woodstock kind of thing?" Before he can
say much, Walter elbows in, if only to answer Hervey's query

whether she's "a friend" by snapping, "Just another trick, honey."

The last stretch of the movie is a poor man's *Psycho*, what with Walter knifing Eastwood's housekeeper, slashing his portrait, and moving in with Mills, the better to snip off her hair. Director Eastwood smothers what little suspense he's got going—and here's the kind of moviemaking choice that separates the true maker of Bad Movies from the also-rans—with two looooong musical sequences: a lovers' montage set to Roberta Flack's "The First Time Ever I Saw Your Face," followed by a detour to the Monterey Jazz Festival (replete with shots of soulful black people a-dancin' and a-clappin').

Don't miss the only truly scary moment: Eastwood, startled from sleep by a butcher knife embedded in his pillow, investigates the situation dressed only in his BVDs.

Produced by Robert Daly, directed by Eastwood. Screenplay by Jo Heims and Dean Reisner. "Mr. Eastwood's wardrobe by Brad Whitney of Carmel." C, 102 m., V, L

Point Break (1991) ❤ ❤

Something should have told Hollywood that there's a reason why nobody's bothered to make a bigtime surfer flick since John Milius capsized his career in 1978 with *Big Wednesday*—and that movie seems totally rad next to this totally "gonzo" flick about bank robbers who surf.

You've got to love any suspense movie that asks us to buy Keanu Reeves, player par excellence of clueless dudes, as Johnny Utah, a football supernova whose career was detoured by a busted knee. Considering that Reeves suggests a guy who scored too many tackles without a helmet, that's already pushing it, but Reeves's character is also supposed to have won a law degree and graduated at the top of his class. The plot kicks in when he joins the FBI—fer sher!—and gets teamed with bureau burnout Gary Busey (late of—yes!—*Big Wednesday*). Hot on the trail of "The Ex-Presidents," guys who rob banks disguised as crooks Lyndon Johnson, Richard Nixon, Jimmy Carter, and Ronald Reagan, our slow-witted heroes stumble over an astounding fact: the baddies only pull jobs during the summer. Hmmmm, they wonder, so what could they be doing the rest of the year? Sitcom actors on hiatus? Shrinks who don't summer in the Hamptons? Nah, surfers.

So Reeves infiltrates a subculture of wave-riding Cro-Magnons around whom the movie tries (and fails) to build a mystical, Robin-and-his-Merry-Men aura. Reeves meets Bodhi (Patrick Swayze, in a bad Ozzie Osbourne dye-job), whom we spot at once as the head of the bank robbers—who wouldn't guess it, since the billing demands it? Reeves, that's who, since he's busy shooting the curl, falling in love, and absorbing Life Lessons from Swayze, who talks like Shirley MacLaine. Swayze yammers about the perfect wave ("Accept its energy"), extolls the magical mystery of surfing ("A place where you lose yourself, find yourself"), and justifies his crimes ("This is about us against the system—we show that the human spirit is still alive"). Somebody, quick, deprogram this poor bro'.

After reels of pumped-up chases, car crashes, and explosions, Reeves finally manages to finger the crooks but, apparently lured by Swayze's charisma, gets pulled into committing a caper with them. So very Patty Hearst, only without the sex. The delirium reaches fever pitch when the skydiving-happy bank robbers, aware Reeves is a fed, kidnap him and toss him out of a plane: "Whoa, fuckin' amazin'!" Reeves quips in that signature voice that sounds like he swallowed too much Sex Wax. As they plummet earthward, Swayze gets off a way cool farewell line ("Johnny, I'll see you in the next life!"), and you think—no, chant—that the movie's over at last. No way, dude.

With Lori Petty, James Le Gros. Produced by Peter Abrams and Robert Levy, directed by Kathryn Bigelow. Screenplay by W. Peter Illiff, based on an original story by Rick King and Illiff. C, 115 m., V, L

Sleeping With the Enemy (1991) ❤

"Does it give you that much pleasure to humiliate me?" Patrick Bergin asks about some imagined slight, knocking wife Julia Roberts to the ground and then kicking her. "You aren't suggesting I enjoy that?" he asks later. "Oh no," Roberts replies, "that would make you a monster." Which Bergin clearly is, since the brute also selects Roberts' clothes, forces her to align the food items in the pantry, wants all the towels hung evenly and—it's too dreadful—likes to play the *Symphonie Fantastique* by Berlioz during sex.

Far more objectionable is Bergin's acting, which reaches new heights of hamminess when Roberts is seemingly washed away during a storm: "Laura!" he bellows—fourteen times—before one last "Lauuuraaaa!" "That was the night that I died," Roberts helpfully explains, "and someone else was saved." She's staged her own death, see, and hightails it to Iowa where—with a new name and maybe, oh, an inch cut off her long mane—she starts life anew: she wantonly messes up her towels to show us she's free.

When the drama coach next door, Kevin Anderson, says, "I don't know how to feel what I'm feeling when I don't even know your name," Roberts tells him, "People never really know each other." Which would probably explain why Roberts phones her invalid mother, Elizabeth Lawrence, then covers the receiver to say, "I miss you, Mom, I love you" while Lawrence mutters, "Hello? Hello? Is anyone there?" Meanwhile, Bergin discovers Roberts' wedding band right where she left it (that's right, in the toilet) and, realizing he's been duped, hires a private eye to track Roberts down.

Anderson and Roberts start opening up to one another—"I had a husband and he hurt me, and I guess I'm just really afraid," she confesses; he too digs deep and reveals, "The closest I ever got to Broadway was tending bar at Sardi's"—which leads, inevitably, to one of Roberts' try-on-clothes-and-hats music montages. Anderson dresses Roberts up as a man but not, alas, for a *9½ Weeks/Wild Orchid*–style sex scene—it's so she can visit her *blind* mother. Though Bergin's in line behind Roberts at the hospital water fountain, the disguise is so good he doesn't recognize her. (But then, after all, he was only married to her for "three years, seven months, six days"!)

Pretending to be a cop, Bergin tricks Lawrence into divulging Roberts' whereabouts by saying that Bergin is on her trail. "He's a crazy man," Lawrence says. "I know that," Bergin says about himself. "He's very dangerous." This leads to the movie's unintentionally hilarious high point, when, after a local carnival, Roberts returns home to find Berlioz on her tape deck, the towels in the bathroom straightened and the food in her kitchen cabinets lined up neat as a pin. *Who* could it be?

Produced by Leonard Goldberg, directed by Joseph Ruben. Screenplay by Ronald Bass, from Nancy Price's novel. C, 99 m., V, L

Tattoo (1981) ❤

This hilariously pretentious mishmash of *Psycho* meets *The Collector* meets *Woman in the Dunes* meets *Taxi Driver* is the sad saga of psycho tattoo artist Bruce Dern, one of society's misfits. He's the kind who caters to the likes of teen hooker Cynthia Nixon: "Hey Rembrandt," she jibes, "how 'bout stickin' your needle where it counts?" Dern gets hired for a fashion shoot by flamboyant photographer Leonard Frey to paint temporary tattoos on such models as Maud Adams. "I've seen your designs and I think they're brilliant," enthuses Adams, yanking off her blouse, "I hate to sound like I know everything but they remind me very much of Japanese prints—especially of Utamaro."

She invites him to dine with her, where he regales her with tales of such past jobs as (get this) disinfecting public telephones. "You do that for a little while," Dern says, bugging his eyes, "and you never want to put your mouth to a receiver again." Such conversation would send any sensible supermodel running, but it only sparks in Adams such musings on fame as, "Well, it won't last forever; everybody's famous for at least fifteen minutes these days." (Ain't it the truth, Maud.) Later, when she suggests they make it, Dern snaps, "Are you asking me to have intercourse with you?" and throws her out.

But soon he's making nutty phone calls to her—with a handkerchief over the receiver, of course—and, when her boyfriend John Getz leaves her alone one night, Dern chloroforms Adams and schlepps her to his family's picturesque Ocean City beach house, and then, night and day, against her will, decorates her naked body with his ugly tattoo gun. (Don't miss the moment when Dern lifts his tattoo gun to the unconscious Adams and Barry DeVorzon's music score suddenly goes *Psycho*.)

Discovering he's tattooed her—"You goddamn freak," Adams howls, "what the fuck is this?"—Adams looks for ways to kill him. When she's finally tattooed within an inch of her life, he tells her—a real smoothie with sex shop lingo—"Take your hands and undo the sash of your robe . . . touch yourself . . . feel yourself." She screams, "You're sick, you're twisted. Well, you're not going to turn me into a freak, too!" Strong words but, in fact, finally they merge, tattoo to tattoo, and indulge in some steamy—and, incidentally, some of Hollywood's most *rumored*-about ever—humping, which leads to a mad, screaming orgasm, the flash of a murder weapon, and one less fetishist.

Produced by Joseph E. Levine, Richard P. Levine, directed by Bob Brooks. Screenplay by Joyce Buñuel (daughter of the great Luis Buñuel), story by Brooks. C, 103 m., V

CHAPTER 2

Trash Yourself Cinema

Perhaps taking a cue from Mae West, who advised, "Keep a diary and someday, it'll keep you," Bad Movie Stars We Love know exactly what to do when their off-screen pecadilloes spark ugly front-page headlines. When scandal pounds down the doors, when fame turns to notoriety, just package the whole mess and sell it, that's what! Your neglected teenage daughter kills your young lover? Rake in millions by starring in a movie in which your neglected teenage daughter vies for the affection of your young lover. You're a full-fledged sex goddess who's as notorious for being many times married as for making suicide attempts? Make zillions as a scarlet woman by starring in movies moist with scandal, bed-hopping, and suicide attempts.

We'll admit it: some of the Bad Movies We Love *most* invite us to watch the stars play out their private lives in public. Ready for a peek?

Bad Influence (1990) ❤

When Lana Turner and Elizabeth Taylor stopped making features, Bad Movie fans feared the demise of "Trash Yourself Cinema"—those irresistible flicks where stars eagerly reenact their own latest off-screen scandals—forgetting that Hollywood is filled with celebrities in need of quick career rehab. We're anticipating future contributions to the genre from Drew Barrymore, but "Trash Yourself Cinema" already staged a hooty comeback when Rob Lowe rushed in to pick up the Lana/Liz mantle, showing surprising smarts with the all-important sense of timing—knowing just the right moment for self-exploitation. Fresh from his true-life notoriety as the purported despoiler of underage girls he seduced while (gasp!) videotaping a ménage à trois, Lowe here videotapes—yes, you guessed it—an innocent person having sex, and then wreaks havoc by making the tape public. That the "victim" isn't a young lady (it's James Spader) didn't fool anyone; in fact, since the script posits that Lowe may be the Devil, he's ideally cast—at the time, concerned parents of jail bait everywhere feared that Lowe actually was Evil Incarnate.

Preppy Spader runs into Lowe (outside the men's room on a pier, wouldn't you know) and unwittingly strikes a bargain to whip his career and love life into shape. Before you can say "Faust" (or "*Strangers on a Train*," for that matter), Lowe terminates Spader's dreary engagement, gets him the promotion he sought and, best of all, has Spader picking up beauties at hilariously decadent parties where Lowe always knows the ever-changing password, whether it's "Dominant Athletic Female" or "Gay White Male."

When Lowe takes Spader on a crime spree—robbing burger stands!—Spader snobbishly decides Lowe's the *wrong kind* of sociopath, and gives him the heave-ho. The rejection drives Lowe to kill Spader's gal, Lisa Zane, cleverly framing Spader with his ever-ready camcorder. Here, Lowe is clearly having fiendish fun going way over the top and—considering America's then-recent frenzy to view a bootlegged tape of his true-life sexcapades—Lowe becomes an icon of High Camp when he commands, "Don't touch that dial!"

Spader's brother Christian Clemenson turns up to deliver the movie's falling-down-funny message: "If you get into bed with the Devil, sooner or later you have to fuck." Speaking of which, Lowe finally strips down for the de rigueur sex scene with two partners; no video cameras, alas, but Spader is watching in secret, and afterwards he tells Lowe, "You make a very funny face when you come." Spader beats Lowe at his own game by videotaping the bad boy's murder confession, but just then, Lowe falls off the pier into the ocean, disappearing without ever resurfacing. Was he really the Devil? or maybe a mystery man with extraordinary lung capacity? or perhaps just a lucky "Brat Packer" who got off easy? You decide.

With Kathleen Wilhoite, Sachi Parker (Shirley MacLaine's daughter). Produced by Steve Tisch, directed by Curtis Hanson. Screenplay by David Koepp. C, 99 m., V, L

Butterfield 8 (1960) ❤ ❤ ❤

"Face it, Mama," Elizabeth Taylor cries out, "I was the slut of all time!" Sure, this overripe dialogue might be from the novel by John O'Hara, but we suspect the familiar "gifts" of co-scenarist John Michael Hayes, whose other laugh-out-loud scripts include *Peyton Place, The Carpetbaggers, Torch Song,* and *Harlow.*

Although "Trash Yourself Cinema" wasn't actually invented for Liz Taylor, one would be hard pressed to name another star who made so much money so many times for wallowing so deep in this kind of plush, overproduced pigsty. Taylor was notorious, at the time, as a "brazen hussy" who "stole" Eddie Fisher away from wife Debbie Reynolds, which makes this movie's opening sequence irresistible: Taylor awakens alone in her married lover's bed, wraps herself in only a sheet, lights a cigar, drains a glass of whiskey, discovers her torn dress on the floor, brushes her teeth with booze, finds an envelope with $250 cash, scrawls "No Sale" in red lipstick across a mirror, leaves the money and instead steals the absent wife's mink coat, calls her answering service, and hails a cab to the apartment of . . . Eddie Fisher (by then, he was the real-life Mr. Taylor).

True to form, spineless Fisher greets Taylor with a namby-pamby observation: "Sunday morning, and there's scotch on your breath." "Well," shrugs Taylor, "it's *good* scotch." Later, Fisher's girlfriend, Susan Oliver, will want to know about Taylor: "Is she or is she not a tramp?" Mumbles Fisher, "I've never liked that word."

It's hard to fathom why Taylor won an Oscar for this performance, though there's a brief flash of real acting when her character claims that she's not interested in rich men: "I've had more fun in the back of a '39 Ford than I could ever have in the vault

of the Chase National Bank!" Oh, sure. But catch Laurence
Harvey as the married sicko who can't help lovin' dat Liz, no
matter how badly she treats him (when she grinds her stiletto
heel into his foot, it's clear he digs it).

With Dina Merrill, Mildred Dunnock, Betty Field, Jeffrey
Lynn, Kay Medford. Produced by Pandro S. Berman, directed
by Delbert Mann. Screenplay by Hayes and Charles Schnee, from
the O'Hara novel. C, 108 m., V, L

The Fan (1981) ❤

With her patented haughty glare, overconfident Lauren Bacall
transparently thinks that she's outclassing this formulaic slasher
flick, and single-handedly she turns it into a prime slice of "Trash
Yourself Cinema." An aging Hollywood glamour queen better
known for her former show biz husbands and her digs in a land-
mark apartment building than for any of her creaky, Broadway
musical "star vehicles," Bacall here is playing—how did you
know?—precisely that. When servants sing "Happy Birthday,"
Bacall snaps, "As of today, I'm going to be forty-five *forever*."
Secretary Maureen Stapleton mutters, "Forty-nine," and Bacall
admits to "Fifty," but since none of these figures seem remotely
plausible, it's all the stranger that young, hunky Michael Biehn
sends mash notes that blather, "We'll be lovers soon and I have
all the necessary equipment to make you very happy."

Stapleton writes back, admonishing Biehn's "tasteless pornog-
raphy," making Biehn worry—in voice-over, to us—about Stapleton's "possessiveness," asking, "Has it occurred to you that
she might have lesbian tendencies?" Bacall snarls at Stapleton,
"We've had lots of weirdos. What about the guy who kept trying
to jump into a taxi with me? Don't upset my fans." Stapleton
(who has the upper hand because she can act) replies, "Ever occur
to you that my job isn't exactly heaven? [meaning, presumably,
costarring with Bacall] I'm a Secret Service escort, a butler, a
nurse, a letter-writing machine, a floor mop . . . ten, twelve hours
a day!" While we're mulling that one over—"a floor mop"?—
Bacall simpers, "What would I do without you?"

Cue Biehn to start rampaging around with a razor, slicing up

Stapleton, Bacall's maid, and even the choreographer of Bacall's new show. The loss of the latter certainly helps explain opening night of the musical: Your jaw will drop as one tough-to-top, insane routine follows another, with sparkling chorus boys praising—in "you've never heard of 'em before, you've never heard of 'em since" tunes by Marvin Hamlisch and Tim Rice— the charms of the ageless Bacall. (The show is, of course, a triumph.)

Later, Biehn chases Bacall—swathed in an evening gown— through the empty theater. Finally he stands over her, razor in hand, and Bacall snaps, "You're pathetic. Here's your chance to be like one of those hoodlums who kill their victims for nothing, a thief who murders little old ladies for a quarter. Don't you think the world's had enough of people like you? I've had it," and— having apparently monologued him into submission—she grabs the razor and kills Biehn, then exits the theater, heading for her opening-night celebration.

The movie warns, "Think twice before sending fan mail to Lauren Bacall," but after seeing her hammy self-parody here, who'd want to?

With James Garner, Hector Elizondo, Griffin Dunne, Dana Delaney. Produced by Robert Stigwood, directed by Edward Bianchi. Screenplay by Priscilla Chapman and John Hartwell, from Bob Randall's novel. C, 95 m., V, L

Imitation of Life (1959) ❤ ❤ ❤

Without a doubt, here's the most accurately titled movie in the entire oeuvre of "Trash Yourself Cinema," so boldly does it parallel Lana Turner's then-recent off-screen trials and tribulations when her daughter killed Turner's lover. The first hour charts Turner's rise to Broadway fame. "Aren't you a little late getting started?" suitor John Gavin asks. "I'm going up and up and up," spits Turner, "and nobody's gonna pull me down!" Years later, triumphant Turner laments, "It doesn't seem worth it," but her longtime black housekeeper and close pal Juanita Moore says, "You need show business as much as it needs you."

The storyline finally kicks in when Turner's daughter, Sandra Dee, and Moore's daughter, Susan Kohner, grow up to be troubled teens. Kohner, in her nightie and high heels, is a hot-blooded bad girl whose only desire is to pass for white. No "busboys, cooks, chauffeurs" for her, Kohner sneaks out at night to romance Troy Donahue, who, when he learns her mother's black, beats Kohner senseless in an alley, while frenzied jazz blares on the soundtrack.

This is a high point of hotcha sin in Bad Movies, but it's topped by the scene that follows. Moore, back at the homestead, tells Turner what friends she'll want at her funeral. Turner, lighting a cigarette to show off the fur-trimmed sleeves of her Jean Louis creation, brings the movie to a dead halt with her observation, "It never occurred to me that you had any friends." *Whew!* Turner flies off to Europe to act for the great Italian director "Fellucci," leaving errant, squeaky-voiced Dee to vamp Gavin (whose name, don't you know, is "Steve"—the same first name as the man who fathered Turner's real life daughter, Cheryl).

The movie reaches the first of its crazed climaxes when Kohner runs off to L.A., where she works as a white chorus girl, doing a frenzied routine with a prop champagne glass. Moore turns up in her dressing room only to be turned away by Kohner: "Please go. And if, by accident, we should ever pass on the street, don't recognize me." Meanwhile, Turner returns home to find herself competing with Dee for Gavin's attentions.

Did this movie imitate life, cashing in on the Turner scandal blow-by-blow? No, that's *Where Love Has Gone*. But this flick drifts perilously close when Turner and Dee square off for their showdown. "I haven't been a good mother," Turner confesses, stating the obvious. "You've given me everything but yourself," cries Dee. "If Steve is going to come between us," sighs Turner, "I'll give him up. I'll never see him again." Dee wails, "Oh mama—stop acting!" (These two carry on as if one of them had killed Gavin.) Turner has the final, world-weary word: "It's funny, the way things turn out." Funnier to us than you, Lana, dear.

With Robert Alda, Dan O'Herlihy, Mahalia Jackson. Produced by Ross Hunter, directed by Douglas Sirk. Screenplay by Eleanore Griffin and Allan Scott, based on Fannie Hurst's novel. C, 124 m., V

Love Has Many Faces (1965) ❤ ❤

Lana Turner's "million-dollar wardrobe" received star billing in the publicity for this south-of-the-border potboiler, which should have been called "Lana Has Many Costume Changes."

Turner, an aging jet-set movie star who'd made headlines with her notorious romances, plays an aging jet-setter known for her notorious liaisons with hunky gigolos, who becomes involved in a scandal involving the death of one of the hustlers—in other words, this was a real acting stretch for her. We're meant to wonder who killed the beach boy: Was it lacquered Lana? Was it the gigolo Lana married, Cliff Robertson? Or was it the gigolo who's in line to be Lana's next husband, Hugh O'Brian? (Actually, the lad committed suicide—if we'd been cast in this movie, we would have too.)

O'Brian serves up a taste of what we're in for when he greets the dead boy's sister, Stephanie Powers, as she arrives at one of Turner's fabled wild soirees, with "Welcome to nothingland." Powers confronts Turner by asking about her late brother, "You mean you didn't love him?" and Turner, squashing out a cigarette, sneers, "That depends on what you mean by 'love.'"

Strutting around in high heels, a black swimsuit, and a zebra-print chiffon cape, belting back booze, and snarling, "You didn't use to despise money so much" at her rent-a-hubby, Turner tries her damnedest to embody all the tabloid headlines written about her—but since she can't act, she comes across instead like a *female* drag queen (Joan Crawford, without balls).

Posing on her yacht in a flame-colored cocktail ensemble, Turner's asked where she would like to go. "Anywhere that isn't here," she snaps. "I need to be . . . somewhere else." We know just how she feels, but we wouldn't want to leave and miss the scene in which another unhappy Americano, Ruth Roman, asks O'Brian, "What do I like about you?" and he replies, "Want me to tell you—or show you?" Nor would we want to miss Turner's retort when O'Brian suggests that he replace Robertson in her bed. "You might fill the days," she says, sighing, "but never the nights."

By the time Turner shows up wearing a sequin-encrusted,

emerald green shorts and halter-top outfit with matching earrings, bracelet, and floor-length stole, it's clear that costume designer Edith Head has been out too long in the Acapulco sun.
She's not the only one, however; in dim hopes of explaining why
Turner so hates herself, the screenwriter has concocted a supremely hilarious monologue ("I spoil everything I touch!") that
sends even Turner's faithful maid running for cover, pleading
"Forgive me, Señora, I should not hear thees. *It ees not good.*"

In the crazed climax, Turner topples from her horse and gets
gored by a bull, which nearly kills her but, worse, completely
ruins her outfit. Not to worry, though—she has just the night-
gown to wear in the hospital.

With Virginia Grey, Ron Husmann. Produced by Jerry Bresler, directed by Alexander Singer. Screenplay by Marguerite
Roberts. C, 105 m., V

Madame X (1966) ❤ ❤ ❤

Scandal has wreaked havoc on many a star's career, but it gave
Lana Turner a third-act career boost. La Lana's audience
wanted—and got—scenes like the one here in which she's told
by her live-in mother-in-law, Constance Bennett, "You're an unfit
mother, guilty of adultery. Your prosecutor will say you killed
your lover. Even if a clever attorney gets you off, the mud will
cling!" (Never mind that Turner hadn't killed smoothie Ricardo
Montalban—in fact, she'd been in the midst of calling him "A
contemptible, rotten . . ." when he'd replied, "A contemptible,
rotten what? Never end on a dangling insult!" and just then had
fallen down a convenient staircase to his death.)

To protect her son, and husband John Forsythe, from the
scandal that would drag them all down, Turner agrees to fake
her death and start life anew in Europe. This hoary plot has made
the rounds since the silent era, but this is the deluxe edition,
pumped up by its producer with gowns, jewels, and wigs, in hopes
that we won't notice that Turner's too old for the role. The over-
the-top script keeps us laughing out loud as Turner spends the
next twenty years going from man to man, drink to drink, trying
to forget.

When she runs out of dough, Turner ships out on a Mexico-bound tramp steamer, where she downs absinthe with scummy Burgess Meredith, telling him "I've come a long way down. 'Would you prefer the Rolls or the Mercedes this morning?' they used to ask me." Old enough to recognize this plot from earlier *Madame X* movies, Meredith realizes who Turner is and tricks her into returning to the United States, so he can blackmail her husband. Figuring out Meredith's game, Turner tells him, "Listen, scavenger, I crawl in the same gutter, but I'm not a beast of prey!" and then proves her point by shooting him dead.

When she's tried for murder, she's defended by her own grown son, Keir Dullea, who does not realize that she's his own mother! "I don't have much to leave my son," Turner says on the stand, "only a lie that his mother was clean and good. I killed to keep my son from knowing what I'd become. If time were turned back, I'd kill again." Turner, Forsythe, Bennett and even a jury member weep copiously throughout this speech—there's not a dry eye on the set. Turner collapses and dies, but not before telling Dullea, "When you marry, it's important to live alone"—as if that's how she got into this mess.

With Virginia Grey, Warren Stevens. Produced by Ross Hunter, directed by David Lowell Smith. Screenplay by Jean Holloway, based on the play by Alexandre Bisson. C, 100 m., V

Portrait in Black (1960) ❤ ❤ ❤

Of the celluloid cheese Lana Turner churned out after her front page scandal in 1958, *Portrait in Black* is her four-course Velveeta banquet. The onetime "Sweater Girl" cats about as hot-blooded Sheila Cabot whose lover, Dr. Anthony Quinn, coldbloodedly injects a lethal air bubble into the gnarled veins of Sheila's loathsome invalid husband, Lloyd Nolan.

It looks like a perfect crime until Lana receives a note: "Congratulations on the success of your murder." Next ensue scenes of our diamond-heavy heroine thrashing in bed—mussing not a hair, mind you—to suggest (utterly unconvincingly) guilt; Quinn swooning during surgery when he hallucinates that his murder victim awaits on the operating table; and a second murder and nearly a third—alas aborted, since the intended victim is Sandra Dee, who chirps such lines as "If I'd known we were going to a beatnik joint for coffee and word jazz, I'd have worn my tights."

Connoisseurs of the overwrought will savor such set pieces as the row during which Quinn shatters Turner's mirrored reflection with a candlestick and the moment where Quinn—driven yet again to the breaking point—crushes a syringe in his hirsute paw. And the dialogue? Turner and Quinn cling tightly, murmuring "David," "Sheila," "Sheila," "David." And do not miss several scenes played in shadow, allegedly because the star arrived on the set visibly battered by a too-ardent admirer.

We know and love such late-era Turner epics for what they are: exercises in mutual exploitation by a manufactured, scandal-wracked star and her creators. Here, pushing forty, shot in gauzy soft focus, sporting fourteen Jean Louis getups, and, according to the typical Ross Hunter–style publicity, "$1,175,000 worth of jewels—using 4,200 real diamonds, 700 pearls, 250 emeralds," Lana is the last of the great zircon icons, forever Miss Rhinestone.

With Richard Basehart, Anna May Wong, John Saxon, Ray Walston, Virginia Grey. Produced by Hunter (the veritable Baron of such Bad Movies We Love as *Imitation of Life*, *Airport*, the 1973 musical remake of *Lost Horizon*, etc.), directed by Michael Gordon. Screenplay by Ivan Goff and Ben Roberts. C, 113 m., V

The Sandpiper (1965) ♥♥♥♥

People who murmur the age-old maxim "No one ever sets out to make a bad movie" haven't seen *The Sandpiper*: From first frame to last, this low-grade, high-budget rehash of Somerset Maugham's *Rain* was custom-built to ride the crest of international headlines that exploded when married movie star Elizabeth Taylor broke up the marriage of her *Cleopatra* co-star Richard Burton. The question is not why the couple made this movie (money, of course) but how they both managed to keep straight faces while shooting it.

Taylor, as a free-love-endorsing, barefoot, beatnik Big Sur painter, is asked by the straitlaced, married man-of-the-cloth Burton, "What's your attitude toward marriage?" The audience circa

1965 knew full well that Taylor had, at that point, already been married five times, so imagine their peals of knowing laughter when Taylor replies, "I'm withholding judgment until I see a happy one," and then adds, "How's yours?" Later, one-time child star Taylor drops to her knees and confesses to the good Reverend Burton, "Men have been staring at me and rubbing against me ever since I was twelve. I see myself, perhaps tomorrow, perhaps next year, being handed from man to man as if I were an amusement for men who've only had me, never really loved me." Burton, of course, says just what you hope he will: "I want you, I want you," which he intones in that playing-to-the-second-balcony voice that was trained for the other kind of classics. "Do you want me as a woman or just as a whore?" asks Taylor, a query Burton wisely avoids answering.

After he's watched her mend the wing of an injured sandpiper, the holy man and the wanton finally make love, which leads to the howlingly funny highlight of the film: as they're lying by the fire, the sandpiper flutters over and nests in Taylor's hair. "I've never known anything like this," marvels Taylor. "Does this happen to married people?" (You pray that Burton will answer: "No, most married couples keep their birds in cages.") Just like in real life, Burton can't help confessing to his wife what's happened: "We made love—even in motels, God help me!" So, though Burton loses both wife and mistress, don't be sad: He's learned something. So has Taylor: "I never knew what love was before." Uh-huh.

Meanwhile, both Burton and Taylor clearly gleaned from this whole experience that it would be better to trash themselves in tonier material. They went on to make that tribute to couples-from-Hell, *Who's Afraid of Virginia Woolf?*, and then made the title-tells-all *The Taming of the Shrew*.

With Eva Marie Saint, Charles Bronson, Robert Webber as the gentleman caller Liz must fight off with a hatchet, and restaurateur and producer (*sex, lies and videotape*) Morgan Mason as Liz's illegitimate son. Produced by John Calley, directed by Vincente Minnelli. Screenplay by blacklist victim Dalton Trumbo and Michael Wilson. C, 116 m., V

The Star (1952) ❤ ❤ ❤

Bette Davis made only one foray into "Trash Yourself Cinema," but it's such a firecracker of self-exploitation, she didn't need to make another.

Aging, frumpy, and broke, Davis stands outside the auction house where her personal effects aren't selling. "What am I bid?" the dealer barks. "One dollar? This stuff belonged to Margaret Elliot. She was your favorite movie star. She made you laugh, she made you cry. Secretly you were in love with her." Davis's agent walks out—holding a hideous candelabra—and she rants, "Be a scavenger! Pick my bones! Don't touch me with your ten-percent hands. Always reaching, grasping . . . you can do anything but get me a picture!"

Davis visits teen daughter Natalie Wood, who's living with Davis's ex-husband. "My six months with Daddy are up," Wood smiles. "You did come for me, didn't you?" Well, no. Davis begs off, explaining her new apartment is too tiny and she's too busy —neatly anticipating Davis's real-life daughter later penning a nasty, neglected kid's tell-all book. Rushing home, Davis grabs her Academy Award and says, "C'mon, Oscar, let's you and me get drunk!" She places the statuette on her dashboard and takes it on a boozy tour of the stars' homes. "On your right, ladies and gentlemen," Davis slurs, "is the home of Mitzi Gaynor, rising *young* movie star." Stopping outside a mansion, Davis says, "And that, Oscar, *was* the home of the wealthy, glamorous Margaret Elliot. Going . . . going . . . gone!"

When this bender gets her tossed in jail, Davis hollers, "You don't seem to know who I am!" An inmate asks, "Whatta ya in for, honey?" and we expect Davis to blurt, "Bad choice of script." Her bail's paid by Sterling Hayden with whom, he reminds her, she once costarred in "the worst picture ever made." (Worse than *this?*) "Where to?" he asks, and Davis shrugs, "Isn't this the end of the line?" Well, yes. But since it's not the end of the movie, Davis shacks up with Hayden, recalls her studio battles when she "was sick of the tripe they were forcing me to play," and—whenever anyone else tries to get a word in edgewise—again mutters, "Going . . . going . . . gone!"

Hayden helps her get a department store job selling lingerie but, when one customer says to another, "It's a disgrace for a respectable store like this to hire a jailbird," Davis snaps. "It is a disgrace," she thunders, "waiting on a couple of old bags like you!" She begs her way back into her movie studio, agrees to do a screen test for a supporting role, but when the cameras roll, the ham takes over. "Your fans would love it," the director says sarcastically, but Davis—thinking she's employed—hurries home and says to her Oscar, "You're going to have a baby brother!" Go rent this, right now.

Produced by Bert Friedlob, directed by Stuart Heisler. Screenplay by Dale Eunson and Katherine Albert. Gowns by Orry-Kelly. B&W, 91 m., V

Too Much, Too Soon (1958) ❤ ❤

Dorothy Malone, a '50s-era Faye Dunaway, danced a mad mambo and won an Oscar for *Written on the Wind*. That Bad Movie led to this one, featuring Malone playing Diana Barrymore, the alcoholic daughter of screen legend John Barrymore, impersonated here by broken-down screen legend Errol Flynn. Decide for yourself whose self-exploitation is the most ghoulish in this entry of "Trash Yourself Cinema." Is it Diana's, for blazing the trail in celebrity tell-all books? or Malone's, for thinking she could class up Diana's back-alley saga? or Flynn's, for imitating one of his closest pals? or Warner Bros.', for casting burned-out lush Flynn—who'd once made zillions for them as a matinee idol—as a burned-out lush?

Sad, teenage Diana (thirty-three-year-old Malone) reunites with Flynn, her long absent Dad, aboard his yacht—the *Infanta*—but he'd rather get soused with his buddies. So Malone becomes a society deb (squired by nice, dull, filthy rich Martin Milner) who, dreaming of stardom, parlays a bit role on Broadway into a Hollywood movie deal. A news photographer hikes up the hem of her skirt at the train station and leers, "Now, how about a little of that Barrymore genius?" Bad Movie regular Efrem Zimbalist, Jr., who plays (of all things) a talented actor, wows her with such sweet talk as, "Someday, those ears will be enshrined in cement at Grauman's Chinese."

Malone helps sober up Flynn, but he dies the night of her first film's disastrous premiere. Lucky him. When hubby Zimbalist's away, Malone throws a wild party where her wicked cha-cha, performed soaking wet in her bathing suit, arouses the attention of sexy, slimy gigolo Ray Danton. Divorced, she marries him, starts drinking, and hits the skids. What to do for money? "The name's all we've got left," Danton sneers, "unless you want to peddle girdles over a counter," just before he lobs a tennis ball at her.

Divorced again, she hits rock bottom. Strap yourself in for the tour de force that Malone thought would get her another Oscar: She staggers drunkenly onto a burlesque stage to imitate Greta Garbo and Marilyn Monroe, then, when the crowd heckles her, begins to bump and grind! Thrown into rehab, she then gets dumped, penniless, back onto the streets and runs smack into faithful old beau Milner. In one of the more bizarre scenes in film history, Malone pours out to him a lifetime of abuse and degradation, but Milner, apparently feeling that fate hasn't treated him much better, removes his hat to reveal . . . his bald head! Malone sympathizes, "Oh, I guess I'm not the only one life played dirty tricks on." *Whew!*

Produced by Henry Blanke, directed by Art Napoleon. Screenplay by Art and Jo Napoleon, from Barrymore's book. B&W, 121 m., TV

The V.I.P.s (1963) ❤❤

This swanky trashfest is sort of *Grand Hotel* set in an airport lounge; as the airline exec who must tend to the pampered types hired to star in this movie puts it, "I have these awful film people to see to." Orson Welles plays the hilariously named filmmaker Buda, who blusters, "It is not the purpose of the modern cinema to entertain. We use our cameras today as a surgeon uses his scalpel."

Indeed, someone's been scalpeling headlines out of the tabloids of the day, for Elizabeth Taylor and Richard Burton helicopter in—fresh from the set of *Cleopatra*—to play a fabulously wealthy, fabulously famous married couple caught up in the psychodrama of infidelity. (Where ever do these screenwriters get their ideas?) All of Taylor's dialogue seems to come from her off-screen life. "We're not hiding away—we've done enough of that," she tells the lover she's running off with. "His face! I'll never forget it as long as I live!" she exclaims over her husband's expression when he learns he has lost her. "Oh please," Taylor's lover, Louis Jourdan, finally implores, "don't talk like a woman's magazine." (Taylor knows, however, that the audience wants each and every detail to mirror some aspect of her countless marriages.)

When her getaway flight is fogged in, Burton returns so the pair can do what they've both been so fabulously overpaid to do—the anything-for-money, dog-and-pony show of playing themselves. Burton: "I've come to abase myself, to grovel at your feet, to beg you to forgive me." Taylor: "You'll find someone else." Burton: "What can he give you that I can't? I'm told he's a very skillful maker of love. Is he? Is he all that much better than me?" Taylor's response required some real acting skill, for here at last was a situation she had never found herself in: "I don't know. That hasn't come into it yet." Burton, speaking up for everyone in the audience, responds—one carefully enunciated word at a time—"I . . . do . . . not . . . believe . . . you." They struggle, and Burton smashes Taylor's wrist into a full-length mirror (mirrors being a telling metaphor for the sure sign of trouble in the marriage of two vain movie stars, dating all the way back to the finale of Welles's marriage to Rita Hayworth in the shattered hall-of-mirrors climax of *The Lady From Shanghai*).

When push comes to shove, of course, Taylor kisses off Jourdan and hurries to find Burton. The film ends with Burton and Taylor hailing a commoner's ordinary taxi cab to ride home, so that we'll know that from now on, they'll be leading a simpler, more down-to-earth existence. It's the funniest gag in the movie.

With Elsa Martinelli, Rod Taylor, Maggie Smith, Margaret Rutherford. Produced by Anatole De Grunwald, directed by Anthony Asquith. Screenplay by Terence Rattigan. C, 119 m., TV

CHAPTER 3

Slip Us a Mickey

We first caught Mickey Rourke's punchy, mumbly, self-amused, tough Palooka act in *Diner* and *Body Heat*. Some critics sized him up as a latter-day James Dean or Marlon Brando. Others thought he was a contender for the crown of leading character actor of his generation. Then, somebody read Rourke his reviews and, when moviemakers offered him leading man roles, Rourke went soft. He made hootily pretentious potboilers for Michael Cimino, and even more hootily pretentious sex potboilers for Zalman King. His moist, distant routine, which had seemed to say, "I'm cooler than you," turned into a bunch of poses and mannerisms. His mutterings became incomprehensible. He quit shaving and washing his hair. Voilà: an instant icon, a superstar. In France, anyway.

In America, he turned into our contender for the crown of most enjoyably hammy character actor of his generation. Whenever we grow weary of Master Thespian turns from Brando, Olivier, Clift, Nicholson, and De Niro, we say shamelessly, "Slip us our Mickey."

Desperate Hours (1987) ♥

Talk about *two* accidents waiting to happen: teaming up Michael Cimino with Mickey Rourke seems almost divine inspiration. To date, the Bad Movie gods have let director and actor make two flicks together; the first was *Year of the Dragon*. In *Desperate Hours*, you know you're in for some serious moviewatching dementia when lawyer Kelly Lynch pleads in court for the parole of convict client Rourke, who's serving a ten-year manslaughter sentence, by boasting that he's "completed the Johns Hopkins Creative Writing Workshop," has character references from two "nationally known authors," and that his "IQ has been measured about 130." Rourke tops this by jumping up to scream, "I demand to represent myself! My life is in jeopardy from every guard in the place!" (The guards had obviously seen other Rourke movies, so who can blame them?)

Lynch helps Rourke stage a daring escape that hinges on, among other things, ripping her blouse to expose her breasts. Fleeing, Rourke kisses Lynch and we know this is a Mickey Rourke movie because Lynch has to pretend that she loves him. Rourke happens on the home of estranged marrieds Anthony Hopkins and Mimi Rogers, but unlike the con in standard criminal-terrorizing-innocents flicks, Rourke's a kinder, gentler psychopath. "You probably can't absorb any of this right now," he croons to Rogers, who has opened the door to him though she's wearing next to nothing. "Go upstairs and put something else on." In a competitive Bad Actor act-off, Hopkins does his customary Richard Burton imitation while Rourke does his customary Marlon Brando imitation. When Lynch fails to show up chez Hopkins as planned, Rourke decides to stay for dinner. Slipping into one of Hopkins's Armani dinner jackets, Rourke offers up murderer's etiquette tips, like "A man is not a gentleman unless he knows how to mix a martini."

The real fun comes from Cimino and Rourke straining to ram Important Statements down the throat of a poor little thriller: When a home repairman arrives too late to do his work and Rogers agrees to pay him anyway, Rourke says, "That's why America's becoming a second-rate country. I wouldn't pay him." Then, when he spies that Rogers has written "Help us" on the check, Rourke remarks, "Mendacity is the great sin that's destroying America, and I'm a living reproach to you 'cause I'm an honest man."

There's much more foolishness to savor. Stay alert for the moment when dependably bad Lindsay Crouse, as an FBI boss, tells the topless Lynch—who has agreed to wear a "wire" to help bust Rourke—"I just put my ass on the line. Now, you get out of here. My earrings are killing me. I'm in a real bad mood. You be careful." Desperate hours, indeed.

With Shawnee Smith, Danny Gerard, Elias Koteas, David Morse. Produced by Dino De Laurentiis, directed by Cimino. Screenplay by Laurence Konner, Mark Rosenthal, and Joseph Hayes, based on Hayes's novel and play and the 1955 movie. C, 105 m., V, L

Harley Davidson and the Marlboro Man (1991) ❤

"High concept" movies—that's Hollywoodspeak for two-sentence descriptions used by screenwriters to convey the entire idea of a proposed film to catch a studio executive's interest—have been providing us with Bad Movies We Love for years now. "Picture this," went some writer's hard sell in a meeting. "An all-star cast at an opening night party atop the world's tallest building. Fire breaks out below, the sprinkler system doesn't work yet, and only Steve McQueen and Paul Newman can save them."

Not every no-brainer sales pitch results in *The Towering Inferno*, however. High concept meets rock bottom with *Harley Davidson and the Marlboro Man*, which surely was sold with something like, "Picture this: a remake of *Butch Cassidy and the Sundance Kid*, set in the future, with motorcycles instead of horses, and we don't kill the heroes at the end. Here's the beauty part—we've got two product placement tie-ins right in the title alone. Doncha love it?" We sure do, but not for the reasons that the writer might have guessed.

The movie opens with Mickey Rourke flashing his bare buns, then lovingly revving up his Harley. Like your homoerotic associations more deliberate than that? You have only to read the names of cast members like "Big John Studd" and "Tom Sizemore" to start collapsing with mirth. When Rourke (dressed in leather lad regalia, replete with tattoo and earring) bumps into his ol' high school pal Don Johnson (dressed in cowpoke drag, including Stetson, boots, and whiskers), we suspect the pair must have attended Village People High. When Rourke ponders, "If there is a God, I'd like to meet the dude, I'd like to go hang out with him," it's hard not to cry out to the screen "Yo, Mick—you're already in Bad Movie Heaven, and you're God there."

Though *Harley*'s all tricked out with costly high-speed chases, helicopter footage, and leaps off Vegas hotels, it never passes muster as a *Lethal Weapon* clone, and the two stars are the reason why. They're just B actors time-warped into the wrong period of movies: both belong in the mid-'60s, when America was the land of drive-in movies, and Roger Corman was churning out cheapo *Wild Angels* biker flicks. "It's better to be dead and cool than alive and uncool," the stars tell each other, oblivious to the fact that, as actors, they're already both dead and uncool.

At movie's end, Rourke pulls over his Harley for a shapely starlet with her thumb out. "Where you heading?" he asks. She says, "Nowhere special." "C'mon," says Rourke, "I'll take you there." Indeed, nowhere special is where Rourke always takes us, down that long lonesome highway, headed straight for Unintentional Laughter, U.S.A.

With Chelsea Field, Vanessa Williams, Daniel Baldwin (who does a dead-pan take on brother Alec doing Steven Seagal). Produced by Jere Henshaw, directed by Simon Wincer. Screenplay by Don Michael Paul. C, 98 m., V, L

9½ Weeks (1986) ❤ ❤ ❤

"You'll be putting an ad in the personals," newly single Kim Basinger is told by her roommate Margaret Whitton, " 'Divorced white female, beautiful blonde, witty, cultured, owns own vibrator.' " But Basinger can't wait: out on the street, she picks up Mickey Rourke, who promptly utters the line that ought to be emblazoned across giant banners hung over the entrances to all theaters playing the films he stars in: "Don't say I didn't warn you, okay?" (No *problema*, Mick, since we're there expressly for that highfalutin', low-voltage sneer you give to every immortal word of dialogue, from "May I blindfold you?" to "Spread your legs for Daddy.")

The most perverse thing about this soft-core kinkfest is the casting. Dour, expression-free Rourke and pouty, expression-free Basinger engage in competitive underplaying to demonstrate who can give the less lifelike performance, and together they send a chill right down the spine of this hothouse, hubba-hubba humpathon, which manages to get one worked up, all right—worked up to smirks, tee-hees, and finally, peals of laughter. What's it like to have sex with Rourke? Basinger tells her co-workers, "I sprayed Lysol under my arms this morning." Draw your own conclusions.

The movie's delirium hits a feverish peak when Rourke makes Basinger sit on the floor of her kitchen, her eyes closed, while he force-feeds her olives, cherries, champagne, cough syrup, pasta, Jell-O, jalapeño peppers, milk, and then rubs honey all over her naked thighs. Never mind the obvious—nobody keeps all this stuff on hand (c'mon, a Jell-O mold?)—and note instead that Basinger squeals, shrieks, and does Rourke, right then and there, while Whitton's in the very next room!

Certain now that Basinger's a slut, Rourke goes further, forcing her to shop for whips, crawl on all fours while picking up cash off the floor, and—best of all—making her cross-dress as a man, so they can neck in public. When toughs from a passing car call them "faggots," Basinger taunts them to give chase; she kicks one in the crotch and then stabs the other in the butt with his own switchblade. Rourke and Basinger are so aroused by this, they go at it on the wet pavement. (This deranged, gender-bending interlude gives earlier dialogue new meaning: "How'd you know I'd respond to you?" Basinger asked, and Rourke replied, "I saw myself in you." Guess so.)

Finally, Rourke goes too far (by hiring a hooker who touches the blindfolded Basinger and then—here's the rub—stops touching her), but by film's end you, too, will be screaming in heat: "Don't stop, don't ever stop!" Teasemeisters extraordinaire, the filmmakers have been promising a sequel for years.

With Roderick Cook, and—if you don't blink—Corey "thirty-something" Parker and Dan "Wonder Years" Lauria as janitors who lust after Basinger. Produced by Anthony Rufus Isaacs and Zalman King, directed by Adrian Lyne. Screenplay by King & Patricia Knop, and Sarah Kernochan. C, 117 m., V, L

Wild Orchid (1989) ❤❤

We're living in an era when film buffs have managed the seemingly impossible feat of restoring butchered classics: thus, *Lawrence*

Of Arabia, Spartacus, even the 1954 *A Star Is Born* can be seen the way the filmmakers intended. Happily, now Zalman King's *Wild Orchid* is available in all its soft-core splendor; though more of this movie isn't exactly better, it sure is even funnier than it was in theaters. Blank-faced beauty Carré Otis (who, we're asked to believe, speaks six languages, though she's barely mastered her native English) lands in Manhattan the day after she passes the bar, and her first job is flying to Rio with Jacqueline Bisset to deal in international real estate deals with screen history's most unlikely male sex symbol, Mickey Rourke (cast here as a Harley-riding, Howard Hughes–like billionaire who just happens to share Rourke's own off-screen penchant for Harleys and for wearing bandanas around his head).

Initially, Otis doesn't warm to the manipulative Rourke—after all, he tries to nuzzle her while wearing a giant bear's head, forces her to watch another couple making love in the back seat of a limousine, then makes her lose her virginity to a virtual stranger for cash—but soon, they're trading intimate secrets: "I'm not used to men in masks biting my neck," she confides; he admits, "I'm just not very good at being touched." Bisset, meanwhile, does her level best to remind one that long before she was a talented actress, she was once a swingin' London go-go girl: though forty-something, she does the twist in a fringed dress, she cross-dresses only to do a striptease come carnival time, and—best of all—she picks up a handsome Brazilian stud on the beach, then asks Otis to translate for her. "Tell him to take off his pants," Bisset instructs. "Ask him if he understands what tremendous pleasure women get looking at naked men."

Just as things get interesting, Rourke breaks in and yells at Otis, "You're the lawyer! We're not talking circumstantial evidence here. We're talking getting caught with a smoking gun in your hand. *Bang!* You're guilty . . . of being just like the rest of 'em!" Otis forces Rourke to confront his feelings—and boy oh boy, does he ever, in a sub-Brando mumble that qualifies as the worst acting even he's ever done: "I had a father for a while," Rourke says, fighting tears. "When he disappeared, I barely spoke for years. I stayed in the third grade for a long time." Well, faced with such a heart-rending confession, what would you do? Otis unbuttons her blouse and offers up the standard telephone ad copyline, "Just reach out and touch me." This leads to the steamy sex scene that, er, climaxes the film, but long before the lovers have nearly died from bliss, you'll have died from laughing.

With Assumpta Serna, Oleg Vidov, Bruce Greenwood. Produced by Mark Damon, Tony Anthony, and Howard Worth, directed by King. Written by King and Patricia Louisianna Knop. C, 100 m., V, L

What Will the Neighbors Say?

One of hypocritical America's favorite little fantasies is that our small towns are an Andy Hardy–land of upright, God-fearing, apple pie–eating, 4-H club–type model citizens. *Please*. In a giddy spate of sex-drenched epics set in rural or suburban America, Hollywood has spelled out what some of us don't like to admit: that behind the closed doors of small towns—just as in the big, wicked cities—lurk lust, sin, adultery! (You know—many of the very things that make Bad Movies We Love worth watching.)

By Love Possessed (1961) ❤

Had it not been based on a bestselling novel, this would surely have been titled "By Lana Possessed," since it's the saga of one of those steamy Saturday nights when an otherwise respectable father and son (Efrem Zimbalist, Jr., and George Hamilton) both succumb to their baser instincts and try to make time with aging "Sweater Girl" Lana Turner. The movie neatly combines the two pressing questions posed by most Bad Movies We Love, circa 1960: "What happens when animal passion rears its head in a small New England town?" and "Can Lana be had?" (The answers are, respectively, "Someone's gotta die for our sins" and "You betcha.")

Turner is cast as hard-drinking Marjorie, unhappily married to gimp lawyer Jason Robards, Jr. As Robards tells partner Zimbalist, "There are two Marjories. Marjorie 'A' runs the house like a duchess, reads books (not just reviews of books), and is the sort of girl you want your best friend to marry. But I married Marjorie 'B'—she's wild, restless, full of impulses, urges, and needs. Not the kind of needs that can be met by a cripple." Gee, what's a pal to do?

With Zimbalist's wife, Barbara Bel Geddes, conveniently tucked away in the hospital (laid up, no doubt, after reading the script), adultery's in the air even before Turner and Zimbalist run into each other in the middle of the night and exchange the ripest existential pickup dialogue in movie history: "Somebody switched all my signposts along the road," he tells her. "Well, somebody painted arrows on mine," she replies. "They all say 'This way to nothing.' " After they've made it in her stable, Turner says, breathily, "You've made me feel alive again," though you'd scarcely guess it from her acting.

That same night, Hamilton walks out on nice girl Susan Kohner, looking instead for—you know—a good time. When Lana brushes him off, he picks up hash house waitress Yvonne Craig, of whom the local doctor says, "She's been around more in her twenty years than the moon in its millions." Craig urges Hamilton to stop drinking, with an argument they should have used in the "Just Say No" campaign: "If I get drunk and pass out, it's no fun for me. If you get drunk and pass out, it's no fun for me."

Ever wondered why the movies they select to show on airplanes are invariably awful? Well, *By Love Possessed* was the first movie ever shown as in-flight entertainment, setting a precedent that has been followed carefully in the decades since. (And when you see that it's *By Love*'s Zimbalist who turns up in a bit part as the pilot who gets creamed in *Airport 1975*, you'll know the score has been settled.)

With Thomas Mitchell, Everett Sloane. Produced by Walter Mirisch, directed by John Sturges. Screenplay by John Dennis, based on the novel by James Gould Cozzens. C, 116 m., V

The Chapman Report (1962) ❤ ❤

The opening credits suggest a classy movie—directed by George Cukor under the aegis of two Zanucks—but the film's very first line of dialogue tips us off that this will be a deliriously overwrought smutfest. At a press conference with the noted sexologist Dr. Chapman, a reporter asks, "Is the average American male more obsessed with sex?" Well, no more obsessed than this movie, that's for sure.

"Inspired," if that's the word, by America's fascination with the sex surveys conducted by then-hot Dr. Kinsey, *The Chapman Report* purports to show what happens when four suburban housewives agree to take part in Dr. Chapman's next study. The housewives are frigid widow Jane Fonda ("Help me, I don't want to be half a woman"), adulterous wife Shelley Winters ("Of course I'm sure my husband and I only do it once a week—Saturday night only comes once a week"), happily married poet Glynis Johns ("Am I abnormal?"), and nympho divorcee Claire Bloom ("I really wanted my husband, but I wanted everyone else too").

Though separated from interrogator Efrem Zimbalist, Jr., by a screen, Fonda primly drops her handbag when asked about her "preliminary loveplay" experiences. Zimbalist returns it to her home, where she screams, "They told me it would be anonymous, and now the interviewer's in my house!" Zimbalist, apparently attracted to noisy neurotics who wear their hair in symbolically tight French twists, takes her out to dinner.

At the beach, Johns is reading her own poetry into a tape recorder when touch-football stud Ty Hardin falls atop her. "What a magnificent animal," she utters, aloud. "He needs a woman who's better than he is." This is the kind of movie where "better" means "richer": She *pays him* to make love to her, and then offers him loveplay advice: "You can't just toss me around like a football."

When a married musician drops by neighbor Bloom's hacienda and leers, "You look awful hungry," they fall to the floor moments later. That night, he and his jazz-playing buddies gang rape Bloom, then toss her from a moving car into a cul-de-sac. But *The Chapman Report*'s pot really boils over when Bloom telephones her rapist and says, "Why should I be mad? How're the boys? I'll leave the door open." Mercifully for us, she overdoses on pills and booze.

When Zimbalist asks Fonda to marry him and she says she can't, he changes her mind by telling her, "You're not the first woman to find the physical act repellent." This melts her heart, and she kisses him, warmly, so we'll know that her problems are now solved, and they'll live happily ever after.

With Andrew Duggan, Harold Stone, Ray Danton, John Dehner, Cloris Leachman, and Chad Everett as the delivery boy who catches Bloom's roving eye. Produced by Richard Zanuck, directed by Cukor (who insisted that Darryl F. Zanuck ruined the movie by recutting it. Wouldn't you cop a plea, too?). Screenplay by Wyatt Cooper and Don M. Mankiewicz, from the Irving Wallace novel. C, 125 m., V

Desire Under the Elms (1958) ❤

Sophia Loren, in one of Hollywood's most ludicrous miscasting coups, plays the vixen who brings a New England family to ruin—a tragedy that created a scandal when playwright Eugene O'Neill introduced them to the stage in 1924. Of course, O'Neill didn't write that woman as a Neapolitan, any more than he envisioned twitchily oversensitive Anthony Perkins as the virile young buck who beds his own stepmother, fathers her son, and willingly undergoes arrest with her for the baby's murder. That's only the beginning of what makes this one a classic of botched casting, direction, and production.

Burl Ives—completely unconvincing, but, at least, trying for a New England accent—plays the patriarch of the family who lives by the creed "God is hard," and proves the good Lord isn't the only hard one by bedding Loren, who, the much revised dialogue explains, is a twenty-five-year-old former waitress and "greenhorn." "A home's got to have a woman," Ives grunts, to which lovely Loren, unsure of her English, croons, "A woooman's gotta to have-a home."

Though two of Ives's other sons—Frank Overton and "Bonanza" son-to-be Pernell Roberts in a very bad wig—crack that

Loren should be put "in the pen with the other sows," it's the supposedly studly son Perkins who catches Loren's eye (while he does manly things like chopping wood, shirtless, which has the undesired effect on us of making him look even more boyish than before). Lord knows there's no missing her, as she shoves out her breasts at him, hands on hips, and advises him not to clash so much with Ives. "I know how to make it easy for you with him," she says tantalizingly. Perkins puts her off, but Loren knows he can be had. "Ever since the day I came here," she drawls, "you've been fighting nature, trying to tell yourself I'm not pretty to you." She goads Ives by saying of Perkins, "It's lust eatin' his heart," and then, declaring, "I'm tired of old men," she's soon making hay in the hayloft with Perkins.

Although everyone in the village but Ives seems wise to whose baby gets a big christening party months later—"Unto him," an old geezer says of Perkins, "a brother is born"—the corn hits the grinder when Loren, angered that Perkins rejects her once the baby is born, smothers the kid and tells Ives what really happened. Perkins, vowing that he will endure "death, Hell, anything" (alluding, of course, to his later, even more disastrous screen teaming with Melina Mercouri), gets carted off with Loren to receive God's judgment. Everyone involved acts like they're making Art, which makes the awfulness all the more sublime.

Produced by Don Hartman, directed by Delbert Mann. Screenplay by Irwin Shaw, based on O'Neill's play. B&W, 111 m., V

The Long, Hot Summer (1958) ❤ ❤ ❤

Long and hot, sho' nuff. Whenever Hollywood tore into the high-toned works of William Faulkner, the results were inevitably Southern fried sex, sex, sex (think of *The Story of Temple Drake, Sanctuary, The Tarnished Angels*), resulting in some of the most entertaining Bad Movies you're ever likely to mosey into.

Wealthy "Big Daddy" Orson Welles—in a performance as broad as, well, Orson Welles—caresses Joanne Woodward, his spinster daughter, and drawls, "That's what I like. There's bones there, but the bones is covered up by plenty of real woman." Welles, so rich he owns the county's only town, frets that Woodward's repressed womanliness (she wears her hair in perhaps filmdom's tightest bun) is wasted on her mama's boy beau, Richard Anderson, who will leave her, Welles barks, the "best-looking old maid in the country." Everyone else in the cast is merrily rutting like mad. Woodward's weakling brother, Anthony Franciosa, spends most of the movie frolicking about like L'il Abner after his Daisy Mae, the luscious Lee Remick. Even Welles has a good thing going with backstreet gal Angela Lansbury.

Into this mint julep–flavored *Peyton Place* struts sexy drifter Ben Quick, Paul Newman, whom Franciosa hires on as a farmhand. "Don't you know what Quick means in this county?" bellows Welles to his son. "Hellfire! Ashes and char! Flame follows that man around like a dog. He's a barn-burner!" Realizing that Newman may be just the one to ignite Woodward's pilot light, Welles invites him to a grand family dinner. Out on the porch, Remick's presence sets local boys to a-hootin' and a-hollerin'. Woodward, shuddering, carps, "Listen to that—if those boys don't sound like a bunch of tomcats yowling at the moon." Franciosa commands Remick to get out of the light and chases them off—yelling, "Trash! Trash!"—but Welles snarls, "They don't have to see her. They can *smell* her."

Welles takes such a shine to Newman that he tells Woodward he's tired of waiting for male heirs and commands her to marry "that prize, blue-ribbon bull, that hand-grown, hand-picked, hand-selected-by-me fella." Woodward tries resisting Newman's animal magnetism, but late one night, Newman tells her to go for it: "The world belongs to meat-eaters, Miss Clara, and if you have to take it raw, take it raw." To facilitate that, Welles actually moves Newman into the Big House, sticking him in the room next to Woodward's; standing outside her bedroom window clad only in briefs, Newman howls her name. Woodward warns he's "barkin' up the wrong girl," but Newman assures her that, once she's tried him, she'll "wake up in the morning smiling."

Need a reminder of how much more fun Hollywood's sex sagas were in the '50s than nowadays? Watch the long, tepid 1985 TV remake starring Don Johnson and Cybill Shepherd.

Produced by Jerry Wald, directed by Martin Ritt. Screenplay by Irving Ravetch and Harriet Frank, from *Barn Burning*, *The Spotted Horses*, and *The Hamlet* by Faulkner. C, 118 m., V, L

Lucy Gallant (1955) ❤

A train carrying Jane Wyman gets stranded in a godforsaken
Texas oil boomtown, where farm owner Charlton Heston falls
instantly in love with her, because the script demands him to.
When he reveals he has a little ranch, Wyman says, "I didn't
know there was anything little in Texas." Posing his body for her
inspection, Heston drawls, "We do talk sorta big. Mostly true,
too."

Wyman, proper and prim in her Edith Head–tailored costumes, puts Heston off, so the other guys in town mistakenly
believe—because the script demands them to—that she's the
newest addition to the "saloon" of good-time gal Claire Trevor.
That's funny enough, but funnier still is how Wyman makes a
killing by selling off, to Thelma Ritter and the town's other dowdy
female population, her wedding trousseau. Announcing that
"Women can't wear derricks," Wyman purchases Trevor's sin pit
and transforms it into a chic, Manhattan-style dress shop that,
natch, makes her a fortune.

She teases Heston about wearing the right color boots with
his farming duds, but though he's sweet on her, he wants to make
a fortune on his own before marrying her. The oil companies long
to buy his idyllic farmland—envisioning an oil derrick on his
acreage, Wyman says, "I could see one right about here, trimmed
in chintz"—and Heston sells out. Though he loves Jane, she won't
have him—she reveals how her father's suicide left her stuck,
see, at the altar by her bridegroom—and Heston snarls, "You're
off men for life now?" Trevor tries to console Heston, saying,
"Don't you know the only way to forget one is to find another
one? . . . Okay, bleed to death!"

While Heston trudges through a World War II montage, Jane
and the town grow even richer, building ever-grander estates.
Heston turns up to propose to Wyman, but since he wants her
to quit working, they part. "You want to wind up a rich old maiden
lady warmin' your feet at night on a monogrammed hot water
bottle?" warns Ritter, who must have come to Texas by way of
Brooklyn. Yes, apparently, for Wyman opens the biggest, most

swank department store in all Texas, flying all over Europe to find the best designer clothes.

Hang on for the high point when Jane, together with her shifty suitor and business partner Tom Helmore, hosts the grand opening of her fabulous store and throws a whale of a fashion show, attended by no less than the real then-governor of Texas and, as the celebrity moderator, Miss Edith Head. Helmore tries swindling Wyman out of power, but when Heston saves the day, she consents to marry him. You can tell this is the '50s for, when Heston asks who will mind the store while they enjoy wedded bliss, Jane gushes, "What store?"

Produced by William H. Pine and William C. Thomas, directed by Robert Parrish. Screenplay by John Lee Mahin and Winston Miller, from *The Life of Lucy Gallant* by Margaret Cousins. C, 104 m., TV

No Down Payment (1957) ❤

Movies about sex in a small town reached a loony apex in 1957, when 20th Century-Fox and producer Jerry Wald churned out both *Peyton Place* and this suburban exposé that suggests even regular Joes in G.I. Bill tract homes go bad, too.

"Here's to Sunrise Hills, the place for better living for young lovers," toasts sloshed salesman Tony Randall at a barbecue with his long-suffering wife, Sheree North, and his immediate neighbors, who are gas jockey Cameron Mitchell and his wife, slatternly Southern belle Joanne Woodward, atheist Pat Hingle and his religious-minded missus, Barbara Rush, and nice new arrivals Jeffrey Hunter and his good—but bored—bride, Patricia Owens. Everything's not as hunky-dory as the movie's pristine sets: North snarls at Randall, "All you do is chase after every tramp in town." Hingle asks Rush to enlist her church to help his Japanese employee get into their closed community, and she rages, "You want to strike a bargain with God before you even believe in him? Well, God doesn't do business that way!" Woodward nags Mitchell about the child they put up for adoption and he barks, "I tried to get that baby back, I tried!" Owens craves "excitement" and Hunter sneers, "What kind of excitement? Like when you were eighteen and the phone kept ringing and you'd get singing telegrams and guys came around, six deep, and I had to wait in line?"

Is it any wonder Randall asks the fellows plaintively, *"You ever fight with your wives?"* We'll say—in real life, Rush was Hunter's ex! The tensions bubble higher during another patiofest where, when Woodward drawls to Hunter, "Hey Dave, you rock," she's not assessing his stiff-as-a-board acting, she's asking him to dance. They bop to the hilariously hep ditty "The Drive-In Rock."

When, the next day, Mitchell isn't named police chief because he doesn't have a college education, he commits the ultimate act of '50s violence—he kicks in his own TV screen! Then he sends Woodward out to pick up a man. Then he goes next door and rapes Owens. "Other men have disappointments," spits Rush, "but they don't become animals!" The next morning, Owens tries telling Hunter that "something happened last night" but—in a touch so mad it prefigures the sharp satire of John Waters's films—she has to scream this over the drone of Hunter's electric razor. Hunter confronts Mitchell, who growls, "I might be the first but I ain't gonna be the last!" making Woodward hiss, "I never want to see you again as long as I live!" which she proves by shoving Mitchell under the car he was repairing and—as the car's heard the whole sordid thing—it obligingly crushes him to death.

Produced by Wald, directed by Martin Ritt. Screenplay by Philip Yordan, based on John McPartland's novel. B&W, 105 m., TV

Peyton Place (1957) ❤ ❤ ❤

After all these years—plus a sequel, a weekly series, and even a TV "reunion" movie—this film of Grace Metalious's bestseller remains the ne plus ultra of Bad Movies about sexy secrets hidden just below the placid surface of a tiny town. This is due, in part, to the hilarious miscasting of aging sex bomb Lana Turner as the prim matron who goes bonkers when she comes home to find her teenage daughter, Diane Varsi, kissing (in the dark, at her own birthday party) rich rotter Barry Coe. He explains: "We were just playing a game called 'Photography'—you turn out the lights and see what develops." Turner throws all the kids out, barking, "I knew this would happen." Varsi remarks, "Everything has to be learned, even kissing—," and Turner snaps, "And *sex*? Is that what you're going to practice at your next party? I don't want you to get a reputation." Varsi wises Turner up: "I already have one—the wrong kind. If any man would seriously ask me, I'd become his mistress!"

The 1001 delights of *Peyton Place* come from the fact that this exchange is not an over-the-top highlight: *everyone* in town talks this way. Here's what bad girl Terry Moore says when Varsi opines that Moore's new dress is "a little fast": "Just remember, men can see much better than they can think. A lowcut neckline does more for a girl's future than the entire Britannica encyclopedia!" Indeed, Moore lands wealthy Coe, telling him, "I think you're ten percent man and ninety percent talk." Coe's comeback? "You're one hundred percent woman." Moore corrects, "Two hundred and fifty percent. Maybe five hundred percent. It's going to take a lot more than money to keep me."

Across town, white trash Hope Lange calls her drunken stepfather, Arthur Kennedy, "You dirty filthy animal!" but that doesn't stop him from having his way with her and—oh, the shame—calling Lange "a little wildcat" too. She becomes pregnant, murders Kennedy, then suffers a miscarriage. Meanwhile, Varsi learns from Turner that she's illegitimate and runs to her room in hysterics, where she finds that their maid—Betty Field, Lange's mother—has hanged herself in the closet.

Wait, there's more! The new principal, Lee Phillips, spots what's bothering Turner. "It isn't sex you're afraid of—it's love," he says. "And that's what you're offering me," she asks, "with your hands all over me?" Later, she turns up at his place in a hot-mama, red cocktail dress to pant, "I wanted you more than you ever could have wanted me," and then adds the howler that few Bad Movies can hope to duplicate. "I've always been so afraid of *scandal*," says the star whose very name was—and is—synonymous with the word. Incredibly, unbelievably, astoundingly, Turner was Oscar-nominated for this performance!

With Lloyd Nolan, David Nelson, Leon Ames, Mildred Dunnock, Russ Tamblyn. Produced by Jerry Wald, directed by Mark Robson. Screenplay by John Michael Hayes, from Metalious's novel. C, 157 m., V

Return to Peyton Place (1961) ❤❤

"To coin a cliché," Manhattan publisher Jeff Chandler tells neophyte novelist Carol Lynley, "I'm going to make you the hottest writer in America, an overnight celebrity, a household word. Before I'm through with you, you're going to be sorry you learned how to spell!" Lynley (who, like everyone else in the cast, is pinch-hitting for the performer who originally played her character in *Peyton Place*) races to New York, leaving behind the sordid small town she has immortalized in print.

Her best pal, Tuesday Weld, recovers from murdering her stepfather just in time to have her heart broken when her former beau, Brett Halsey, returns home with a bride, Luciana Paluzzi. Far unhappier is Halsey's "possessive, evil, meddling mother," Mary Astor, who snipes about Paluzzi, "Maybe it's just the way she dresses." Astor then hides inside a closet, the better to hear the newlyweds making love. Come morning, Paluzzi knows the score and tells Astor, "What you'd like to do is change places with me." Astor snaps, "You have a *filthy* mind"—but in this movie, who doesn't?

In the Big Apple, Lynley seems destined to repeat her mother's mistakes (have wild affair with married man, shamefully produce an illegitimate offspring) but since Chandler's such a smoothie, who wouldn't swoon? "Seldom has the writer of a first novel gotten me as excited," Chandler pants at Lynley. "Your descriptive passages—they're sheer poetry."

Though this is novelist Grace Metalious's account of what happened when *Peyton Place* was initially published, we doubt that's what any esteemed publisher had to say about her writing. We'd guess it went something more like what happens when Lynley's home town reads the just published masterwork. Lynley's mother, Eleanor Parker, announces, "It's *cheap* and *dirty* and *vulgar!*" Astor proclaims, "It's *lewd*, a *lurid* piece of *trash!*" then dumps it in the wastebasket. Weld, hearing her sleazy, bad girl life reduced to sleazy, bad girl pulp when her boyfriend Gunnar Hellstrom reads Lynley's book aloud, goes further than Parker or Astor—Weld goes insane. "Like all the rest, you want to know all the dirty, perverted details of a sex act!" she screams, brandishing a fire poker at Hellstrom, who gets in a memorable query ("Was it dirty?") before he gets offed.

Lynley returns when her stepfather, principal Robert Sterling, loses his job for the single craziest thing in the entire crazy movie: he wants Lynley's book in the high school's library! In a choice mother-daughter showdown, Parker sneers at Lynley, "You've sold a lot of things for success. You can't buy back your decency, your friends, your self-respect!" then slaps Lynley (hard), who hisses back, "I hate you for that!" Lynley then loses Chandler to his wife, apparently without ever having actually consummated their "torrid" affair. So Lynley's still got that one thing that's more important than decency, friends, or self-respect—her virginity.

Produced by Jerry Wald, directed by José Ferrer. Screenplay by Ronald Alexander, based on Metalious's novel. C, 122 m., V

Ruby Gentry (1952) ❤ ❤

"Don't let it shake you—it's just *anatomy*," advises rich Karl Malden when the new doctor in town spies Jennifer Jones posing with her hip thrust out in the doorway of her pappy's hunting lodge. No, actually, it's just miscasting in this overheated sex drama from director King (*Beyond the Forest, The Fountainhead*) Vidor. Jones, a narrator solemnly tells us, "was born on the wrong side of the tracks, and though she struggled valiantly to overcome this stigma, the townspeople never let her forget it." You'll never forget the spectacle of Jones playing yet another sexy hellcat for Vidor who, after directing her hilariously bad performance in *Duel in the Sun*, really should have known better.

Rich Charlton Heston returns home after years in South America, and drawls at Jones, "Let's see what I've been missin'. . . . You grown any?" Jones eyes Heston hungrily, but snaps, "You can't come back and treat me like part of the scenery—I'm not just a North Carolina dame." She wants respectability, see, but

Heston's engaged to proper Phyllis Avery. Jones's Bible-toting brother James Anderson condemns her ("You wanton fool!"), but her trashy father advises, "At the right time, give him the right bait," so Jones shacks up with Heston. The morning after, Heston drawls, "It's been so sweet and wild and crazy," but . . . he's gonna marry the rich Avery. "Yeah, she's got brains and breedin'," Jones hisses. "Both of you, like a pair of pedigreed hounds."

On the rebound, Jones marries Malden, and though he throws a huge party to break her into society, the local snobs spurn her. Finding Jones and Heston dancing intimately, Malden growls at his wife, "You little tramp! You're dressed up to look like a lady. It's a pity you can't behave like one!" Malden up and drowns, making Jones the richest woman in town; she's determined to bring the citizenry to its knees. "They tramped over my life," she bitches, "treatin' me like I was trash!" She offers to underwrite Heston's plantation, emasculates him, and as they hunt together in the bayou, he stalks her, growling, "Why do you have to ruin everything you touch?"

Then, in a demented replay of the finale of *Duel in the Sun*, Jones and Heston, pursued by her religious fanatic brother, crawl through the fog and swampy waters, until Anderson shoots Heston, and Jones shoots Anderson and kicks his body into the water.

Don't miss the hasty epilogue in which we learn that Jones—hair cropped and looking mad as a hatter—is now a sea captain. "Yes, Ruby Gentry was born on the wrong side of the tracks," explains the narrator in case we missed it the first forty times, "and the people of Braddock never let her forget it." Neither will you.

Produced by Joseph Bernard and Vidor, directed by Vidor. Screenplay by Silvia Richards, from a story by Arthur Fitz-Richard. B&W, 82 m., V

Strangers When We Meet (1960) ❤❤

Neighbors Kim Novak and Kirk Douglas seem destined for an extramarital affair, because their friends keep saying they're, well, the type. Architect Douglas's pal Walter Matthau envies Douglas working at home. Matthau leers, "You get a chance to watch the procession, the itchy foot club—tramp, tramp, tramp! They want romance. There's nothing romantic about the slob they see shaving in his pajamas. You and me, we're furniture in our own homes, but if we go next door—aha! we're heroes. Any place you got a housewife, you got a potential mistress." Novak's mother Virginia Bruce couldn't agree more, telling Novak, "I'm not a tramp—what happened to me could happen to any woman." And does, from the moment Douglas and Novak eye each other at their kids' bus stop.

She's soon visiting the lot where he's building a house for author Ernie Kovacs. As those two-by-fours start going up, both find reasons to get out at night. Novak asks her husband, as she's leaving, "Suppose I'm going to meet another man? It happens," only to be told, "Not to someone like you." Wearing designer Jean Louis's form-fitting, tomato red dress that fairly screams "yes," Novak flees from her rendezvous with Douglas. He catches her in the parking lot, where she pants, "Don't, please don't kiss me. . . ." and then, after he does, "Oh yes! Yes! Yes!" *Costumes never lie.*

One day at "their" motel, Douglas comes to blows with some stud trying to pick up Novak. Afterwards, Douglas asks, "How'd he know your name?" He's a truck driver who stopped up at her house one day, Novak explains, and after he left—even though she knew he was coming back—Novak took sleeping pills. "I tried to fight him," she says. Douglas, shocked, says, "You took those pills to make it easy . . . you wanted what happened, you—," but before he can finish that thought, Novak drives away. Ashamed, Douglas goes to Novak's house, then into her bedroom, to beg forgiveness, and Novak's mother says, "So it happened to you."

Torn up over whether to stay with wife Barbara Rush or start anew with Novak, Douglas confides in Kovacs. "I'm such a phony," Douglas says. "I've got a drawer full of manufactured labels: 'architect,' 'husband,' 'father,' 'son.' " (Though he doesn't throw in "actor," we're happy to.) "I sew them into my clothes . . . the suits never fit." When Matthau tries raping Rush in a last-minute plot device, Douglas defends hearth and home—and realizes it's Rush he loves. Novak, understanding, comes to see the finished house Douglas built and says goodbye, driving off, no doubt, in search of that truck driver.

With Kent Smith, Helen Gallagher, Roberta Shore, Nancy Kovack. Produced and directed by Richard Quine. Screenplay by Evan Hunter, based on his novel. C, 117 m., TV

The Stripper (1963) ❤

"Look, there's Jayne Mansfield," says an old biddy on one of those Hollywood Star Homes tour buses as she spots a bubble-haired platinum blonde in skin-tight Capri pants. "No, it isn't, it's Kim Novak," argues her companion. "No, it isn't," snarls the bus driver, "it's nobody." Actually, it's Joanne Woodward, shoved into one of the many parts intended for Marilyn Monroe before she died.

This one—from a William Inge play—casts Woodward as a third-rate showgirl who blows into "Squaresville" with her scuzzy boyfriend/manager Robert Webber, and fellow troupe members Louis Nye and Gypsy Rose Lee. Taking a long look at the grease monkey who helps her with those terribly tricky Coke machines ("I'm just terrible with mechanical things," she purrs), Woodward declares, as they drive off, "Funny, he reminds me of somebody." (Could she mean that the pump jockey, Richard Beymer, reminds her of Warren Beatty, who'd originated the role on Broadway but was too old by the time the movie was ready?)

Meanwhile, dewy Carol Lynley and lonely widder Claire Trevor, Beymer's mom, have their different hopes pinned on Beymer's future. Trevor invites Woodward to dinner and Beymer—practically convulsed with lust—walks Woodward back to her hotel, during which she recalls her past beauty contest triumphs as "Miss Look-alike Betty Grable, then in San Bernardino, I was Miss Look-alike Rita Hayworth, and in Pomona, I was Joan Crawford's spittin' image." She shows Beymer a strip of celluloid she carries in her purse from her unsuccessful screen test. "A lot of stars get started late," observes Woodward—whose movies, at the time, despite her having won an Oscar for *The Three Faces of Eve*, tended to be financial duds—"especially these days."

Later, Woodward shacks up with Trevor and Beymer, to whom she admits, "It's awful hard livin' in the same house with you." She tries to head him off by saying, "Once, I took sleeping pills and they had to give me shock treatments" but Beymer has his way with her, then dumps her. So Webber books Woodward into dives doing The Twist covered in balloons and singing "Something's Got to Give" (the title song, incidentally, of Marilyn Monroe's last, unfinished movie). Like Monroe doing "That Old Black Magic" in *Bus Stop*—also by Inge—Woodward's supposed to be touchingly awful, but instead she's, well, just plain awful.

When Woodward decides to strike out solo, Webber tells her, "You're going to be cruisin' street corners, looking for any trick you can find and when you can't find any, you're going to start taking those sleepin' pills of yours. Maybe this time, you'll just jump out a window at some fleabag hotel!" Instead, Woodward stayed clear of hokum like this and wound up a Grand Lady of TV and the Cinema.

Produced by Jerry Wald, directed by Franklin Schaffner. Screenplay by Meade Roberts, from Inge's play *A Loss of Roses*. B&W, 95 m., V, L

Two-Moon Junction (1988) ❤ ❤

From the fevered imagination of Zalman (*9½ Weeks*, *Wild Orchid*) King comes this howler that introduces us to bleached-blonde Southern deb Sherilyn Fenn, crouching at a peephole to watch guys in a shower, then going all glazed-eyed and masturbating as she slides to the bottom of the tub. Mega rich, partial to white outfits that match her BMW, and destined to inherit practically the entire universe, Fenn is also engaged to a handsome, moneyed bozo, Martin Hewitt (understandably absent from the screen since *Endless Love*). "Keep him wild as long as you can," counsels Fenn's grandmother, Louise Fletcher (terrifying in a wig that looks as if it's made of Dream Whip), whose family estate, she boasts, has hosted everyone from "Civil War heroes to Betty Ford, after her rehabilitation."

But no sooner has a carnival slipped into town than Fenn practically salivates at the sight of Richard Tyson, the sinewy, silent drifter in low-slung jeans, who mostly lets his pecs do the talking. Before you can say "convenient plot device," Fenn's parents, Don Galloway and Millie Perkins, zip away on a trip, leaving Fenn to find the dark and dangerous Tyson in her shower stall, shampooing himself in the strangest come-on in movie history: Watch Me Wash Myself. From then on, though, Fenn's too far gone to stop her stud from videotaping their MTV-style cavorting on the living room rug, or prowling the fairgrounds by night ("I couldn't sleep," she murmurs, looking him up and down), or shacking up in motels. Naturally—the course of true lust never did run smooth—Fenn is soon calling her boytoy a "hollow, manipulative piece of shit," telling him, "everything you own is between your legs!"

Three guesses which man Fenn ends up with, but trust us, the supporting cast alone makes for Bad Movie bliss: Herve Villechaize ("Fuck you!" is his only line), Burl Ives, and the indispensable Juanita (*Imitation of Life*) Moore. And don't miss Kristy McNichol's eye-popping turn as Patti-Jean, the truckdriving hairdresser, who encourages Fenn to exchange underclothes with her and seduces her into some dirty dancing at a honky-tonk. "It's at times like these," McNichol asserts, "I can see why guys like women so much." But Millie Perkins, a long, long way from *The Diary of Anne Frank*, snags the movie's choicest moment when she lays on her daughter—the night before her wedding—a Louis Vuitton caseful of contraceptives.

Sex-mad director King could lay claim to being the postmodern Russ Meyer—except that he actually seems to take his crackpot oeuvre seriously. Apparently, so do others; in France, *9½ Weeks* and its star Mickey Rourke are revered.

With Dabbs Greer, Milla, Screamin' Jay Hawkins. Produced by Donald Borchers, directed and written by King. Screenplay by King, from a story by King and MacGregor Douglas. C, 104 m., V, L

Vanity, Thy Name Is Lucy

To celebrate the sheer, demonic, egomaniacal insistence of Lucille Ball—who became legendary as TV's "Lucy Ricardo," the funniest but most untalented nonsinger, nondancer in show biz history—on playing the worldly Manhattan madcap in the all-singing, all-dancing movie musical *Mame*, we've dedicated this chapter which recalls stars whose egos have led them—and the studios (or husbands) that backed them—way, way down South. Watch any flick in this chapter and revel in the knee-slapping spectacle of what happens when a powerful star or star director gets in way over his or her pampered head.

And God Created Woman (1988) ❤

A beautiful blonde convict makes a daring prison escape, flags down a passing limousine, quaffs champagne with the gubernatorial candidate inside, gets returned to the Big House and breaks back in, makes love with a hunky construction worker while standing up, complains that her break for freedom was a fiasco ("Hey," replies her cellmate, "at least you got laid"), then joins the other hardened inmates for an impromptu a cappella song-and-dance number—and that's just the first ten minutes of this self-indulgent Roger Vadim extravaganza. The film, Vadim's overhaul of his own sexy 1957 French hit (which, though pretty bad, at least had the compensating factor of making an international sensation out of Brigitte Bardot), earns a special place in the history of cinema as, of all things, the worst movie remake of a film by the same director as the original.

Now, admittedly, there's some fierce competition in this doofus sweepstakes of inflated egos: Howard Hawks turned his great 1941 comedy *Ball of Fire* into the feeble 1948 musical *A Song Is Born*; Jean Negulesco turned his 1954 soap opera *Three Coins in the Fountain* into the feeble 1966 musical *The Pleasure Seekers*; Mitchell Leisen turned his 1939 comedy *Midnight* into the feeble 1945 musical *Masquerade in Mexico*. Vadim, however, cops the coveted top spot not only because he, too, turned his flick into a feeble musical but because he went the others one better (well, not exactly *better*) and decided that the movie, instead of just being filled with lots of cheapo sex scenes, should showcase the acting and singing skills of Rebecca De Mornay. (After her career-stalling debacle playing a rock 'n' roller in *The Slugger's Wife*, one would have hardly bet that De Mornay would think it prudent to warble onscreen again.) Luckily, the movie boasts more than its fair share of crazed plot twists to make amends for the error of Vadim's ways.

To get outta prison once and for all, De Mornay pays Vincent Spano, the hammer-and-nails stud she screwed in the slammer, to marry her, but then she won't come across, telling him "I'm not that kind of wife." The thrust of the plot—and *thrust* is indeed the operative word here—concerns how long the husband will wait before jumping her (and if you guess that it will finally happen in an empty art museum, maybe you should be directing unintentionally hilarious movies yourself.)

Till then, De Mornay stays busy as that kind of cheating wife: sitting on a pool table with her thighs spread apart, she orders married politician Frank Langella to "Get down on your knees" and—suffice it to say—indeed he does. Sated, De Mornay gives Langella a hot-tub hand-job, which we suppose is sort of a safe-sex "thank you" note.

With Donovan Leitch. Produced by George G. Braunstein and Ron Hamady, directed by Vadim. Screenplay by R. J. Stewart, based on Vadim's original script. C, 100 m., V

Butterfly (1981) ❤❤❤

This saga of a penniless dad willing to do anything, *anything*, to get into the pants of his short wild child is niftily paralleled, offscreen, by the saga of a sugar daddy willing to do anything, *anything*, to make his short starlet child-bride happy. Whoever said that money can't buy happiness doesn't know how Meshulam Riklis's untold fortune bought his wife Pia Zadora a James M. Cain novel to trash on screen, paid for actors like Stacy Keach and Orson Welles to drag their names even further down, purchased a costly ad campaign to help win Zadora an undeserved Golden Globe award, and—with the spare change left over—snapped up the writing, producing, and directing skills of one of Jayne Mansfield's ex-husbands.

All pudgy baby fat in her Bob Mackie–designed "white trash" wardrobe, Zadora meets up with Keach, the father who abandoned her, and pouts her thick lips to utter, "Don't it get lonely out here? Or is milking that cow good enough for you?" with unmistakable intent: Why not milk this cow? Learning that she's pregnant and unmarried, Keach calls Zadora "bad," and she responds, "The first time I ever had a dollar bill in my hand, I was twelve. I let one of the boarders spend the night with me. Maybe that was bad, but the things I bought with that money was good. I want good things for me and my baby, and if that's bad . . . *then I want to be bad!*"

Does she ever! Zadora climbs nude into her bath and asks Keach to rub her shoulders: "You got good hands," she sighs, as—in a meant-to-be-mouthwatering close-up—he cups one of her bare breasts, then says "It ain't right." Zadora cries, "Feels good to me!" grabs his hand and thrusts it way below the surface of the water. Their idyll is interrupted when Zadora's mother, hooker Lois Nettleton, turns up with the louse who really fathered Zadora, James Franciscus. Before you know it, they're both conveniently dead and Keach (who knows he's not Zadora's father) can finally have sex with Zadora (who doesn't know, and doesn't care).

The police arrest them for incest which, Judge Welles pontificates, "is a crime against nature, shocking and repulsive." To

get her set free, Keach claims he forced himself on Zadora, but
she stands up in court and cries out, "He never forced me to do
anything! What we did was bound to happen from the first day
we met, and when it did," she pants, "it was good for both of
us"—as if testimony about mutual orgasm will sway the jury and
get them off. But it's not to be: Welles decides, "You're going to
reform school," causing visions of Pia Zadora reform-school-girl
movies to swim before our eyes.

With Edward Albert, Stuart Whitman, Ed McMahon, June
Lockhart. Produced and directed by Matt Cimber. Screenplay by
Cimber and John Goff, based on the Cain novel. C, 105 m., V, L

Communion (1989) ❤ ❤ ❤

Christopher Walken's way out there performance as novelist
Whitley Strieber—who not only claims to have been abducted,
examined, prodded, and probed by little blue creatures, but also
wrote the screenplay to capture every "true" detail as no one else
possibly could—is enough to ensconce this *very* late entry in the
'70s space-epic cycle into the "must-see" Bad Movie pantheon of
Egos Run Amok.

In the opening, Walken bolts upright in bed, muttering,
"Something's here . . . Umm! Ummm!" Then we're treated to a
typical work day for a famous New York author: Walken mumbles
aloud his latest "Knock-knock" jokes. Suddenly, his computer
conks out—gee, a whole day's "Knock-knock" jokes down the
tubes!—and in pops his annoying wife, Lindsay Crouse, who, as
the real life ex–Mrs. David Mamet, certainly knows about being
married to a Living Legend. Walken rambles, "Oy vey, what a
day, what a schmeer! . . . I lost, you know, I lost another day.
What I lost was gold, gold in an ocean is erased, smoke dreams,
phantoms. What I crave is, you know, consolation . . ." (His son,
Joel Carlson, rolls his eyes and moans, "Oh, brother," seconds
after we do.)

Guessing Walken needs a breather from the immensity of his
gifts, the family's off to their swell country house. While everyone's snoozing, the rooms suddenly flood with blinding white
light—you know, the kind from Spielberg movies—and Walken

spies an ugly little space thing who shoves a surgical probe through his skull. (Don't you hate it when that happens?)

From here on in, Walken seems even nuttier—if that's possible—than before, and Crouse insists they get help. We're thinking, right, what these two need is a nice long stay in Bad Actor Rehab, but no, she ships Walken off to shrink Frances Sternhagen. Under hypnosis, Walken undergoes flashbacks in which he dances with space creatures, fantasizes himself as a magician, and gets to wear intense mascara. "Somebody came and took me," he mumbles. "They were small, bluish-skinned . . . and . . . others . . . long, thin faces and big eyes . . . I think I'm hallucinating, major, maybe psychotic, hallucinations . . . I had some kind of rectal probe . . ."

You'll think you're hallucinating, too, when Crouse bellows, "My shoes hurt!" and flings them across the room. (Crouse-watchers will savor what has become a motif in her performances: in *The Desperate Hours*, she complains about earrings that hurt.) You'll love it when Walken free-associates with his alien visitors: "Can we talk this over? It looks like you're going to sing *White Christmas* . . . You've broken my mind!" But nothing tops the moment when Crouse stands—amazed—as Walken tells her he's going out for a pack of cigarettes, then does a song and dance to "Puttin' on the Ritz," leaving her to mutter, "You don't smoke."

Produced by Phillipe Mora, Whitley Strieber, and Dan Allingham, directed by Mora. Screenplay by Strieber, based on his book. Main theme composed and performed by Eric Clapton. Clothes for Walken, Crouse, and Sternhagen by Perry Ellis. C, 100 m., V

The Game Is Over (1966) ❤

Roger Vadim directs movies of such idiosyncratic, hypnotic awfulness, they almost make other directors' movies seem quaint in their insistence on such trivialities as plot, characters, coherence.

This made-in-Paris Vadim vanity affair based on Émile Zola's *La Curée* is built around Vadim's then-wife, sexpot Jane Fonda, doing her take on Vadim's "eternal woman," this time round, the capricious trophy wife of wealthy Parisian Michel Piccoli and playmate of Peter McEnery, her stupid stepson. Vadim knew a thing or two about turning his girlfriends into sex kittens (think what he did for Brigitte Bardot and Catherine Deneuve) and he had Fonda pegged from the jump: in her first scene, Fonda works out with fierce self-absorption in her exercise room, while trying to ignore McEnery, who follows her around with a movie camera. (It was years before Fonda saw the possibilities in combining the two.)

For reasons clear only to the director, Fonda, naked underneath her coat, stalks McEnery with a rifle and starts shooting up his bedroom. "Your wife tried to kill me," McEnery casually informs Piccoli. "Unfortunately," Fonda snaps, "I missed." With Piccoli away, McEnery, dressed as Genghis Khan, slinks into Fonda's room where she's half-naked, her face bizarrely painted in "a cream for preventing wrinkles." The two chase each other, she does a self-conscious hootchy-koo with a silk scarf, and they make love. At a swank party later that night, Fonda gets so worked up over seeing McEnery with his girlfriend, Tina Marquand, she stuffs her mouth with flowers and starts chomping. The next day, Fonda slaps McEnery's face and asks, "You don't like my hair, do you?"—then, in a robe with a cigarette dangling from her lips, dances to African drums.

Our illicit, incestuous lovers go for a drive across the entire French countryside, taking a short-cut McEnery knows. Vadim actually keeps the sound and cameras rolling while Fonda hilariously inserts the word "short-cut" into the lyrics to "Alouette," "Oh, Susanna," "The Battle Hymn of the Republic," and "For He's a Jolly Good Fellow." Here's one eternal woman you never want to car pool with.

You haven't really experienced the endless possibilities available in Bad Movies till you've seen Fonda, with a bad Carol Burnett haircut, turn up at Piccoli's "Green Ball," staring through the windows like Stella Dallas as dancing extras samba. She hurls herself into a pond, then—hair dripping and mascara running—walks zombie-like past the revelers, embarrassing both Piccoli and McEnery. (After all, she isn't wearing green!) In the end, she stares blankly at the camera—*New Wave* enough for you?—but, in the real world, Fonda survived to work again.

Produced and directed by Vadim. Modern adaptation of Zola

by Jean Cau, Vadim, with the collaboration of Bernard Frechtman; dialogue by Cau. C, 96 m., V

The Jazz Singer (1980) ❤ ❤

Quick, name the pop singer who made the biggest fool out of himself when he unwisely tried his hand at making movies. If you answered, "Roger Daltrey in *Lisztomania*," "Paul Simon in *One-Trick Pony*," or "Madonna in *Who's That Girl?*" then you've never seen the third version of *The Jazz Singer*, which makes Neil Diamond the all-time champ chump.

"So vat's da rush?" asks Diamond's father, Laurence Olivier, when Diamond cuts out of cantoring at the shul earlier than usual. But how can Diamond explain that he's unsatisfied with the five-generation family tradition of being a cantor, so he's hurrying uptown to a Harlem nightclub where he performs, in black face, for an all-black audience? This being Diamond's own vanity movie, the black audience loves his music—it's the telltale sight of his lily-white hands they don't care for. "That's a white boy!" cries an understandably outraged man. A fight breaks out, and Diamond is jailed. When Olivier bails him out, he asks his errant fortysomething unmarried son, "It's not tough enough being a Jew?" Diamond explains, "God doesn't pay so good." All this, in the film's first ten minutes!

Diamond flees to L.A. to break into show biz. There he meets record company flunky Lucie Arnaz, who becomes his manager by holding a big-time agent at gunpoint until he'll listen to Diamond's demo tape. (Since she's required to deliver dialogue like, "Is *schmuck* a Jewish word? I just wanted to say something in Jewish to you," Arnaz should have held her own agent at gunpoint to get out of this movie.) If you've guessed that what comes next is a falling-in-love montage, you probably haven't guessed that it goes thus: walk on the beach, she converts to Judaism, *then* they get naked by the fireside.

When Olivier turns up in L.A. to tell Diamond "Come home vit me, now," Diamond replies, "I can't, Pop, I just cut my first album." When he realizes that his son's living in sin with Arnaz, Olivier stops the movie cold with his line reading of four little words, "I hef no son!" In movies this bad, it's not the stars who can't act (Arnaz, Diamond) that do real damage, it's the stars who can act that bring the film to its knees. *The Jazz Singer* had been a Bad Movie twice before, but it took the participation of a full-blown hamola like Olivier to turn this dross into a Bad Movie We Love.

All ends happily, of course. By the time the requisite Neil Diamond-in-sequins concert ending rolls around, Olivier's out in the audience sitting cozily with Arnaz—he's part of the family again, now that there's an illegitimate lovechild as his grandson. If nothing else, *The Jazz Singer* is definitely a notch above Diamond's previous venture in moviemaking—supplying the treacly pseudospiritual soundtrack for *Jonathan Livingston Seagull.*

With Catlin Adams, Sully Boyar, Franklyn Ajaye, Paul Nicholas, Mike Kellin. Produced by Jerry Leider, directed by Richard Fleischer. Screenplay by Herbert Baker and Stephen H. Foreman. C, 115 m., V, L

Mame (1974) ❤ ❤

Among connoisseurs of unintentionally hilarious movies, *Mame* separates the men from the boys. It's so terrible that it's not just funny, it's frighteningly funny. Watch it and wonder, "What were they thinking of?" *Sunset Boulevard* aficionados will quickly realize that this movie, rather than the *Salome* that Norma Desmond hoped would return her to glory, is the faded Hollywood star's vanity production nonpareil, and that Lucille Ball as Auntie Mame is a good deal scarier than Gloria Swanson as Desmond. The difference, of course, is that Swanson was *supposed* to be scary.

Ball allegedly sank a large chunk of her personal fortune into the making of this musical *Titanic*, which is the only possible explanation for how anyone in Hollywood could possibly have offered her the title role. A movie chorus girl way back in the years before she was TV's Lucy Ricardo, Ball envisioned a triumphant return to the silver screen in Jerry Herman's hit Broadway musical (based on the earlier play and movie *Auntie Mame*). But to put it kindly, it had been so long since she'd sung or danced, every number in *Mame* had to be s-l-o-w-e-d d-o-w-n for Ball's minute vocal range and one-two terpsichorean talents.

The results are like watching a musical taffy pull. It's a model of self-deception: Ball, trying to look young enough for the role, employs every trick of the trade to tautly pull her wrinkles and lines into a mask-like visage of middle age. When she dons a plastic Santa Claus face for the song "We Need a Little Christmas," the eerie effect of one mask over the other sends chills up the spine—it stops the show, all right, but not the way Ball and company imagined.

Maybe you won't want to watch *Mame* all the way to the end, but do: The conclusion is a loony montage of earlier scenes showing Auntie Mame hugging one co-star after another—a movie first and, one hopes, a movie last.

With Jane Connell, who stepped in to recreate her Broadway role of the nanny Gooch after Ball had Madeline Kahn fired (perhaps Ball realized that it was Kahn who should have been playing *Mame*?), Robert Preston, Beatrice Arthur, Bruce Davison, Joyce Van Patten, John McGiver, and as the young Patrick, the utterly resistible Kirby Furlong. Produced by Robert Fryer and James Cresson, directed by Gene Saks. Screenplay by Paul Zindel, from the play by Jerome Lawrence and Robert E. Lee, based on the novel by Patrick Dennis. C, 131 m., V, L

Revenge (1990) ❤

If you know your Bad Movies, then you know that there are certain rules. For example, if a retired flyboy makes love to a raven-haired woman belonging to an Anthony Quinn–esque hambone, then the lovers must die! (Anyway, that's how it goes in *The Other Side of Midnight*, which you'll wish you were watching before *Revenge* is over.) Here, Kevin Costner is the flyboy, Quinn himself is the Quinn type, and his raven-haired wife is Madeleine Stowe. Costner and Stowe go at it while standing up in a coatroom at a party, and then while he's driving his open-air jeep, but their affair causes a problem: Costner wants to be viewed as the movie's hero even though he is playing the movie's heel, but since Costner is the film's executive producer, well, Costner's character just becomes the hero, even though he's the heel.

The movie goes loco when Quinn and his henchmen catch the couple in the act, but both Costner and Stowe survive the, er, fatal beating they're given. Peasant shamans find Costner's bod in the desert; they nurse him back to health, apparently by wrapping him in just enough chiffon so that the famed Costner tush can be glimpsed (millions will miss it when Costner finally retires it from the screen). Stowe, on the other hand, is spirited away to a whorehouse where she gets turned into a junkie—or something (since Stowe's acting here, whether she's playing alive, drugged, aroused, or dead, is all pretty much the same, it's hard to tell). Costner, bent on revenge, befriends James Gammon, a wheezin' TB-ridden cowpoke who becomes Costner's roommate (oh—don't ask). Getting ready to go out on the town, Gammon suggests Costner come along: "A little poontang might ease your mind a bit." But Costner, suffering existentially, replies, "I killed a man I hated today." "I got ya," grins Gammon. "You don't want to mix your pleasures."

Gammon dies (Costner probably had him killed off for stealing the picture), only to be replaced by touring rock has-been Sally Kirkland, who tosses off such bon mots as "I was certified dead in 1982" and—this, to Costner—"I thought you were gonna say you're gay." Finally, Costner tracks down Quinn, and when the onetime best friends meet again, does Costner kill him, as he's sworn he will? Well, no. That'd be kinda unsympathetic, so instead Costner apologizes for stealing Quinn's wife, and hey—this is the '90s, isn't it?—all is forgiven. Not by us, however, who are moved by the film's swoony finale, where Stowe dies in Costner's arms; moved to gales of laughter, that is.

With Miguel Ferrer, Tomas Milian. Produced by Hunt Lowry and Stanley Rubin, directed by Tony Scott (to whom the project fell after John Huston wisely bailed out). Screenplay by Jim Harrison and Jeffrey Fiskin, based on Harrison's novella. C, 124 m., V, L

Stella (1990) ❤

Bette Midler's not the first actress to take a crack at playing the vulgar, workin' class ma who sacrifices everything for her daughter's shot at going uptown. Belle Bennett, then Barbara Stanwyck got there first. Midler, anxious to demonstrate to Hollywood her range, wound up coming in last, and how: she's the only one to interpret this Olive Higgins Prouty chestnut as an occasion to do a bump 'n' grind atop a bar, imitate Carmen Miranda, stage a food fight, and refer constantly to her breasts while insisting that other characters rave over her sex appeal. Our forty-five-year-old star doesn't even look surprised when Stephen Collins, who's seen her dance, speaks up—no, not to offer midlife crisis counseling—but to ask for a date. Though Midler thinks med student Collins "just a little too fancy" for her (leaving aside "just a little too young"), soon she's preggers and spurning his marriage offer.

Bartender John Goodman, hellbent on spewing his lines louder and more insistently Blue Collar than Midler, proposes wedlock, too. He says, "Marriage is: I come home from work, we have beer, eat some spaghetti, then we roll around on the sofa for twenty minutes—ya like that, doncha?—till we're all sweaty. Then we watch 'All in the Family,' take a shower, and eat some ice cream in bed. That's marriage." Understandably, Midler elects to raise her illegitimate tyke on her own, and—despite Midler's terrifying propensity for transforming herself into Betty Hutton, Ruth Gordon, and Jerry Lewis rolled into one—her daughter grows up to be pretty Trini Alvarado.

Midler locks horns with local bigwig Eileen Brennan, who, when she cracks wise about Midler's outrageous getups, gets this dose of Midler's mouth: "You probably haven't had a good lay in years. Your legs have been together longer than the Lennon Sisters." Midler's blowsy ways grate on her kid (and boy, do we sympathize) but Collins invites Trini to meet Marsha Mason, his fabulously wealthy wife-to-be, with whom she does some serious Movie Bonding (i.e., clothes shopping). Trini tells Midler that Mason's "different," and Midler snaps, "How's she different? She got three tits?" Scraping together enough money for Alvarado and her to join Trini's boyfriend on spring break in Florida, Midler—imagine Sylvia Miles dressed as Baby Jane Hudson—mortifies the Palm Beach set (and us) by dancing a madcap meringué with a waiter.

Finally realizing she's sabotaging her daughter (not to mention her own movie career), Midler convinces Alvarado that she should live with Collins. Thus, the famous finale, where Midler stands in the rain, outside a ritzy joint watching her daughter marry a rich guy right in front of a convenient window. While Stanwyck shredded hearts with the scene, Midler makes you wish someone in Hollywood had the guts to remind her that even supertalented divas can't play everything.

Produced by Samuel Goldwyn, Jr., directed by John Erman. Screenplay by Robert Getchell, from the Prouty novel. C, 106 m., V, L

Viva las Divas

Stars attain Diva status when they demand that their movies become orgies of self-adoration. From that moment on, no plot is too ridiculous, no amount of overemoting is too over-the-top, no hairdo too outré. In the mood for all-stops-out scenery chomping? For big, fat, gauzy close-ups while the background music goes nuts? Ready for a dizzying array of costume and coiffure changes to match what the stars perceive to be their infinite variety?

Then strap yourself in for a trip to Diva Heaven, where Bette Davis, Joan Crawford, and Olivia de Havilland reign supreme.

Another Man's Poison (1951) ❤❤❤

"If only you were human," Bette Davis coos to her horse, then tells it (and us), "maybe I'm not human, either." That would explain the out-of-this-world performance she gives in this barmy thriller made right after *All About Eve*—demonstrating the peril of selecting a project because it offers a role for one's latest husband (her *Eve* co-star, Gary Merrill).

Davis is the most successful mystery writer in the universe and when Merrill breaks into her English manor, demanding to see her husband—they've just committed a bank heist together, see?—Davis rolls her eyes, puffs on a cigarette, plays "Stardust," then announces: "I *killed* him. I *hated* him. I brought him his drink—I'd put something in it. It was *all* over very quickly." Conveniently needing a new identity, Merrill offers to dispose of the body and take his place: "I'll make a good husband, better than he ever did."

When Davis's secretary Barbara Murray and Murray's fiancé, Anthony Steel—but really Davis's lover (are you getting all this?)—turn up unannounced, Davis kicks into histrionic over-drive. "Did my faithful little secretary think I might suddenly have a juicy *murder* to dictate? Yes, the night air *teems* with unexpected guests. *Sounds* like Shakespeare, but it isn't." Merrill introduces himself as Davis's husband—oh, did we mention that no one had ever met the real one?—making Davis snarl, "I could kill you." "We're in this together," Merrill tells her, "for better or for worse, in love or in loathing, we're married!"

Just when you think it can't get any loonier, it does. Davis, out riding with Steel, says, "For a man, you have *disgracefully* long eyelashes." His response? "I want you and I hate you," he pants, kissing her, "both—together!" Merrill warns Steel they have "a rival" in Davis's horse, then recites this dilly of a poem: "I do not like the human race / I do not like its silly face / But give me a puppy for a friend / And I'll be faithful to the end." Stomping around in jodphurs, brandishing a whip and chain-smoking, Davis snaps at Murray about Steel, "You've asked a *pretty* question and I'm giving you the *ugly* answer. I've wanted him ever since the first moment I saw him. No suicides or anything melodramatic!" (That's her turf.)

While Merrill's off shooting her horse, Steel tells Davis they had "an infatuation—nothing more," prompting Davis to cackle madly and say, "This is a very funny thing that's happening to me, and when I'm amused, I *laugh*. I'm deeply in love with you—a nice woman wouldn't say things like that, would she? Well, I'm *not* a nice woman!" In the end, of course, both Merrill and Davis accidentally drink the poison, and yes, Davis grimaces, "Till death do us part."

With Emlyn Williams. Produced by David Angel, directed by Irving Rapper. Screenplay by Val Guest, from Leslie Sands's play *Deadlock*. B&W, 89 m., TV

Autumn Leaves (1956) ❤ ❤

"I've been told, 'You're so attractive,' 'So lovely,' 'So this, so that.' Then they assume I'm . . . all tied up. Makes me feel like I'm a package. And I'm left, alone . . ." Spinster typist Joan Crawford just can't seem to land a date in her autumn years; in a flashback, we see young Joan breaking a date with her fiancé to tend to her sick father, saying, "Don't worry about me. There's plenty of time." Back in the present, Joan wanders into a cheap café where she orders a chicken salad sandwich—then plays the ever-present theme song on the jukebox—and gets picked up by young Cliff Robertson, who takes her to the beach to neck in a shameless imitation of Deborah Kerr and Burt Lancaster in *From Here to Eternity*. (What makes this even loonier is that Crawford was originally to have played the Kerr role, but quit.) Knowing the folly of her ardor, Joan advises Cliff, "Find a girl your age, there must be lots of them," adding, hilariously, "It's a big city."

Then she comes home one day to hear "Autumn Leaves" playing on her phonograph. "Isn't it strange," she says to Robertson, who's bought her the record, "how that lovely song reminds you of chicken salad?" He explains that though he meets lots of girls, they don't hold a candle to Joan. "Are you sure you're meeting live people?" she asks, while we wonder the same thing. Recklessly, they wed in a Mexican ceremony, and the plot jerks into a thrill-less thriller as Robertson subjects Crawford to pathological lies and scary mood swings.

Out of the woodwork crawls Robertson's scheming ex-wife Vera Miles and Robertson's shifty daddy, Lorne Greene, who is Vera's (say it isn't so!) lover, neither of whom Crawford knew existed. When Crawford confronts Robertson with the fact that he'd told her his father was dead, Robertson mutters, "Well, I just felt he was dead." When Greene advises Crawford to commit Robertson to the nuthouse, Crawford turns on him and Miles, snarling, "Where's your decency? In what garbage dump? And yours, you tramp? You, his loving, doting, fraud of a father and you, you slut! You're both so consumed with evil, your filthy souls are too evil for Hell itself!"

Crawford changes her tune after Robertson smashes her hand

with her own typewriter, and in retaliation, she forces him to endure months of shock treatments. But it's no easier on us: we're forced to endure life-threatening mega-closeups of Joan screaming, wide-eyed, with her hands over her ears trying, no doubt, to shut out yet another rendition of that theme song! It all ends up fine, with Robertson—miraculously cured of schizophrenia—kissing the very hand he smashed.

Produced by William Goetz, directed by Robert Aldrich. Screenplay by Jack Jevne, Lewis Meltzer, and Robert Blees. B&W, 108 m., V, L

The Dark Mirror (1946) ❤ ❤

"Sisters can hate each other with such terrifying intensity," psychiatrist and twin specialist Lew Ayres observes about the twins played by Olivia de Havilland, one of whom killed the doctor who was courting her. Audiences wise to the animosity between real-life sisters Olivia de Havilland and Joan Fontaine must have howled gleefully over such lines that run throughout this creaky, ridiculous thriller in which conniving, Fontaine-like twin de Havilland makes life hell on earth for sweet, de Havilland-like twin de Havilland.

Good Olivia runs a magazine stand in the lobby of a skyscraper where hot stuff bellboy Richard Long asks her out for a date, saying insinuatingly, "When I get out of this monkey suit, I ain't such a bad-looking guy." Bad Olivia, whom shrink Ayres calls "a paranoiac—capable of anything," vamps anyone in pants. They're a couple of lulus, these two, sporting matching hairdos, nightgowns, even street clothes (except for hilariously tacky necklaces with giant letters that spell out their names) and cheerfully admitting that they've switched places on jobs (and Lord knows where else).

As police guy Thomas Mitchell enlists Ayres's aid in cracking the murder case ("One of our young ladies is insane!" Mitchell helpfully informs him), the shrink trots out all the tricks of his trade—inkblots, word association games, lie detector tests—that, presented straight-faced, come off as hilariously hokey. The deeper Ayres probes, the more the crackpot sister unravels. "If you ever suspected me," bad Olivia warns good Olivia, menacingly fingering a knife, "I don't know what I'd do. I really don't."

When the shrink gets romantically involved with good Olivia, the bad sister starts in *Gaslight*ing her, complete with encouraging her to dope herself up with sleeping pills and flashing lights in her eyes when she's asleep. "The minute the doctor falls in love with the patient," Mitchell warns Ayres, "he's about as useful as a papoose." The good sister won't believe a negative word anyone has to tell her, insisting that she and her twin "have never been rivals. Never. Not in the slightest," but the finale, in which the soulful Olivia hears sinful Olivia selling her down the river, hits a new high in absurdity. The only improvement we could possibly suggest is that Olivia and Joan had played the twins.

Produced by Nunnally Johnson, directed by Robert Siodmak. Screenplay by Johnson, from the story by Vladimir Posner. B&W, 85 m., V

Dead Ringer (1964) ❤ ❤

How do even powerhouse performers get themselves into movies this bad? After her triumphant comeback as the eponymous loony hag of *Whatever Happened to Baby Jane?*, fifty-six-year-old, difficult Bette Davis decreed that she would look good again on-screen, and that she would not work with difficult co-stars like *Baby Jane*'s Joan Crawford. Hence, *Dead Ringer*: Davis picked the project because she got to sashay about in expensive-looking clothes, and because she was her own co-star. She plays the dual roles of identical twins, Edie and Maggie, who meet again after twenty years at the funeral of the man that one sister stole from the other.

Wealthy widow Maggie takes poor cocktail hostess Edie back to Beverly Hills, where she offers up her cast-off gowns and furs. "They'll all be out of style before I'm out of mourning," she explains. But Edie won't settle for Maggie's Diors, she wants Maggie's entire pampered lifestyle. "You never loved anyone but yourself!" Edie says before coolly shooting Maggie dead. And after disguising the murder as her own suicide, she smoothly assumes Maggie's identity. Now, since Davis makes no attempt whatsoever to differentiate between the twins—they have the identical voice, walk, and bad wig—it's one of the movie's hilariously grievous shortcomings that the plot turns on whether anyone can spot that Edie's winging it as Maggie. The good cop, Karl Malden, who loved the supposedly dead Edie, is easily fooled. But Maggie's Great Dane, Duke, knows the difference at once, and before long Maggie's gigolo lover Peter Lawford sniffs out the truth, too.

When Edie-as-Maggie learns that Lawford and the real Maggie murdered Maggie's husband, Edie-as-Maggie realizes that she has killed Maggie only to take on the identity of a killer. Anyway, just then, Duke (make that Duke ex machina) attacks and kills Lawford, leaving Edie-as-Maggie all alone to face the officer who's come to arrest her for murdering Maggie's husband. If you guessed that the flatfoot is Malden, maybe you won't be amazed by what happens next—but don't bet on it. "Don't ya know me?" Davis says, heaving her body at Malden. "I'm not Maggie, I'm Edie." "Nice try," Malden says, "but Edie was sweet and kind. She would never have killed her own sister. I was planning to ask her to marry me." Inexplicably touched by this, Edie-as-Edie asks, "Did you ever tell her?" then toughens up again to claim she was just kidding about not being Maggie, whereupon she departs nobly to face Maggie's certain death sentence—instead of just telling Malden that he's a lousy judge of character.

With Jean Hagen, Estelle Winwood, George Macready, Phillip Carey, George Chandler. Produced by William H. Wright, directed by Paul Henreid, a universe away from his (and Davis's) glory days in *Now, Voyager*. Screenplay by Albert Beich and Oscar Millard, based on the story "La Otra" by Rian James. B&W, 115 m., V, L

Flamingo Road (1949) ❤

Everyone, a narrator tells us, hopes one day to live on Flamingo Road, "the street of social success, the avenue of achievement, the golden goal for all who struggle and aspire to reach the top and sometimes find that, from the top, there's no other place to go." Joan Crawford was on the road to hand-me-downs when she played a hootchy-koo dancer in this manic melodrama. Stranded in a Southern town and taken up by deputy Zachary Scott, Crawford explains why she's ditched the carny life: "I got tired of being on the wrong end of a rabbit hunt—I was tired of moldy tents, one-night stands, greasy food, sick of people looking at me like I was cheap."

Soon, Crawford's slinging hash at the local dive and making time with Scott. One night, at a shady roadhouse run by scene-stealer Gladys George, Scott finds Crawford singing torchily at a piano, takes her to shady waterside and . . . well, makes her fall in love with him. But when powerful sheriff Sydney Greenstreet takes over Scott's life—he's planning to further his own political career by maneuvering Scott into a senator's seat—he forces him to marry wealthy Virginia Huston, then gets Crawford (whom Greenstreet calls "that stray cat from the carnival") fired from her job.

Crawford figures out that Greenstreet is trying to keep her from seeing Scott by running her out of town, but she won't budge. "I'm going to stay here if it kills me," she says, eyes burning. "I'm not a carnival girl anymore!" At this point in her life, Crawford was anything but any kind of girl anymore, but that doesn't stop her from landing millionaire power broker David Brian, who, no sooner than she sobers him up, feeds him, and drives him to his construction site, gushes, "I'm crazy about you, Lane. What's your last name?"

Wait, that's not all. He marries her and moves her—that's right—to the best house on Flamingo Road. So what if she's just done time for a trumped-up morals charge? Crawford makes Brian happy and fends off the enormous Greenstreet's threats by comparing him to a mad elephant she remembers from her carny days. "Had to be shot," she snaps, "you wouldn't believe how much trouble it is to dispose of a dead elephant." Things spin into delirium when Scott, who's taken to drink, shoots himself in Crawford's mansion, bringing on the inevitable scene where local yahoos tear up her yard and try to scare her out of town. Instead, toting a gun, Crawford wins the day—and, despite all odds, gets to stay on Flamingo Road after all.

Produced by Jerry Wald, directed by Michael Curtiz. Screenplay by Robert Wilder, from his novel and play (co-written with

Sally Wilder), with additional dialogue by Edmund H. North.
B&W, 94 m., TV

Female on the Beach (1955) ❤ ❤ ❤

Over the railing of a fabulously tacky Newport Beach waterfront
house tumbles alcoholic Judith Evelyn—literally head over heels
for the gigolo-next-door, yummy, prematurely gray Jeff Chandler. Enter the next morning, the cynical gambler's widow Joan
Crawford, an ex-Vegas "specialty dancer" there to claim the property from her dead tenant. That the role of a streetwise but
supposedly still stunning showgirl is played by fiftyish Crawford
as though she were still twentyanything is a clue to the utter
madness of this movie, which stakes its hopes on pretending that
if Crawford believes she can pull it off, why then, so will you.

The craziness hardly stops there: When Crawford asks chirpy
blonde real estate agent Jan Sterling why the porch railing is
torn away and why the local cops are combing the sand for clues
to Evelyn's mysterious death, Sterling shrugs it off as "some
government thing." What isn't? *Female on the Beach* is vintage
late middle-era Crawford, in which fellow actors dutifully brown-
nose the star by referring to her—straight-faced—as a "girl" and
where the fetishistic cameraman shoots her at panty level every
time she takes, like, twenty minutes getting out of bed. (And
never in the same negligee twice: the film's scant suspense is
generated by your wondering, "What will Joan wear next?")

Crawford moves into the beach house, and in no time flat,
Chandler is displaying his pecs and annoying the poor widow by
revving the motor of his long, greasy boat. Chandler keeps
pressing—what we know, but Joan doesn't, is that he and his
tony pimps, Cecil Kellaway and Natalie Schaefer, are flat
broke—but Joan won't come across. Well, not *too* quickly, anyway. She reads the dead woman's diary, and she comes across
this entry about Chandler: "He takes my money—but I love him!
Love him!" Despite such dire warnings from the beyond, Crawford up and marries the louse anyway, the better to spend the
rest of the movie caught in that B-movie heroine fix: "Will he kiss
me or kill me?"

And the dialogue? Pass the Cheese Whiz. Before they've married—in fact, before they've even met—Crawford finds the gigolo making breakfast in her kitchen and snarls, "You must go with the house, like the plumbing." When he mumbles that he's just "being friendly," Crawford calls Chandler "about as friendly as a suction pump." Why, she flares, "I wouldn't have you if you were hung with diamonds, upside down!" Anytime things slow down, the irresistibly awful Crawford thrashes about, shoving cigarettes between those sour-milk lips and cranking up jazzy records (but never, alas, to revive for us her Vegas "specialty" number), leaving no prop—or co-star—unchewed. Our favorite moment in Joan's orgy of self-adulation: the telephone scene during which she keeps rubbing her bum.

Produced by Albert Zugsmith, directed by Joseph Pevney. Screenplay by Robert Hill and Richard Alan Simmons. B&W, 97 m., TV

Johnny Guitar (1954) ❤ ❤ ❤

Packing a gun, dressed head to toe in desperado black, and freed from the constraints of having to make even the tiniest concession toward acting feminine, Joan Crawford looks like she's having the time of her life playing "Vienna," the wild west's snarliest, toughest, butchest bitch, in this most Freudian of shoot-'em-ups. Symbolism runs rampant in this riotously purple-with-passion melodrama, and the whole cast goes way over the top, playing people driven mad by the frustration of not getting what they really want.

Crawford, for example, is the onetime saloon gal who's ready to open her own gambling joint, if the railroad ever blasts its way through that damned mountain that's blocking the way. In the meantime, she's playing footsy with both psycho Scott Brady and former psycho turned music man Sterling Hayden, but it's really wild-eyed, hard-breathing, she-cat Mercedes McCambridge— who snarls dialogue like "You're nothing but a railroad tramp" and "I'm not satisfied!"—that heats Crawford's blood to the boiling point. "I'm going to kill you," McCambridge says, as the two women stare longingly at one another; "I know," pants Crawford, "if I don't kill you first." Incredibly, none of this is played for subtext—the entire movie is bursting to come out of the closet. As one of Crawford's male employees says about her, staring into the camera lens at us, "Never seen a woman who was more a man. She thinks like one, acts like one, sometimes makes me feel I'm not." And he's not the only one walking funny down Main Street: John Carradine eyes Hayden and tosses off a pickup line worth memorizing: "That's a lot of man you're carrying in those boots, stranger." In a scene heretofore unknown to westerns, saddle tramp Ernest Borgnine can't help noticing Hayden's lips. Brandishing a bottle of whiskey, Borgnine says, "Open your mouth, I'll feed you. I said open your mouth, guitar man!"

When the screenplay halfheartedly tries to play it both ways —and insists that we believe that Crawford and Hayden were lovers long ago—the pair give this dialogue their best, you-guess-what-it-all-means once-over: "How many men have you forgotten?" Hayden asks, and Crawford replies, "As many women as you've remembered." There's nothing halfhearted about Mc-Cambridge, however; whip in hand, she knows what she wants —to see Crawford hung. Bound on a horse, Crawford's neck is in the noose before Hayden shows up in time to cut the rope— treating us to the ultra-bizarre sight of Crawford making a get-away, in bondage. The two women finally meet in a showdown and, ahem, shoot it out. Before McCambridge dies, we expect her to look up at Crawford and ask "Was it good for you, too?"

With Ward Bond, Ben Cooper. Produced by Herbert J. Yates, directed by Nicholas Ray. Screenplay by Philip Yordan, based on the Roy Chanslor novel. C, 110 m., V, L

Lady in a Cage (1964) ❤ ❤

After *Whatever Happened to Baby Jane?* revived Bette Davis and Joan Crawford's careers, half of Hollywood's aging stars raced to enter the Fallen Great Ladies of the Silver Screen sweepstakes. *Psycho*-inspired, *faux* Saul Bass credits punctuate this film's opening tableaux of Our Society Gone Mad: a rollerskater runs over a drunk's leg, motorists pass a dead dog, a couple necks while a radio evangelist wonders, "Have we an anti-Satan missile?"

Wealthy poet Olivia de Havilland—suffering from a broken hip—assures her mama's-boy son, Charles Seal, as he leaves for the weekend, that she'll phone "the ice company if I need ice, the coal company if I need coal, and the happiness people if I need happiness." (Better she should call the *direction* people.) A power failure traps her in an elevator in her mansion, clearing the coast for de Havilland to hog the screen, singing "Alouette," indulging in eye-rolling and hair-yanking the likes of which you've seldom seen, then deciding, "I'll write a poem in my head." Brace yourselves, kids! "Oh I had worshipped thee, false god, for thou art false—electricity!" she coos. "But one day, our god Kilowatt left us; could we then go back to the gods of our childhood? To reindeer? Santa Claus?"

Just when we're thinking, "She must have married well because she sure can't be living high on publishing royalties," into this one-woman Hamathon crashes bum Jeff Corey and floozie Ann Sothern. When Corey paws her bloated body, Sothern drawls, "Can't make up your mind, can ya? Repent one minute, slobber the next!" Momentarily upstaged, de Havilland watches as lean, hungry newcomers James Caan, Jennifer Billingsley, and Rafael Campos race in next, and you know they're bad news because Billingsley is a bleached blonde who smokes. "Me, I'm an animal," Caan menaces de Havilland, doing his best Brando imitation in vain hopes of stealing scenes from her, "right now, I'm all animal." Don't dare miss de Havilland's retort—after Caan's related his history of reformatories, foster homes, and work farms—"I see, you're one of the many bits of offal produced by the welfare state! You're what so much of my tax dollars goes for the care and feeding of!"

By the time the heathens stab Corey, pulverize Sothern, and bend de Havilland's mind by reading her a kiss-off letter from her son, you'll be alternately howling for mercy and howling for more. When de Havilland protests to Caan that her son has many girlfriends, Caan snarls, "Yeah, women friends he made in public shower rooms, I'll bet!" At last, our heroine drags herself out of the house, jabs prongs into the eyes of Caan who naturally goes hurtling into traffic, where a car runs over his head (shown in closeup). As the cops restore order, de Havilland is left trembling, weeping, and pondering, no doubt, what ever happened to movies like *Gone With the Wind*?

Produced by Luther Davis, directed by Walter Grauman. Screenplay by Davis. B&W, 97 m., V

Queen Bee (1955) ❤ ❤ ❤

From the moment Joan Crawford makes her grand entrance into this overblown penny dreadful, wearing just the gown a female impersonator would have chosen and asking "Well, do I look fairly human?" it's clear why this is the movie most beloved by the star's fans as well as by her detractors—and for exactly the same reasons. There's not an inch of film wasted on anyone but Crawford, who vamps around her mansion in hostess gowns, fur stoles, and opera gloves while she cuts the rest of the cast down to size, remarking to one, "You look sweet—even in those tacky old clothes," asking another, "Aren't I wicked?" and commenting to husband Barry Sullivan, "Darling, a party is to women what a battlefield is to men—oh, I'd forgotten, you weren't in the army, were you? Something about drinking, wasn't it?"

Cast here as a neurotic diva who married into an unhappy Southern clan, Crawford amuses herself by ruining their lives. Cousin Betsy Palmer tells new arrival Lucy Marlow, "I read a book about bees. There's a whole chapter devoted to the queen who stings all her rivals to death. She'll sting you one day. So gently, you hardly feel it—till you fall dead." Marlow doesn't need that book: Crawford destroys Marlow's guest room with her riding crop while explaining, "I'm an outsider and they hate outsiders. You don't know the things they've made me do trying to protect myself. And how ashamed I've been, sometimes, because of it. You don't know how they are, as if you have to be from the South to be any good. I wish I could get rid of them as easily as this trash!" Noticing that she's reduced the room to rubble, Crawford shrugs her shoulders and says, "I don't know when I've been in such a temper."

At night, her children cry out, alone in the darkness (was

Christina Crawford's memoir *Mommie Dearest* inspired by this movie, or was the film copying Crawford's home life?), while Crawford is downstairs wooing her old beau John Ireland: "Isn't there anything left of us?" When Ireland responds, "You're like some fancy kind of disease—I had it once, now I'm immune," Crawford lies to his fiancée that "*Any* man's my man if I want it that way." The distraught woman hangs herself, causing even Crawford to admit to Marlow, "I'm not a very nice person. Once I was a great deal like you—young and innocent." When Marlow remarks, "That must have been a very long time ago," Crawford snarls, "Sounds like something I might say. You see, there's a little bit of me in every woman." Perish the thought! One of her co-stars finally drives Crawford off a cliff, but this fire-breathing characterization was too strong to die. It returned from the dead when Faye Dunaway played Crawford in the film of *Mommie Dearest*.

Produced by Jerry Wald, directed by Ranald MacDougall. Screenplay by MacDougall, from the novel by Edna Lee. B&W, 98 m., TV

A Gaggle of Starlets

From the toe-tapping *Golddigger* musicals of the '30s to the eardrum-bustin' *Satisfaction* musicals of the '80s, Hollywood has built an entire cottage industry on the idea of throwing together a bunch of comely young hopefuls—the Yvettes, Connies, and Julias of the moment—and, depending on the zeitgeist, sending them off on the flimsiest pretexts to photogenically far-flung locations, jeopardizing them on the flimsiest pretexts with supernatural forces, or having them confront on the flimsiest pretexts some pressing social ill. Watching these nymphets in action goes far toward explaining the old axiom: "Where starlets go, trouble follows."

The Best of Everything (1959) ♥ ♥ ♥

Sometimes it seems that filmmakers who've made Bad Movies We Love have done so quite by chance: surely such hilarity, goes our thinking, is indeed unintentional, just a random collision of terrible taste and utter lack of knowledge about what makes good movies good. Other times, however, we wonder if there aren't talents who set out to make them on purpose. What else could possibly explain this whole delirious genre, "A Gaggle of Starlets" Cinema? You know—A Passel of Starlets Go to Europe (*Three Coins in the Fountain*), A Brace of Starlets Go to Hollywood (*Valley of the Dolls*), A Clutch of Starlets Go to Flight School (*Come Fly With Me*), A Bushel of Starlets Go to Fort Lauderdale (*Where the Boys Are*), and so on.

Rona Jaffe, high priestess of this bestselling swill, sent notes to director Jean Negulesco: keep everything "real, real, real!"

But no, as a trio of secretaries trying to make it in the starlet-eat-starlet world of Manhattan publishing, Hope Lange, Diane Baker, and Suzy Parker lounge around their apartment drinking champagne. Lange says if she's not wed by twenty-six, she'll "have to take a lover." Baker agrees, "If you're that old, you have a right to live." Parker proposes a toast: "Here's to men. Bless their clean-cut faces and their dirty little minds."

The gals all work for hard-as-nails Joan Crawford, who answers Lange's query if she wants a report "typed" by snarling, "No—beat it out on a native drum!" When she gets an unsolicited manuscript, Crawford scrawls across the title page, "Trash . . . No!"—you can't help thinking that she must have scrawled "Trash . . . Yes!" on this movie's script. Crawford is secretly carrying on with a married exec: "I waited and waited," she overacts into the phone receiver. "You were home? But one night a week is all we have. She did the same thing last week. How many headaches can she have? You and your rabbit-faced wife can both go to hell!" Another editor, Stephen Boyd, advises Lange to "Get out quick—and *love* happily ever after"; instead, she drunkenly throws herself at him. "Please make love to me," she begs. "Twenty-six is too far ahead!" But she passes out cold, and in the morning finds she's been given both a promotion and a raise— the rewards that go to good girls who wait.

Parker and Baker don't fare as well. Parker meets brilliant playwright Louis Jourdan, and though you've guessed that he'll begin his seduction by murmuring "Act One, Scene One" (and will later kiss Parker off with "end of Act Three, end of play"), who'd guess that this blank dullard could drive Parker mad? She takes up living on his fire escape, and when her high heel catches in the grating, she plunges to her death. This is preferable to the fate worse than death which awaits Baker. She no sooner falls for playboy Bob Evans's come-on than she finds that she's pregnant. On the day they're to elope, Evans says he's really driving her to have an abortion. Baker screams, "Let me out!" then climbs out while his convertible's speeding. (Well, that's one way to get rid of a love child.) Baker lives, if only to spell out the movie's message: "I'm so ashamed, now I'm just somebody who's had an affair."

Back at the office, Lange lands Crawford's job when Crawford resigns because she's found true love. But she's back in a flash, explaining, "It was too late for me." Lange realizes "This could happen to me!" and rushes to find Boyd.

With Brian Aherne, Martha Hyer. Produced by Jerry Wald, directed by Negulesco. Screenplay by Edith Sommer and Mann Rubin, from Jaffe's novel. C, 121 m., TV

Change of Habit (1969) ❤❤

By the late '60s, the formula of packing off a bundle of starlets to a picturesque clime was getting stale, so—believe it or not!—someone came up with the "relevant" twist of A Gaggle of Starlets Go to the Ghetto Where They Work in a Free Clinic as Nurses. What's more, the three starlets in question are (get this) nuns who are going out into the world to make it a better place, undercover.

The film's title sequence features all three starlets shedding their nunnery drag for up-to-date fashions, resulting in a virtual holy striptease: they drop the wimples, try on nylons, and get new coiffures as we listen to Elvis Presley sing the title tune. (Sister Mary Tyler Moore isn't far from wrong when she observes, "It's music to exorcise evil spirits by!") When Elvis—who is, of all things, the free clinic's resident doctor—meets the three lookers, he can only assume they're "Park Avenue" types who've come downtown to him for abortions. "All three of you?" he asks. "Just out of curiosity, was it the same guy?"

During a duet that must be seen and heard to be believed, Elvis falls in love with MTM, never suspecting she's already betrothed to Christ. This being an Elvis pic, there's a block party, but it's not quite the usual frug-out we're expecting—a white thug slugs black Sister Barbara McNair square on the jaw, which provokes rioting in the streets. When MTM returns to her convent, Elvis finally learns that she's a nun but proposes marriage nevertheless: "This place is not a prison—you can get a release, y'know." She's, well, undecided (an Elvis movie first) and the film ends with her coming to hear him sing in church. As they eye each other, a priest mutters, "The Lord moves in mysterious ways"—but not more mysterious, certainly, than the studio execs who were moved to greenlight this trash classic.

With Jane Elliot, Regis Toomey, and as a local cop, MTM's future TV series boss, Edward Asner. Produced by Joe Connelly, directed by William Graham. Screenplay by James Lee, Eric Bercovici, and S. S. "Paddy" Schweitzer, based on a story by John Joseph and Richard Morris. C, 93 m., V

The Pleasure Seekers (1964) ❤

After *How to Marry a Millionaire*, *Three Coins in the Fountain*, and *The Best of Everything*, trio-of-starlets specialist Jean Negulesco directed this musical remake of *Three Coins*. In dim hopes of "updating" the material to give it that "now," 1964 feeling, it's set in Madrid instead of Rome, and there's even less emphasis on the career girls' careers.

At a news bureau, Carol Lynley spends her time pouring coffee and flirting; Pamela Tiffin simply wanders through art museums trying to look soulful; and Ann-Margret, we're told, has "gone native, even a little gypsy, sings, dances, a little modeling, a little bit of *everything*." Whatever their sources of incomes, this trio can afford a soundstage-sized apartment and have money to burn on shoes. (The film's a foot fetishist's fashion show as these career women parade around in stiletto heels and towels, stiletto heels and baby dolls, stiletto heels and sweatshirts, and stiletto heels and bikinis.)

These are not, however, the only heels in the movie. Lynley's torn between her married boss Brian Keith and bachelor reporter Gardner McKay; in the Prado, Tiffin's picked up by playboy Anthony Franciosa; outside, Ann-Margret's run down by motorcycle-riding doctor André Lawrence.

Bits of the first film's story keep turning up—here's the office cocktail party—but there are countless "What could they have been thinking of?" additions, like Ann-Margret entertaining the guests in a skintight flamenco dress, throwing around her red mane like she's suffering a seizure, and lip-synching the fall-down-funny title song.

Troubles brew when the gals fall in love: Keith takes Lynley to a party, but instead of the privacy they seek, they run smack into the biggest peril that working gals come across in the workplace, the boss's wife. Breathing fire as Keith's missus, Gene Tierney corners Lynley in the ladies room, and snarls her way into the annals of high camp. "What's the goal, sweetie, a nasty little love nest? That's all you'll get—if that," Tierney steams. "No cold-eyed, calculating little viper's going to do me out of a thing. He doesn't give a damn about you, you little tramp!"

Realizing the error of her ways ("She called me a 'little tramp'!"), Lynley decides to return to the United States, and when they're wronged by their fellas, so do Tiffin and A-M. The film's unintentionally hooty highlight comes when A-M tells Tiffin—while each is wearing five pounds of eye makeup—that "It's over. He can't afford me." Tiffin sniffles sympathetically but says, "Don't—my mascara will run." A-M tries to fight back her tears, too. "What am I doing?" she says aloud, "I'm not wearing any mascara."

Produced by Sol Siegel, directed by Negulesco. Screenplay by Edith Sommer, from John Secondari's novel *Three Coins in the Fountain*. C, 107 m., TV

The Stepford Wives (1975) ❤ ❤

What happens when starlets grow old? Why, they move to Stepford, where their horrible husbands turn them into robot starlets! Since they're played here by such Bad Movie vets as Katharine (*The Swarm*) Ross, Paula (*Where the Boys Are*) Prentiss, and Tina (*God's Little Acre*) Louise, who can possibly tell the difference?

New arrival Ross is certain that something's wrong, and Prentiss agrees. "It's like maids have been declared illegal and the housewife with the neatest place gets Robert Redford for Christmas," Prentiss blathers (unaware that, in palmier days, Ross got Redford). "If that's the prize, I'd enter, but no one will tell what the contest rules are." Ross's husband, Peter Masterson, has become a sex fiend since the move—he says, "I'd like to christen every room in the house" so we'll know he's a monster—helping

Ross to decide that what's needed is a consciousness-raising group. "I messed a little bit with women's lib in New York," she tells Prentiss. "I'm not contemplating any Maidenform bonfires, but they could certainly use something around here."

Getting the Stepford wives to join up is another matter. "I've never been much of a joiner," one explains. "I've just been so busy with baking. I know I shouldn't say this, but I just love my brownies." Another is busy all day long pleasing her husband: "Oh, you're the best," we hear her moan—thankfully, off camera—"you're the king, the champion, the master!" Louise tells Prentiss and Ross she thinks it sounds like "a bitching session," and she'd much rather dish her housekeeper, Dee Wallace, explaining sotto voce, "She's a German Virgo. Their thing is to serve!"

When neighbor Nanette Newman runs amok at a party telling every guest, "I'll just die if I don't get that recipe," Prentiss becomes convinced "There's something in the water that turns us into hausfraus," tipping us off that she's next. Indeed, when Prentiss is (hilariously) turned into a heavily made-up domestic, Ross flees to a psychiatrist. "Don't ask me to explain it, I just know there'll be somebody with my name and she'll cook and clean like crazy, but she won't be me. She'll be like one of those robots in Disneyland," Ross says. "If I'm wrong, I'm insane, and if I'm right, it's worse than if I'm wrong."

Funnier, too, for Ross tests out her theory by stabbing Prentiss in the stomach. Prentiss doesn't bleed—she malfunctions! ("I thought we were friends," Prentiss mutters over and over, trying but failing to serve coffee, dropping one cup after another while she bumps into the counter, "I thought we were friends.") For the finale, Ross—now an Audio-Animatronic dummy, too—leads the wives through a crazed supermarket ballet, decked out in picture hats and long gowns while dreamily pushing shopping carts. A screwball classic.

With Patrick O'Neal, Mary Stuart Masterson. Produced by Edgar J. Scherick, directed by Bryan Forbes. Screenplay by William Goldman, from Ira Levin's novel. C, 115 m., V

Three Coins in the Fountain (1954) ❤

Here is proof positive that they really don't make movies like
they used to: before the main titles even come on, the movie
opens with a five-minute sequence with Frank Sinatra's voice
seductively crooning the title song, backed by a heavenly choir,
as CinemaScope cameras roam over each and every breathtaking
fountain ever built in Rome, with mugging extras playing romantic lovers at every site. For all the splashy window-dressing,
it's just Fox's frequently filmed old chestnut about starlets
seeking husbands. This time the babes are expatriate American
secretaries sharing a soundstage-sized flat—virginal Maggie
McNamara, comely Jean Peters, spinsterish Dorothy McGuire—
but it's the same old preposterous primer on How to Land a Man.

Forbidden to date fellow employees where they work, Peters
and Rossano Brazzi are both fired when it's learned they went
on a picnic together. Heartbroken that she's cost him his job,
Peters does what any right-minded girl would do in the same
situation: she beds him. McNamara thinks this is no way to win
a man, and so pursues her intended, "predatory prince" Louis
Jourdan, by tricking him into thinking they share common interests. McGuire gives her a ten-second crash course in Jourdan's
passion, modern art: "There's really only three phrases you need
to know," McGuire advises, " 'Neoimpressionism,' 'harmony of
color,' and 'infinity.' " Shortly after hearing McNamara blabber-
ing like this, Jourdan proposes! To reel him in, McNamara plays
hard-to-get, and delivers one of the best howlers in Bad Movie
history: she tells the vacant-faced pretty boy Jourdan, "I'm afraid
of you. I've discovered you have an exciting mind, something
handsome men rarely have—and the combination might be too
much for me."

Observing these pairings, McGuire muses, "I'm glad I'm not
young and vulnerable anymore," but just then, her employer, the
fey and never-married Great Author Clifton Webb (sporting a
preposterous goatee so we'll know he's a serious writer), proposes
a marriage of convenience. "Isn't it ironic?" McGuire asks her
roommates. "You're both so young and lovely, but of the three
of us, I'm to be the bride!"

For a minute there, all three romances look like fizzles: Brazzi's penniless, Jourdan finds he's been duped, and it turns out that Webb's dying of Incurable Movie Disease. Even so, on the very morning that our three starlets are leaving for home, the three sets of lovers are reunited in front of the Trevi Fountain. Sure, two couples look likely to divorce and the other gal will soon be a widow, but the starlets got their men—and in 1954, that was a happy ending.

With Howard St. John, Kathryn Givney, Cathleen Nesbitt. Produced by Sol C. Siegel, directed by Jean Negulesco. Screenplay by John Patrick, from the novel by John H. Secondari. C, 102 m., V, L

Where the Boys Are (1960) ❤ ❤

"Experience," explains on-the-make Ivy Leaguer George Hamilton, "that's what separates the girls from the girl scouts." This is the great-granddaddy of movies where school-age starlets head for the shore to *Follow the Boys* while *Looking for Love* (to name only two of its immediate knock-offs). Hollywood's been remaking this movie ever since—as *Shag, Satisfaction, Mystic Pizza*, and so on.

When college pals Dolores Hart, Paula Prentiss, Yvette Mimieux, and Connie Francis arrive in Fort Lauderdale, the entire plot is spelled out: "Just think, twenty thousand kids out there!" says Mimieux. "Yeah," agrees Francis, "and eighty percent of them boys!" Since Mimieux's set her cap for a "Yale man," she can have her pick of a flock of them downstairs—and does, *one after another*. Prentiss, dogged by eccentric Jim Hutton, says, "He certainly is persistent. He keeps knocking on the door. It's just a question of how long I can keep it locked." Francis hooks up with jazz groovester Frank Gorshin so she can bleat Neil Sedaka's throbbing title song (which single-handedly made this movie a hit).

The movie goes loco when, at last, wise-beyond-her-years Hart meets world-weary Hamilton, who picks her up by—we swear—drawing a question mark in the sand. They then go for drinks, where *she* draws a question mark on the table top. Their volleys are the ripest, over-the-top chatter to ever turn up in a glossy teen makeout movie. She: "No girl enjoys being considered promiscuous—even those who might be." He: "Sex is a pleasant, friendly thing, like shaking hands or making sure you catch a person's name when you're introduced." She: "I've divided boys into three types—the sweepers, the strokers, and the subtles. I'll have to figure out a new classification for you." He: "What's your IQ?"

We're just about to agree with local cop Chill Wills as he moans "I wish I were dead!" when, happily, Mimieux staggers back into the movie. Her hair askew and her dress undone—those appliqué daisies on her bodice tell the whole sad story of innocence lost—Mimieux dazedly leaves a low rent motel and walks straight into oncoming traffic. Though Hamilton risks his own life to save Mimieux, Hart turns on him and snarls, "I blame all of you who think of a girl as something cheap and common just put here for your personal kicks!" (Guess *that* answers your question mark in the sand, eh, George?)

In the hospital, Mimieux tearfully tells Hart the words every young girl needs to hear sometime: "I lived it up, didn't I? I sure lived it up. Why didn't I die, why didn't I die? I feel so old, so old. You want to hear a big joke? They—they weren't even Yalies." Hart breaks down and cries—and we break down and laugh till we cry.

With Barbara Nichols. Produced by Joe Pasternak, directed by Henry Levin. Screenplay by George Wells, from Glendon Swarthout's novel. C, 99 m., V, L

Where the Boys Are '84 (1984) ❤

"I love cheap grandeur," says one of four college girls arriving in Florida for spring break. We do, too, and there's nothing quite like the cheap grandeur of vulgar, trashy remakes of bad starlet flicks. In updating *Where the Boys Are*, the screenwriters realized that modern mores made it impossible to follow the original formula (three nice girls, one tramp) and so made all four into tramps. Thus, other factors besides sex were needed to create separate personalities for each gal, as demonstrated in a sequence when the foursome needs to find a bathroom: Wendy Schaal wants to "pee-pee"; Lisa Hartman prefers to "tinkle"; Lorna Luft needs to take a "leak"; Lynn-Holly Johnson says she's gotta "piss." The latter shows us what she's packed for the trip ("One bottle of hundred-fifty-proof rum, birth control pills, some Midol, my father's American Express card, king-size bottles of Alka-Seltzer II, one sexy black teddy, a lid of grass, and a quarter—just in case I have to call home"), which helps to prepare us (if anything could) for the scene where all four gals smoke weed, talk orgasms, and decide to help Schaal learn to have a climax.

How? A handy inflatable male doll is hauled out, and while Schaal French-kisses it, Johnson helpfully advises, "Just pretend it's Richard Gere." (We can't help imagining that this delirious scene was used during auditions, and that somewhere in a vault there are videotapes of every young actress in Hollywood, tonguing a blow-up doll in hopes of landing this movie.)

Schaal winds up in jail (don't ask), and to raise bail Luft enters a "Hot Bod" contest, which is one thing, but wins Second Place, which—after you've seen her bod—is another thing altogether. Johnson lands a date with the buffed boy of her dreams, who's a hustler. Non plussed, she says, "Get undressed—if I'm buying a piece of meat, I sure as hell intend to see what's under the wrapper." He does, and she asks, "Where's the rest of it? I'll see you in small claims court."

To distract us from a subplot in which Hartman must choose between rich Daniel McDonald and poor Russell Todd, Louise Sorel and Alana Stewart (who's related to the original movie by a divorce from George Hamilton) swagger on as Fort Lauderdale society harpies, giving the film some unexpected drag queen pizazz. At a "wild" party, where a leather-clad dominatrix mingles with blue-haired dowagers, Howard McGillin propositions Stewart by asking, "How would you like to have an affair with a younger man?" and she retorts, "Only if it's brief and meaningless." In other words, only if it's just like this movie! Saving the hilarious worst for last, Hartman "sings" the famous Neil Sedaka title song over the end credits.

With Christopher McDonald, Asher Brauner. Produced by Allan Carr, directed by Hy Averback. Screenplay by Stu Krieger and Jeff Burkhart "suggested by Glendon Swarthout's novel." C, 95 m., V

All This, and
Troy Donahue Too

Beachy, blond, bland, eye-searingly handsome Troy Donahue was the teenage wet dream of the late '50s and early '60s—the predecessor of such TV pinup boys as Johnny Depp, Richard Grieco, and Luke Perry. Unlike them, Donahue attained certified movie star status in huge box-office hits. Donahue couldn't act his way past a pink gel, but when he looked like that, he didn't need to.

Palm Springs Weekend (1963) ❤

"I propose a toast," announces wealthy Robert Conrad to the cast of this soundstage-bound extravaganza. "I drink to the Easter orphans, to all of us wicked little children banded together on the beaches and resorts from Florida to California to observe the rites of spring. Here's to sex, sand, and suds!" Little children? The average age of these performers—including Troy Donahue, Connie Stevens, Stefanie Powers, Jerry Van Dyke and Ty Hardin—is twenty-five, *if* their studio bios are to be believed. The players converge on this pasteboard Palm Springs to try to act young while discovering the mysteries of, well, sex, sand, and suds.

Sex rears its head when med student Donahue meets local gal Powers and he explains that "the girl you have an affair with can never be the girl you marry," then it pops up again when compulsive liar Stevens wants moneyed cad Conrad to quit pawing her. "Don't, stop that, I'm scared," pouts Stevens, and Conrad sneers, "Why don't you drop that line? Look, I've been waiting for this since the minute I first laid eyes on you, and you're not gonna back out now!"

To relieve all this tension, we're treated to two stupendously terrible musical interludes—besides Donahue's vocalizing on the title tune, that is. Hardin, in his swim trunks, sporting a Stetson and his guitar, sings "Bye Bye Blackbird" accompanied by Van Dyke on his banjo while extras dressed in swimsuits do "The Twist" poolside—a real high point of how out of touch these movies were with teenagers of any era. This is topped, later, at a party when Powers and Donahue do "The Twist" (conclusive, irrefutable, filmed proof that white people have no sense of rhythm).

Suds turn up when Van Dyke spills soap into the pool, covering the whole set in mountains of bubbles. Don't miss Donahue's rescue effort: Sitting astride Van Dyke, he presses on his stomach to make soap bubbles emit from his mouth.

Sand figures into the plot on the last night of vacation, when Donahue and Powers wander by a blatantly artificial painted backdrop as she tells him of the "haunted dunes." It's visited, Powers explains, straight-faced, "by ghosts of thousands of kids who come down here for Easter week, fall in love, and then when it's over they go out there to say good-bye. They write their initials in the sand. It's always sad to me to come by later, after the wind has swept the sand smooth again." Their love, of course, is different. "I never thought I could feel like this," pants Powers. "It's easy to see how people get themselves in a mess." Donahue begs her, "Help me, Bunny—I'm no hero." They swear eternal devotion, you'll be glad to know, and we're certain they waited (nice twenty-five-year-olds do).

Produced by Michael A. Hoey, directed by Norman Taurog. Screenplay by Earl Hamner, Jr. C, 100 m., V, L

Parrish (1961) ❤ ❤ ❤

Studio head Jack Warner envisioned a steamy adult drama when he lured director Joshua (*Picnic*) Logan to *Parrish*, and Logan signed up newcomers Warren Beatty and Jane Fonda to make their film debuts; but when all three read the shooting script, they headed for the hills. What Warner got instead was just another unintentionally hilarious hothouse teen soap opera from Delmer Daves, who put his pet player, Troy Donahue, into the title role.

One hundred percent tanned blond beach hunk Troy arrives in tobacco country and utters in his surfer-boy drawl, "Back home in Boston, we don't grow tobacco, we just smoke it." This monumental miscasting is just the tip of the iceberg: The film's chock full of shapely studio contract players who look like they've wandered in from the set of Donahue's TV series "Surfside Six." Troy's faced with having to choose between the three babes who lust after him: wanton field hand Connie Stevens ("When it gets hot, I sleep raw"), nice rich girl Sharon Hugueny ("If I were a dog and somebody made me beg, I'd bite"), and bad rich girl Diane McBain ("I'll buy what I want—even a lover").

Talk about wandering onto the wrong soundstage: Claudette Colbert, of all people, turns up as Troy's mother. It's been speculated that having to play scenes opposite Donahue was reason enough for Colbert to retire after *Parrish*, but an even likelier reason lies in the fact that Colbert is cast opposite another seasoned pro, Karl Malden. Colbert probably took one look at his career and realized that things were only going to get much worse for actors their age, about which she was dead right. Malden's film career from *Parrish* on reads like a primer titled "When Bad Movies We Love Happen to Good Actors." (He also turns up in *Come Fly With Me, Dead Ringer, Hotel, Meteor, Beyond the Poseidon Adventure*, and *The Sting II*, for starters.)

By the time of the Colbert-Malden wedding, director Daves stops pretending to present the storyline straight-faced: Troy confronts his stepbrother with the news that Troy knows he fathered Connie's illegitimate baby, just as a band singer croons "My secret love's no secret anymore." (Would we lie to you?) Disgusted by the mores of the very rich, Troy runs off to join the Navy. He seems mighty happy during his two years on a sub, and when he returns it shows. Looking Troy up and down, a local farmer observes, "You left your boyhood behind you." "Yes," says Troy with a knowing smile, "one night under the ice at the

North Pole . . . it separated the men from the boys." However, before we're given a chance to dwell on that, Troy hurriedly picks out Hugueny—the only female in the cast left—and Daves rushes us to the happy ending. (Still, we're left wondering, What happened on that sub?)

With Dean Jagger, Madeleine Sherwood, Hampton Fancher. Produced and directed by Delmer Daves. Screenplay by Daves, from Mildred Savage's novel. C, 137 m., TV

Rome Adventure (1962) ❤ ❤ ❤

In what must be a Bad Movie first, *Rome Adventure* begins as a librarian at a women's college gets fired because she let a senior read the very novel that is the basis for the movie we're watching. Suzanne Pleshette tells off the faculty board: "I'm going to where they know what love's about—Italy!" Suzanne's mother worries, "What if something happens to you there?" Suzanne replies, "What if nothing does?" Not to worry: The ship hasn't left port before she's being romanced by Euro-smoothie Rossano Brazzi.

Once in Rome, Suzanne moves into a pension for expatriate Warner Bros. contract players—among them Troy Donahue, who races to the train station when he learns that he's being dumped by Angie Dickinson. Hats off to Delmer Daves for giving Angie (as a character we've *never seen before*) one of the great, unintentionally hilarious monologues in Bad Movie history: "I wish you hadn't come," she tells Troy. "I hate good-byes. Don't try to understand me. No man ever has, no man ever will. Got a cigarette? Remember your first nickname for me, 'Frigid Bridget'— you said if I sat on an iceberg, it wouldn't melt. It was just as true then as it is now. I'm no good for you, I was never any good. You're lucky to get rid of me. Good-bye." Troy can only ask, "We'll never meet again?" Angie sighs, "There's never any never. Kiss me."

What's a blond surfer lad to do? In the movie's most (in)famous sequence—clearly lifted from the puppy-love-over-spaghetti scene in *Lady and the Tramp*—Troy romances Suzanne over pasta, murmuring, "Forgive me for being profound, but it's good to be alive" just as a crooner wanders out to belt the movie's swoony make-out theme "Al-di-La." (This hummable tune did more than merely melt movie audiences, it apparently had the same effect on Troy and Suzanne, who were married—albeit briefly—after making this movie.)

Troy and Suzanne run off together, and the throbbing love song follows them everywhere: When they're atop the Alps (where Troy whispers, "Now I know how Shakespeare felt when he said, 'Alone at last' "), "Al-di-La" blares out of a loudspeaker. Back in Rome, Angie tells Suzanne: "If you've never made love to 'The Stars and Stripes Forever,' you haven't lived!" Realizing that she can't hope to compete with a woman of such highly developed musical tastes, Suzanne takes a boat bound for America. There on the dock in New York waits Troy, armed with roses, a marriage proposal, and "Al-di-La" playing in the background. Apparently unfamiliar with the various modes of travel available in 1962, the year this film was made, Suzanne asks how it's possible he's there. "Out of the blue I flew," says rhyme-happy Troy. "I love you!"

With Constance Ford, Hampton Fancher, Pamela Austin, Al Hirt, Chad Everett. Produced and directed by Delmer Daves. Screenplay by Daves, from the novel *Lovers Must Learn* by Irving Fineman. C, 119 m., V, L

A Summer Place (1959) ❤❤❤❤

In most 1950s Hollywood flicks, sex is subtext, but in *A Summer Place*, sex stands front and center at rigid attention. Delmer Daves throws together six people bleary-eyed with lust under the roof of a summer guest house in photogenic Maine. The oldsters include badly married Dorothy McGuire, reduced to taking in renters, and Arthur Kennedy, her blue-blooded souse of a husband, who sets the overripe tone by describing Pine Island as "a perverted Garden of Eden where the pines and the salt air seem to act as an aphrodisiac." Into the mix come filthy rich, equally badly married vacationers Richard Egan and his wife, played to dykey perfection by Constance Ford.

Before one can say "old flames," McGuire gazes longingly out her bedroom window at Egan—the ex-lifeguard who deflowered her in her teens but was too poor to marry her, now the humpiest research chemist ever to strain the seams of a LaCoste. In no time flat, the old lovers are stealing away to deserted boathouses. "I'm hungry," McGuire confesses, "for everything that hasn't been." Teen lust has its day, too. When Sandra Dee whines about the "armor-plated bra" and "cast-iron girdle" her mother buys to hide her budding curves, Papa Egan—with whom Dee likes to snuggle in bed to confess "naughty" thoughts—hurls them into the ocean. Ford reasserts her authority by commanding Dee, upon arriving at her room in the inn, to "Get the disinfectant and clean this bathroom. And don't forget the toilet seat!" But we know what repression breeds, right? Barely after they've been introduced, Dee and Troy Donahue (the innkeepers' pouty glam-bomb of a son) dive into a tacky soundstage woods to hold hands and dry-hump. Although Troy and Sandra strike zero romantic sparks, Max Steiner's famous, lilting theme does the trick.

Dee's mother spies on the young couple ("You can't let him think that your kisses come cheap!"), and after the teens spend the night together, she greets her daughter with a waiting doctor, bellowing, "Take off every stitch and let him examine you!" The director zooms in on Dee for a big, fat, hissy-fit closeup. "I want my fatha! I want my fatha!" she screams. Yes, doll, we know that, but all you're going to get is pregnant by Troy.

The couple finally finds acceptance with her father and his mother, now married. The chintz moment supreme, the scene that put the Production Code seal of approval on all the heavy breathing that has preceded it, comes when the director cuts from an exterior of Egan and McGuire's spectacular Frank Lloyd Wright love nest to a living room interior where our four stars, cozily domesticated, talk sex and chow down on TV trays.

With Beulah Bondi. Produced and directed by Delmer Daves. Screenplay by Daves, from the novel by Sloan Wilson. C, 130 m., V, L

Susan Slade (1961) ❤ ❤ ❤

"We've been sinful," whispers Connie Stevens to Grant Williams, with whom she's gone all the way during a shipboard romance.

It seems that Stevens, the stammering, shy daughter of engineer Lloyd Nolan and former "sophisticated fashion model" Dorothy McGuire, spent ten years too long up the Amazon, and her parents know it—that's why her father is returning the family to America. Though they have zilch in common besides the same dark roots ("You go for deserts while I'm hot for peaks," Williams observes, "and not just through doors, either"), it's okay that they're doing it because Williams wants to wed Stevens. Right after his next mountain climb.

So in love that she forgets to stammer, Stevens waits in vain for word from Williams. "I'm the woman God forgot," she chirps, too preoccupied to notice the charms of Monterey locals like rich boy Bert Convy or, for that matter, dreamy Troy Donahue, playing a poor stable boy and budding novelist. Connie marvels, "Oh, he's big! Oh, he's beautiful!" but she's only talking about her new horse.

Horrified to learn she's preggers, Connie lets Troy take her to dinner where, apparently suffering from early pregnancy delirium, she predicts: "I think one day in Monterey, they'll put a very big sign saying 'Robert Louis Stevenson and John Steinbeck and Hoyt Bricker wrote here.'" During a gala, Connie gets the bad news: Williams fell off the mountain. Watch for some swell scenery chewing when Connie tears at her party dress, rides her horse madly, and tries to drown herself, only to be rescued by faithful Troy.

Once Connie confesses that she's been sinful, her folks whisk her off to Guatemala, where her menopausal mother passes Connie's baby off—okay, *don't* believe us—as her own. Her father's death returns them to America, where Connie, hating the lie she's forced to live about her little "brother," grabs every chance to emote like blazes. "Everybody is taking my baby from me!" she wails to McGuire. "I want to take my son and go someplace where nobody knows me." Ever-understanding Troy, having finished his first book, tries to cheer her up. "How'd you like me to saddle up your old boyfriend?" he asks, in one of the movie's unintentionally riotous moments (he means her horse, of course).

Meanwhile, McGuire urges Stevens to wise up and marry wealthy Convy. "I can hardly walk down an aisle with a somewhat soiled gown," says Connie. "It's supposed to stand for purity.

Well, let's face it, I'm not." Shortly after Stevens warbles "Brahms' Lullaby," the baby—well, a plastic dummy, actually—sets himself ablaze with a cigarette lighter. At the hospital, the horrified mama blurts out the truth to Convy, who flees, clearing a path for a big fat Troy and Connie kiss. Director John Waters cites this Delmer Daves–directed zircon as perhaps his favorite movie.

Produced and directed by Daves. Screenplay by Daves, from Doris Hume's novel. C, 116 m., V

CHAPTER 9

Bad Girls

Not every screen queen exists to be a good wife and mother, to wait breathlessly on the sidelines while the hero has all the fun, or to get in touch with her inner child. Nah, some girls—bless 'em all, from Barbara Stanwyck and Gene Tierney to Sigourney Weaver and Drew Barrymore—live to scheme and plot, talk trashily, pout, glare sultrily, use up guys and toss 'em out like Kleenex, and wear great hairstyles. Certain kinds of moviewatchers (you know we know who you are) can't resist reveling in the bad girls' every delightfully malicious move.

Baby Face (1933) ❤

"I'm a tramp and who's to blame? My father!" complains Barbara Stanwyck, whose papa does indeed run a speakeasy-cum-brothel, where he warns she'd better be nice to the boys. He growls, "Whaddya think we're running here?" and, looking over the clientele, she replies, "It looks to me like a zoo."

But Stanwyck balks at cozying up to a sleazy politician to whom her father has sold her in exchange for police protection and so runs off to the Big City. Spotting a chic woman climbing out of a sleek car in front of the Gotham Trust Company, Stanwyck says, "What I want to find out is, how did she get 'em?" She's got a rough idea, however, and follows the dame inside, where Stanwyck vamps every man on the payroll. In Personnel, when Douglass Dumbrille asks, "Have you had any experience?" Stanwyck volleys, "Plenty." Hired! Next, Stanwyck works her wiles on young bit-player John Wayne, which gets her booted up to the Filing Department. (The camera pans up the side of the sky-scraper every time she makes another conquest.)

At quitting time one day in the Mortgage Department, her lechy boss makes a move on her—"Not here, somebody might . . ." she scolds—and then, her boss's handsome young superior, Donald Cook, intrudes on their interlude just as she's coolly reap-plying her lipstick. "What could I do?" she coos. "He's my boss and I have to earn my living."

Soon, she's risen to Accounting, working day and night, um, under Cook—who's engaged to the daughter of bank president Henry Kolker. Stanwyck makes sure the fiancée "accidentally" discovers them, and Kolker calls her on the carpet, where Stan-wyck throws herself at the old goat's mercy: "I haven't any friends and I haven't any money. My telephone number is Schuyler 32245," she says. Kolker, natch, sets her up in style. One night Cook, still mad about her, discovers her in her love nest with his prospective father-in-law, shoots him dead, then kills himself. (Are you getting all this?)

The front-page scandal so rocks the bank that its new presi-dent, handsome playboy George Brent, buys off Stanwyck with a job in the Paris branch, where he visits her, inviting her to tour the château country. "And see all those lovely fourteenth-century ceilings?" she says, two steps ahead of him. When she tells him the only thing she wants "is a 'Mrs.' on my tombstone," he weds her and showers her with wealth. She nearly walks out when he faces financial ruin, but after he recovers from a self-inflicted gunshot wound, we learn in a tacked-on ending that Brent is now a happy laborer in the Pittsburgh steel mills. That leaves us to guess what Stanwyck's happy doing. This is the real *Working Girl*.

Produced and co-written by Darryl F. Zanuck (who, under-standably, took his name off the film), directed by Alfred E. Green. Screenplay by Gene Markey, Kathryn Scola, and Mark Canfield (i.e., Zanuck). B&W, 70 m., L, V

Back Street (1961) ❤ ❤ ❤

Susan Hayward, as a hungry fashion designer, fights off the advances of a businessman who leers, "I can help you get ahead, but it's not a one-way street." Though she looks plenty able to take care of herself (and gets off a snappy retort, "Not one way . . . dead end!"), Hayward is saved from this compromising situation by total stranger John Gavin. "You know the worst part?" Hayward tells Gavin, "He was trying to seduce me with domestic champagne!" To prove her gratefulness, Hayward sleeps with Gavin, telling him (and us), "This is crazy, but I love you."

Crazy is the word, all right, for this plush "jewels by David Webb, furs by Alexandre" fantasia, spun from Fannie Hurst's creaky old novel, in which Hayward learns that Gavin's married, rejects him, and goes on to become a successful, chic dress designer. (How chic? The drapes in her dream apartment match her cape and gown, actually the creations of Jean Louis.) When Gavin pursues her, Hayward explains, "I'm not cut out to be the other woman," and flees to Rome, where she presides over *la dolce vita.*

When Hayward and Gavin meet again in a Rome restaurant (get this!) over the drunk body of Gavin's alcoholic wife, Vera Miles, somehow it's clear to them (if not to us) that their love was meant to be, so Hayward selflessly moves to Paris to be near Gavin. Among her couture clients is—you betcha—Miles, who knows there's another woman, but doesn't know who. However, Gavin's son guesses, telling Dad, "I'd like to kill her! She's a no-good, dirty . . ."

Hayward doesn't want to wreck their family, but the show must go on, so, out of the blue, right in the middle of this overwrought tearjerker, there's a lavish charity fashion show. If you've already guessed that Hayward ends the show by introducing her "personal favorite," a bridal gown, you'll probably never guess (let alone believe, even after you've seen it) that the dress is purchased by Miles, who storms down the aisle in front of *tout Paris,* announcing, "It's not for me. I'd like it delivered. Doesn't matter how it fits, she'll never get to wear it. You've all tried to guess, 'Who is the other woman in my husband's life, that mysterious creature he hides away on some back street?' "

Miles says the gown's to go (gasp!) to Hayward, and the scandal ruins her career (how times have changed—today such headlines would make Hayward a fashion goddess). "Everyone's laughing," Hayward tells Gavin, seemingly unaware that's been the case since the movie began. "Everyone knows. It's become cheap and vulgar and dirty. Other people's love affairs are always funny." This one, anyway, is hilarious.

Produced by Ross Hunter, directed by David Miller. Screenplay by Eleanore Griffin and William Ludwig, from Hurst's novel. C, 107 m., V

The Bitch (1979) ❤

"You'd never believe I'm supposed to be a jet-setter, would you?" asks aging sex kitten Joan Collins, in flight from New York to London with shifty, Omar Sharif–wannabe Michael Coby. The film that this is the sequel to—*The Stud*—is, that's right, the movie being shown in-flight, about which Coby says, "I can't make up my mind whether it's funnier with the sound or without." Collins says, "It's not meant to be funny."

Whatever this movie is meant to be, it's nothing but funny. After Coby slips a priceless, hot diamond ring into Collins's fur coat to get it through customs, Collins loses him at the airport, unwittingly taking the swag with her.

She's got other problems—for instance, that she's actually reduced to hiring "customers" to dance at her passé disco—so old pal Sue Lloyd cheers Collins up by presenting her with a new young chauffeur, Peter Wight. "Would you imagine me in the sack?" Collins asks him. "In the hay? In the pit? That's very apt, don't you think? The snake pit. The writhings of snakes? Fucking like rattlesnakes. Do you like to fuck, Ricky?" Such a movie— from a tome by Collins's equally talented sister, Jackie Collins— is predicated on every man lusting after our star so, before she and Wight hit the sack, she needlessly struts her stuff in a fur coat, chauffeur's hat, and black lingerie.

Not for nothing does one of Coby's crooked pals describe Collins as "the best-known cradle snatcher this side of the Atlantic."

Out on the town, Collins runs into Coby who, after they've had sex, searches for the ring through the pockets of her dozens of fur coats. Collins catches him and snaps, "You just take your cheap Italian ass and hustle it somewhere else."

Her accountant Kenneth Haigh proffers dire warnings about Coby ("Is it serious?" he asks. "Is anything serious?" she wonders, world-wearily puffing a cigarette) and then he asks, "Where are you going to be in ten years' time? It's cold out there." Old trouper Collins, perhaps trusting that she'd be fighting off the cold with an international hit TV series, "Dynasty," not to mention her own bestselling memoirs (which make little mention of movies like this), ignores his advice and spends a sex-filled weekend with Coby at Lloyd's among the horsey set.

The simulated sex isn't quite as good as in *The Stud* but still, there are lots of naked revelers in the swimming pool and the instantly forgettable disco title tune. God help us all if the Collins sisters decide to team up again.

Produced by John Quested, directed by Gerry O'Hara. Screenplay by O'Hara, based on Jackie Collins's novel. C, 93 m., V

Caged (1950) ❤ ❤ ❤

"File out, you tramps, it's the end of the line!" So arriving prisoners are greeted in the opening line of *Caged*, a women-in-prison exposé whose special charm derives from the fact that its over-the-top stereotypes—forever afterwards played by drag queens like Divine and drag queens manqué like Sybil Danning—are here essayed by actual women. What's more, two of them, Eleanor Parker and Hope Emerson, were nominated for Academy Awards for these scenery-chewing antics (1950 must have been a very slow year for actresses).

"Welcome to Lysol Lane," a longtime inmate tells first-timer Eleanor Parker, a teenage newlywed, when she arrives in the slammer. The movie kicks into high gear when six-foot, two-inch Emerson roars on as a hard-drinking, no-nonsense prison matron about whom one inmate opines, "Her first name is Filth." Emerson squares off against prison reform advocate Agnes Moorehead, telling her, "This place ought to be run with a rubber hose— break 'em in two if they talk out of turn."

It's hard to believe this movie was co-written by a woman, but screenwriter Virginia Kellogg keeps the howlers coming fast and furious. "You stay in here too long, you don't think of guys at all," one con tells Parker. "You just get out of the habit." Another seventy-one-year-old inmate sighs, "What I wouldn't give for a sink full of dirty dishes"—the movie's subtle warning to dissatisfied suburban housewives everywhere.

Meanwhile, novice inmate Parker discovers she's pregnant, finds that her best gal pal has hung herself, is shocked into giving birth prematurely, and learns she must give up her baby for adoption. What keeps her from losing her mind during all this is (yes!) finding a helpless pussycat outside in the snow. When matron Emerson tries to take the kitty away, they get into a hair-pulling, costume-tearing cat fight that results, deliriously, in a "cell-block riot"—this entire movie gives a new meaning to that phrase! Furious, Emerson takes revenge by cutting off Parker's hair. The director zeroes in for a big panicky closeup of Parker's eyes—Do anything, but don't touch my coiffure!

Shorn, she toughens up and eggs on another con to kill Emerson. You keep thinking, "What else could possibly happen?" Plenty, sister, plenty. A mannish old broad finds Parker to be "a cute trick," gives her a rhinestone compact and teaches her basic shoplifting skills, so Parker will have a career outside the prison walls. On the day she's paroled, Parker throws her wedding ring into the trash, and says, "I certainly got myself an education." With a worldly sigh, Moorehead tells her secretary, "Keep her file active. She'll be back."

With Ellen Corby, Jan Sterling, Jane Darwell, Lee Patrick. Produced by Jerry Wald, directed by John Cromwell. Screenplay by Virginia Kellogg and Bernard Schoenfeld. B&W, 96 m., TV

Duel in the Sun (1946) ❤ ❤

We who love Bad Movies positively worship David Selznick's overproduced, overwritten, overwrought *Duel in the Sun*. This film was Selznick's futile effort to make a sex symbol out of his Oscar-winning girlfriend Jennifer Jones by casting her as a wanton half-breed Injun gal who makes men's blood turn to, well, firewater. You've got to wonder about the private life of any famed movie producer who writes a script expressly for his young actress protegée that includes self-appraisals such as: "I'm trash, I tell ya, trash!" and "I know what ya think, that I'm trashy like my ma!" and, best of all, "Trash, trash, trash, trash, *trash!*"

This two-hour-plus saga of what happens when half-caste Jones is brought to live within the walls of the McCanles homestead—wild son Gregory Peck goes insane, nice son Joseph Cotten leaves home, decent mama Lillian Gish expires from all the excitement, and sinister father Lionel Barrymore cracks such one-liners as "Is that what they're wearing in wigwams these days?"—lends itself irresistibly to the interpretation that this is a Hollywood insider's look at the effect Jones actually had on the married Selznick's home life when their romance began. How else to explain away the self-indulgence of Barrymore begging for Gish's forgiveness as she is dying? "It don't seem possible but I musta been wrong about a whole lotta things," weeps Barrymore—a thought that apparently never occurred to Selznick when writing this script.

And for that matter, what on earth was Selznick telling himself as he watched the dailies of Jones, all heaving breasts in off-the-shoulder gypsy blouses, whispering, "I wanna be a lady. Will ya learn me?" Happily, no one can, so she falls in love with the handsome but psychopathic Peck, who nicknames her his "bobtailed little half-breed" (she calls him "varmint"). Peck loves her so much he kills every one of her decent suitors, including his own brother. (Presumably, things weren't quite this out of hand around Casa Selznick, since all the kids survived.)

The jaw-dropping, justifiably infamous finale of *Duel in the Sun* has these two bad-for-each-other lovers shooting it out on a mountaintop, then crawling—slowly, s-l-o-w-l-y (the sequence lasts a mind-boggling eight minutes!)—across the rocky terrain for one last embrace. "Lemme hold ya, little bobcat," Peck says, before they kiss and die. Incredibly, unbelievably, both Jones and Selznick worked again after *Duel in the Sun.*

With Walter Huston, Herbert Marshall, Charles Bickford,

Tilly Losch, Joan Tetzel, Harry Carey, Otto Kruger. Produced by Selznick, directed by King Vidor (quite a maestro with crawling scenes: see *Beyond the Forest*). Screenplay by Selznick and Oliver H. P. Garrett, from the Niven Busch novel. C, 138 m., V

From the Terrace (1960) ❤ ❤ ❤

A more accurate title might have been *From the Furnace*, for this laugh-out-loud soap opera is downright feverish as it demonstrates how much it hates the very, very rich—why, almost as much as the very, very rich hate themselves.

Returning war hero Paul Newman overhears his parents fighting (Workaholic father Leon Ames: "You could stay with him and me, the same night? You're a pig!" Alcoholic mother Myrna Loy: "You drove me to it, I needed love wherever I could find it!") and resolves that he'll be different. He's right, of course—he'll be even less happy than his folks. Society deb Joanne Woodward ("Fancy pedigree, papers on both sides," someone says about her. "She's really saving it, that one is.") looks like Newman's ticket to a happier life, but she no sooner dumps her fiancé to marry Newman than she too turns out to be a boozy tramp: Rolling around on their bed, she pants, "What do you call me . . . 'a hot number'?"

Newman, in tried-and-true sins-of-the-father fashion, throws himself into his work, driving Woodward into the arms of her former fiancé, psychiatrist Patrick O'Neal. Away on a business trip, Newman yells into the telephone, "I don't want that guy in our apartment!" and Woodward, clad in a pink negligee, says, "I'll tell him," hangs up, and gets back into bed with O'Neal: "You're not to come up here anymore," she purrs.

Meanwhile, Newman meets nice girl Ina Balin, but women just seem to go slutty when they're around him: Before you know it, she's moved to the city to become Newman's mistress. "I think I'm going to remember this night for all time," Balin says. "And some day, when we finally part, I'll go to Spain and live with my memories" (whereas we only have to go to the VCR for the memories of the days when Bad Movies were this deliciously funny).

When the two women meet (Woodward in a fur coat and a

tiara, Balin in a plain cloth coat), and Woodward observes, "She has something I haven't got—niceness," Newman knows what he must do: dump Woodward so he can turn Balin into his next boozy tramp of a wife. Before she's given the heave-ho, we're treated to what's meant to be a horrifying glimpse of Woodward's future life as a fallen society matron: At a charity ball, a swank but sleazy gigolo waltzes Woodward around the dance floor, whispering into her ear "I know all about you. You won't be the first dissatisfied wife I've made happy." We can't help thinking, it sure looks better than marriage to Newman.

With Elizabeth Allen, Barbara Eden, George Grizzard. Produced and directed by Bad Movies We Love maestro Mark Robson (who also gave us *Peyton Place* and *Valley of the Dolls*). Screenplay by Ernest Lehman, from the John O'Hara novel. C, 144 m., V, L

Go Naked in the World (1960) ❤❤❤

In this film's opening second, dressed-to-kill Gina Lollobrigida gets eyed by a slatternly streetwalker who gives her a sisterly wink. Then Gina hurries into a nightclub where the maître d' whispers, "If you're free later this evening . . ." and Gina laughs, saying, "I'm never free, sweetie." Suddenly, her "date" must depart, saying "I don't like leaving you alone," and Gina says with a shrug, "I haven't been alone ten minutes since I was twelve."

This laugh-till-it-hurts saga of a San Francisco call girl who's loved by a zillionaire father and his son was no doubt developed for MGM contract star Liz Taylor (who hardly made a wiser choice by making *Butterfield 8* instead). The movie has Taylor's fingerprints all over it, down to the Helen Rose gowns topped with what look like Cadillac fins to emphasize an ample bosom. (Perhaps Gina got this role because she could step right into the costumes—it certainly can't have been her acting.)

Tony Franciosa, home from the army, boasts, "I can make love in twelve languages," but he's the first soldier in history who's never heard of prostitution, for, though Gina is "the highest-priced woman in captivity," he never guesses it (even with her hints like "Girls like me don't fall in love" and "You make me feel like being honest, and honest women have lonely nights"). At his parents' anniversary party, Franciosa tells pop Ernest Borgnine that they're in love. "Love?" rages Borgnine, "We're talking rent! There's a dozen men in this room who know that call girl better than you—including me, you dumb kid." Gina confirms it's true ("I sell myself"), but says she does love Franciosa ("It was free"). He pelts her with dollars and fumes, "I want to be like the others, I want to have a hard time remembering your name!"

Though he gets drunk and winds up on skid row, he can't forget her: "I'm hooked by a hooker!" Borgnine has problems of his own—his teen daughter stays out all night, his wife says she's leaving him—and, just then, Franciosa returns home to say he's decided to wed Gina. Thunderstruck, Borgnine mutters, "It's the moon, that's what it is."

That's as good an explanation as any we could offer, but nothing could possibly explain what happens next: Franciosa and Gina run off to Acapulco, where they can be alone to whisper sweet nothings. "How many?" he asks her. "Did you ever count?" She replies, "Why count waves in the ocean?" He proposes marriage, but knowing that he'll never forget her sordid past, Gina pretends to stop caring. "I'll see you around," she tells him as she packs. "And if you don't say hello, I'll understand." Heartbroken, she then goes out on the town, gets gang raped, and commits suicide. But don't despair: father and son reconcile their differences over her lifeless body.

With Luana Patten. Produced by Aaron Rosenberg, directed by Ranald MacDougall. Screenplay by MacDougall, from the Tom T. Chamales novel. C, 103 m., TV

Half Moon Street (1986) ❤❤

Enjoy the spectacle of watching esteemed, personable actors make hash of their reputations? Then take a detour down *Half Moon Street*, in which prim Ph.D. Sigourney Weaver lectures on petrodollar politics at London's elite Middle-Eastern Institute by day and by night sells herself for the "Jasmine Escort Service." It seems Weaver was having a tough time living in a crummy bed-sitter on her small monthly salary. "You could hock that video," she complains, sitting naked in a tub full of freezing bath-water when her Jamaican landlord tells her he doesn't have the cash to fix the plumbing. "And you, doctor," he retorts, "could hock your ass." Good idea!

But Mistress Sigourney becomes no ordinary, trick-turning, whip-wielding rent-a-dominatrix: This movie would have us be-lieve she actually gets her clients off with feminist harangues on racism, sexism, and vegetarianism. (She also deliberately wears her brainy glasses on dates, and is so politically correct, she charges double for smokers.)

Her pimp wonders aloud (as have we), "What have you got that makes you so popular?" and Weaver explains, "Something you don't have. Brains." A sample of her smarts? Her first words upon meeting Michael Caine, a titled statesman and antiterrorist with a yen for hired girls, are: "Don't worry, I'm naked under-neath." Caine is fascinated by tales of Weaver's stay in China, where she and a lover "stayed up all night arguing T. S. Eliot." Despite their generating zero screen chemistry, they continue seeing one another; Weaver confides, "The men I see don't want a woman. They want me to be a thing. They want me to be a pillow. Or a table. Or a pet rabbit."

Whatever Caine wants Weaver to be gets left, thankfully, to our imaginations. When she's not philosophizing with Caine, Weaver's slipping between satin sheets with a Palestinian she wows by observing, "You're not a bit like the sheik in *Beat the Devil*." When Caine fails to meet her for a birthday rendezvous, she shacks up with a sexy Frenchman. "I know: 'something came up,' " she screams at Caine when he tries to apologize. "Well, same here. I got laid. It was fantastic."

Though Caine's the center of terrorist threats, he risks it all to visit Weaver in her apartment. When she notices him eyeing her exercise equipment, she asks, "Do you want me on the bi-cycle?" Caine, alas, demurs, saying "No. In the bedroom. Like lovers." It all ends with Weaver quitting the agency and out-smarting the terrorists who're trying to snuff her. The fadeout suggests that she and Caine will drive each other to ecstasy with intellectual parry and thrust. Blame this one on the moon.

With Keith Buckle, Karim Nadim Swalha, Vincent Lindon.

Produced by Geoff Reeve and Edward Pressman, directed by Bob Swaim. Screenplay by Swaim and Edward Behr, from Paul Theroux's novella *Doctor Slaughter*. C, 90 m., V, L

Poison Ivy (1992) ❤❤

"I never knew anyone that looked that much like a slut," Sara Gilbert remarks about teen psycho Drew Barrymore, who literally swings into Gilbert's life on a rope across a significantly deep ravine. "Not that I'm a lesbian," Gilbert says. "Well, maybe I am. I told my mother I was and she said, 'Fine, as long as you don't smoke.' " But everyone *smokes* in this swoony saga of the havoc a gal who's been denied hugs can wreak on one wealthy family—like Cheryl Ladd who, as Gilbert's dying mom, breathes fire when she demands, "Give me the Percodan!" or asks Barrymore, as she's trying on Ladd's oxygen mask, "Aren't you afraid of catching death?" Nope, it's Bad Acting that one might catch from this flick, which showcases Barrymore wishing, "I hope that when I die, I'll have had a sports car, a family, and a home. One day with the top down is better than a lifetime in a box."

Barrymore, being tattooed by some sleazeball, urges Gilbert to get one, too; Gilbert shrugs, "I'm not the type," causing Barrymore to rant, "Oh, but I am low class?" Gilbert responds, "You don't have any class," then demonstrates her class by suggesting that instead of borrowing Gilbert's money to pay for the tattoo, Barrymore should "suck his dick—maybe he'll give you a deal." Barrymore avenges herself by arranging for Gilbert to be away when her father Tom Skerritt (fresh from his *Wild Orchid 2: Two Shades of Blue* triumph) throws a big soiree. Barrymore, looking luscious in Ladd's gown and jewels, helps out instead, asking Skerritt, "Care for anything?"

This leads to the first of the movie's many tasty highlights when, post-party, Barrymore and Skerritt converge on Ladd in her bedroom. Barrymore hands Ladd champagne to wash down her painkillers, gives another glass to recovering alcoholic Skerritt, then—when Ladd, more or less unconscious, drops her glass—Barrymore grinds her high heel into the fragments.

Skerritt, kneeling at her feet, kisses his way up, up, up her thigh, making Barrymore moan "Ooooh!" as she fingers Skerritt's toupee.

Gilbert, sensing that Barrymore is trouble, snaps, "My dog's a traitor!" and challenges Barrymore to a duel that will test the hound's loyalty. This hilarious "showdown" has the poor dog running back and forth while Barrymore and Gilbert act and act and act variations on "Here, Fred . . . c'mere, Fred."

We haven't even yet mentioned what happens later, like Skerritt making love to Barrymore atop his Mercedes in the rain; like Barrymore killing Ladd, then taking her ashes for a spin in a sports car with, yes, the top down; like Gilbert hallucinating when she catches Barrymore and Skerritt doing it; like Barrymore French-kissing Gilbert; like Gilbert killing Barrymore; like Gilbert telling us, "I miss her." Deranged, demented, delightful.

Produced by Andy Ruben, directed by Katt Shea. Screenplay by Ruben and Shea. "Limousines provided by Elite limousine service." C, 92 m., V

The Shanghai Gesture (1941) ❤ ❤

Raving beauty Gene Tierney is side-splittingly *out there* in Josef von Sternberg's monumentally screwy fantasia about a British society playgirl who goes to rack and ruin in a sin-laden gambling house in naughty Shanghai. Dragon lady Ona Munson, the Oriental proprietress of the joint (whose cantilevered hairdos make even Patti Labelle and Cher at their most outré pale by comparison), is fixated on Tierney from the moment the stunner looks around the place and says, "It smells so incredibly evil. . . . It has a ghastly familiarity, like a half-remembered dream. Anything could happen here, any moment." Nothing much does happen, as it turns out, but all of it is preposterous.

Munson's blood boils when she learns that millionaire Walter Huston plans to run her out of business. "Find his mistakes," Munson says—coming on like equal parts Gloria Swanson in *Sunset Blvd.*, Arletty in *Children of Paradise*, and Marlene Dietrich in other, better von Sternberg movies—"If he's successful, he makes quite a few." Meanwhile, Tierney becomes a lush and a roulette wheel junkie. Coke-eyed Arab Victor Mature asks, "I wonder how you look with your hair down," and soon finds out.

Then Tierney, stoned out of her gourd, starts carousing in the casino, picking fights, and yelling to the bartender, "Bring me some brandy and sulphur to chase away the evil spirits!" Munson reprimands Tierney: "Behave yourself. You're in China and you're white. It's not good for us to see you like this." (However, it's deliriously good for *us* to see her like this.)

As Munson predicted, it turns out that Huston does have a few secrets. Ogling muscle-bound Mike Mazurski, Huston says, "You likee Chinee New Year?" Mazurski smiles, "I likee," and the two vanish to do Buddha only knows what.

Munson amuses her thirteen dinner guests with such delights as an auction of caged girls and a doll representing each guest at his or her place at the banquet table. When one of the guests notices a doll with a missing head, Munson purrs, "That represents a very distinguished young lady who's being sobered up so that she can take her place at this table." Guess who? In staggers Tierney, druggy and slatternly, to learn that Huston and Munson were once married and she—oh, the horror!—is their mixed-blood daughter. When Munson breaks this news to her, Tierney sneers, "I have no more connection with you than with a toad out there in the street," and Mama puts her out of her sweet misery. And ours.

With Maria Ouspenskaya, Eric Blore, and, as it reads on a lengthy credit (honest), "a large cast of Hollywood Extras who without expecting credit or mention stand ready to do their best and who at their best are more than good enough to deserve mention." Produced by Arnold Pressburger, directed by von Sternberg. Screenplay by von Sternberg, with the collaboration of Geza Herczeg and Jules Furthman, from a play by John Colton. B&W, 90 m., V, L

The Stud (1978) ❤

"I'm tired of putting it in everything that winks at me," boy-for-rent Oliver Tobias moans to his mates at the private London disco he manages for sexually voracious boss lady (and zillionaire's wife)

Joan Collins. Collins demands that sexy, younger Tobias service her all kinds of ways in the elevator of her posh manse and commemorates the event for posterity on videotape.

Naked under a masseur's paws at a posh health club, Collins sings the praises of Tobias to her salivating pal, Sue Lloyd: "I have turned a common waiter into one of the most fancied young men in London. More or less with my bare hands. Clothes, hair, even sex. Especially sex. When I first met him, Tony thought that 'sixty-nine' was a bottle of Scotch!" Soon every woman in London's competing for Tobias's charms and, after he's bedded a sexy black dancer who overhears Joan insisting he return to her place to do her again, the dancer asks if he takes Diner's Club. "It's not often," she purrs, "that I get to eat that much." Collins promises to give Tobias to Lloyd for a Christmas present, explaining that she's not jealous because that'd be like "being jealous of a turnstile at Regent's Park Zoo."

Every generation gets the music it deserves, so, between all the pseudosexy badinage and soft-core humping, there are riotous, endless disco numbers staged to a series of nonhits.

Tobias falls instantly in love with Collins's horse-faced daughter, Emma Jacobs, but is whisked off by Collins to a jet set orgy at the Parisian "Palace of Delights" owned by Lloyd and her ambisexual writer husband, Mark Burns. This place—the entire first floor is a sunken swimming pool—sets the stage for a movie high point: naked Collins and Burns merrily riding, for what seems like hours, on a swing over the water.

When Tobias tires of popping pills, ogling naked bodies, and finding Burns fellating him underwater, Collins dumps him. When he asks how he'll get back to London, Collins sneers, "Fuck yourself there, darling." Tobias races back to true love Jacobs but she screams, "You think I don't know about you and that cheap slut who owns you? You're what she deserves, a cheap gigolo in a little nightclub!" So Tobias ends up tossed out like a cheap paperback novel—rather like, well, Jackie Collins's novel, *The Stud*—and Joan ends up tossed out by her rich husband, treating her like a desperate, aging movie star cast by her own sister in a hilariously trashy movie.

Produced by Ronald S. Kass, directed by Quentin Masters. Screenplay by Jackie Collins, from her novel; additional material and dialogue by Dave Humphries and Christopher Stagg. C, 95 m., V

Sylvia (1964) ❤ ·

Who is Sylvia? Not *Laura*, that's for sure, although that's clearly what was hoped for by the filmmakers, who constructed this would-be spellbinder as if private eye George Maharis were Dana Andrews on the trail of fascinating Gene Tierney, here understudied by less-than-fascinating Carroll Baker. Producer Joseph E. Levine, in this second of three attempts to turn Baker into a sexbomb, even hired *Laura* composer David Raksin to compose the score.

Wealthy Peter Lawford hires Maharis to unlock the closet of secrets surrounding his mysterious fiancée, Baker, who makes her living as—oh, watch the movie yourself if you don't believe us—a grower of prize roses and, yes, a poet. "I got pie in the sky and I got sin," goes a selection of Baker's *Moon Without Light*, "a bellyful of sin, a dark blue, syncopated sin." From this, Maharis sniffs something earthier than just rose petals in Baker's past, so he goes down the Flashback Trail, first meeting Viveca Lindfors (a sexually ambiguous, overacting librarian) who reveals that Baker was raped by immigrant stepfather Aldo Ray.

The path next leads to the madam who employed Baker, Ann Sothern, who pockets the movie simply by listening, straight-faced, as Baker utters, "I'm full of hate and anger and frustration, and I know that it's going to take all the gold and silver and diamonds in the world to cure me." Next, Maharis locates burlesque doll Nancy Kovack who, changing in her dressing room, announces, "I'm neurotic, I like to get dressed with men in the room," and lets drop how she and Baker once did time after a whorehouse raid.

Joanne Dru, another ex-hooker pal of Baker's, tells Maharis ostensibly about Baker but perhaps cluing us in to how actors get through movies like this, that she "trained her mind and soul to be somewhere else." We meet Baker's next employer: drag queen, bar owner, and entertainer Paul Gilbert, who finishes singing Harold Arlen's "Love and Learn" by karate-chopping a board

("And that, you lovely things," she tells her boys, "is what Lola calls a bang-up finish"). Baker met all kinds among Gilbert's screwball clients, but none slimier than Lloyd Bochner who, when he asks her reaction to his bound volume of erotica and she observes "It belongs in the trash!" growls, "You're paid for!" and beats her up.

Then Baker refines herself with "travel, Europe, and culture." Soon, of course, Maharis finds himself gazing into Baker's eyes, treating her (hilariously) to "mile-long" hot dogs, commiserating with her about modern angst—"I've felt that way," he tells her, "dry and dead"—and refusing to spill the beans on her to Lawford. "You know all about Sylvia," she utters to Maharis, breathily, "why don't you kiss me?" The only real mystery here: How did these people ever think they would get away with it?

Produced by Martin H. Poll and Joseph E. Levine, directed by Gordon Douglas. Screenplay by Sidney Boehm, from the novel by E. V. Cunningham. B&W, 115 m., TV

Two Mules for Sister Sara (1969) ❤

Director Don Siegel had originally set Elizabeth Taylor as Clint Eastwood's co-star in this warped western that begins with a mercenary saving a nun from being raped and, with notable nods to *The African Queen* and *Heaven Knows, Mr. Allison*, gets screwier from there. When Taylor dropped out, Shirley MacLaine—perhaps her sole rival in having been most often cast as a hooker or a loose woman—took the role, assuring that the "surprise" finish as to the holy sister's true vocation could come as a surprise only to someone who'd never seen a movie before.

Grizzled Clint pays no mind to Sister MacLaine's eyeliner and false eyelashes—nuns followed such a different dress code in the Old West—yet, as they travel together, he can't help but observe, "Maybe a nun ought not to be so good-lookin'." But, she warns, "The way I look is of no importance. I'm married to our Lord, Jesus Christ." That doesn't keep her from occasionally sneaking off in the wilderness to smoke or take a belt of booze, though. So on their way to help the Mexicans fight off French invaders, he persists: "Haven't you ever wanted to be a whole woman? Have a man make love to you? Haven't you ever laid awake at night wondering what it would be like?" She replies, "When we get these feelings, we pray until they pass."

And you'll be praying that the ridiculous plot complications will pass, too—like Sister MacLaine having to remove an Indian arrow from Eastwood's shoulder, a scene that director Siegel milks for what seems like an eternity. Eastwood's soon saying more sweet nothings to Sister MacLaine, such as, "Every night, when we bed down next to each other, I think of you that way," which he recites so unconvincingly he might as well be talking to his horse. In fact, for all the heat the two generate, each of them could have done their closeups from two separate locations.

When Eastwood and Sister MacLaine take a shortcut through her old place of employment and Eastwood marvels (duh!) that it's a cathouse, Sister MacLaine throws off her nun drag and bellows, "Oh no, this is no cathouse, this is the best whorehouse in town!" It all ends with the stars frolicking in a tub and riding off together into the sunset.

Produced by Martin Rackin and Carroll Case, directed by Siegel. Screenplay by Albert Maltz, from a story by Bud Boetticher. C, 116 m., V

Wild Orchid 2: Two Shades of Blue (1992) ❤

Ready for "a piggyback ride straight to Hell"? That's what junkie Tom Skerritt (appropriately named Ham) tells daughter Nina Siemaszko he did for her mama, and that's precisely what filmmaker Zalman King has in store for us Bad Movie addicts who need his flicks the way Skerritt needs his fix.

To score Skerritt his heroin, Nina offers her virginity to sleazy Joe Dallesandro (who, decades before, was playing *her* role in Andy Warhol movies). Skerritt dies, Nina needs moolah, so Dallesandro introduces her to classy madam Wendy Hughes with this farewell, "Fucking whore—just like your mother," and we're plunged deep inside the steamy psyche of King's silly sex fantasies. On a tour of the brothel, Hughes deadpans one zany aside after another, from "Dominique was trained in Paris. Her technique is impeccable" to "Naked women sitting on straight-backed chairs—what could be more beautiful?"

Nina's introduced to her work by a john who ravishes her while she's sitting in a shoeshine chair in a men's lavatory. In the next scene, when Nina stares into a mirror, muttering, "Don't think about it. Just do it," we assume she's convincing herself to go back and continue filming this deranged, funny movie. The other working girls tell Nina, "There's girls you fuck and girls you marry, and never the twain shall meet," so, naturally, Nina meets the love of her life, Brent Fraser, when his father pays for him to be deflowered.

Torn between her conflicting desires, Nina goes wild the night of the Hooker's Sock Hop: Half-naked, she ruins the party by, um, spreading out on the dance floor and howling like a banshee. Hughes, slapping Nina silly, warns what really waits for her in the outside world: "A baby sucking on each tit, varicose veins running up and down your leg, and a husband who abuses you!"

But when Hughes sends Nina out to make a porno film for senator Christopher McDonald—who waves handcuffs around and says depraved things like "Show me your claws!"—Nina makes a break for a better life, sets up house in a neighboring town, and enrolls in high school. On her first day, Nina's English teacher brings the movie to its knees with her remark, "Tell the class a little about yourself."

Even if you've guessed that schoolmate Fraser fails to recognize her, falls in love, and admits "I'm a fake" (so she'll say, "I'm a fake too"), there's no way you could imagine their first date. Fraser drives Nina to a field in the middle of nowhere, shows her his brass bed, and asks, "Mind if I air out the sheets?" A nice girl at last, she rebuffs his advances, and he does handstands to win her heart. Since King's turned to TV with his riotous show "Red Shoe Diaries," we're hoping someone will bankroll another King series—"Wild Orchid 90210," anyone?

Produced by David Saunders and Rafael Eisenman, directed by King. Screenplay by King. C, 111 m., V

The Price
of Fame

Hollywood, fame's epicenter, is seldom loonier or more lovable than when its moviemakers slash away at the glitter and artifice to get at the real tinsel. Most of the would-be cautionary tales in this chapter drip with sin, betrayal, degradation, and the horror of getting a bad table at the Brown Derby. Sure, they follow timeworn scenarios (ambitious overachiever claws his way to the top, steps on everyone around him, ends up in the gutter), but each is as irresistible as a celebrity tell-all autobiography—with all the dull parts cut out.

Beloved Infidel (1959) ❤ ❤

Fresh off the boat, ladylike Deborah Kerr heads to a Manhattan editor with samples of her writing. "Debunking celebrities seems to be your ruling passion," he says. "It sells newspapers, doesn't it?" Kerr retorts. Since she's playing Sheilah Graham, the gossip columnist who romanced the very married F. Scott Fitzgerald, then cashed in by writing a tell-all memoir, then sold the rights so we could be watching this movie, the obvious answer to her question is, You betcha!

When Kerr becomes the top dish queen in Tinseltown, one female star inquires, "Tell me, how did a girl as pretty as you ever get to be the biggest witch in Hollywood? And that word is spelled with a capital *B*!" Kerr snaps, "Not the biggest—the second biggest."

At a dinner party, Kerr and Gregory Peck—stupendously mis-cast as Fitzgerald—make bedroom eyes at one another. Though she's engaged and he's married, they're drawn together. "This is a mistake," Peck pants, and Kerr readily agrees, but soon they're lovers, with Peck murmuring such howlers as, "You look more attractive every day. Today you look like tomorrow."

He's a great writer, though, so there are probing, insightful questions, too: his query, "How many times have you been in love?" inexplicably unleashes a hurricane of hysteria. "I cannot go on lying to you," Kerr blubbers. "I was brought up in a slum! There was no one to tell me right from wrong!" Later, Peck reveals his plans for a new novel: "I've always felt that Hollywood had a wonderful kind of foolish grandeur. It's got its kings, clowns, wicked princes, and clever mistresses, all in a ferment of ambi-tious motion." (Gee, isn't this just how Fitzgerald must have really spoken?)

At their Malibu love nest, Peck wonders why Kerr's never mentioned marriage. Answers Kerr, who's just come from inter-viewing Greta Garbo, "A Graham is a trusting animal. It makes a fine house pet, it's easily trained and likes to play games. And it never asks questions."

Their romantic idyll cannot last, of course. Soon Peck's boozing it up (he's so wooden, the only way we can tell he's supposed to be tipsy is whether or not his hair is mussed), and Kerr's screech-ing, "I didn't drag myself out of the gutter to waste myself on a worthless drunk like you! Worthless! Worthless!" They split up, but reconcile just in time for Peck to say, "I owe you so much, Sheil-o," and then—drop dead. Surprisingly, the movie doesn't end with Kerr racing directly to the typewriter to pound out this exploitative tale; instead, she wanders along the beach, listening to a heavenly choir sing the impossibly-difficult-to-come-up-with-a-rhyme title song.

Produced by Jerry Wald, directed by Henry King. Screenplay by Sy Bartlett, from Graham's book (co-authored by Gerold Frank). C, 123 m., TV

Harlow (1965) ❤ ❤

"I'm not a person to them, I'm a thing; just hair and legs—no face, no feelings." It sounds like an actress refreshingly wise to herself and Tinseltown, but nah, it's just Carroll Baker, waxing melancholic on what a drag it is being a love goddess, in producer Joseph E. Levine's bogus whitewash of Hollywood's platinum blonde, Jean Harlow. Not that Baker got to learn first-hand about being the wet dream of millions, but it wasn't for lack of trying. Levine pulled out the publicity stops for his movie of *The Carpetbaggers*, starring Baker as Harlowesque "Rina Marlowe," then, when the cash rolled in, he tried his luck again with *Harlow*, one of two movies "inspired" by a trashy best-selling biography by Irving R. Schulman.

Playing one of the snappiest, raciest gals in movies, Baker radiates all the charisma of a crash test dummy as John Michael Hayes's Lonely-Actress-at-the-Top script staggers from cliché to cliché. You'll be hooting right from the moment Baker, in a bad wig and Edith Head–designed padded dresses, tries scoring her big break without losing her virginity. "Honey, you're no Sarah Bernhardt," advises a moviemaker. "You've got to make the most of what nature gave you."

It's no picnic at home, either, what with stepfather Marino (Raf Vallone) mooching off her and eyeing her like she's the blue plate special. Angela Lansbury, as Mom, isn't much help either, consoling her daughter with such wisdom as "Acting is hard." (Apparently, good acting is, under the circumstances, impossible.)

When top director Leslie Nielsen gives Baker a guided tour of his bedroom, replete with round bed and Ziegfeld-like draperies, hold on to your corn nuts for the moment when she repulses his advances by screaming, "You're a dirty animal of a person!" to which he retorts (you guessed it), "You were nothing when I picked you up and you'll be even less when I drop you."

Things get weird after Baker weds effete producer Peter Lawford who—considering his impotence on their wedding night— must have been trying for irony when he had revealed, on meeting her, "You've made me a firm believer." Lawford shoots himself, and Baker hits the skids—boozing, shacking up with studly greasers, behaving the lurid way you'd hoped she would in a movie like this. "Tell me truthfully, mama," she asks, chewing on a cigarette holder and most of the scenery, "is Marino that exciting?"

She never finds out for, just then, Baker up and expires! Never mind that, in real life, Harlow's husband was a bigamist, that he may have beat her to a pulp, or that he may have been murdered. When Baker's agent, Red Buttons, claims, "She didn't die of pneumonia, she died of life," we wish they'd made *that* movie. If Levine had really wanted to come up with gimmicks to promote the hell out of *Harlow*, he should have insured audiences against death by laughter.

Produced by Levine, directed by Gordon Douglas. Screenplay by Hayes. C, 125 m., V

The Legend of Lylah Clare (1968) ❤ ❤ ❤ ❤

The plot seems just a retread of *Vertigo*—guy remakes girl in the image of his dead love then, when he falls for her, she falls from a height to her death—but this Hollywood hothouse melodrama directed by Robert ("Over the top? Never heard of it") Aldrich is a laugh-till-you-ache classic.

Manufactured '50s sex goddess and *Vertigo* star Kim Novak again plays dual roles: dead Lylah, a Dietrich-style superstar, and the mousy actress that agent Milton Selzer is certain is the girl to star in Peter Finch's movie of Lylah's life. Director Finch, Lylah's von Sternberg–like mentor and lover, arranges to meet Novak, but first she's hours late, then she stares obsessively at Lylah's portrait, unleashing a goofy flashback of Lylah being accosted by a crazed fan on her staircase (the very staircase under which Novak now stands) first killing her admirer, then toppling to her death.

The laughs kick in when Finch demands Novak walk down that same stairway—"You're moving like a deeply offended Tibetan yak!" he snaps—and when he manhandles her, Novak, badly dubbed, suddenly growls, "Keep your feelthy hands off me!" She's supposed to sound just like Lylah, but instead she's a soundalike for Linda Blair dubbed by Mercedes McCambridge in *The Exorcist*.

At a gala press conference to introduce Novak, gossip columnist Coral Browne—who sports a rose in her iron leg brace! —purrs to Finch, "Aren't you borrowing a little heavily from *Sunset Blvd.?*" and on inspecting Novak with her cane, calls her "a grubby little slut." Predictably, Novak, suddenly badly dubbed again, calls Browne "the Wicked Witch of the West, throw water on her and she shrivels, she melts!" Finch later introduces Novak to Gabrielle Tinti, his studly, shirtless Italian gardener, for, as Finch observes, "I've never seen a woman yet who hasn't got a whore locked up inside her somewhere."

But it's Lylah who's locked inside Novak, and as Finch begins directing his protégée, the dead woman "commands" Novak to pitch temper tantrums, seduce her directors, and require thirty-three takes per scene (much like certain manufactured '50s sex goddesses). Novak can't play Finch's ending, so Finch rewrites it to sidestep the sordid details of Lylah murdering her attacker—who was actually a transvestite!—and instead invents (get this) a grand finale on a trapeze in a circus.

Novak, hours late, bellows to the waiting crew, "Tell them Lylah's comin'—soon as she gets her harness on!" then, when Finch demands a retake of a perfect scene, she falls to her death. It all ends, astoundingly, fittingly, with a TV commercial for dog food, followed by a Frank de Vol theme song, wordless except for a chorus who occasionally whisper, "Cha-cha-cha."

With Rosella Falk. Produced and directed by Robert Aldrich. Screenplay by Hugo Butler and Jean Rouverol, from a TV play by Robert Thom and Edward de Blasio. C, 130 m., TV

The Lonely Lady (1983) ❤ ❤ ❤

Let no one say that this Harold Robbins show biz potboiler doesn't begin with a bang: On the very day that Valley High student Pia Zadora wins an award as "most promising English major," she parties with fast Beverly Hills High students, one of whom— weed-smoking Ray Liotta—fondles her award ("Looks like a penis!"), fondles her breast ("Valley girls are anxious to please!"), throws her onto the lawn ("I'm gonna give you something special!"), and rapes her with the nearby garden hose. All this in the film's first fifteen minutes! (You may think it can't possibly continue at this crazed, trashy pace—but you are wrong: In the seventy-six minutes left, there are eight nude love scenes, two lesbian encounters, two showers, one hot tub, one Jacuzzi, and one pool table yet to come.)

Zadora, who wants to be a writer, marries the first Oscar-winning screenwriter she meets, Lloyd Bochner. When a has-been begs Bochner for a part in his next film, Zadora gives what she hopes we'll think is a literary shudder as she wonders, "Who would want to be an actress?" Bochner, speaking as one who knows (to one who *ought* to), replies, "In this business, you can't afford self-respect." When Bochner starts waving around that same garden hose, asking "Is this your kick?" Zadora divorces him.

She falls for (well, actually, she drops to her knees for) married movie star Jared Martin, who cold-shoulders her when she announces she's pregnant. She gets an abortion and, broke, works as a waitress for disco owner Joseph Cali, who promises to fund her script. Zadora believes that Cali "knows a lot of people," but her director pal Anthony Holland scoffs, "So does my garbageman!"

Soon Zadora's doing poppers, doing coke, and doing Cali, who plays pool while Zadora lies nude on the table top, dodging the balls. Cali says she's to write only for him from now on, and Zadora gets off a classic Bad Movie howler when she roars, "If I write for anyone, I write for me!" Zadora's realization that everyone in the film is using her drives her stark, raving mad. How can we tell? It's the only time in the movie that Zadora takes a shower with her clothes on.

She's institutionalized, where an orderly tells Zadora's mother, Bibi Besch, "She was suffering from paranoia and hallucinations, induced by tranquilizers, cocaine, amphetamines, alcohol" and Besch shrugs, "She's always been difficult." Given a typewriter as therapy, Zadora writes the script . . . of the movie we're watching.

Come the night of "The Awards Presentation Ceremony"—Tinseltown's highest honor, we're told—Zadora wins Best

Screenplay and, at the podium, gives the speech that brings the film to its infamous finale: "I don't suppose I'm the only one who's had to fuck her way to the top."

Produced by Robert Weston, directed by Peter Sasdy. Screenplay by John Kershaw and Shawn Randall; adaptation by Ellen Shepard, from Robbins's novel. C, 92 m., V, L

The Love Machine (1971) ❤❤

The indescribably tacky Moss Mabry fashion show that opens this movie version of Jacqueline Susann's novel will have you laughing so hard, you're bound to miss the first fifteen minutes of the plot. Thoughtfully, the filmmakers include a recap: In John Phillip Law's penthouse, model Jodi Wexler shows the front page of *Variety* to her caged bird, saying, "Look, Chipper, after just six weeks with us, we've taken him from a lowly newscaster and made him President of IBC News."

While Dionne Warwick sings "Your dreams will fade, and so will you" on the soundtrack, Law cheats on Wexler with every starlet who passes by, even as he fights programmer Jackie Cooper to improve the quality of TV. Cooper, standing in, no doubt, for talent-free novelist Jacqueline Susann as well as for the moviemakers, claims proudly, "When it comes to schlock, I'm a genius!"

It's not Law's notions of *Hamlet* that get him ahead, but his skills in the sack: while bedding Dyan Cannon, the wife of his boss Robert Ryan, the latter conveniently collapses from a heart attack (we suspect that he was watching the dailies), so Cannon names Law as his replacement. The envious Cooper remarks, "You've come a long way from the six o'clock news." "That's right," Law says, "I'm in your field now—I'm a connoisseur of crap." (Aren't we all?)

There's a price to pay, natch. When Law's too busy for Wexler, she commits suicide. Law would be heartbroken, if only he could register any emotion on his immobile face. Since he can't, he walks down to Times Square and hires a big, big hooker (Eve Bruce, listed in the credits as "Amazon Woman"!). When she calls him "a closet queen," Law beats her senseless and hightails it to (believe it or not!) the pad of David Hemmings, the photographer who loves him. In exchange for giving him an alibi, Law agrees to buy Hemmings "a gold slave bracelet" inscribed any way he likes. (And you thought it was easy being a love machine, didn't you? The problems never end.)

When Cannon finds Law enjoying two naked babes in the shower, she sets fire to his bed. Realizing that she could torch his career, too, Law escorts Cannon to a party and then . . . blatantly ignores her. Why? Probably so that the outraged Cannon will steal Hemmings's slave bracelet—to use as blackmail—and stuff it down her bra.

This leads to the movie's crazed climax, a crockery-throwing, hand-biting, face-slapping melee over the buffet table, but three grown men—Law, Hemmings, and his actor boyfriend—are no match for Cannon. When Hemmings pulls her hair and Cannon cracks him over the head with an Oscar, it's the closest anyone associated with *The Love Machine* ever got to such a statuette.

With Shecky Greene, Maureen Arthur, Sharon Farrell, Alexandra Hay, Claudia Jennings. Produced by M. J. Frankovich, directed by Jack Haley, Jr. Screenplay by Samuel Taylor, based on Susann's novel. C, 108 m., V

Mahogany (1975) ❤ ❤ ❤

"Flash that baby grand of yours you call a smile," Diana Ross coos at Billy Dee Williams in *Mahogany*, the one about the goody-two-shoes ghetto girl who becomes a *supreme*ly jaded jet-set celebrity (gee, Diana, anyone we know?). You can guess what you're in for from the opening scene, when top clothing designer Ross (yes, named Mahogany) receives a standing ovation from the fashion press (!) for a parade of kimonos trimmed with lit neon tubes. (Talk about your Method acting: to get into her role, Ross personally designed every costume in the movie, which is one thing, but took credit for it, which, once you've seen them, is another thing altogether.)

Early on, Ross is happy, so she dons a rainbow-hued gown and dances among bare white department store mannequins;

later, Ross is sad, so at a Roman orgy she drips hot white candle wax onto her tawny bare skin.

This film (with a line of dialogue that instantly entered the annals of kitsch: "Success is nothing without someone you love to share it with") was the beginning of the end of Ross's brief movie career. (*The Wiz* polished her off.) It had no less than three directors: one died during production, one was fired, one came in late but took all the credit (no one really came out ahead).

Anthony Perkins gives a loopy kick to his line readings as "Sean," a control-freak fashion photographer who makes, then wants to break, Ross; he literally tries to *drive* her crazy, trapping her in a speeding sports car as he shoots photos of her hysterical fear, until the car crashes. From her hospital bed, Ross coolly eyes the 8 × 10 blowups of her face in terror, muttering dryly, "Sean wanted to see death—and he did." (If you miss that throwaway line, Perkins just seems to disappear.)

Ross reforms before the end credits roll, so the social climber gets a social conscience—and Billy Dee Williams, too.

With Jean-Pierre Aumont, Nina Foch, Beah Richards, Marisa Mell. Produced by Rob Cohen and Jack Ballard, directed by Berry Gordy (and Tony Richardson, among others). Screenplay by John Byrum, from a story by Toni Amber. C, 109 m., V, L

Marjorie Morningstar (1958) ❤ ❤

"Sometimes I think I can act," Natalie Wood tells pal Carolyn Jones, "and other times I feel I don't have any talent at all." We can commiserate since, watching Wood struggling to play a Jewish teen who dreams of being a great theater actress, we feel the same way about her.

The two have summer resort jobs at South Wind—named, no doubt, after all the hot air expelled by forty-six-year-old Gene Kelly as he tries to pass himself off as a thirty-three-year-old "genius." Watching him direct dancers ("Be a cat!" Kelly suggests), Jones warns Wood, "Careful, he affects young girls the way whiskey hits an Indian."

When Wood's mother Claire Trevor sends uncle Ed Wynn to

keep an eye on her, Wood cracks, "You'd think mother was guarding Fort Knox." Jones says that losing one's virginity is "not a fate worse than death. Take a poll of your graduating class ten years from now, and see how many of them clinched the deal without giving away a few free samples."

Kelly would prefer not to bother, but he's happy to talk (and talk) about why. "I've no time for 'Shirley,' " he tells Wood. " 'Shirley' is a trade name for the respectable middle-class girl who likes to play at being worldly. It's monogrammed all over you the way parents sew camp initials on a child: 'Hands Off, Decent Girl, Object: Matrimony.' " Wood eventually gets a word in—"You think I'm just a stupid kid with a crush on you?"— sending Kelly off again. " 'Shirley' only hugs and paws on a rigidly graduated scale. We're an error in matchmaking. You're on a course charted by 5,000 years of Moses and his Ten Commandments. I'm a renegade."

We have only to hear Kelly croon the swoony song he's supposedly written, "A Very Special Love," or watch the unintentionally hilarious routine he choreographs for Wood to perform, a be-boppin' "Fiesta Rock," to see that Kelly's about as renegade as this expensive by-the-numbers soap straight off the studio assembly line. After that dance, Trevor opines, "Cigarettes, beer, all grown up!" but Wood gets it right when she says, "We may as well face it, I've gone to the dogs."

Though Kelly utters those words that every girl dreams of hearing—"Marjorie, you are your mother"—he can't help changing for her true love. "You've broken me," he claims, "I'm saddled, bridled, bitted, and tamed. Children ride me in Central Park for a dime." But when Kelly, "the Shakespeare of advertising," goes on a week-long bender with goodtime gal Ruta Lee, we know Wood's romance is doomed. Not, however, till Kelly's written a flop Broadway musical, till Wood's chased him through Europe, till they both again return to South Wind where it all began. Sadder, wiser, at fadeout, Wood looks determined to find better scripts.

Produced by Milton Sperling, directed by Irving Rapper. Screenplay by Everett Freeman, from Herman Wouk's novel. C, 123 m., V

Myra Breckinridge (1970) ❤

Novelists rarely wield the clout to put their name above a movie's title, but when they do it's always a sure sign of an enter-here-at-your-own-risk Bad Movie We Love. Take Gore Vidal's *Myra Breckinridge*, with its jaw-dropping opening in which Rex Reed petulantly waits for surgeon John Carradine to make him into a woman—or rather, to make him into Raquel Welch. The only Hollywood pinup to date who's made her bid to be "taken seriously" by playing a transsexual, Welch intones, "I am Myra Breckinridge, whom no man will ever possess." Rarely, if ever, has such unlikely material been so ideally matched to a director as pretentious and untalented as Michael Sarne—his "vision" here was, and remains, one of the most infamous box office disasters in film history.

Welch hits Hollywood to lay claim to the wealth that Uncle John Huston has raked in with his phony dramatic school, and also to lay hunky Roger Herren (in his debut, and simultaneous adieu, to the movies). Reed, on hand as Welch's other half, helps earn his salary by prompting her line readings, on screen: "Your goal is . . . ," he says, and Welch responds, "My goal is the destruction of the last vestigial traces of traditional manhood in order to realign the sexes, while preparing humanity for its next stage"—which, if it meant more movies like this one, thankfully never happened.

Both Mae West and Farrah Fawcett turn up, making this a virtual parade of Sex Symbols of Yesterday, Today, and Tomorrow. "I've come to bring back star quality," Welch asserts, hilariously, but more accurately opines that Fawcett's "mentally retarded." Don't dismiss this idea unless you've seen the film. Fawcett prances about, nude under a chiffon nightie, proffering food to Reed in this demented exchange: "Try this banana," she urges him, then, "Oh, a big bite!" This is topped when Welch kisses her way down—way, way down—Reed's chest, while he writhes and moans, "Oh Myra, yes!"

Another memorable moment occurs when the camera lingers on a trio walking away so we can study, meaningfully, Welch's bottom, Huston's butt, and a horse's ass. Another trio (Welch, Reed, and Fawcett) end up in bed together.

Back from the dead, it's West who makes the movie challenging to sit through: As an embalmed-looking talent agent and famed recording star, she tries but fails to work her way past very bad dentures to bark a song and sink her "teeth" into lines like, "There's no more studs around anymore. Everyone's popping pills and smoking grass." West singles out Tom Selleck for her sexual favors, and he looks even more dumbstruck than usual when he says, "I never did see a bed in an office before," dreading what's to come. Apparently this calamity was not the comeback vehicle West envisioned; she lived—well, sort of—to make an even worse movie, *Sextette*.

Produced by Robert Fryer, directed by Sarne. Screenplay by Sarne and David Giler, from Vidal's novel. C, 94 m., V

Slander (1956) ❤

Kiddie entertainer and puppeteer Van Johnson goes, overnight, from obscurity to becoming the idol of millions of tykes on his own TV show and, just as quickly, is toppled when a scandal erupts. (Sound like any kiddie icons we know, from Pinkie Lee in the '50s to Pee-Wee Herman in the '90s?)

Steve Cochran, ruthless editor of scandal magazine *Real Truth*, snarls, "The public has about as much brains as a halibut steak," goading his staff of boozers, deadbeats, and washouts to dredge up something sensational for their next issue. Cochran wants the scalp of America's biggest female star, Mary Sawyer ("In the minds of the American public, she is practically a nun, right?" he says), and sniffs out that something wicked happened to the box-office princess (whom we never see) as a kid and that Johnson's mother was somehow involved.

So, to get the goods on her, Cochran threatens Johnson (and wife Ann Blyth) with a mock-up of a story layout of a bombshell he plans to reveal: Johnson did four years in the Big House for armed robbery. Johnson refuses to trash the star, even when Blyth snaps, "I want you to make a choice between Mary Sawyer and us!"—even when she packs herself and their kid off to her mother's!

Such hooty dilemmas happen on Park Avenue, too, where Cochran fights with his booze-guzzling mother, Marjorie Rambeau (who, before they hit the bigtime, also came from the wrong side of the tracks): She's ashamed of how he makes his living, but he reminds her that "imported scotch is a lot better for what's left of your stomach than the rotgut you used to drink."

Johnson pays Cochran a visit—to call him, unforgettably, "a new kind of dirt!"—but still refuses to rat on the star. Out comes the cover story ("Our Kids' Hero, A Jail Bird!") and the sponsors pull the plug on Johnson's show. His son, taunted by schoolyard bullies, runs into the path of an oncoming car and dies; distraught, Rambeau comes to see the grieving Blyth, asking whether there was any connection between the accident and the magazine article. In closeup, Blyth, emoting like all get-out, grits her teeth and says, "If it hadn't been for your son, my son would be alive! He'd be alive, do you hear?"

On TV, Cochran and Rambeau watch Johnson get his chance at overemoting, fighting tears as he condemns the public for buying scandal magazines that ruin people's lives: "I hope the next person you help to kill won't be someone you love!" Moved, Rambeau gets out a pistol and puts Cochran out of his misery. Johnson got a first-hand taste of this kind of muck-raking when his stepson, Ned Wynn, revealed in his 1991 book *We Have Always Lived in Beverly Hills* that stepdad Johnson left Wynn's ma for another man.

Produced by Armand Deutsch, directed by Roy Rowland. Screenplay by Jerome Weidman, from a story by Harry W. Junkin. B&W, 81 m., TV

Torch Song (1953) ❤ ❤

MGM came to the rescue of the floundering career of Joan Crawford (who had in the '30s and '40s been one of their biggest meal tickets) after she'd been toiling for ten years in the salt mines of Columbia and Warners. Anyway, that was the plan—"Discover a *NEW* Crawford," screamed the ads, "the *eternal* female!"—until critics and audiences got a look at the movie, as unintentionally funny as any that Crawford ever made.

Here Hollywood's Medusa is cast as Broadway's Medusa, smitten by a blind pianist, played (virtually straight-faced) by Michael Wilding, who tells her that she has the "mouth of an angel" but "the words that come out of it are sheer tramp." Though the studio tried to disguise the preposterousness of it all by giving Crawford Technicolor, dances and songs (dubbed by musky-voiced India Adams), and enough cigarettes to stub from here till social security, her snarly dialogue gives the game away—we're talking pure, unadulterated camp.

"When the talk's about me, I'll buy a ticket," growls our Joan, and "I'm tough. That's why I'll never be lonely." Tough, all right, and never more manly. She sucks up to autograph hounds ("How's your mother, dear?") and supports her free-loading relatives but fires overage chorus boys and advises the sightless Wilding that he ought to "get a nice seeing-eye girl."

Luxuriate in the cheesy '50s splendor of Crawford's getups (one suggests a lampshade that hemorrhaged), up-to-the-minute sets (asteroid-shaped pull-down lamps, pink-and-blue sectional furniture), then blast into kitsch nirvana when Crawford, in black face, orange lips, and a Cyd Charisse wig, sings "Two-Faced Woman" (a song an earlier, wiser MGM cut, with Cyd Charisse lip-synching to the *same* India Adams track from *The Band-wagon*). Don't, however, watch this scene alone. In the finale, Crawford bugs her eyes, makes that mouth, and rips off her wig to reveal orange hair. (Oh, the horror, the horror!) Not even unmasking *The Phantom of the Opera* or discovering Mother's corpse in *Psycho* come close.

Not surprisingly, *Torch Song* didn't make a plug nickel, and according to the director, Crawford, scared witless, downed three vodkas daily before nine a.m. While Marjorie Rambeau, playing Joan's poor-folks ma ("Play somethin' soothin'," she tells Joan's pianist sister), got an Oscar nomination, our Joan instead officially entered the ranks of Superstars on the Skids.

With Gig Young, Henry Morgan, Dorothy Patrick. Produced by Henry Berman and Sidney Franklin, Jr., directed by Charles

Walters. Screenplay by John Michael Hayes and Jan Lustig, from the story "Why Should I Cry?" by I. A. R. Wylie. C, 90 m., V, L

Trapeze (1956) ❤❤❤

The only psychosexual circus movie to date, this Bad Movie *must* presents a triangle of performers who thrust and parry over whether to do, ahem, a "triple."

Burt Lancaster as the drunken, hunky former trapeze star who was crippled trying to perform a "triple" somersault on the bars, bemoans that the big top ain't what it used to be. "Pink lights, ballet girls, blue sawdust . . . a lotta hoopla!" he whines into his beer, and after this lowbrow "hoopla" extravaganza, which earned a bundle, Lancaster went serious-o, teaming with Tony Curtis again to make the highbrow, searing show biz exposé *Sweet Smell of Success*, which made news, not money. Here, however, there's plenty of "hoopla" for any tastes, as Lancaster and Curtis—the boy who wants Lancaster to teach him how to do a "triple"—parade about, bare-chested, in formfitting tights.

"People like spangles, you know?" says Gina Lollobrigida as she squeezes her way into the lads' act by shimmying up a rope above Lancaster, spreading her legs and asking, "How do you like my costume? I wanted to make sure it wouldn't split." She vamps Curtis, too, though Lancaster tells him he preferred it when it was just the two of them: "One flies and one catches, and nobody comes between." Curtis says, "You force me to choose, and I'll leave you."

Lollobrigida hogs more and more of the act, so on opening night, Lancaster warns her, "No more tricks or you're out!" She snarls, "I can take him whenever I want. That trick I've still got." Lancaster growls, "Get out or these hands won't be there to catch you." Just then, natch, they're on. Lollobrigida tells Curtis that Lancaster's "jealous" of their love. Exactly and, to get Curtis back (supposedly to pay more attention to performing a "triple," but draw your own conclusions), Lancaster woos Lollobrigida away. How? He offers to teach her "a new trick" on the bars; when he catches her, he lifts her up, up, up and plants a big, wet one. She can't help it—she's just a trapeze tramp—and she kisses him back.

Emotions reach such a fevered peak that a lion breaks free and mauls Lancaster's wrist. We're wracked by side-splitting suspense in the finale: Can the three make up in time to do a "triple," even though the circus owner has ordered the net to be taken away, even though the ballerinas are dancing on the ground below, even though Lancaster and Curtis get into a fist fight, swinging at one another while swinging from the bars?

Produced by James Hill, directed by Carol Reed. Screenplay by James R. Webb, from Max Catto's novel *The Killing Frost*; adaptation by Liam O'Brien. C, 105 m., V

The Stone Age

Before Sharon Stone came on strong as the leggy, scene-stealing stinker in the otherwise forgettable *Basic Instinct*, she had honed her craft in some real stinkers. Today, while her star grows brighter even as you read this sentence—and before, inevitably, she moves on toward the pinnacle of Sharon Stone, Screen Diva—we suggest that you revisit a few of the career milestones that made the beauteous towhead what she is today.

Action Jackson (1988) ❤

"Some say his mother was molested by Bigfoot, and Jackson is their mutant offspring," a policeman explains—no, not about Michael Jackson, but about the Detroit cop, ex-serviceman, and Harvard Law School grad played by Carl Weathers, who's hot on the trail of psychotic auto magnate Craig T. Nelson (named "Dellaplane"—we couldn't possibly be meant to think him John DeLoreanesque now, could we?). Seems Weathers not only helped put Nelson's bad-news son behind bars but also tore off the kid's arm. Tore off? "So what—he had *two*," reasons Weathers, cluing us in to a cross-examination technique he must have picked up at Harvard.

Weathers, who acts with his torso, is plenty amusing on his own, but the movie takes off into the Bad Movie stratosphere with the arrival of Sharon Stone as Nelson's gorgeous dim bulb of a wife, and Vanity as Nelson's gorgeous dim bulb of a mistress.

Women in these movies exist to be naked, dead, or both—and it's lucky for Stone she gets to do both, since that means she's not stuck in this flick till the end.

She meets Weathers at an awards ceremony for her husband, decked out in a backless dress and enough white lipstick for a mid-'60s *Matt Helm* movie. We know she digs Weathers because she smiles *and* flares her nostrils. Later, at a nightclub, we catch Nelson digging junkie Vanity, a long way down even from her association with Prince, as she sings and bumps and grinds ("choreographed" by Paula Abdul). "I expected a standing ovation," she whispers, sidling over to Nelson's table, who answers, "You're getting one." She berates him for not delivering her a Motown record deal and, when he asks for two good reasons why he should come through, she (yes) pops out her breasts.

Since this is a by-the-numbers Joel Silver production, Stone is gratuitously naked too. Because she gets chummy with Weathers, villainous Nelson has to off her. "I love you," he says before shooting Stone dead, then adds, "*more* than life itself."

Weathers becomes the prime suspect, which sends him and Vanity on the run. With half of Detroit's underworld after them, Vanity coos, "We gotta go back for my purse. I'm not wearing makeup. I look terrible." (Vanity, thy name *is* Vanity.) Weathers can't help but fall for a gal who, badly in need of a fix, mutters, "I feel like my teeth are hollow! My gums are made of rubber! My stomach's trying to start a bonfire in the back of my bloody head!" Commiserates Weathers: "I think I felt that way once. They called it love." It all ends up with more explosions and a "Who asked for it?" encore of the Pointer Sisters singing the theme song. On such trash, Silver got the clout to bring us *Hudson Hawk*.

Produced by Silver, directed by Craig R. Baxley. Screenplay by Robert Reneau. C, 95 m., V, L

King Solomon's Mines (1985) ❤

Sharon Stone's enjoyably terrible—unlike her co-stars, who're just plain terrible—in this expensive, trashy *Indiana Jones*–influenced remake of H. Rider Haggard's jungle adventure.

Stone, an improbable archeology student, hires Richard Chamberlain—even more improbably, he's a rugged adventurer—to track her kidnapped father in darkest Africa. Together, they battle Nazis, deadly snakes, giant spiders, quicksand, tribal priestesses, hilarious hair and makeup jobs, and—backed by Jerry Goldsmith's ersatz *Indiana Jones* score (the score of which was in itself ersatz Erich Korngold)—they swap pathetic witticisms that will have you laughing at them. Consider the repartee when Stone confronts *Indiana Jones*'s John Rhys-Davies with the endearingly saucy, "Where's my father, you cheap-suited camel jockey?" which Chamberlain tops with, "Where is her father, you towel-headed creep?" If you think that's racist and you find Chamberlain lacking in the derring-do department, don't miss the moment when he blunders into a railroad car packed with Nazi soldiers and breaks into "Camptown Races," replete with wide-mouthed "Doo-Dahs!"

Since the stars throw off no sparks together, the script hopes that sending them up together in a runaway plane will fire things up. Clinging to the wing for dear life, trying to tell Stone how to man the throttle, Chamberlain yells, "It's right there between your legs, pull on it!" The movie's single funniest moment comes just then, when Stone, bizarrely, half-sings, half-gargles the line, "There's a lot of smoke coming out of the back, and there's some brown goop leaking out the side!"

Don't miss the scene in which a cannibal tribe dumps the stars into a huge pot of plastic vegetables, prompting Chamberlain to gush at Stone, "Did anyone tell you you look ravishing with onions in your hair?" Clearly unimpeded by their director J. Lee Thompson (who brought us *White Buffalo, What a Way to Go!, Cabo Blanco, Conquest of the Planet of the Apes,* and *The Greek Tycoon*), the stars are so at sea in a script that's going nowhere (but not fast!), you'll be praying the natives make ham hocks out of them.

Keep your eyes peeled during the scene in which a spiked ceiling is closing down on the pair, who stand neck deep in water, and Stone's hair color and coiffure change completely. Imagining that the world would be demanding a sequel, Cannon Pictures (now defunct, and this is why) ordered a follow-up—*Allan Quatermain and the Lost City of Gold*—that was shot simultaneously.

Produced by Menahem Golan, directed by Thompson. Screenplay by Gene Quintano and James R. Silke, based on Haggard's novel. C, 100 m., V

Scissors (1991) ❤

As *Basic Instinct* proved, millions enjoy spending time in the dark with nudity-friendly vamp Sharon Stone, but *Scissors* poses the query, "Would those same millions be willing to put in their time on this tour de *farce* in which Stone, mostly fully clothed, merely acts her way through a tacky *Repulsion* rip-off?"

Stone, wittily cast against type as a twenty-six-year-old virgin who works temp jobs but lives in a stadium-size, high-rise apartment surrounded by antique dolls, meets a red-bearded guy in the elevator—his voice is *so* badly dubbed we know he's got to be a major actor in the movie—who shoves her down and grunts, "You know what I want. Don't scream, bitch, or I'll really fuckin' hurt ya. Come on, spread 'em, spread 'em out!" Luckily, Stone happens to have with her a pair of scissors to stab him, making him vow, as he staggers off, "I'll be back."

Stone befriends her neighbor, Steve Railsback, *so* talented he's been given two roles to play—a TV soap star and his embittered, wheelchair-ridden artist brother. Aside from the wheelchair, you can mostly tell the two brothers apart by their coiffures: the "good" Steve has a Jimmy Swaggartish 'do, while the "bad" Steve wears a pony tail.

Stone keeps seeing menacing red-bearded men and actually fends off an attack from one in a movie theater while watching *Mayerling*. "How 'bout us doing it here, bitch?" he grunts. The good Railsback makes a pass at Stone, but in the end she begs off, declaring, "I can't make love with a man!" Looming mysteriously in the background is Railsback's ex-girlfriend, Vicki Frederick.

All this trauma sends Stone to a creepy shrink, Ronnie Cox, whose creepy wife, Michelle Phillips, is a career-driven politician. For Stone, it's all an opportunity to keep a straight face while playing unplayable scenes, like the one where, under hypnosis, she's repressing some sexual trauma involving her stepfather,

her mother, and a puppet of a little pig (don't ask). All this leads, natch, to her being trapped in a vacant building with, as her only company, a red-bearded man with a knife in his back, a bunch of talking dolls, a caged talking bird that squawks, "You killed him! You killed him!" *and* music composed by Alfi Kabilju that must have been inspired by Muzak-filled elevators. Stone freaks out, hilariously, and faster than you can say *Gaslight*, we learn it's all been a horrible conspiracy by a trusted character (guess which one!) to drive her—and *us*—stark, raving mad. With this jewel, Frank De Felitta proved he could make a lousier, funnier movie than professional directors made of his *Audrey Rose* and *The Entity*.

Produced by Mel Pearl, Don Levin, and Hal W. Polaire, directed by De Felitta. Screenplay by De Felitta, from a story by Joyce Selznick. C, 105 m., V, L

Year of the Gun (1991) ❤ ❤

Early in this thrill-less thriller, American journalist Andrew McCarthy hears a huge explosion on the streets of Rome and asks, "Bomb?" Considering such notorious box-office duds as *Fresh Horses* and *Less Than Zero*, it's a wonder McCarthy didn't ask this question before signing for this movie, which hilariously posits that our Teflon hero is writing a novel that accidentally anticipates every plot twist in the film.

McCarthy's boss, George Murcell, throws a party where he introduces McCarthy to "the hottest talent to hit this town in a long time," internationally acclaimed photographer Sharon Stone who, with her opening line—"What're you doing here in Dodge City?"—reveals that she's even more adept at snappy one-liners than at snapping shots. Just then, the soiree is invaded by gun-toting "Red Brigade" terrorists who (oh, it's too, too horrible!) push Murcell in the pool, steal the guests' jewelry, then shoot their machine guns up into the sky!

Determined to uncover who's behind these loathsome acts of brutality, Stone and McCarthy never think to wonder about the only two Italian characters in the movie, McCarthy's girlfriend Valeria Golino and her cousin John Pankow. Instead, they eat out, make love, and ride around the city on McCarthy's motor-cycle, mouthing such fall-down-funny dialogue that we're tempted to think the movie *is* based on a book penned by McCarthy.

"I had my agent call your agent," Stone tells McCarthy (no, not about getting them out of this movie). "You're writing a book about the Red Brigade and I want in." Claiming that he's writing a restaurant guide, McCarthy protests, "I'm not and never have been a revolutionary." Stone doesn't buy it: "Yeah? Well, the book you're writing is not and never has been about spaghetti!"

Later, though McCarthy thinks Stone is "one of those people who've come to love war," he frolics with her at a student riot after which she coos, "Well, that was a trip to the moon. Doesn't it bum you out not to connect with what's going on in this country?" McCarthy replies, "I don't feel any desire to grab a live wire," prompting Stone to snap, "Don't hide behind wise-cracks. You sound like a refugee from the '60s." McCarthy volleys, "My least favorite decade, ten years of phoniness, a decade-long circle jerk!" When Stone asks him, "What about *your* politics?" McCarthy observes, "Americans in Rome don't need politics—they need American Express cards."

Soon (but not nearly soon enough) they're being chased by the terrorists who've been killing extras. "We're next!" McCarthy exclaims—but no such luck. The duo survives to collaborate on a book called, that's right, *Year of the Gun*, and the movie ends—long after it's over—when they plug the bestseller on "The Dick Cavett Show." Beware: Nobody in this movie is what they seem, but they're not much of anything else either.

Produced by Edward Pressman, directed by John Franken-heimer. Screenplay by David Ambrose, from Michael Mewshaw's book. C, 111 m., V, L

If Joan Collins had actually ever read her sister Jackie's books, would she *ever* have agreed to star in *The Stud* and its sequel, *The Bitch*? We think not.

ABOVE: Hugh O'Brian gives it all he's got, but nothing can keep Lana Turner and her terribly tasteful "million dollar wardrobe" from stealing *Love Has Many Faces.*

RIGHT: Peter Finch fails to conceal his amusement over the sight of "possessed" Kim Novak, who plans to plow new ground with Finch's sinewy gardener in *The Legend of Lylah Clare.*

Plantation owner James Mason thinks up the damnedest uses for his slave boys: there ought to have been rioting in the streets after *Mandingo*. Instead, there was a sequel!

LEFT: Alec Baldwin, as Rev. Jimmy Swaggart, prays for lightning to strike dead the insufferably self-enamored Dennis Quaid, playing Jerry Lee Lewis, in *Great Balls of Fire*. BELOW: Fellow fashion victims Mickey Rourke and Don Johnson in *Harley Davidson and the Marlboro Man*.

ABOVE: Kevin Costner looks undecided as to whether Madeleine Stowe has fainted or died—or is just *under*acting again, in this typically riveting moment from *Revenge*. BELOW: Poker-faced John Forsythe, in *Kitten With a Whip*, figures he needn't bother registering the slightest emotion since scenery-shredding Ann-Margret emotes enough for a cast of thousands.

MGM hoped this *Sandpiper*-inspired fashion line would catch on with slim, trendy Saks shoppers who saw this ad in the May 1965 edition of *Harper's Bazaar*; the sight of Elizabeth Taylor in the actual costumes from the film ensured they'd catch on with Lane Bryant shoppers instead.

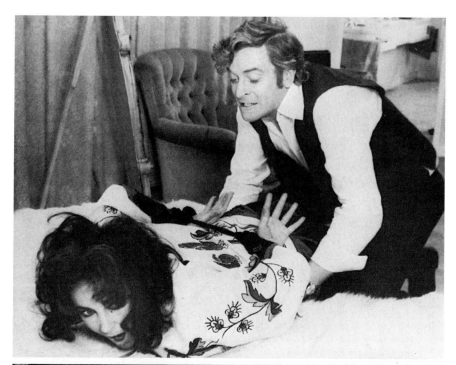

ABOVE: Ties that *bind*. Sadistic Michael Caine ties up masochistic Elizabeth Taylor, then torments her by telling her how much more money *he* got for co-starring in *X, Y and Zee*. BELOW: No, it's *not* a convention of Elizabeth Taylor's ex-husbands. It's the star playing the hooker who's *literally* the toast of New York in *Butterfield 8*.

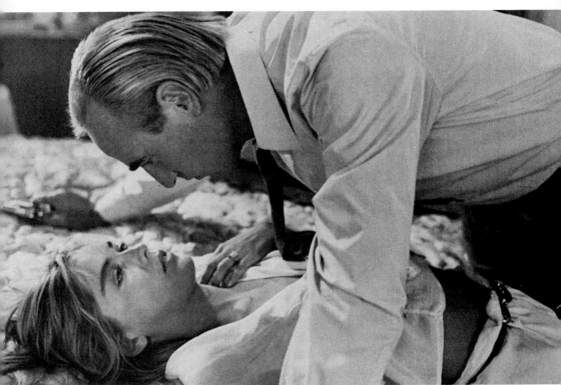

Dead or alive? *Who can tell?* ABOVE: In *Action Jackson*, Craig T. Nelson's just shot and killed wife Sharon Stone *in order to profess his undying love.* BELOW: Andrea Occipinti works overtime to get an expression—*any* expression—out of Bo Derek (to no avail) in this torrid sex scene from *Bolero.*

TOP: In *Point Break*, an aerial and aquatic retelling of *Les Miserables*, hunter Keanu Reeves and hunted Patrick Swayze. MIDDLE: In *Masquerade*, John Glover uses a gun to try to force Rob Lowe *to act*.

Remember the '70s? The Village People and *les boys* demonstrate some—but not all—of the fun things to do at the "Y.M.C.A." in *Can't Stop the Music*.

Remember the '60s? Oscar-winner Shelley Winters psychedelicizes her image in *Wild in the Streets*, modeling the "harpy hippy" look.

Old-style hams Olivia de Havilland, Ann Sothern, and Jeff Corey square off in *Lady in a Cage* against new-style Method hams James Caan, Rafael Campos, and Jennifer Billingsley.

Did some savvy photographer ensure Joan Crawford's swoon of rapture by installing a full-length mirror on the ceiling above her? Her *Autumn Leaves* co-star Cliff Robertson wisely hides his face in shame—too bad he couldn't do that in the movie as well.

ABOVE: The stars of Irwin Allen's waterlogged disaster epic *The Poseidon Adventure* look at something scary: co-star Gene Hackman *acting*. LEFT: By hiding in a boat throughout most of *The Other Side of Midnight*, plucky Susan Sarandon salvaged her career. Her co-stars weren't so smart.

ABOVE: Gina Lollobrigida, blissfully ignorant of her inability to carry off the hooker role in *Go Naked in the World*, vamps befuddled boyfriend Tony Franciosa, blissfully ignorant of how many *real* stars *must* have turned down his role before he inherited it. BELOW: "How much will it cost to get me *out* of this movie?" Laurence Harvey seems to be asking co-star Capucine, the "protegée" of the producer of *A Walk on the Wild Side*.

LEFT: They nominated Diana Ross for an Oscar for *Lady Sings the Blues*, but in *Mahogany* she demonstrated her *real* gifts for eye-bugging and teeth-gritting. RIGHT: Al Pacino in *Revolution* shows that no one—not even Diana Ross—can outdo *him* when it comes to popping eyes and distorting lips.

"Tell Simba to *squish* the bitch," hisses Gloria Grahame to Cornel Wilde as they get scene-hogger Betty Hutton exactly where they want her in *The Greatest Show on Earth*.

We'd guess that Method starlet Ann-Margret got through this scene in *The Swinger* by repeating to herself, "I'm in a Fellini movie, I'm in a Fellini movie. . . ."

ABOVE: Efrem Zimbalist, Jr., wonders why Claire Bloom, Glynis Johns, Jane Fonda, and Shelley Winters give him so much as a second glance in *The Chapman Report*. LEFT: Emoting like this, in *The Lonely Lady*, put the career of Pia Zadora where it is today.

"Don't fuck with me, *retard*," heinous nanny Rebecca De Mornay sneers at handicapped handyman Ernie Hudson in a scene from —*no*, not *Mandingo*— but *The Hand That Rocks the Cradle*.

In this typically suspenseful moment from *Fatal Attraction*, a cute little tyke whispers into Michael Douglas's ear, *"Psssst*, watch your back, Daddy. That curly-haired lady's *stealing the movie."*

LEFT: *We'd* shoot that terrible wig, too, if we were twinsies Bette Davis in *Dead Ringer*. BELOW: Lucille Ball, looking aghast at the latest bit of direction from director Gene Saks *(far right)*, ponders why she thought it'd be such a smart career move to try making a movie out of the Broadway hit *Mame*.

ABOVE: You know you're in trouble if your director asks you to play a love scene in a swamp. Richard Pearce sparked mirth when Richard Gere and Kim Basinger tenderly touched in *No Mercy*, and so did *(inset)* King Vidor when he had Charlton Heston and Jennifer Jones kiss in *Ruby Gentry*. BELOW: Your career's in no better shape, however, if you must make love atop a car in the pouring rain. Teenager Drew Barrymore feigns a passionate frenzy while middle-aged Tom Skerritt feigns a heartbeat in *Poison Ivy*.

ABOVE: Whether freaking out in the nuthouse or *(inset)* belting out a show-stopper, Patty Duke in *Valley of the Dolls* practically *dared* the Oscar committee to revoke her earlier award for *The Miracle Worker*. BELOW: Dorothy Malone, another Oscar-winner whose career went to hell, played Diana Barrymore in *Too Much, Too Soon*.

LEFT: Candice Bergen, playing the world's wealthiest, most pregnant girl in *The Adventurers*, encourages her playboy hubby, Bekim (*who?*) Fehmiu, to swing her higher, *higher, HIGHER*! RIGHT: "Call off the wedding and I'll cancel the shock therapy," Julia Roberts appears to be purring to Kiefer Sutherland in *Flatliners*.

LEFT: "Is this my finger in your pants or are you just glad to see me?" Nicolas Cage seems to be asking Erika Anderson as he explores her shorts in public, in *Zandalee*. RIGHT: Tom Cruise displays, in *Cocktail*, early signs of his acting versatility by simultaneously spinning a bottle and smiling.

No, But I Saw
the Book

It's axiomatic that no one in Hollywood reads much beyond trade papers and *TV Guide*. If they did, why would producers constantly try making movies out of such utterly unfilmable books as these? Be forewarned: when the movies try to go literary, the *merde* flies thick and fast, so it's best to keep your head down, your Reeboks encased in hip boots, and your Kleenex supply handy. You'll be laughing all the way to the fadeout.

Another Time, Another Place (1958) ♥

. . . but the same old Lana. If, as a critic once said, the mere presence of Louise Brooks made her films masterpieces, the mere presence of Lana Turner makes her films quintessential Bad Movie classics (call it Lanavision).

This tearjerker presents her as a war correspondent mad for young BBC reporter Sean Connery. It's London, 1945, and at the site of a bomb that fails to detonate—no one could say the same of this movie—Connery ducks into a car to smooch with Turner. She gushes, "It's crazy, isn't it? You look for love in all the proper places, among all the proper people, and then, there's a war and you find who you were looking for just swimming around in the ocean." Of course, as real-life newspaper headlines would soon reveal, the offscreen Turner hadn't exactly been looking for love among proper people or places.

When Turner reveals that she'd accepted the marriage proposal of her newspaper boss, Barry Sullivan, several months before, Connery drops a bigger bombshell: He's already married and won't be seeing her again. "It can't be true!" Turner says. "Why didn't you tell me?" She tearfully confesses all to sympathetic Sullivan who says, "You haven't been punched enough, is that it? You want to climb back into the ring and really get hurt?" Hilariously, given Turner's real-life predilection for tough guys, she replies, "Sure, I'm looking for a beating."

She can't stop herself from bursting into Connery's hotel just before he's to ship out to Paris to say, as if it were 1945 at MGM, "Oh, darling, I tried to stay away!" Then, Connery (whose agents must have demanded it) dies in a plane crash, and Turner's hospitalized for shock. (We can tell she's really hurting, her lipstick shade grows paler.)

On her release, she heads straight for Connery's boyhood village, to find his widow, Glynis Johns. Turner has a Bad Acting field day as she vibrates to the "presence" of Connery in his chair, books, and notepads. Sullivan arrives to bring Turner back to her senses—"Now that you've lost your sense of direction," he says, referring to Turner's character, not her performance, "I don't want to let you out of my sight"—but, instead, Turner chooses to toil together with Johns on a book about Connery. "It was becoming my village, my people, my life," Turner exclaims, but when Johns learns that Connery had an affair with Turner, the party's over. "What are you trying to do," Johns snaps, "take Mark away from me even after his death?" At the finish, Turner, mink-wrapped, sadder but wiser, ships out to the States where, in the real world, more sex, scandal, and heartbreak await her.

Produced by Lewis Allen and Smedley Aston, directed by Allen. Screenplay by Stanley Mann, from Lenore Coffee's novel. B&W, 98 m., V, L

Chanel Solitaire (1981) ❤

We meet chic *gamine* Marie-France Pisier on the stairway of her grand salon, musing—no, not about how acclaim in French movies led to her disastrous American debut (and farewell) in *The Other*

Side of Midnight—but on how she got stranded in this ludicrously Hollywoodized biopic about Coco Chanel, queen of *haute couture*.

Off we tumble into Flashbackland, where *cher enfant* Pisier is taken in by two aunts, with one of whom, Brigette Fossey, she bonds instantly—after all, Fossey knew what it was like to make terrible American movies, too (or haven't you seen *Enigma?*).

Pisier takes up with rich Rutger Hauer, who brings her to his estate where he breeds horses. Who pops in but our favorite sophisticated Parisian *poule*, Karen Black, who puffs cheroots and, in a Gallic accent that must be heard to be believed, apologizes for her appearance by growling, "I had a very heavy night with a very heavy smoker!" That night, Pisier watches Black steal the movie—someone has to—by croaking in bad French, "Ta-Ra-Ra-Boom-Dee-Ay!" and commenting to Pisier, "What an outrageously ambiguous outfit, my dear! Women in jodhpurs. What next?" Jousts Pisier, "I never ride side-saddle," to which Black replies, "I never ride anywhere but in the bedroom."

Hauer's pal, coal magnate Timothy Dalton, bedazzles Pisier and, in a dinner scene in which the entire cast sports Chanel drag, Black suggests Hauer lend Pisier his French apartment so she can make it a hat salon. "Girls like us," lisps Hauer, dressed as a woman, "are not cut out for business!" Dalton convinces Hauer to fund Pisier with this infallible bit of wisdom: "Women need hats." And, *sacre bleu*, he's right, because soon Pisier is making a killing with chapeaus and with Dalton, who confesses, "I was born on the wrong side of the blanket . . . I'm—a bastard!" He rents her a knockout of a salon and, when he warns her that she's spending way too much, Pisier rouses herself out of *ennui* to declare, "It's my business—mine, mine, mine!"

When Dalton dumps her to marry a lord's daughter, Pisier chops off her hair, which, in bad biopics like this, can only mean she's going to turn lesbian. "That's what I love about you," she tells her female lover, "you're neither a lady or a whore—you fall somewhere nicely in between." Rubbing on her new fragrance, Chanel No. 5, Pisier announces, "The woman who wears no scent has no future."

Dalton returns, woos her madly, makes love to her and, driving to see his wife about a divorce, smashes into a tree, leaving Pisier to find no *joie* in her *vie* and leaving Peter Allen to bleat the theme song: "If I knew how, I'd erase you, but I know there'll be no one who can replace you." *Alors!*

Produced by Larry G. Spangler, directed by George Kaczender. Screenplay by Julian More, based on *Chanel Solitaire* by Claude Delay. C, 120 m., V

Claudelle Inglish (1961) ❤ ❤ ❤

Hey kids! Thinking of having premarital sex? Think again. That's the message here, and though back in 1961 no one used buzz words like "sexual addiction," "safe sex," and "low self-esteem," Erskine Caldwell's cautionary tale offers a timeless lesson for every generation of teens.

Diane McBain plays Claudelle, the dirt-poor sharecropper's daughter who turns town pump after fiancé Chad Everett uses her for sex and then breaks her heart by marrying someone else. McBain's surprisingly sanguine mama, Constance Ford, observes, "You woulda wasted your life on that no-'count, like I wasted mine on your father," and urges her to wed rich old widower Claude Akins who comes a-wooing with a gift of red high heels. Clad in only a tight slip, McBain models them as old Akins pants, "You're kinda flowering all over like a pretty peach tree."

But McBain knows she's damaged goods, so she's not looking for security with some ol' geezer. She prefers backseat sex with every hunky hick who brings her dimestore candy. As she tells one who knocks on her bedroom window in the middle of the night, "If I go out with you, tell me I'm pretty—pretty all over." Next time Akins comes by, mama Ford—who knows a sure thing when she sees it—puts on McBain's best dress and runs off with him. "You want to know where Mama is?" McBain asks her father. "They're down by the willows. We watched them!"

In the movie's heated finale, McBain has sex with the father of her only decent suitor, Will Hutchins, and then—in the midst of Hutchins's subsequent marriage proposal, no less—she goes off to make it with a total stranger who scores just by saying to her, "You're not the marrying kind." The stranger then mows down Hutchins with his car.

Is it any wonder that McBain's father can't figure out how all this happened? "Oh, Papa," cries McBain, "I wanted to be bad—as bad as could be!" Just then, the dead lad's dad arrives. "You're still alive, with your painted lips and your wickedness," he snarls, and shoots McBain dead.

Don't laugh, gals, it could happen to you! This movie dares to show the real danger of having premarital sex: It's not just that once you've done it, boys can tell merely by looking at you (that's bad enough). But then, those boys will write books about you, and studios will make Bad Movie versions of those books, and as you can see, those movies of your promiscuous life will never go away.

You have been warned.

With Arthur Kennedy, Robert Colbert, Ford Rainey, James Bell, Robert Logan. Produced by Leonard Freeman, directed by Gordon Douglas. Screenplay by Freeman, from the Caldwell novel. B&W, 99 m., TV

Cocktail (1988) ❤ ❤

We're truly awed by Tom Cruise. Is there anything he can't do? We gasped when he showed that he could dance in his underwear in *Risky Business*; then he mastered sitting inside a jet for *Top Gun*; then he learned to ride around in a wheelchair for *Born on the Fourth of July*. These triumphs, however, pale next to *Cocktail*: Cruise single-handedly breathes life back into that long-dead genre, Elvis Presley movies.

Opening in tried-and-true Presley fashion, Cruise—fresh out of the service—has those *G.I. blues* till he decides to *follow that dream* and go into the family business, tending bar. Despite his lack of training, studly bartender Bryan Brown wants to hire Cruise anyway. "The waitresses hate me," notes Cruise, but Brown says, "Wait till you've given them crabs—then you'll really know hatred. Stick with me—I'll make you a star." Sure enough, all the *girls! girls! girls!* in Manhattan are soon crowding in to watch these two juggle bottles while they shake their booties and, if Cruise cannot exactly sing like The King, he does a mean lip-synch. In no time, the duo is hired to work at the chic Cell

Block (where the staff wear *jailhouse rock* duds), and Cruise stands atop the bar to deliver a poem that will surely be included among the film clips when he eventually receives his American Film Institute Lifetime Achievement Award: "America you're just devoted / To every flavor I've got / But if you want to get loaded / Why don't you just order a shot?"

Brown steals away Cruise's gal, Gina Gershen, by calling her "an assembly-line hump" so Cruise hightails it to *paradise, Hawaiian style* (okay, so it's Jamaica) where he becomes an island resort bartender. Apparently having started watching the rushes, Cruise says to Elisabeth Shue, "My worthless, useless services are at your disposal." Shue, like the audience, knows that Cruise has got real value (if only he'd take off his shirt, show off his torso, and smile more!) so she gets him to frolic under a waterfall and make love on the beach.

But Cruise's head is turned by wealthy Lisa Banes, who takes him back to New York as her paid gigolo, which we know is a bad thing because she covers Cruise back up in fancy designer suits and, even worse, makes him attend a cocktail party where her friends say, "Heel, boy, heel. You haven't got this one party-broken yet, have you?" Cruise undergoes a *change of habit*, leaves the kept life behind, and looks up Shue, who's pregnant—and a zillionairess to boot.

At their wedding, Cruise says, "You're probably going to want to divorce me in three weeks," and Shue agrees, "Probably"—but the movie quickly ends before their prophecies come true.

With Kelly Lynch. Produced by Ted Field and Robert W. Cort, directed by Roger Donaldson. Screenplay by Heywood Gould, based on his own novel. C, 100 m., V, L

The Driver's Seat (1973) ❤

Search out this offender in the video bargain bin under one of its many titles (*The Driver's Seat, Psychopath, Identikit,* or Lord knows what else), then watch awestruck as it demonstrates how far off course stars' careers can veer.

Elizabeth Taylor, many years and many pounds too late, bursts on screen—hair teased like a Gorgon and wearing, oh, five dif-

ferent outfits, none of which fit—to be asked by a nei
"Where you goin' dressed like that—to join a circus?" ?
catch a taxi to the airport where Taylor murmurs, "I'm
south," while—in jigsaw flashbacks and flashforwards—we?
that Interpol is combing four countries to identify her. (V
Who knows? This is the sort of pretentious Italian thriller g
to raising questions, not answering them.)

When attendants frisk her ample figure for hidden bombs
bowls of chili, Taylor blurts out, "You're all so suspicious! St
picious! Suspicious!" Aboard the plane, Taylor's fellow passeng
flicks out his tongue at her. She, however, only has eyes for Ia
Bannen who, seeing her ogle him, bursts out of his seat—whil
the plane is taking off!—to move away. Watching Taylor's puzzled
reaction, her fellow passenger helpfully explains, "He was frightened of your psychedelic dress." LSD hallucinations, in fact, could
be the only possible explanation for what follows. Debarking into
the airport, Liz makes goo-goo eyes at Andy Warhol, a member
of Eurotrash royalty. "He was afraid of me," she puzzles, "why
is everybody afraid of me?"

Next, Taylor heads for the local Hilton—a nifty touch for those
who remember Liz as a big movie star whose marriage to hotel
heir Nicky Hilton made world headlines. Once there, she berates
a maid, thrashes around the room fussing with her hair, then
paints herself up to go stepping out in yet another godawful outfit.

A woman describes Liz to the police, in another of those flashback or flashforwards, as emitting "some force that all women
feel latent in themselves, stifled. A potential for catastrophe."
That potential is fully realized here, in such scenes as Liz charming a cabbie by asking, "Do you carry a revolver? Because, if you
did, you could kill me." (Are we making all this up? We only
wish.)

Liz runs into Warhol again, but the thrill is gone. "I keep
making mistakes," she tells him. "You're not my type at all." Her
hair now teased into a rat's nest (by one Giancarlo Novelli, who
actually received a screen credit), she muses, "I want to go back
home to feel all my loneliness again." But soon, she meets a
stranger, whom she lures to a park and begs him to stab her to
death, which he does. Repeatedly. Roll credits. End of movie.
End of movie career.

/ith Mona Washbourne. Produced by Franco Rossellini, di-
/ed by Giuseppe Patroni Griffi. Screenplay by Griffi and Raf-
/le La Capria, from the Muriel Spark novel. C, 101 m., V

In the Cool of the Day (1963) ❤❤

Some Bad Movies have s-l-o-w fuses but prove worth the wait,
for when they finally explode, it's fireworks time. Angela Lansbury, in an over-the-top pyrotechnics display here, makes us wish
she'd been given the chance to chew the Grade-A fat that Joan,
Bette, Lana, and Liz consumed on a regular basis.

In a snazzy, film buff's in-joke, Lansbury—who used to star
opposite Judy Garland in the good old days—sits around listening
to Garland warble, endlessly, "Over the Rainbow." (As Peter
Finch's unhappy wife, Lansbury hasn't left the house in twelve
years.) On a business trip, Finch meets Arthur Hill's unhappy
wife, Jane Fonda, who carps, "He's driven me away with his
never-ending goodness. He loves me better ill than well." Then
he must love her very much, for what else but Incurable Movie
Illness could explain Fonda's black Orry-Kelly outfits, heavy black
eyeliner, and a riotous black Cleopatra wig?

Fonda and Finch run into her mother, Constance Cummings,
who—sporting a glittering Balmain turban—waspishly inquires,
"How's your sister? I hear she's unloaded her Bavarian lifeguard."
Finch tells Fonda he wrote a novel once: "It was *Wuthering
Heights* in the Aegean . . . pretty bad," but not worse, surely,
than this. Fonda suggests a trip to Greece. Hill can't make it, so
our three stars go, turning the movie into a triangle travelogue.

Outta that house, Lansbury positively swamps her co-stars,
bitching to Finch, "It's all right if she's in love with you, but you'd
be an idiot to fall in love with her. She's thin as a bean," announcing that Greek peasants are "a bunch of manic-depressives,"
and yawning over museum nudes, explaining, "I'd settle for one
real man in a business suit." She gets her wish when a smarmy
gigolo offers to show her "spots not found in the amusement
guides."

Finch and Fonda are so smitten, they fail to notice this stranger
following them everywhere, smoldering as he lights Lansbury's

cigarette, meaningfully. Finch suspects that something's up when he finds Lansbury packing. "You're always after me to get out, so that's what I'm doing," she chirps. "I'm off to the Riviera!" Cheerfully naming her lover, Lansbury extolls his sexual prowess, adding, "It won't last but I don't care." Finch and Fonda, alone at last, follow Lansbury's example, and on a ferry to Delphi, they go native. It's the career lowpoint for both: they down ouzo, then join the extras for a finger-snappin', throw-back-your-head-and-laugh dance that would embarrass even Anthony Quinn. This full-of-life (well, full of—something) sequence suddenly reminds Fonda that she's supposed to be a dying swan, so she asks Finch, reflectively, "Is one happier, do you think, with ten years of happiness than if one has ten minutes or ten days?" The answer, of course, is that one's happiest with an hour and a half of swoony trash like this.

Produced by John Houseman, directed by Robert Stevens. Screenplay by Meade Roberts, from Susan Ertz's novel. C, 89 m., TV

Mandingo (1975) ❤❤❤

Bad Movies We Love always pose the question, "Can there really be too much of a good thing?" Purporting to show us what the pre–Civil War South was really like, *Mandingo* answers this query: You bet. With more violence, more nudity, more foul language, and more racism than any other flick we've ever seen, you'll hate yourself in the morning for laughing yourself silly, but if you put this maximum offender in your VCR, just try looking away.

In the first ten seconds, slave breeder James Mason observes, about a slave starlet, "She's Mandingo wench. You don't let just any bud get her," to remind his crippled son, Perry King, of his family obligation. Local doc Ray Poole agrees, saying, "She's craving, in the bud o' heat. You pleasure her, she get better." The slave starlet tries to stall the inevitable by drawling to King, "I too black, I not fit for you." Mason settles the matter by stating, "Master's duty to pleasure the wenches first time."

Then it's back to the family mansion, where Doc Poole suggests that Mason's rheumatism would improve if he'd put his feet on black children. So for the rest of the movie, Mason (astoundingly) uses two little slave lads as his foot stools.

King brings home a new stud slave, Ken Norton, another slave to be King's mistress, Brenda Sykes, and—last but not least—a Southern belle whom King will marry, Susan George. King tells his pa, Mason, that Norton is "hung so big he'll tear the wenches," then orders Norton to "shuck down those pants!" When the wedding night's a bust—King sneers at George, "You thinkin' I don't know a virgin when I sleeps with one and pleasures?"—King turns to Sykes, driving George into Norton's bed.

Mason tells George that to win King's affections back, she should "do dirty things to get him in your bed and keep him there." Instead, George—whose incestuous relationship with her brother is her Big Secret—screams at King about Sykes, "That slut! You like that black meat? You'd rather pleasure with a baboon?" and then (there's more), when George learns Sykes is pregnant, she hisses, "You dumb animal!" and pushes Sykes down the stairs. Later, George discovers she's preggers and—as the doctor's wife so eloquently puts it after delivery—"It come, only it ain't white."

King cheers us up by promptly poisoning George, then finds the baby's real dad, Norton. You're not going to believe this— we didn't—King settles the score by shooting Norton, then pushing him into a vat of boiling water, and then pitchforking him to death. In retaliation, one of Norton's pals shoots and kills Mason, ensuring that he wouldn't be able to overact in the sequel, *Drum*. Mesmerizingly heinous.

Produced by Bad Movie maven Dino de Laurentiis, directed by Richard Fleischer. Screenplay by Norman Wexler, from Kyle Onstott's novel and Jack Kirkland's play. C, 121 m., V, L

The Mephisto Waltz (1971) ❤

As the '60s psychedelicized to an end, 20th Century-Fox appeared virtually certain to close its doors for good. A series of mega-expensive bombs—from *Cleopatra* to *Hello, Dolly!*—had sunk their fortunes so low that, at one point, only one movie was even being shot. It was the "can't miss" picture that the top brass knew would engineer their comeback, for it aped the formula of the recent blockbuster *Rosemary's Baby*: Take an urban Gothic, gussy it up in chi-chi demonic trappings, then—talk about imitation being the sincerest form of trying to make a fast buck—cast a star from TV's "Peyton Place" in a leading role.

When journalist Alan Alda comes to interview "zee great pianist" Curt Jurgens, Jurgens is so enamored of Alda's hands he asks daughter, TV bad girl Barbara Parkins, to take a gander. "He has great hands," Jurgens thunders, "Rachmaninoff hands!" Parkins studies Alda's paw, then utters a breathy "Yes." Jurgens is so excited, he seems on the verge of propositioning Alda, or suggesting a three-way, or, at the very least, sinking his fangs into Alda's neck, but no—Jurgens wants Alda and his wife, Jacqueline Bisset, to come to dinner.

At the soiree, Jurgens's jet-set pals banter, "God exists, and the Devil is his vice-president," "I saw your last picture—at least, I hope it was your last picture," and "I have an axiom to grind: Cliché is king!" From this, it's clear that Jurgens and Parkins are either Devil worshippers or talent agents (but what's the difference?).

Their New Year's bash must be seen to be believed: ever-reliable designer Moss Mabry mixes together chiffon gowns, animal masks, *Cleopatra*-eye "creations" on Parkins, a monkey head for Alda, and—so chic!—an actual human face on Jurgens's pet dog. Later, Jurgens announces, "People should be born at seventy and live their life backwards," and before you know it, he's "died" so his soul can "possess" Alda.

After Jurgens's strange funeral, Bisset asks, "What was all that mumbo jumbo?" (a question she should have asked about this script). Bisset notices that Alda's changed but she doesn't mind, since in the sack he now drives her to pillow-biting ecstasy. When she hears Alda play the piano, however, the jig is up. She tells the police, "My husband is not really my husband. Someone's using his body." Figuring, at last, that she'd better turn the tables or be done in, Bisset learns incantations whereby she can cut a deal with the Devil to "kill" Parkins and "possess" her body—to become, in appearance, the woman Jurgens/Alda really wants. (Jeez, what some people won't do for a good lay.)

The ads for the movie queried America: "Have you ever been

afraid? Really afraid?" Guess so, for America, as it turned out, was afraid of spending money to see *The Mephisto Waltz*.

Produced by Quinn Martin, directed by Paul Wendkos. Screenplay by Ben Madden, from Fred Mustard Stewart's novel. C, 108 m., V

Walk on the Wild Side (1962) ♥ ♥ ♥

"I've got the run . . . of the bottom of the barrel," sighs Capucine, and it's hard to tell whether she's talking about the whorehouse where this trash classic is set, or about the movie itself. Though deservedly more famous for its slinky Saul Bass title sequence with a black cat wandering through the alleyways of New Orleans, the movie itself has its own lamebrained charms.

You can't blame writers for trying to capture the seedy poetry of the deep South, but you can blame filmmakers who keep giving ill-advised opportunities to motion picture performers to ham it up with corn-pone accents, honey chile! The casting here is often riotously off—though no one told the actors. Decidedly effete Britisher Laurence Harvey plays the sensitive cowboy stud, Dove, who's looking for his long-lost love, only to learn she's now a hooker (and Capucine, the lady-of-the-evening in question, wears only up-to-the-moment '60s Cardin clothes, despite the film's Depression-era setting).

Patrician Anne Baxter, who ought to be giving elocution lessons, plays the widowed half-breed who loves Dove, a performance that's all off-the-shoulder peasant blouses and an accent like *thees*. Classy Barbara Stanwyck is the lesbian bordello madam who loves Capucine, and her other working girls include Joanna Moore (mother of Tatum and Griffin O'Neal) and Jane Fonda (who made a trilogy of unintentionally hilarious overwrought melodramas set in the South—this, *Hurry Sundown*, and *The Chase*).

Well worth a special mention is the director, Edward Dmytryk, a master of many Bad Movies We Love—his other finest hours include *The Carpetbaggers*, *Harlow*, *Where Love Has Gone*, and *Bluebeard*. Produced by Charles K. Feldman, directed by Dmytryk. Screenplay by John Fante and Edmund Morris, from the novel by Nelson Algren. B&W, 114 m., V

Youngblood Hawke (1964) ❤ ❤ ❤

Don't even think of writing a bestselling novel—that's the advice of *Youngblood Hawke*, which hilariously details the heartbreak of success in the New York literary game. This is a story that can only be told by a writer who's been there, someone like, say, Grace Metalious with her classic *Return to Peyton Place*, or in this case, Herman Wouk telling all after the success of his novel *Marjorie Morningstar*. As written and directed by Delmer Daves, *Youngblood Hawke* seems the work of someone who has never even read a book.

Blond, tanned James Franciscus plays the title character (apparently, Troy Donahue, Daves's regular tanned blond, was otherwise engaged), a dirt-poor but literate coal-mining truck driver from Kentucky who becomes the toast of the Big Apple in one day.

Literary patroness Eva Gabor (!) introduces Youngblood to the cream of the art crowd thus: "I read your book, and I was taller and cleaner, I was younger, I was sadder, I was happier. How did you do this miracle, dahling?" Before he can answer that, he's introduced to married interior decorator Genevieve Page who asks, "What shall I call you, Youngie or Bloody?" but before he can answer that, she takes him home to make love. "When I'm with you," Page says afterwards, "everything seems new again, it's sharp, and good, and food tastes better, and colors seem more intense, and oh, I love you, Bloody."

She installs him in a posh penthouse where they're caught in the act by her young son. ("Tomorrow morning," says mama Page, "you report to military school.") Youngblood runs away from this affair by making a play for his book editor, Suzanne Pleshette, but gives in when Page wants him back ("Kiss me, as only my wild Hawke knows how!"). Then the couple's caught in the act again, this time by Youngblood's widowed mother. "Now she knows what I am," moans Page. Youngblood suggests they break

up. "When that volcanic urge of yours comes back—and it will!
—you'll come to me," Page rages. "I hate you!"

As so often happens in real life, Youngblood's next novel is
published on the same day that his first Broadway play opens.
"One book does not an author make," says a critic to Youngblood's
party guests. "His new book was to be the proof of the pudding.
Proof it is not, pudding it is. I had a premonition that our Kentucky stag would be brought to his knees by the hounds of the
metropolis." (Gee, if people in New York really talked this way,
wouldn't you move there in a second? Maybe not: when Page's
seen-too-much son, off at his military academy, commits suicide
by jumping off—no! yes!—a stack of novels, Youngblood heads
home for them thar hills of Kentucky.)

With Mary Astor, Lee Bowman, Edward Andrews, Don Porter. Produced and directed by Daves. Screenplay by Daves, from
Wouk's novel. B&W, 137 m., TV

CHAPTER 13

Guess Who's Who

Who can resist a movie à clef? You know, those naughty, peek-behind-the-headlines flicks the makers of which (trying to avoid lawsuits) insist that they're not about the private lives of the real-life rich and famous when we know better. In fact, the entire raison d'être of such movies is to tease and titillate us with scandals torn from actual headlines and gossip columns. Many say that much of the mirth of such movies comes from guessing the identities of the characters—"Is Candice Bergen really playing poor little rich girl Barbara Hutton?" "Is Susan Hayward really playing scandal-wracked Lana Turner?" "Is Jacqueline Bisset really playing the White House widow Jackie O?"—but we say, watch these movies and prepare yourself, because that's not the half of it. These are hilariously demented movies—whether or not you know whom they're about.

The Adventurers (1970) ❤ ❤

This Harold Robbins smorgasbord offers kicks for everyone: Orgies! Drugs! Bloodbaths! Miscarriages! Lesbianism! High fashion! Satyrism! Thinly disguised characters based on real celebrities! A private torture chamber!

The fun begins in flashback, when a boy in revolution-torn "Corteguay" shoots the soldiers who raped and killed his loved ones. All this sex and violence must have screwed up "Dax" royally because, when he and his adopted kid sister happen upon a naked couple frolicking in the woods, he observes, "He's raping

her." When the girl suggests, "Let's do it," he refuses. "No, you
are too young, and I think I have to kill you afterwards."

We next meet "Dax" grown into Bekim Fehmiu. (Think how
many stars must have turned down the role before the producers
landed this Yugoslav unknown to play this filthy rich, world-class
legend in the sack.) Before anyone can say "Porfirio Rubirosa,"
Fehmiu is screwing some starlet by Rossano Brazzi's swimming
pool. Apparently desperate to justify the lofty screen credit "A
Lewis Gilbert Film," the director's camera zooms in and out on
the amorous couple, accelerating the tempo as their excitement
peaks, all the while intercutting—and here comes the artsy
part—flashbacks of rape and murder. (*Auteur! Auteur!*)

Fehmiu returns home, rekindles his relationship with Leigh
Taylor-Young—the Latina who wanted him to "rape" her when
they were children—then goes back to Europe and teams with
Thommy Berggren (anyone remember *Elvira Madigan*?) in the
rag trade. "We'll start with a fabulous show," Berggren enthuses,
but all that glitz takes moolah, so Fehmiu sells his bod to rich
American Olivia de Havilland (in a career-ender of a role).

Soon Fehmiu finds a younger fish in Barbara Huttonesque
Candice Bergen, "the richest girl in the world" who, at the finale
of the boys' first fashion show (a kitschfest of horse-drawn chariots
and beefy centurions), ogles Fehmiu and says she'll buy
"Everything—and the collection." They marry, she gets pregnant, then one day she goes hurtling off a swing and miscarries.
"We'll try again," she promises, "I won't even sit on a swing."
But the spark is gone, so, for lack of anything better to do, she
marries Berggren.

Fehmiu returns home and, visiting his old flame Taylor-Young
in the local nunnery, finds that she has borne him a son. Still, he
won't commit. For filler, there's the party where Berggren intrudes on Bergen and another woman making love on the couch;
for laughs, it's hard to top Fehmiu's and Bergen's finding out that
Aristotle Onassisish Charles Aznavour has betrayed them by using their money to ship weapons to "Corteguay," so they tie him
up in his very own private S&M torture chamber.

With Fernando Rey, Ernest Borgnine, Jaclyn Smith (as the
Teen magazine reporter who asks Fehmiu, "Is it true you've made
love to every woman in this room?"). Produced and directed by

Gilbert. Screenplay by Gilbert and Michael Hastings, from the Robbins novel. C, 170 m., V

The Arrangement (1969) ❤❤

"She's got a built-in crap detector," quips an ad man of screwed-up sex bomb Faye Dunaway in this whopper from Elia Kazan, the once-esteemed director of *On the Waterfront* and *A Streetcar Named Desire*, foolishly filming his own *trés autobiographique* novel. No one perusing Dunaway's screen credits would claim Dunaway's got a "crap detector," or what would she be doing here? No one says it of Marlon Brando, either, but he knew enough to bolt this flick just before production began.

Kirk Douglas, everybody's favorite Brando substitute, tries to kill himself for selling the public cancer-causing cigarettes, and while he's recuperating, his wife Deborah Kerr puzzles over why he did it. "It's better than if he were off with some tramp," Kerr tells her shrink. "There are nights when I feel ready to go through the roof"—and you'll be ready to go with her once you get a dose of Douglas endlessly smiling as he dips into flashbacks, like the one where he asks his mistress Dunaway why she wears her violet sunglasses indoors. "They make things happen," she says, which is more than we can say for Douglas, who stares into space pondering, no doubt, the Perils of Materialism and the Meaning of Existence. "I know I'm nothing. I never was," Dunaway observes to Douglas. "But you—you could have been—" "What?" he asks. If you guess that Dunaway answers, "a contender," you're thinking of other, good Kazan movies because, in this one, she says, meaningfully, "What you could have been."

In a choice that separates the merely mediocre bad actor from the real McCoy, Douglas in one scene does a Groucho walk and, in another flashback, Kazan—in a choice that separates the merely overpraised director from one in a career freefall—shows Douglas fantasizing he's thrashing a rival by filling the screen with comic book titles: "Sock! Pow! Biff! Zonk! Crash!"

Though Dunaway has a boyfriend and a baby, she occasionally beds Douglas, explaining, "The fact is there's something about a bastard. Like they say, it's always a trombone player. The one who turns you on is the one that does you in." Here, the one that turns her on is the one that does us in. Eventually, Douglas completely unravels and Kazan comes at us full-tilt: we get scenes of the old, corporate Douglas arguing with the new, freaked-out Douglas, fast motion, slow motion, the works.

When Douglas asks Dunaway to marry him, she rages, "Love? Love's a word they say before they pull your guts out." When Douglas tells Kerr, "I want to do one small good thing before I die," she shoots back, "Such as wallowing in that tramp?" Finally fed up, Kerr writes off Douglas as "an ego run wild." Precisely.

With Richard Boone. Produced and directed by Kazan. Adapted for the screen by Kazan, from his novel. C, 127 m., V

The Carpetbaggers (1964) ❤ ❤ ❤

Half the fun of watching this Harold Robbins potboiler comes from guessing who are the real-life figures (Howard Hughes? Jean Harlow? Jane Russell? Gary Cooper?) being fictionalized in this big, fat, supremely silly soap opera.

When zillionaire Leif Erickson drops dead, George Peppard bursts into the bedroom of his dad's gal Carroll Baker who—dressed in a Harlowesque, feather-trimmed robe—gushes, "I'm yours any way you want me. Love me!" He won't—he's too busy expanding the empire he's inherited—but Baker doesn't take "no" for an answer. "How do you like my widow's weeds?" she inquires, dressed in a tiny black lace nightie. "Get your revenge over with," she hisses. "Mistreat me, please, it has to be done. Anything. Everything. Then, throw me out!"

That he does, for when Peppard's surrogate father figure, Alan Ladd—the frailest-looking cowboy ever (perhaps from, as we are told, having "satisfied more women than a cavalry regiment on leave")—comes home, he finds Baker asking how old he is. When Ladd, the '40s star of *The Blue Dahlia*, replies, "Forty-three," Baker marvels, "You look thirty!" (Ladd was actually fifty and looked sixty). When Baker says she's twenty, Ladd snaps, "You look thirty!" (Actually, she was thirty-three.) "You always talk with your body?" he drawls, and she boasts her body "speaks several languages fluently."

Guess that includes French, for soon Baker's the wildest jazz baby in Paris, dancing on chandeliers, plucking out the feathers of her costume and wailing, *"Vive la France!"* Peppard's not interested, having taken up with playgirl Elizabeth Ashley, who purrs as she spins, "Wing spread thirty-seven, fuselage twenty-five—and hand-rubbed, by the way—tail is simply thirty-six. Shockproof landing gear and never stalls in a dive."

Meanwhile, Ladd inexplicably becomes an action movie star and Peppard, to help him, hires Baker as the female lead. "Don't be ridiculous, I'm no actress," Baker chides—right on the money—but she becomes, in the words of agent Robert Cummings, "the biggest thing to happen in this town since the Spanish landed." And the biggest lush.

Peppard's dalliance with movies ruins his marriage to Ashley, and when Baker dies in a car accident, Cummings unearths hooker Martha Hyer whom Peppard signs up to replace Baker and to whom he proposes marriage as part of the deal. Cummings tries blackmailing Hyer with a stag reel she's in, but Peppard says he's seen it (twice). "That's why I wanted you," he explains. "You were beautiful and no good, and that made it better!" Hyer snaps, "One of us is crazy—I'm not sure which one it is," and soon we learn what's driving ruthless Peppard: he had a twin brother who died insane!

In the end, he gives it all up for Ashley, and sermonizes the narrator: "So ended the Jonas Cord legend, leaving its aspirations and its scars on those who lived under his creative genius as well as his tyranny."

Produced by Joseph E. Levine, directed by Edward Dmytryk. Screenplay by John Michael Hayes from Harold Robbins's novel. C, 150 m., V

Eureka (1981) ♥ ♥ ♥

Shelved for years, this mad Nicolas Roeg jigsaw soars into the wild, purple yonder alongside the nuttiest of von Sternberg, Vidor, Ray, and Sirk.

Based on the jet set's most famed unsolved murder—the beheading of zillionaire Sir Harry Oakes so his private isle could become the gambling getaway Paradise Island—this self-indulgent insanity begins full-tilt with prospector Gene Hackman slogging into a mining town's whorehouse (run by psychic madam Helena Kallianiotes), where he mumbles, "Gold smells stronger than a woman!" Well, not this woman, who keeps confusing Hackman with her dead lover, musing, "Tonight, I took a bath, maybe because of you . . . My Jack had all the nuggets we needed right between his legs . . . With you, gold is everything. We had a crock of gold between us: his cock and my crack! . . . Then, one morning . . . Jack was dead, dead inside me, dead in bed. That must have been when I started to smell bad."

After finding gold, Hackman rushes back to ask Kallianiotes, "What happens now?" She replies, "A mystery—the end and the beginning." Flash forward to white-haired Hackman on his estate on his private island, married to chic alcoholic Jane Lapotaire, to whom he expounds, "Once I had it all, now I just have everything." Lapotaire snipes, "If only your father could see you now. The world's richest man, crazy like a fox, wearing a dress, with parrot shit on his shoulders."

Hackman, being squeezed into a crooked deal by Mafia guy Joe Pesci and lawyer Mickey Rourke, rages over daughter Theresa Russell's obsession with titled gigolo Rutger Hauer who, at a dinner party, swallows a nugget of Hackman's gold and tells Hackman, "It's only gold. Like all things, it will pass and when it does, I'll send it back to you." Russell (director Roeg's wife) keeps calling herself "a jinx," and when Hackman storms into her and Hauer's bedroom, she screams, "I don't want your gold. I want flesh. I want to kiss it. I want to suck it!"

Don't miss the astonishing sequence in which Hauer takes a couple of army men's wives to a voodoo orgy where a woman deep-throats a snake. The same night, Hackman gets slaughtered and decapitated by Pesci's goons, but Hauer is arrested and tried for the murder. Acting as his own counsel, he questions Russell, who stops the show with a soliloquy about "true love," which can be found "in the shore, in the sand, in the back of a car. Then, it's in the bed. It's an electric bed, isn't it? An electric chair. As you would say, it's switched on, as though neither of us can stop it. Shouting and shuddering electric bed on and on and on until you think you're dead." You'll think you're dreaming when you hear Russell ask Hauer about her father, "Did you cut off his head?" A dreamily delirious crackpot classic.

Produced by Jeremy Thomas, directed by Roeg. Screenplay by Paul Mayersberg, based on the book *Who Killed Sir Harry Oakes?* by Marshall Houts. C, 129 m., V

The Goddess (1958) ❤ ❤

Knowledge of obscure showbiz trivia can add a crazed kick to watching all Bad Movies We Love, especially Bad Movies We Love That We Know Are Really About Marilyn Monroe. Such trivia lends a giddiness to watching *The Goddess*: In the film's opening scene, where Monroe's desperate mother is trying to palm off her little girl on in-laws, the aunt who doesn't really want to take in MM as a member of her immediate family is played by Joan Copeland, who in real life was the sister of Arthur Miller, and hence, actually the real MM's sister-in-law. What's more, the MM tyke is played by Patty Duke, who would later star in *Valley of the Dolls*, which features a bosomy blonde character who ODs on sleeping pills, based in part on the adult MM. (Wait, there's more.) When the Duke character grows up to be the adult MM, she's played by Broadway legend Kim Stanley, who—having lost her own greatest stage role, "Cherie" in *Bus Stop*, to MM when the movie version was made in 1956—had her own score to settle when she agreed to play this unflattering portrait of MM. (But even that's not all.) Lloyd Bridges, who is cast here as the has-been athlete (read Joe DiMaggio) who marries MM at the peak of her career, would turn up twenty-odd years later in one of the MM TV minis playing Johnny Hyde, the real-life agent who loved and launched MM, but died before she met and married DiMaggio.

Got all that? Good. *The Goddess*, however, stands on its own as a preposterously overwrought and—this is vintage Paddy Chayevsky, after all—overwritten account of the Price of Fame. It's guaranteed to give you the giggles from its dialogue alone. When making out on Lovers' Lane with a backwoods teen, "Emily Ann" (as Norma Jean Baker is called here) says aloud, "I'm going to Hollywood someday. I am, I am," establishing the film's penchant for never showing us anything without first telling us about it, twice if possible. "You don't know what loneliness is," her first husband says. "You don't know the great, ultimate ache of desolation, of desolation." Oh but she will, she will, and when she does, she'll talk about it, and talk about it.

The laughs really erupt when "Emily Ann" moves to Hollywood, gets renamed, marries the athlete played by Bridges, and goes bonkers. Chayevsky invents things that are even nuttier than MM's true saga. You doubt that's possible? Consider his conceit that the couple honeymoons in a bungalow at the Beverly Hills Hotel, but never leaves it to move anywhere else during their entire marriage, though God knows they talk about wanting to: This is Hollywood's notion of *No Exit*, where there's room service.

With Steven Hill, Betty Lou Holland. Produced by Milton Perlman, directed by John Cromwell. Screenplay by Chayevsky. B&W, 105 m., V, L

The Greek Tycoon (1978) ❤❤❤

The eponymous hero's a white-haired, faintly sinister shipping billionaire given to well-publicized love affairs with famous, tempestuous women. The heroine's the chic young wife of a slain American president, the sister-in-law of an ambitious senator turned attorney general, and the most famous woman in the world. Before they get married, they sign a contract that grants her $50,000 in mad money a month and $10 million for every year they stay married in exchange for ten connubial nights a month. She can't abide his affair with a flamboyant world-famous diva, but remains steadfast and loyal until his death. (Who on earth could they possibly be? Not Aristotle Onassis and Jacqueline Kennedy, surely, because the characters played by Anthony Quinn and Jacqueline Bisset are named, respectively, "Theo Thomasis" and "Liz Cassidy," and Quinn's teeth-baring, hair-tossing lover, played by Marilu Tolo, is named "Matalas," not Callas.)

The howls begin when Quinn meets Bisset and her then-senator husband James Franciscus aboard Quinn's yacht where, when Bisset asks why he so prizes a nude statue, Quinn answers, "Because she has great tits." Later, as Quinn romances Bisset—

dancing with her in a shamelessly *Zorba*esque scene that defies belief—his long-suffering wife, Camilla Sparv, serves him with divorce papers. Years after Bisset's husband is ambushed while strolling with her on a beach (conspiracy buffs note: the single bullet strikes him from the rear in the back of the neck!), she tells her brother-in-law she's fed up with widow's weeds. "You'd rather I continue the deception," she asks, "Liz Cassidy, public shrine?"

As soon as she's accepted Quinn's businesslike marriage proposal, the couple gets told off by Quinn's playboy son, Edward Albert, Jr., and then they're shocked to learn that Quinn's brother, Raf Vallone, is marrying Quinn's ex-wife. "My beautiful Simi with that hunk of shit?" he bellows. But that's nothing compared to the wedding night when, jealous of mistress Tolo, Bisset seethes, "Ten nights a month, isn't that the contract you wanted? Well, tonight is just not one of those nights. Now, get out of here!"

Hang on for a laugh-out-loud scene in which, after he has humiliated Bisset before guests at breakfast, she rounds on Quinn, "You're an animal. How dare you? You bastard," and pounds the tar out of him until, blocking a kick to his groin, he won't let her leg go. "God, what a woman," he huffs and puffs, "let's go and make love!"

After a gooey Lovers' Montage that's accompanied by a mind-bendingly gooey, Roberta Flack-ish song, Bisset becomes the perfect wife, even tolerating Quinn's last *Zorba*-type dance in a Greek fishing village before he kicks off, leaving her one of the world's wealthiest women. One big, steamy hunk of feta cheese.

Produced by Allan Klein and Ely Landau, directed by J. Lee Thompson (see *King Solomon's Mines*). Screenplay by Mort Fine. C, 106 m., V

Once Is Not Enough (1975) ❤❤

"These scripts they send me! This one belongs in intensive care," barks a Hollywood mogul, neglecting to mention that this script from Jacqueline Susann's tripe bestseller belongs in the terminal ward. Aging filmmaker Kirk Douglas is supposed to be easily recognizable in this jet-set exposé, but in 1975, Hollywood was so overrun by bearded Young Turks that Douglas could be playing virtually any desperate-for-a-hit hack, including this film's producer.

Penniless, Kirk romances Barbara Huttonish Alexis Smith, though the real love story lies elsewhere. "Gee, I hope nobody thinks we're father and daughter," purrs Deborah Raffin when papa Kirk meets her plane in New York. "I hope they think you're a dirty old man and I'm your broad." Raffin's shocked that Douglas has married a cold fish like Smith. He offers, "It's difficult not to feel a little something for a woman with all that money."

Dewy young Raffin gets a call from her "old classmate," Brenda Vaccaro (and we do mean old, since Vaccaro is clearly pushing forty) who, when Raffin marvels at her transformation, explains, "I had a nose job, my tits were lifted, my ass was flattened and my knees were straightened. My navel, I'm proud to say, was untouched. It's perfect." (Helen Gurley Brown, perhaps?)

Vaccaro, "the youngest editor *Gloss* magazine has ever had," promises to teach Raffin "writing, screwing, everything!" but stepmother Smith imperiously wants Raffin "taught to want the right things." (In Smith's case, the "right things" include her longtime affair with Garboesque Melina Mercouri, who overacts broadly even when she's merely eating grapes.)

Raffin falls for hard-drinking, Norman Mailer–like David Janssen (who wows Raffin by remarking, "Forgive me, but I can't take my eyes off your ass"). Vaccaro, on the make, gets Janssen to her apartment, inviting him to peruse her record collection—"How's this?" she says, " 'Music to Get It Up By'?"—but he climbs the fire escape to Raffin's apartment, explaining, "Silicone tits and a computerized brain is not my idea of a sexy combination."

Vaccaro confronts Raffin: "It'd be a lot healthier if you just got it over with and went to bed with your father. Why don't you ask him?" Raffin doesn't, choosing instead to chat with Dad's ex-maid. "I worked for your father twelve years," she tells Raffin, "and it was just one long parade of poontang."

After such a remark, there's nowhere to go but down, so Douglas and Smith die in a plane crash, leaving Raffin an unfulfilled heiress. Just then, Janssen dumps Raffin, saying, "You gave a middle-aged guy his last pretense of being a stud. For that I'll always be grateful." We hoped the movie would end with Janssen doing the truly Maileresque thing: killing Raffin. For blowing that, we'll never forgive the moviemakers.

With George Hamilton (as—of all things—a Wall Street wizard). Produced by Howard W. Koch, directed by Guy Green. Screenplay by Julius Epstein, from Susann's novel. C, 122 m., V

Where Love Has Gone (1964) ❤❤❤❤

"Somewhere along the line," Bette Davis says with a sniff of disdain, "the world has lost all its standards and taste." *She* should talk, considering that she's in the movie version of Harold Robbins's trashy rehash of the scandal that erupted when Lana Turner's teenage daughter Cheryl stabbed Mom's gangster beau. The story is "disguised"—the central character is a sculptress, not an actress, and the newspaper headlines read "TEENAGER SLAYS SOCIETY MOM'S LOVER"—but it's so laughably transparent that one critic, in his review, congratulated the filmmakers for not offering the lead to Turner.

Playing this untamable tramp, Susan Hayward—fresh off a remake of *Stolen Hours*, Davis's earlier *Dark Victory*—squares off against Davis, as her disapproving society mother, in a battle of the battleaxes that is a Bad Movie must-see. "You have made it publicly obvious that you have only one concept of love," Davis declaims, finding new syllables in every word, "a vile and sinful one!" Hayward tosses her red mane and gives as good as she gets, snorting like a dragon, "When you're dying from thirst, you'll drink from a mudhole!"

The movie's crazed theory—that Hayward cannot sculpt great statues unless she's whoring around (spelled out when art critic DeForrest Kelly tells her, "With you, sex and art go hand in hand. Sculptor . . . pagan . . . alleycat!")—is all the funnier when you apply this psychology to Lana Turner's generally hapless performances: what might her career have been like without her sex life? (The mind reels.)

In flashbacks, we see Hayward with husband Mike Connors, taunting him, "Take your rights, I want you to! Sometimes it's better that way. You're not the first today—I'm just getting warmed up!" Connors slaps her, raging, "I've heard about them, I've laughed about them, I've even joked about them, but I never thought I'd end up married to one. You're not a woman—you're a disease!"

Their teen daughter, Joey Heatherton, is cut from the same mold. "How about it, kid?" a reporter asks as she's led into the courtroom. "Was he your lover, your mother's, or both?" Connors, who's neglected his daughter for years, says he didn't know Heatherton smoked. Pouting her lower lip, undulating in her cashmere sweater, and sighing, Heatherton says, "There's a lot of things you don't know, Daddy. The worst is yet to come."

Brother, she ain't just whistling Dixie: The climactic courtroom showdown's a lulu, what with Hayward growling, "It's been decided that I'm an unfit mother, an ungrateful daughter, and an irresponsible wife," then revealing that her lover died because he stepped "in front of me, and got what I should have gotten," because Heatherton "was trying to kill me!" After that, Hayward uses the murder weapon to off herself. Davis shrugs, "She was destined for tragedy."

Produced by Joseph E. Levine, directed by Edward Dmytryk. Screenplay by John Michael Hayes, from Robbins's novel. C, 114 m., TV

Written on the Wind (1956) ❤ ❤ ❤ ❤

"Down there, I'm a guy with too many chips—throw 'em up in the air and a few land on my shoulders," says tortured playboy Robert Stack, piloting classy secretary Lauren Bacall on a joyride in his private plane. This zanily overwrought classic—about the mysterious death of the heir to an American dynasty—had lawyers for the tobacco-rich Reynolds family working overtime. But instead of trying to stop the moviemakers (it's a heavily veiled account of the Reynoldses' son marrying torch singer Libby Holman and then meeting a sudden demise), the clan ought to have sued for a better script: No matter what happened in real life, it can't possibly have been this divinely silly.

"Are you looking for laughs or are you soul-searching?" asks Rock Hudson, Stack's devoted childhood pal, of nice girl Bacall.

Actually, as audiences of the mid-'50s already knew, she's out to demonstrate again that she knows how to marry a millionaire. When she and Stack return to the family mansion from their honeymoon, Bacall's alarmed to find a gun stashed under Stack's pillow, perhaps because it's not the only Freudian symbol on hand: they're living in the shadow of the most insistently phallic oil wells in movie history. Hudson's so hot for Bacall that a character quips that Hudson's, er, "torch is burning."

Sizzling out of control, too, is Stack's floozy sister, Dorothy Malone, who ogles Hudson like the slab of prime rib he is, and reveals there's bad blood between her and her brother. "I hate him so," she drawls, "for taking you away from me. I'm desperate for you . . . marriage or no marriage." Malone sneaks off from a society blowout in the newlyweds' honor to ask Hudson, "I've changed since we last swam in the raw, haven't I?" When he mutters, "I was an idiot boy then," Malone storms back to the party and achieves Bad Movie immortality by dancing the maddest, most furious mambo *ever*.

The madness accelerates when Malone picks up gas station attendant Grant Williams, who tells her tycoon father, Robert Keith, "Your daughter's a tramp, mister." Turned on by all the action, Malone mambos again—in front of a framed portrait of Hudson—as her father drops dead. Then, Malone goads Stack, who's taken to booze when he finds he may not be able to father a child with Bacall, that he'd better keep an eye on Bacall and Hudson. When Stack calls her "a filthy liar," Malone snaps, "I'm filthy—period!"

It all ends, as of course it must, with gunplay, a courtroom trial, and Malone—head of the family at last—crumpled at her father's massive desk fondling a miniature oil derrick. The following year, Malone stood onstage at the Oscar ceremonies similarly fondling her Best Supporting Actress award. Meticulously filmed, utterly sublime, here's the *Giant* of Bad Movies We Love.

Produced by Albert Zugsmith, directed by Douglas Sirk. Screenplay by George Zuckerman, from Robert Wilder's novel. C, 99 m., V

Bring On
the Bimbos!

We don't mind Hollywood's never-ending search for new faces. Who knows when the next Demi Moore or Daniel Day-Lewis might turn up? But, as the here-today-gone-today "stars" of these movies prove, would-be starmakers would be wise to insist on a little acting talent, charisma, and personality before they try to push their latest "discovery" on the public from the seemingly endless supply of pretty faces that don't make the grade.

Bolero (1984) ❤ ❤

After blank-eyed beauty Bo Derek achieved stardom playing a contemporary wanton in the 1979 hit *10*, her Svengali, husband John Derek, took her red-hot career in hand and went further than he had with his earlier, lookalike wives, Ursula Andress and Linda Evans: he became Bo's exclusive *auteur*, miscast her as period-piece virgins, and with just two Bad Movies We Love, brought her reign as a love goddess to a screeching halt.

In the second of these gems, *Bolero*, Bo is a '20s heiress who tells school pal Ana Obregon, "In the ways of love, we're kindergarten toddlers." Bo wants to head for Morocco to "learn of ecstasy. What a beautiful word: E-X-T—" "No, no," Obregon interrupts to correct Bo's spelling, but if you ask us, Bo knew full well what she was spelling—"Extasy," the name of the '80s "hug drug" that could go a long way to explain this frenzied love-in of a movie. "Let's go wallow in it, do the backstroke in it!" Bo exults. Yes, let's.

Desert sheik Greg Bensen slurps honey off Bo's naked torso, but then passes out cold, leaving Bo to complain, "I'm all dressed up with no place to go!" So Bo tries her luck in Spain, chasing after matador Andrea Occipinti. In a sex scene of jaw-dropping exhibitionism that is exceeded only by later scenes in this same film, the naked Occipinti pulls apart Bo's legs, and we recall (not for the first time, and certainly not for the last) that it is Bo's husband who has staged and photographed this sequence. In case we're unable to follow what's happening as the actor gamely humps away atop her, Bo helpfully remarks, "I'm not a virgin anymore." (Thank you for sharing, Bo.) As often happens in real life, the matador is then gored by a bull . . . yes, *there.*

In John Derek's signature "I wonder if the idiots who watch my movies can possibly follow the plot?" style, he has Obregon ask Bo the obvious: "You don't care if he can never make love to you again?" A foolish question, if you know Bo's healing powers. Certain that "the doomsday doctors" are wrong, Bo goes to her lover's side to tell him, as she points at his crotch, "That thing is going to work!"

(How? Glad you asked.) Bo learns to fight a bull, natch, bringing a whole new meaning to the term "bareback" as she rides around the bullring in the buff. This accomplished, she returns to Occipinti and commands, "I want ecstasy," whips her wet hair across his naked torso, climbs astride him, and applauds. (You'll want to cry "Bravo!" but you won't need to—Bo does that, too.) Their lovemaking is so fine, dry-ice smoke wafts in, colored lights flash, and a neon sign comes on, reading "EXTASY." (So we won't mistake Bo for a tramp, the movie ends with the couple getting married.)

With George Kennedy, Olivia D'Abo, Ian Cochrane. Produced by Bo, directed and photographed by Derek. Screenplay by Derek. C, 104 m., V

Endless Love (1981) ❤

Filmmaker Franco Zeffirelli, hoping to reignite his lukewarm career with a swoony, romantic teen tragedy (aping his earlier smash, *Romeo and Juliet*) only pulled off the swoony part with this misguided, hooty attempt to launch '70s prepubescent pinup Brooke Shields into adult stardom. Saddled with Shields and newcomer Martin Hewitt—two dreamy-looking dead weights who'd make better bookends than film stars—Zeffirelli tries, hilariously, to divert our attention from their inability to act by encouraging the film's other players to overact up a storm. "Too much self-dramatizing around here!" snaps Beatrice Straight, as if (1) she'd just come from watching the rushes, and (2) she weren't guilty as sin herself.

The movie, a yarn about star-crossed Chicago teens who go mad when torn apart (already laughably preposterous when *Splendor in the Grass* was filmed twenty years earlier), throws together the son of two politically aware do-gooders with the daughter of two "free spirits," whose home "is the joke of the neighborhood—into drugs, into everything—a relic of the '60s."

Earth mama Shirley Knight likes that Hewitt is spending nights in fifteen-year-old Shields' bedroom; she asks hippy hubby Don Murray, "Aren't you happy that someone has the courage to wake up Sleeping Beauty?" (Shields looks to us like she's sleepwalking from beginning to end.) Knight explains, "He hides in the house till they think we're asleep, and he scuttles away at dawn. They're rather sweet—like bats."

Bats is the word, all right, for the sequence where Zeffirelli whips up a veritable operatic quartet of Bad Acting: Murray screams at Shields, "I don't want him in your room!" Shields wails, "You're just jealous!" Knight shrieks at Murray, "You're a hell of a doctor—she's hysterical!" and Shields' brother, James Spader, shouts, "There's something wrong with that guy!"—all at the same time.

Forbidden to see Shields (or even her nude body double), Hewitt goes off the deep end, takes the advice of arson enthusiast Tom Cruise, and sets fire to Shields' house—taking the notion of "carrying a torch" a tad far. Hewitt's sent to a psychiatric hospital (where he has "visions" of Shields in earlier scenes) and, as is so often the case when a teen torches a house, the marriages of both families fall apart.

"Get me out of here!" Hewitt rages to his folks—a sentiment you'll share before the movie's over—so (get this) they do, and Hewitt hotfoots it to Manhattan, where he gets vamped by the divorced Knight, chased by Murray (who, mercifully for us, is hit by a taxi and killed), and reunited with Shields, who hasn't learned one single thing about acting in all the years they've been apart. What any of this has to do with *love* is anybody's guess, but it's certainly *endless*.

With Richard Kiley, Penelope Milford, Jami Gertz, Teri Shields. Produced by Dyson Lovell, directed by Zeffirelli. Screenplay by Judith Rascoe, from Scott Spencer's novel. C, 115 m., V, L

Flashdance (1983) ❤ ❤ ❤

From its crazed opening, where welder "Alex" removes a protective face mask and turns out to be (gasp!) pouty Jennifer Beals, to its crazed climax where Beals's interpretive ballet turns out to be the work of (gasp!) a dance double, this is the ridiculous—and ridiculously popular—musical that gave birth to that "What was the world thinking of?" fashion trend, the torn T-shirt. Despite her dazed, dopey performance here, Big Things were predicted for Beals, and her relative obscurity today suggests that—maybe, just maybe—the old adage "Only the public can make a star" is true.

Just how bad is Beals? Well, when her boss, Michael Nouri, asks, "What's a dancer doing working as a welder?" the question on our minds is, "What's an untalented girl like you doing in a big hit like this?" Convinced that we can be force-fed Beals as an '80s sexpot, the filmmakers offer up unintentionally amusing, heavy-handed scenes like her jazzercise workout, replete with cutaways to her dog, his tongue hanging out.

When Beals isn't welding, confessing in church ("I've been thinking about sex"), or insulting street hustlers ("Did you know that the smallest penis ever measured was 1.1 inches?"), she's bumping 'n' grinding at a tawdry blue-collar bar where the patrons crowd in to watch tarts like Beals, uh, *not* strip. "Bring on the bimbos!" hollers one rowdy, and out they come—hair spiked, bared skin glittering, faces slathered in white Kabuki makeup. They shimmy, they crawl, they pour gallons of water on themselves, but they're nice-girl bimbos, not like those bad-gal bimbos up the street, who bare their titties for cash. When Beals refuses to date her boss (principles, see?) Nouri says, "Okay, you're fired. Pick you up at eight."

At dinner, Nouri gets aroused just watching Beals eat lobster—the movie's zany high point. "I'm not hungry," she pants, butter literally running out of her mouth while, under the table, she runs her stocking-clad foot up into his crotch. "You like phone booths?" she asks. "You probably just like doing it in beds, right?" Just then, to heighten the hilarity, Nouri's ex-wife approaches the table and says, "You two look cozy. You're not really a welder, are you?" (Even the characters in the movie can't believe it.)

Somehow, between all the MTV-influenced dance numbers and the montages of our lovers romping through a steel mill, Nouri learns Beals is afraid to apply to ballet academy, but he changes her mind by uttering the line that became instant kitsch: "When you give up your dream, you die." What someone should have told her was, "Sometimes, when your dreams come true, and you land the starring role in a movie, you die." A better title would have been "Flash-in-the Pan."

With Lilia Skala, Belinda Bauer, Cynthia Rhodes. Produced by Don Simpson and Jerry Bruckheimer, directed by Adrian Lyne. Screenplay by Tom Hedley and Joe Eszterhas, from Hedley's story. C, 95 m., V, L

Lipstick (1976) ❤

You haven't lived until you've witnessed stuporous fashion mannequin Margaux Hemingway race away from a Francesco Scavullo fashion shoot in a slinky red dress and heels, grab a rifle from her car, and blast the bejesus out of her psycho rapist Chris Sarandon. This knock-down-drag-out-funny thriller was designed by no less than superagent-producer Freddie Fields to present to the world the movie debut of stunning (that is, stunningly untalented) Margaux. It became obvious during production that it was another Hemingway, little sister Mariel, who was stealing the show and would be heard from again.

Mariel invites her creepy music teacher, Sarandon, to come to one of Margaux's nude photo sessions—posing for lipstick ads—because though Mariel has a crush on him, he's got a crush on Margaux. He turns up at their apartment, plays Margaux his shrieking avant-garde music, gets positively nutsy when she tries to blow him off, then attacks her. Growling about her lipstick, "I want it on me," Sarandon ties Margaux to her bed, beats her, and subjects her to rough sex of every possible persuasion, then cutting her loose, advises, "Listen, don't do this with anyone else."

Hemingway gets a lawyer (an embarrassed-looking Anne Bancroft) and decides to prosecute Sarandon. "You hard-sell her all over this country," bellows Bancroft to Perry King, Margaux's photographer boyfriend. "We're allowed to look and we're allowed to buy, but don't touch!" She's trying to warn Margaux that she'll "be abused again in court," provoking a response from Margaux about her rapist: "He wanted to kill me . . . with his cock! I hate him!"

The jury acquits Sarandon, which so rattles the victim that she and Mariel decide to escape to a rural life. "We'll be the first sister team," jokes Margaux, "to make a living by starving." After a ridiculously prolonged chase sequence through L.A.'s Pacific Design Center, Sarandon assaults Mariel, prompting hot revenge from big sis Margaux, who literally blows him away. "Crime is expected since humans are never perfect," Bancroft says, addressing the jury on Hemingway's behalf, "but the failures of justice may be more damaging to society than crime itself." Still, there is justice; after this big debut, Hemingway next starred, four years later, in *Killer Fish*. Later still, she changed the spelling of her first name to "Margot," but honey, you haven't fooled us.

Produced by Fields, directed by Lamont Johnson. Screenplay by David Rayfiel. "Ms. Hemingway's hair designed by Harry King; Ms. Hemingway's makeup created by Way Bandy." C, 90 m., V

A Night in Heaven (1983) ❤

When Christopher Atkins bared his all with such abandon in *The Blue Lagoon*, somebody mistook him for The Next Big Thing and made this student-by-day, male-stripper-by-night howler that sent Atkins into instant bimbo oblivion.

"You say what you say well," speech teacher Lesley Ann Warren tells Atkins after he's bluffed his oral finals, "but you have nothing to say." The same goes double for Joan (*Nashville*) Tewkesbury's script, in which Warren runs into Atkins at the Heaven nightclub—he's billed as "Ricky Rocket" and acts like Luke Skywalker on Extasy—and she hollers to sister Deborah Rush over the disco din, "I just flunked that kid in my class." To which their pal Alix Elias bellows, "What? You did what in his ass?"

Atkins, natch, rams his groin into Warren's face, prompting Teach to consider those other types of oral exams. (What makes this all the loonier is that ladylike Warren's played her fair share of strippers, plus, here she's married to Robert Logan, who—twenty years earlier in trash like *Claudelle Inglish*—was the wooden, pretty-boy Atkins of his day.) Logan's Cape Kennedy co-worker, erstwhile "Dance Fever" go-go host Denny Terrio, moonlights as a disco instructor. After class, one instructor muses, "Most of the women in this world must be lonely," prompting Terrio to nudge him and say, "Good thing, or we'd be dancing with each other."

Meanwhile, poor Warren returns to the club where Atkins disrobes and disrobes and disrobes, while the MC barks, "Buns, buns, hot-cross buns!" But lest we write off Atkins as just another pretty pair of hot-cross buns, he pleads to retake the final exam. Atkins's dream, see, is to study hotel management, so he can spring waitress mom Carrie Snodgress from behind the counter of a coffee shop! "I'm not grading your mother's life, I'm grading your . . . performance," Warren explains, as she, along with us, suppresses mirth, since by now, we all know that Atkins isn't even remotely capable of anything resembling a performance.

Logan loses his job, providing a convenient plot device for driving Warren into Atkins' hands. Well, actually, Atkins puts

Warren's hand on his crotch, then strips, and drives her to bliss while she remains fully clothed. Logan comes gunning for Atkins, snarling, "Come on, I want to see you dance!" then holding him hostage on a skiff—get this, Atkins is naked—bellowing, "Where do you get off fucking my wife?"

It all ends anticlimactically as the sadder but wiser marrieds patch things up and put the whole misadventure behind them. Would-be '80s sexpot Atkins didn't have the same option. Trivia buffs may want to note that would-be '90s sexpot Andy Garcia is listed in the credits as "T. J. The Bartender."

Produced by Gene Kirkwood and Howard W. Koch, Jr., directed and edited by John G. Avildsen. Screenplay by Joan Tewkesbury. C, 80 m., V

Summer Lovers (1982) ♥

One of the spoils of a huge box-office hit—and Randall Kleiser had two, *Grease* and *The Blue Lagoon*—is the shot at making a movie that expresses who a director really is.

"Oh, wow!" observes Daryl Hannah, "All right!" pronounces Peter Gallagher, our young lovers, on arriving at the Greek seaside villa they've rented, leaving no doubt that Kleiser is a writer-director after our own hearts. "What are you thinking about?" Hannah asks Gallagher, who mutters, "Time," as he gets misty-eyed at the sight of an ancient ruin. "It's about two-thirty," Hannah chirps, but Gallagher is thinking, like, eternity: "I meant centuries. I was thinking about the guy who made this. His work is still here after two thousand years. What was he thinkin' when he chipped right there?"

But what were these people thinking when they made this movie is more to the point, especially when Gallagher follows around French gamine Valerie Quennessen, an archaeologist who sunbathes topless. Hannah—sensing that Gallagher thinks she's a prude—reads *Imaginative Sex* and *Nice Girls Do*, and winds up tying him up and dripping hot candle wax on his chest.

Later, he advises, "Don't hunch your shoulders, you have beautiful tits—pull 'em back," prompting her confession, "I used to dream I was a mermaid" (perhaps explaining why producers later cast her in *Splash*), then she adds, "I fantasized about being tied up and ravished by the entire swim team." Gallagher, in turn, fantasizes about having both women—how daring!

Covering Quennessen's naked breasts with pebbles, he tells her, "Making love to you is like riding a horse." With smooth talk like that, is it any wonder that Gallagher persuades both women to spend the day with him? He tells them, "When you two went in opposite directions, I wanted to follow you both." Quennessen (so soulful, so deep, so French) says, "People are like gas . . . I mean, gas fills whatever space it's in . . . and people do too." The movie teases all the time—Will the women make it together? Will they merge in a menage à trois? Will Gallagher make it with the drag queen they meet at a party? Will any of the cast members learn to act before the fadeout?—until, finally, the three of them wake up in bed together the morning after. After this movie, Quennessen vanished without a trace, but Gallagher, who graduated to acclaimed stuff like *sex, lies and videotape* and Broadway roles, will spend the rest of his career living this one down. Hannah may spend what's left of her career living up to it.

With Barbara Rush, Carole Cook. Produced by Mike Moder, directed by Kleiser. Screenplay by Kleiser. C, 98 m., V, L

Where Danger Lives (1950) ❤

"I have nothing to live for! Why should I live?" wails sloe-eyed rich girl Faith Domergue when dedicated doctor Robert Mitchum saves her life after a suicide attempt. (And those lines were uttered before Domergue read what critics had to say about this *film noir* designed for her by her Svengali, billionaire Howard Hughes.)

Domergue, who by comparison made the acting skills of Maria Montez seem protean, plays a wicked mantrap who beguiles Mitchum away from a date with his sweet nurse girlfriend, Maureen O'Sullivan (wife of this movie's director). As they go out dancing and clubbing night after night, she reveals, "When we're not together, I feel like I'm suspended in midair with nothing down beneath except the end of the world." Actually, there was nothing down beneath Domergue except Hughes and his fortune, and at the end of her world, roles in cheap horror flicks, but in this, her brief heyday, beefy Mitchum and suave Claude Rains spar over her.

"I'm bleeding," she sobs. "He tore the earring from my ear!" when Rains, her millionaire husband, learns that she and Mitchum are hot to trot. After Rains dies under suspicious circumstances and Mitchum suffers a concussion, Domergue—swathed in mink—drives them like blazes for the border.

Things get really wiggy on the road, what with Mitchum hocking her rich girl trappings for a beat-up truck ("Where's my mink coat?" she screams) and Domergue inhaling the scenery when she wakes up screaming and runs into the desert. And then the pair get busted in a hick town where it's temporarily illegal for anyone to be seen without a beard! After he marries Domergue, Mitchum's just about to finally learn that he's got a nutcase on his hands when Domergue tears the telltale radio from their motel room wall.

It gets worse: When she figures that Mitchum's head wound might slow them up a bit, Domergue smothers him with a pillow and then lights out for her big getaway. But in classic Bad Movie fashion, it turns out that Mitchum's only *slightly* dead, see, because he crawls after her and shoots her, which sets the scene for the hilarious finale in which Domergue, pinned photogenically to a barbed-wire fence, snarls, "Nobody pities me." Or misses her, she might have added.

Produced by Irving Cummings, Jr., and Irwin Allen, directed by John Farrow. Screenplay by Charles Bennett, from a story by Leo Rosten. B&W, 84 m., TV

CHAPTER 15

Overacting in Sensurround

Many a star's career went to hell in a handbasket when, throughout the '70s, such producers as Irwin Allen cranked out a series of end-of-the-world extravaganzas that elevated special effects to the status of stars. So, what's a fading supernova or an overcured ham to do when audiences clamor to see them decimated by scene-stealing deadly plagues, raging fires, marauding swarms of killer bees, sunken pleasure boats, and crashing planes? Why, do as these players did: emote, emote, emote, then take the money and run, run, run!

Airport (1970) ❤ ❤

The makers of this movie have lots to answer for. Already a "recycled" product in the first place (there'd been scads of earlier airplane-in-distress flicks), *Airport* influenced a decade's worth of imitators and knockoffs with its casting formula: Sign up as few box office names as you think you can get away with, add some stage players for "tone," then fill up the marquee with "recycled" celebrities you saw at last night's cocktail party. Thus, box office draws of the day like Burt Lancaster and Dean Martin and slumming theater divas like Helen Hayes and Maureen Stapleton are surrounded by an eclectic assortment of so-called "stars" who never even had their allotted fifteen minutes of fame. (Think about it—did you ever see Jean Seberg, George Kennedy, Van Heflin,

Dana Wynter, Lloyd Nolan, Jessie Royce Landis, Barry Nelson, Gary Collins, or Barbara Hale on "Hollywood Squares"?)

The story is about two brothers-in-law, airport honcho Lancaster and airplane pilot Martin, who're forced to choose between their wives and their mistresses. Martin's missus, Hale, knows that Martin cheats, but he always comes home ("I'm his disaster insurance," she chirps, making Lancaster mutter under his breath, "More like group insurance"). Martin, meanwhile, can't figure why his lover, stewardess Jacqueline Bisset, is being so aloof. "You get me up to full throttle, then throw me into reverse," he whines. "You could damage my engine that way." His engine's fine—she's preggers. Martin asks, "You're sure?" and Bisset snaps, "Am I sure I'm pregnant, or am I sure you're the father? The answer to both is yes." Martin comforts her, "I'll make sure you don't go to some butcher two flights up over a drugstore."

Speaking of flights, just then the duo must take to the skies, with mad bomber Heflin aboard. On earth, Lancaster is reminded by his mistress, former stew Seberg, that he'd "promised to call your wife back." This is shrewish Wynter, who barks, "I'm not a ball game where you keep score, I'm your wife!" (How wrong Wynter is—her character *is* a ball game, and her score is "Three strikes, you're out.") The two sagas intersect when Seberg's charge, stowaway Hayes, escapes to hop on the departing plane and sits next to Heflin.

Since Hayes is shamelessly bad as a dear little old lawbreaker, our hopes are raised that she'll be killed when Heflin's bomb goes off. Alas, it's Bisset who's hurt—a warning to promiscuous stewardesses everywhere: sleep with Dean Martin and pay the consequences—while Hayes is not only uninjured, she also later waltzed off with an Oscar! If this movie was destined to win Academy Awards for the cartoonish histrionics on display, one should have gone to Kennedy who, as ace engineer "Petroni," overacts so broadly that he even makes hammy Lancaster seem human. Instead, Kennedy scored the ultimate booby prize: a recurring role in every *Airport* sequel.

Produced by Ross Hunter, directed by George Seaton. Screenplay by Seaton, from Arthur Hailey's novel. C, 137 m., V, L

Airport 1975 (1974) ❤❤❤

Two nuns watch silent screen diva Gloria Swanson wend her way through an airport, surrounded by the press. "It's one of those Hollywood persons," observes Sister Martha Scott. "You mean an actress?" asks Sister Helen Reddy. Scott shudders, rolls her eyes, and replies, "Or worse." *Airport 1975* is proof that not much is worse than "those Hollywood persons" who grace the Bad Movies We Love known as "disaster films."

As the passenger parade continues—Myrna Loy, Susan Clark, Sid Caesar, Jerry Stiller, Norman Fell, Conrad Janis, Efrem Zimbalist, Jr., Roy Thinnes, Erik Estrada, Karen Black, just for starters—you keep thinking, it can't get any more cut-rate than this. Then Linda Blair rolls on in a wheelchair! The laughs start when Sister Reddy, guitar in hand, serenades the ailing Blair, whom no one has told that patients in dire need of organs don't beam like contestants in a Junior Miss contest. Though the movie's in contemporary drag—a novice stew who gets called "a teenager" shoots back, "It's *Ms.* Teenager, please. I'm emancipated, liberated, and highly skilled in Kung Fu"—it's really just Arthur Hailey's stale chestnut about the plane that must be piloted back to earth by (you guessed it) Someone Who Doesn't Know How!

Desperate to give the tired old plot device some added suspense, somebody decided to put cross-eyed Karen Black into the driver's seat. (Dana Andrews turns up as an in-joke, piloting the plane that crashes into Black's jet; in *The Crowded Sky*, Andrews played the pilot whose plane was struck; in *Zero Hour*, Andrews played Black's role!) When Black's radio breaks, her boyfriend back on earth, pilot Charlton Heston, knows that someone's gotta go up there and bring that plane down. "You mean to tell me you're going to try to transfer a pilot into a 747 in flight?" asks an incredulous extra. "It's going to be like trying to put a raw egg back into its shell!" Heston, who knows that he's nothing if not a raw egg, helicopters over and prepares to literally drop in. Reaching out her arms to help him, Black makes one of those actor's "choices" that distinguishes her from all the others who've played this part: She sticks out her tongue! She then runs down the aisles shouting, "There's nothing to be alarmed about, nothing!"

Just when you're thinking it can't get any goofier than this, there comes the sight of sixty-nine-year-old Myrna Loy actually hurtling down the emergency slide exit, a high point of unintentional hilarity—and, too good to be true, it's topped by the body double for seventy-seven-year-old Gloria Swanson, who comes down at warp speed, her dress hiking up high enough to show a tantalizing flash of white undies.

With George Kennedy, Ed Nelson, Larry Storch, Beverly Garland, Guy Stockwell, and Sharon Gless. Produced by William Frye, directed by Jack Smight. Screenplay by Don Ingalls, "inspired by the film *Airport*, based on the novel by Arthur Hailey." C, 106 m., V, L

Airport '77 (1977) ❤ ❤

"I have now become the foremost collector of toy booze," rasps Lee Grant as she swaggers through *Airport '77*. "I have a mini margarita and a teeny martini. Aren't they cute?" Not as cute as she is, that's for sure: Grant's hilariously over-the-top performance is permanent evidence of the spontaneous laughter that is produced when the full weight and training of Method acting is brought to bear on a script that would hardly pass muster as a made-for-cable-TV movie.

This is the one about the plane that crashes into the Bermuda Triangle. As Darren McGavin says, "Some choice we've got— either we all drown, or we all suffocate." (The latter danger would seem to be from Grant, who reels around, acting, acting, acting, no doubt sucking up the entire oxygen supply. But since her husband is portrayed by Christopher Lee and her lover by Gil Gerard, who can tell whether or not they're unconscious?) You, too, will be left gasping—with hilarity—when Grant notes that the plane's sinking, by theatrically pointing to the water rising outside the windows and intoning, "Look! Look! Look!"

The cast is peppered with pros who know a thing or two about scenery chewing, but not even Jack Lemmon, Brenda Vaccaro, or Olivia de Havilland can get a word in. Grant trembles, rattles her diamond-covered fingers, swills straight out of those bitsy liquor bottles, and asks, "What's going to happen to me?" Apparently, she's unaware that it's already happened—her career as an Oscar-winner has slipped so far she's in an *Airport* sequel on the bottom of the ocean. Who can blame Lee when he decides to join Lemmon in an attempt to scuba up to the surface—sure, they may get killed, but is that really worse than having to share more scenes with Grant?

And what scenes they are! Supposedly in grief but looking, to us, as if she's just staggered out of the dailies in shock, Grant tries to open the airplane door, muttering with real conviction, "I have to leave." Vaccaro stops her with a solid right hook which, mercifully for us, knocks Grant out cold. If that doesn't have you cheering with glee, this will: As penance for her performance, Grant drowns at the end. Maybe there is a God in Hollywood, after all.

With James Stewart, George Kennedy, Joseph Cotten, Robert Foxworth, Robert Hooks, Monte Markham, Kathleen Quinlan, James Booth, Pamela Bellwood, Tom Sullivan, Arlene Golonka, George Furth, and Monica Lewis as the world's oldest stewardess. Produced by William Frye, directed by Jerry Jameson (who'd later work their same special magic on *Raise the Titanic!*). Screenplay by Michael Scheff and David Spector, story by H. A. L. Craig and Charles Kuenstle, "inspired by the film, based on the novel by Arthur Hailey." C, 114 m., V, L

Avalanche (1978) ❤ ❤

Mia Farrow made a spectacle of herself in this absurd "disaster movie" before making an even bigger one of herself the next year in *Hurricane*, but that's just part of the goofy pleasure to be derived from producer Roger Corman's big star snowjob.

"Holy cow, are you going to turn into a swinger?" Jeanette Nolan (who once played Lady Macbeth for Orson Welles) asks *Vogue* magazine editor Farrow when she breezes into the swank ski lodge owned by her ex, Rock Hudson, who plays Nolan's son.

Nolan—certain she's on her way to a supporting actress Oscar for outmugging Helen Hayes in *Airport*—tells Farrow when she asks about Hudson's whereabouts that he's "up to his ass in celebrities." Up to his ass in would-be celebrities is more like it, such as environmental-minded photographer Robert Forster who, after witnessing ladies' man ski champion Rick Moses narrowly escape a mini-avalanche, warns Hudson against chopping down more trees to accommodate his expansion plans. "Things aren't normal," warns Forster, adding, "There's a heaviness and it's growing. I can feel it."

But Hudson pays no heed because he's too busy skinny-dipping in a hot tub and trying to rekindle Farrow's passion for him. "David, you're like the weather," Farrow muses to Hudson, "you just happen." Later, Farrow dances (badly) at the lodge with Forster (who dances worse) while Nolan bellows "Aloha!" and guzzles drinks with her willowy "companion," Steve Franken.

Outside the lodge, snow is falling faster than the reputations of the actors cavorting inside. "You stifle me! I need some space," Farrow flares at Hudson when he wants her to pay less attention to Forster, just about the time you're praying that this veritable blizzard of Bad Acting will be buried alive in snow. But first, Farrow must wander about Forster's mountain hideaway, marveling, incomprehensibly, "I want to see your—what do you call it?—you do your printing here?" having never, it seems, wandered into *Vogue*'s darkroom.

Any time the action and dialogue sag, which means every ten seconds, the director cuts to hilarious shots of snow piling up, underscored by ominous music. The Big Slide comes during the athletics competition, which creams crowds of overacting extras and sets the snowbound stars to attempting to rescue each other. Nolan and Franken get trapped inside the resort but, unfortunately, get rescued, and when Farrow—riding with Nolan in an ambulance—tries to replace Nolan's oxygen mask, Nolan rips it off and growls, "I don't want that, I want a Bloody Mary!" You'll shout for anesthesia too for the last gasp of the movie, which features Farrow perilously dangling from a bridge while the ambulance goes up in flames in the river below. "We survived," Farrow says to Hudson after he rescues her. Not quite, Mia.

Produced by Corman, directed by Corey Allen (who's since given us TV's *The Ann Jillian Story*). Screenplay by Allen and Claude Pola, from Frances Doel's story. C, 98 m., V

The Cassandra Crossing (1976) ❤❤

Aboard a transcontinental train, renowned physician Richard Harris—inventor of a process that "rejuvenates defective brain cells in retarded kids"—gets a desperate assignment from Army ace Burt Lancaster at the World Health Organization: Find the stowaway terrorist carrying a highly contagious plague virus. It couldn't possibly be the guy staggering around the train sweating bullets, now could it?

It's a pity Harris didn't first develop a process to rejuvenate his defective brain cells—or those of fellow passengers Sophia Loren (Harris's ex, who writes best-sellers about him), Martin Sheen (as a heroin-addicted, mountain-climbing gigolo), Ava Gardner (Sheen's wealthy, wed keeper), O. J. Simpson (a narc masquerading as a priest), Lee Strasberg (hamming it up in the Helen Hayes slot as a quirky old concentration camp survivor)—all of whom race from car to car mouthing some of the zaniest dialogue this side of Bad Movie Heaven.

Loren slinks into Harris's train compartment to proffer a copy of her new book, *Brain Sell or: Dr. Jekyll Where Are You Now That We Need You?* and says she's not really sure why she's there: "Just to take a look, perhaps?" Harris replies, "It's rather cold in here for me to drop my pants." Gardner tries (but fails) to look interested in Sheen, whom she met, she tells Harris, when "he decided he'd climb this sheer mountain face in Baden ten thousand feet up." Observes Harris, "He obviously made it." "Yes," she says, "and me."

Hippy Ann Turkel (then Harris's real-life squeeze) is bedding her boyfriend when Harris bursts in on them: "Do you mind?" she whines. "First some sweaty, puffy pervert. And now—" Harris shoots back, "Which sweaty pervert?" After all, this train's crawling with 'em.

Our contaminated terrorist guzzles water out of Gardner's pet pooch's bowl and, in one of our very favorite moments, he sneezes, then hurls chunks of mucus into a bowl of rice on a kitchen countertop. Do "disaster movies" get any more demented? Though (nonstar) passengers drop like flies, our heroes trap the disease carrier (who's practically foaming at the mouth) and Strasberg asks, "You're sure it isn't measles?"

Panic (and hilarity) erupt when men in white suits seal off the entire train. "I'm not coming back to Europe—that's it!" bellows a shamelessly mugging extra. When you think things couldn't get any nuttier, Strasberg, hearing that the train is being rerouted over an unsafe bridge in concentration camp Poland, runs amok with a scalpel, sneaks off the train, gets shot dead by armed guards—only to turn up in later scenes! "I think the bullet passed through," Harris explains, to cover one of the craziest continuity gaffes in screen history. (As always, only the biggest stars survive in the fadeout—if you call that living.)

With John Phillip Law, Ingrid Thulin, Alida Valli. Produced by Lew Grade and Carlo Ponti, directed by George Pan Cosmatos. Screenplay by Tom Mankiewicz, Robert Katz, and Cosmatos. C, 129 m., V

The Concorde—Airport '79 (1979) ❤❤

Let us now consider the plight of those Hollywood powers hounded by wives who want to act in the films they make; then let us consider the roles those wives have played in the subsequent demise of a series of movies once considered "surefire" moneymakers. A coincidence—or justice? You be the judge.

Universal honcho Sidney Sheinberg showcased wife Lorraine Gary in the *Jaws* movies; as her role grew more prominent, the movies came to a screeching halt. Producer Irwin Allen gave bits in *The Poseidon Adventure* and *The Towering Inferno* to Sheila Mathews; a few years later, she was Sheila Allen—and had a substantial role in *When Time Ran Out . . .* , which would prove her husband's swan song to feature films. Monica Lewis, wife of Universal exec Jennings Lang, had small roles in *Earthquake* and *Airport '77*, but by the time of *The Concorde—Airport '79*, she hogged more screen time than co-stars Cicely Tyson, Martha Raye, Mercedes McCambridge, or Charo. But could any of them have played a jazz great quite the way Lewis did? She smiles so demurely when newscaster John Davidson gushes, "I really enjoyed your farewell concert at Carnegie Hall."

Lewis and blues-blowing Jimmie Walker are en route to "the Moscow jazz festival," and their midflight scat session has to be heard to be believed. Lewis stops suddenly and says, "Maybe I don't have it anymore." (*Maybe?*) "Does Ella still have it? Does Sinatra still have it?" Walker asks. "You're like fine wine, you get better with age—and you're going to get those Russians drunk!" Needless to say, this is the only *Airport* movie with a "story" written by (you guessed it) Lewis's husband.

Giving credit exactly where it's due, Lang thought up so many things the series needed: Robert Wagner as a mad scientist who invents an attack missile that might blow the Concorde out of the skies; George Kennedy deciding—at the speed of sound, mind you—to lean out of the Concorde's window so he can shoot at the bad guys; the unforgettable scene where first mate David Warner (who once starred in *Morgan!* as a guy who thinks he's an ape) confides to pilots Kennedy and Alain Delon, "Last night I dreamt I was chased by a giant banana."

Bibi Andersson turns up as a hooker paid by Delon to have sex with Kennedy; afterwards, she assures him: "See, you didn't forget very much." Kennedy agrees, "I guess it's kinda like swimming." She exclaims, "Just like a happy fish!" a metaphor that would haunt you long after the film is over, if it weren't immediately followed by this jaw-dropping exchange: stewardess Sylvia Kristel says to Delon and Kennedy, "You pilots are such men!" and Kennedy leers back, "They don't call it the cockpit for nothing, honey!"

With Susan Blakely, Andrea Marcovicci, Sybil Danning. Produced by Lang, directed by David Lowell Rich. Screenplay by Eric Roth, from a story by Lang, "inspired by the film based on the novel by Arthur Hailey." C, 123 m., V

Delta Force (1986) ❤

The glory part of this stinker from now-extinct Cannon Films is its first hour, a knee-slappingly funny "disaster movie" extravaganza. We meet our starry, happy travelers in the airline terminal where silver wedding anniversary couple Lainie Kazan and Joey Bishop—Jews, we are told, so unsubtly one expects the soundtrack to break into "Hava Nagila," disco-style—who befriend fellow Jews Shelley Winters and Martin Balsam, who are traveling with their daughter, Susan Strasberg, and their obnoxious little grandchild.

Once aboard the plane, it's a regular world expo of international hams: We get "disaster movie" veteran George Kennedy, playing a Catholic priest from Chicago, traveling with two nonstar nuns, plus German art-film star Hannah Schygulla on hand as the stewardess and, faster than you can say "Airport '86," along comes Robert Forster, thickly covered in Mideast terrorist makeup, bellowing, "I'm a commander in the New World Revolution. You will take orders from no one but me or I will blow up this airplane!" The terrorists want their hostages' jewelry, which is all the cast need to start upstaging each other in desperate hopes of Oscar nominations that were not to be. "Harry, Harry, my ring—it's Hebrew!" Kazan says, mugging shamelessly. Replies Bishop, already weeping, "One thing is certain: we'll always remember our silver wedding anniversary."

The ham gets sliced thicker still when the terrorists demand that Schygulla collect and separate "the Jewish passports." Schygulla, free at last from the understatement required of her by such directors as Rainer Werner Fassbinder, explodes, "No! Not me! Don't you see I'm German?" Forster growls, "What does that mean?" She hisses, "The selections! The Nazis! The death camps! I won't do it!" Not about to be outdone, Winters sputters, "This c-c-c-can't be happening. N-n-n-not again!" while hubby Martin Balsam tries to cover his concentration camp tattoo.

Meanwhile, back in the Pentagon, General Robert Vaughn (fresh from his Swedish Formula hair restorer TV commercials) announces, "Israel is America's best friend in the Middle East!" and dispatches a crack team of testosterone boys that includes Arab-bashing Colonel Lee Marvin and elite Delta Force captain Chuck Norris to rescue our stars from the Beirut airport.

The sweaty, nasty American-hating terrorists turn loose half the passengers—"Thank God the women are safe," declares a mugging Bo Svenson—but corral the men to a village hideaway.

Joey Bishop, staring out a window at war-torn Beirut but obviously reminiscing about his Rat Pack days with Frankie, Dean, and Sammy, muses, "It was the Las Vegas of the Middle East. Beirut was beeyoo-tee-ful then. Beeeyooo-tee-ful."

The rest of the flick, a flag-waving, wish-fulfilling bone-cruncher about how, despite overwhelming evidence to the contrary, we really kicked butt in the Middle East, is as simplistic and jingoistic as one would expect, but nowhere near as much fun as the first half.

Produced and directed by Menahem Golan. Screenplay by Golan and James Bruner. C, 129 m., V

Earthquake (1974) ❤ ❤ ❤

Ava Gardner makes her entrance in this movie—under a rumpled wig, wearing a negligee that can't hope to disguise her overweight figure, and boozily roaring the very first line of dialogue, "Goddamn it!"—as if she's ready to play Vera Charles in a bus-and-truck touring company of *Mame*. No such luck, however, for the onetime pinup girl has come further down than that, cast here as the neglected wife of cheating hubby Charlton Heston and also the daughter of magnate Lorne Greene. This must be the wildest mismatch of performers playing parent and child in film history: Greene is only seven years older than Gardner—and he looks seven years younger. (In *Harlow*, Angela Lansbury was only six years older than Carroll Baker, but Lansbury could act, so who knew?)

"If it wasn't 7:30 in the morning," Gardner slurs, "I'd have a drink." Instead, she tries to commit suicide—anything to get out of this picture—but is interrupted by an earthquake tremor. Heston hurries to see Genevieve Bujold, a widowed extra, and this dialogue in a clinch is supposed to establish that they are star-crossed lovers: "Don't worry, I'm not a nympho," she assures him. "Mind you, I'm not Mary Poppins either." Heston replies, "I'm not Billy Graham exactly, but I'm no satyr."

At a neighborhood bar, local drunk Walter Matthau sits up from time to time to call out, apropos of nothing, "Spiro T. Agnew," "Peter Fonda," "Bobby Riggs," like a player in an unseen game of Trivial Pursuit. When the Big One finally hits, we're treated to such cheapo special effects as a distortion lens trying to make a building appear to be swaying, the tried-and-true "shaking the camera" so it'll look like the ground is rumbling, and (the film's riotous low point) some red paint splattering on the camera lens so we'll understand that some extras are *finito*.

Though all of L.A. has been totaled, such cast members as Victoria Principal, George Kennedy, Marjoe Gortner, and Richard Roundtree keep bumping into each other as if the city were the size of, well, the Universal back lot. Sadly, as is often the case in real life, some people help others (Monica Lewis nobly contributes her pantyhose to one survival effort) while others take advantage (Principal is caught, redhanded, in the act of looting doughnuts).

As if things aren't bad enough, the Hollywood reservoir dam gives way—and Gardner, who was merely washed up when the film started, is washed away when it's over. For sheer swill thrills, watching this flick on video can't quite compare with having seen it at the Chinese Theatre in Hollywood, which is located directly in the area just below that dam, but even without that anxiety to help induce nervous yucks, *Earthquake* registers a 7.0 on the Richter Scale of bellylaughs.

Produced and directed by Mark Robson. Screenplay by George Fox and Mario Puzo. C, 129 m., V, L

The Poseidon Adventure (1972) ❤❤❤❤

Here is the "disaster movie" touchstone, a laughathon that for years sent diehards rushing out to see each new *Meteor* or *Hindenburg* in hopes that it might deliver the kind of "so-bad-it's-good" goods that this gem does.

On New Year's Eve, a wave flip-flops an ocean liner upsy-daisy, and the Not-Quite-All-Stars aboard must climb "up" through the ship before it sinks. They're led by "renegade" preacher Gene Hackman, doing a perfect impersonation of man-of-action blowhard Charlton Heston. The cast starts their escape by climbing a Christmas tree (don't ask), which allows us to watch two Oscar-winning pros like Hackman and Shelley Winters honing their "craft": When the fat Winters gets stuck, Hackman uses his meaty paw to give her maxi-buttocks a hefty Method shove.

Red Buttons finds ship thrush Carol Lynley sobbing over her brother's body, and urges her to come along. "Your brother's dead," Buttons explains, which results in one of the great non sequiturs in Bad Movie history—Lynley asks, "Did you like his music?" The movie is filled with visual non sequiturs, too: When Hackman says Pamela Sue Martin can't crawl around the ship in her evening gown, she drops the skirt of her formal to reveal that she's wearing color-coordinated hot pants underneath.

These unexpected twists of dialogue, costuming, and plot reach a hard-to-match zenith in the peerless performance of Winters. Overacting in a gray wig that makes her resemble Miss Piggy's grandmother, Winters performs the most crazed of the film's many madcap surprises. When Hackman is trapped underwater, Winters waddles forward to exclaim, "I was the underwater swimming champ of New York for three years running. Swimming through corridors, and up and down stairwells—I'm the only one here trained to do things like that!" (Honorable mention must be awarded to Stella Stevens, who snaps, "Will you shut up?")—Winters then dives in and saves Hackman, while doing an underwater ballet that is unparalleled in Bad Movie madness: her dress floats up over her head, showing off Winters's mind-bending pantyline and buns.

There is (natch) still more: Winters rises out of the water in time to die of a heart attack, but not before she utters the very words that are on the tip of your tongue: "Enough is enough." However, there's no such thing as "enough" in a movie as over-wrought as this one, which Hackman demonstrates in his screaming match with God (who remains, inexplicably, off-camera): "What more do you want of us? How much more blood? How many more lives?" Did Hackman guess that we'd be rooting for just one more death—his? Happily, we get our wish, and then— oh, seven years later—the boat sinks. (We hope to get around to *Beyond the Poseidon Adventure* in *Bad Movies We Love, Part 3*.)

With Ernest Borgnine, Jack Albertson, Roddy McDowall, Leslie Nielsen. Produced by Irwin Allen, directed by Ronald Neame.

Screenplay by Stirling Silliphant and Wendell Mayes, from the Paul Gallico novel. C, 117 m., V, L

The Swarm (1978) ❤

Arguably the zaniest of all "disaster movies," the threat here isn't fire, flood, sinking ships, or falling planes. It's bees—"African killer bees," to be exact—who can't be tricked into eating "poison pellets." Why not? We're told "they seem to sense it's something that will kill them," an instinct for survival clearly not shared by the film's stars when they read the movie's script. (How else to explain Katharine Ross turning down *Airport*, but agreeing to be in this? Coming off, back then, a formidable one-two punch— *The Graduate* and *Butch Cassidy and the Sundance Kid*—Ross chose unwisely, inevitably hurtling down the Hollywood Slip 'n' Slide to wind up here—indisputably rock bottom.)

This is that rare "disaster" flick to be treasured because most of the hammy stars—from Olivia de Havilland, Henry Fonda, and Jose Ferrer to Richard Chamberlain, Fred MacMurray, and Ben Johnson—get offed. (But not Lee Grant or Patty Duke Astin, presumably because if your career has survived *Valley of the Dolls*, you can survive anything.) The dead are the lucky ones, for when the bees sting but don't kill, survivors wind up hallucinating giant bees, as if they're trapped inside a cheesy '50s drive-in sci-fi movie (which they are). Never mind that this conflicts with what noted immunologist Fonda has told us, that the bees' poison has "the highest toxic content I've ever found, even more virulent than the venom of the Australian brown box jellyfish." (You can practically hear producer/director Irwin Allen salivating, "If *The Swarm*'s a hit, there's my next picture—*The Blobbies!*") When the bees get up a full head of steam, they can derail speeding trains, knock helicopters out of the sky, and explode a nuclear power plant.

Finally, noted entomologist Michael Caine realizes it's a man-made "sonic alarm system" that's driving the bees to destroy, for the sound's "an exact duplicate of the duet between the Queen bee and the young Queen bee challenging her domain." (Ah, yes—well, now—that explains everything . . . except, perhaps, General Richard Widmark's response: "Okay, I'm convinced!")

Caine orders up a massive oil spill on the waters of the Gulf, then lures the bees out there, and torches them. The movie ends with a reassuring title card—"The African killer bee portrayed in this film bears absolutely no relationship to the industrious, hard-working American honey bee to which we are indebted for pollinating vital crops that feed our nation"—put there at the last minute, we'd guess, to keep angry, politically correct American honey bees from staging buzz-ins outside the theaters.

Produced and directed by Allen. Screenplay by Stirling Silliphant, from Arthur Herzog's novel. C, 116 m., V, L

The Towering Inferno (1974) ❤ ❤ ❤ ❤

Faye Dunaway looks so ravishing in this film, you'll probably want her dieting tips, and even if you don't, she offers them up in her first scene anyway. Pulling lover Paul Newman into the bedroom adjacent to his office, she pants, "It's my lunch hour," and he quips, "I'm not a cheeseburger, you know." Dunaway says "You're better—all protein, no bread. All I need to go with you is about eight glasses of water." Newman's wrong, of course—he is too a cheeseburger, and so is everyone else in this all-star BBQ, a film that makes us wonder, Who will escape medium rare, who will only get charbroiled, and who's gonna get burned to a crisp?

Unbelievably, it took two studios, Warner Bros. and 20th Century-Fox, plus two novels and two powerhouse stars to assemble this fireball hoot, the most overproduced glossy swill in "disaster movie" history. When Newman and Steve McQueen couldn't come to terms over billing and salary, they didn't team for *Butch Cassidy and the Sundance Kid* but decided instead to join forces here as, respectively, the architect and the fireman who try to rescue the cast from a party atop the world's tallest burning building. Before the wienie roast begins, an MC exclaims as the guests arrive, "The list of luminaries reads like a Who's Who," but, in fact, it reads more like a list of Who Used to Co-

Star with Who: Newman and Robert Wagner (*Harper*); Jennifer Jones and William Holden (*Love Is a Many Splendored Thing*); Holden and Dunaway (*Network*); Dunaway and Richard Chamberlain (TV's *The Woman I Love*); and so on.

Every star's brush with death illustrates a different lesson about careers in Hollywood: When Susan Flannery smells smoke and asks Wagner "Did you leave a cigarette burning?" we learn that actors with the stupidest dialogue are the first to go; then, when Jones kicks off her heels and does an ungainly shimmy down a scaffolding in a blown-out stairwell, we learn that winning an Oscar doesn't guarantee dignified roles in later years. McQueen teaches us his Golden Rule, "Anything for a buck," as he performs the movie's goofiest stunt: suspended midair from a helicopter, he flies over to the glass elevator that's hanging by a thread and airlifts it up and off the building, all the while holding a dangling fellow fireman with his other free hand.

But it's Holden who gets off the film's most giggly, out-and-out ridiculous line of dialogue, and he's just the aged ham to do it justice. Told by McQueen that the cast is being burned alive, and that his party guests must be evacuated at once, Holden glowers and responds, deadpan, "I think you're overreacting."

With Fred Astaire, Susan Blakely, O. J. Simpson, Robert Vaughn, Sheila Mathews. Produced by Irwin Allen, directed by John Guillermin. Screenplay by Stirling Silliphant, from the novels *The Tower* by Richard Martin Stern and *The Glass Inferno* by Thomas N. Scortia and Frank M. Robinson. C, 165 m., V, L

When Time Ran Out . . . (1980) ❤

Irwin Allen created a veritable "Who Used to Be Who" of '70s trash cinema with his final masterwork, starring players from other disaster epics: *The Towering Inferno*'s Paul Newman, William Holden, and Sheila Allen; *The Poseidon Adventure*'s Red Buttons and Ernest Borgnine; *Airport*'s Jacqueline Bisset; *Beyond the Poseidon Adventure*'s Veronica Hamel; and, for icing, such Bad Movie vets as *Madame X*'s Burgess Meredith and *The Greek Tycoon*'s James Franciscus and Edward Albert.

On a lush island where Holden has built a new resort, Bisset's a career gal torn between old-enough-to-be-her-father Newman and old-enough-to-be-her-grandfather Holden. When Newman asks, "Are you putting him out to pasture, or you going to race us both?" she briskly sidesteps the remark with perky, businesswoman dialogue like "I'd like to show you the volcano campaign."

Things, as they say, start heating up when native Franciscus breaks the law of the island's gods by fooling around with native Barbara Carrera, who's been "sworn since childhood" to native Albert. Franciscus and Newman descend into the island's long-dormant volcano—in a glass-bottom elevator!—and it roars to life, bouncing the box against the volcano walls. (To make sure we grasp that they're in trouble, we're shown closeups of a big button flashing "MALFUNCTION" and Franciscus yells, "Hit the heat shields!")

Narrowly escaping death, Newman observes, "This thing's a powder keg," but instead of leaving the island pronto, picnics with Bisset. "I don't need wine," she coos. "You get me drunk." In a moment we've long dreamt of (but never thought we'd actually see) when these two lovers kiss, the volcano blows its top. Back at the resort, Bisset tells everyone, "The lava is coming directly toward the hotel," in a tone of voice that indicates "It's in my contract to say this line, but they haven't paid me enough to mean it." Guests like retired circus aerialists Meredith and Valentina Cortesa panic: "What shall we do, darling?" she worries. "My darling," he soothes her, "you have lived through the collapse of burlesque and vaudeville . . . twice!" That's hardly preparation for this, the collapse of "disaster movies," with fantastically tacky special effects: the volcano belches fireballs, there's a tidal wave, and—most terrifying of all—in the hotel lobby, death by a falling tiki.

Newman leads a few hardy co-stars on a hike to safety, which brings them to the requisite, rickety-wooden-suspension-bridge-across-a-river-of-molten-lava finale. When producer Allen's wife, playing a hefty-sized madam, crosses the shaky bridge, she overacts so badly that it angers the island's gods, and they claim the lives of both her boyfriend Pat Morita and one of her working girls, but you can bet that she lives. This so angered the "disaster movie" gods that she and her husband were never seen on the big screen again.

Produced by Allen, directed by James Goldstone. Screenplay by Carl Foreman and Stirling Silliphant, based on the novel *The Day the World Ended* by Gordon Thomas and Max Morgan Witts. C, 121 m., V

CHAPTER 16

The *Other* Kind
of "Disaster Movies"

Check out our previous chapter for earthquakes, ocean liners on their way to the bottom of the sea, runamok airplanes, and skyscrapers going up in flames. Here's the place to come for earth-shaking overacting, for mighty reputations on their way to the bottom of the sea, for rampaging egos, and major careers going up in smoke. Welcome to the dizzying world of grand-scale, full-tilt career calamity: you'll find not even one box office moneymaker here, just some of the ripest, most rip-roaring entertainment that proves, once and for all, that the Bad Movie Gods Must Be Crazy.

Bluebeard (1972) ❤ ❤

Director Edward Dmytryk, in his autobiography, put the blame for this all-star fiasco squarely on Richard Burton's daily drinking, but we suspect otherwise: Anyone trying to act the script that Dmytryk co-authored needed a stiff drink, and more than a few, if expected to perform opposite Joey Heatherton. Despite the film's period setting, Heatherton is not only wearing the shag hairdo of the day and white lipstick left over from the '60s, but she also earns the singular distinction of being Burton's worst-ever co-star (in a career that includes Joan Collins, Linda Evans, and in this very film, Raquel Welch). Though *Bluebeard* is crammed with "international" starlets who didn't cut it as stars —Virna Lisi, Sybil Danning, Nathalie Delon, Marilu Tolo, Agnostino Belli, Karin Schubert—Heatherton is worse than all of them rolled into one. Her misguided self-assurance that she's Burton's equal proves true, but not the way Heatherton intended, as she acts her way into Bad Movie heaven.

She tells Burton, about being a showgirl, "The life is dull and fascinating at the same time." (In other words, it's just like this movie.) After they've wed, Burton takes photos of Heatherton bare underneath a revealing black lace bodysuit—just the outfit for wandering through the mansion to find a servant brushing the hair of Burton's long-dead mother. "It will not happen again," Burton intones. "Mother's body has been put back in the crypt."

Heatherton stops the movie cold with the scene in which she talks directly into the camera: "So I'm not as happy as I should be. You wanna know why? My marriage . . . okay, on my wedding night, I was too sleepy. Then came the shock, my nervous breakdown, and so, we still haven't been in bed together. Do you understand?" This is before she finds the deep freeze containing the corpses of Burton's other co-stars.

As Heatherton serves him Jell-O, Burton explains why he had to do 'em all in (and the terrible acting in the flashbacks convinces us). Addlebrained Lisi sings songs like "You're Driving Me Crazy" a capella till we're rooting for Burton to off her. Delon proffers one of her bare breasts and asks Burton, "Like it? Want to kiss it? Its name is Jasmine. But I can't let you—because Cyclamen will get jealous." Former nun Welch confesses to Burton, "I must tell you everything," and then names every man she ever slept with. Schubert nags Burton, "I'm fed up with being an undeflowered wife!"

Heatherton, having heard all and knowing she's next, snaps. "You're a monster! Let me get this off my chest and die happy," she says, racing toward one of our all-time favorite lines: "*I spit on you, darling.*" Burton threatens her—"I shall give you to my dogs!"—blissfully unaware that his career had gone to the dogs long before hers.

Produced by Alexander Salkind, directed by Dmytryk. Original story and screenplay by Ennio De Concino, Maria Pia Fusco, and Dmytryk. "The furs are creations of Sergio Soldan Gepova."
C, 125 m., V

The Bride (1985) ❤ ❤

The history of rock, from Elvis to Madonna, is a l-o-n-g parade
of singers certain they have a date with destiny—movie stardom—but don't. Sting, ludicrously self-enamored and hammy,
is Dr. Frankenstein in this remake of *The Bride of Frankenstein*,
material which was handled more deliberately wittily fifty years
ago.

On a stormy night in a lab, Sting twirls dials and pulls switches
while his assistant, Quentin Crisp, purses his lips as they try to
animate a mate for monster Clancy Brown who, in chains, yells,
"For me! For me!" Crisp, in his only line, snaps in reply, "Don't
be impetuous!"

Things run horribly amok, so Sting and Crisp think their new
female creation is dead—but no, she only seems that way because
she's played by Jennifer Beals, the media-created "star" of
Flashdance. Beals bats her mascaraed lashes—which, for her, is
positively animated—to signify she has come to life, then spurns
Brown, who brings down the lab and shuffles off into the stormy
night. Before you can say "Pygmalion," Sting, all Byronic and
foppish, is staring at his comely creation, and muttering, "She
might be made into anything." Tomorrow's Malcolm McDowell
today, Sting flares, "I might make the new woman . . . a woman
equal to ourselves!" Exactly.

Beals is soon walking stark naked around the castle, to the
horror of maid Geraldine Page, who teaches her manners while
pulling vinegary faces, undoubtedly because Sting is leaving so
little scenery for her to chew. Beals becomes the belle of the ball
thrown by countess Veruschka, at which she and Cary Elwes eye
each other—till Beals sees a kitty and lets fly with mad screech-
ing. ("You never told me about cats," she explains to Sting. "I
thought it was a tiny lion.")

Meanwhile, her soulmate, Frankenstein's monster, has been
befriended by little David Rappaport, with whom he becomes a
stellar circus attraction, but keeps longing for Beals and she,
unknowingly, for him. When Rappaport dies, Brown tells Beals
he's going far away and she says, "Like the Congo, you mean?
Or like America?" He gives her a memento, Rappaport's souvenir

medallion of Venice, where he dreamed of going. Now Beals spits at Sting, "I have a life of my own—you didn't create me!" Replies Sting, "As a matter of fact, I did. I sewed you together out of corpses. And I can uncreate you, too."

Finally, overcome with lust, Sting chases Beals through the castle and leaps on her. You'll cheer when the monster hurls Sting to his death on the roof below, but don't miss the finale in which Beals rides a gondola in Venice, for it's cut in such an odd way that we think Brown at one time might have been shown riding with her. What a finish that would have made.

Produced by Victor Drai, directed by Franc Roddam. Screenplay by Lloyd Fonvielle. Music by Maurice Jarre. "Hair Consultant, Leonard of London." C, 118 m., V, L

The Chase (1966) ❤

A flock of Hollywood high-fliers sure scorched their wings with this hugely expensive, highly touted, laughable dud. Directing a screenplay by Lillian Hellman, no less, Arthur Penn was apparently unable to exert any control over his costly cast, which includes Marlon Brando with an incomprehensible accent as the Texas sheriff tracking down escaped con Robert Redford, Jane Fonda as the bartender's trampy stepdaughter, Janice Rule as the trampy wife of bank clerk Robert Duvall, Martha Hyer as the trampy wife of Richard Bradford, and a star-filled, trampy Texas town of racists, rednecks, Bible-thumpers, and crackers including Angie Dickinson, E. G. Marshall, Miriam Hopkins, Henry Hull, Diana Hyland, and even gnomish songwriter Paul Williams. Since this is a movie with nothing much happening—but plenty on its mind—we're treated to a five-course BBQ of bad Southern drawls, ludicrously overproduced party and riot scenes, and more hams per square inch than you'd find at a county fair.

Things heat up over on the po' side of town, where miserably married Duvall and Rule are a-chewin' the scenery while hosting a drunken, disorderly, distinctly *Who's Afraid of Virginia Woolf*-ish bash. "All you need to come to my party is a pistol, and you've got one," drawls Rule, sizing up sheriff Brando, who struts in to broadcast the news about homeboy Redford's jailbreak. Unlike every other able-bodied man in town, Brando puts her off, quipping, "With all the pistols you got there, ma'am, I don't believe there'd be room for mine." Later, drunken Hyer—watching Rule perform a wild shimmy with her hubby—bellows, "I guess you two are the sexual revolution all by yourselves."

Meanwhile, Redford's woman, Fonda, is shacked up with James Fox, the spineless rich boy who's loved her for years but wouldn't dare defy his tycoon father to marry a hussy from the wrong side of the tracks. But since all these lovers seem to want to do is gab about scene-stealer Redford, when Fox confesses to Fonda, "I love him, too," we don't doubt it for an instant. (Later, when they find fugitive Redford and he doesn't even make a pass at Fonda, explaining, "Jail took things like that away from me," he wins Fox's undivided attention.)

Legendarily temperamental screen queen Miriam Hopkins storms on as Redford's ma and, seeing that there's no director around to curb her, indulges in titanic overacting with Brando. "Liar! Liar! Liar!" she keeps screaming while he screams back, "Shut up, you damn crazy woman!"

It all ends with a mind-bogglingly inappropriate restaging of the assassination of Lee Harvey Oswald, as Redford gets shot by a crazy. Producer Sam Spiegel, as famed for his yachts as his films, said this movie was about "the consequences of affluence." We'd say it's more about the consequences of affluent moviemakers' self-delusions.

Produced by Spiegel, directed by Penn. Screenplay by Hellman, from Horton Foote's novel and play. C, 138 m., V, L

Exorcist II: The Heretic (1977) ♥♥♥♥

"You realize what you're up against . . . eeeevil," Richard Burton warns Louise Fletcher, the psychologist assigned to debug demonically possessed Linda Blair. "Evil is a spiritual being," Burton adds, "alive and living, perverted and perverting, weaving its way insidiously into the very fabric of life!"

Assigned by Cardinal Paul Henreid to investigate the death of exorcist priest Max von Sydow, Burton is forever screaming to Fletcher that Blair, four years after she vomited pea soup and levitated in her bed, only appears to now be a boringly normal Pia Zadora lookalike. When Fletcher nearly suffers a coronary after hooking up Blair and herself to a harebrained-looking gizmo that permits the doctor to relive old footage from the first *Exorcist*, Burton bellows, "Your research has proven that there's an ancient demon locked within her! We must help her!" But there's no help once the hilarity erupts when director John Boorman steers this calamitous, head-scratching sequel to one of the all-time box-office shockers into goofball metaphysics.

"I am Pazuzu," growls a possessed little African boy, "king of the evil spirits of the air!" In one of the movie's many loony highs, Burton is shown scaling the heights of an ancient city in search of the kid, when suddenly the director jump-cuts to closeups of Blair, beaming, tap-dancing, and singing "Lullaby of Broadway." Now, *that's* scary. Later, Burton hooks up with helicopter pilot Ned Beatty (the '70s John Goodman) who flies him to "a mud city with golden walls" that he's dreamed about. "I've flown this route before," Burton murmurs, mystic-eyed to Beatty, "on the wings of a demon."

After what seems like hours of intercutting between Burton and Blair, both muttering, to the point of rendering us giddy with mirth, "Cacumo . . . Cacumo," Burton tracks down the possessed black boy to equatorial Africa, where he has grown into James Earl Jones, who studies locusts for a living and tells Burton that "good and evil are struggling within" Blair. (Quite a surprise.) Suddenly, Burton, too, becomes possessed, able to make a plane carrying Fletcher and Kitty Winn, Blair's very odd nanny, take a nosedive—but alas, not crash.

Hang onto your sides when everyone converges on the Georgetown house that Blair and her actress mom Ellen Burstyn lived in back in the first flick, because the whole rollicking mess turns into an Irwin Allen movie, what with an attack by locusts, raging fire, and an earthquake, while Burton strangles and punches Blair with utter delight, ending in hasty credits underscored by a disco song. Whatever possessed them?

There are apparently two versions of this movie, one of the all-time colossal flops, but to date, no one has asked Boorman to restore the film with a "Director's Cut."

Produced (with Richard Lederer) and directed by Boorman. Screenplay by William Goodhart. C, 117 m., V

Eyes of Laura Mars (1978) ❤ ❤ ❤

"I've never been wrong," sings Barbra Streisand in the opening line of the theme song for this comically trendy, pretentious slasher movie about a photographer famous for sexy, brutal, Helmut Newtonesque images who "sees" violent visions of the murders of her associates before they actually happen.

We'd say Streisand's made plenty of questionable career moves, but it didn't take a clairvoyant to see that she was right to turn down the lead in this one, produced by her then-boyfriend, Jon Peters. Instead, wide-eyed, overwrought Faye Dunaway shreds the scenery with detective Tommy Lee Jones as they slog their way through the "mystery" (which ought to be obvious to anyone in this couple's first scene together) and, absurdly, fall in love, all the while swirled in the world of high fashion, dated disco, and hilarious "improvisational" scenes.

When kinky models Darlanne Fluegel and Lisa Taylor get stabbed in the eyes, Jones suspects that Dunaway is the killer. "You think," Dunaway asks him, "I committed the murders and then recreated them in photographs? I don't buy it!" Well, neither will you, but stay aboard for Dunaway wondering, "Am I hallucinating all of this?" when, after the double wake, she—who we've seen photographed by hungry press through the entire movie— suddenly covers her face with her black bag and dives into a limo. Now, that's the kind of acting "choice" that separates Bad Actors from Bad Actors We Love.

But you'll be sure you're hallucinating in the scene where Jones and a distraught Dunaway walk through the woods, pacing madly, uttering inanities about how, in the midst of all this tragedy, they can't stop thinking about each other, till Dunaway suddenly blurts out, "I'm completely out of control!" and director Irwin Kershner doesn't yell, "Cut!" but instead lets Jones confess, "I know. Me too!"—then kiss her.

Later, after they make love, Dunaway marvels, "To live your whole life without someone and be doing more or less okay and then, suddenly, you find them." When Jones corrects her, "You recognize them," she continues, "You recognize them and you know without them . . . ," and he finishes her sentence: "It's terrifying."

Lots more terrifying than the none-too-surprising conclusion when Dunaway, who's been assured by Jones that the stalker's dead, must go one on one with the maniac. You'll be on the edge of your seat—with mirth.

With Raul Julia and Brad Dourif (as two very hammy red herrings). Produced by Peters, directed by Kershner. Screenplay by John Carpenter and David Zelag Goodman, from a story by Carpenter.

Not surprisingly, Dunaway's photographs were shot by Helmut Newton. C, 104 m., V, L

Fear City (1984) ❤ ❤

"I can't even look at 'em anymore!" says Manhattan bar owner Michael V. Gazzo about the overexposed breasts of Melanie Griffith who, playing a bisexual stripper and junkie, is busily bumping and grinding out her heart for a smoky club full of losers. Pretty as they are, we're tired of looking at 'em too, just as we've OD'd on the sight of Tom Berenger's chiseled pecs, but that doesn't stop either of them—or such fellow burlesque queens manqué as Griffith's lover, Rae Dawn Chong—from whipping 'em out whenever the action flags in this slasher movie about a scissor-wielding sicko who's attacking the stable of club girls managed by "agents" Berenger, Jack Scalia, and their rival, former "Ed Sullivan Show" comic Jan Murray.

Berenger plays Griffith's ex, a prize-fighter haunted by slo-mo *Raging Bull* ripoff flashbacks, whom homicide cop Billy Dee Williams loves to hassle. Williams (sporting a Reverend Al Sharpton bouffant) hilariously spits out his dialogue as if he learned acting from old Kirk Douglas flicks: "There's a thin line greaseballs tread!" After Chong is killed on one of those deserted New York subway platforms so beloved by directors of Bad Movies like this, Griffith locks herself in her dressing room and, out of respect, refuses to peel. Berenger arrives, soothes her and—show biz trouper that she is—Griffith goes on stage for an eye-poppingly slutty strip. You can't help thinking, "What a pro."

Later, she and Berenger rekindle their passion. She: "You should have talked to me more." He: "Sometimes, I can't find the right words." She: "Sometimes, there aren't any." Then, scrunching up her face in torment, Griffith cries, "Shit." Meanwhile, strippers are dropping like flies, forcing Gazzo to book for his overweight, middle-aged club patrons an overweight, middle-aged bimbo of whom Gazzo says, "She couldn't give a hard-on to a rapist."

Mobster Rossano Brazzi, a universe away from his Latin lover days in *Three Coins in the Fountain* and *Rome Adventure*, offers his help to Berenger, who says about the killer, "I want him so bad, I can taste his blood in my mouth!" The tension makes Williams snap, too. After firing a small arsenal into a target, he tells his sergeant—delivering one of director Abel Ferrara's half-baked messages about the Decline of Western Civilization—"Just think of it this way—we're the only thing between that bastard and innocent people."

But everyone here is guilty—of Bad Acting: Griffith crawls back alleys to score heroin, Berenger stalks the streets, and the killer is seen practicing martial arts in the nude (is there any other way?). The *L.A. Times* called this "The best thriller since *The Terminator*," and since there's a discrepancy about the film's running time (on the video box, it's 93 minutes, in video guides, it's 96), we demand a fully restored "Director's Cut"—now.

Produced by Bruce Cohn Curtis, directed by Ferrara. Screenplay by Nicholas St. John. "Hair stylist to Mr. Williams, Bruce Johnson." C, 96 m., V

52 Pick-Up (1986) ❤

This Elmore Leonard novel got trashed twice in Bad Movie versions, but how could the merely bad *The Ambassador* (made in 1984 with Robert Mitchum, Ellen Burstyn, and Rock Hudson) compete with this transcendentally bad version (filmed two years later by the same company!) starring Roy Scheider, Ann-

Margret, Vanity, John Glover, Clarence Williams III, Doug McClure, and the future Mrs. John Travolta, Kelly Preston?

Scheider's a steel magnate whose wife, Ann-Margret, has just been asked to run for city councilperson. Trouble is, Scheider's being squeezed by porn maven Glover for $100,000 in exchange for those incriminating videotapes of him frolicking with mistress Preston. Think it's easy being one of those "Live Nude Model" babes? "I'm really tired of my life," Preston confesses to fellow nude playmate Vanity. When Scheider turns over the "money," the bag's stuffed with newspapers and a note: "Bag your ass." In retaliation, Glover kidnaps Scheider, straps him to a chair, and subjects him to a "snuff" video starring nude Preston, whom they slaughter on camera. (Considering what comes next, she's the lucky one.)

Scheider—emoting in the teeth-clenching, eye-popping style beloved by fans of Kirk and Michael Douglas—tracks down Vanity and pays her for a "private session" where she notes, "You're after something—and it ain't my pussy, is it?" He offers her $500 and she hoots, "I make that in five minutes with shoe clerks," but tips him off, anyway, to Glover's whereabouts. Scheider shows Glover his tax records and offers the only money he's got—$52,000—while Williams smothers stoolpigeon Vanity.

Reaffirming her permanent standing in Bad Movie nirvana, Ann-Margret wails, when she finds Scheider fooling around with his prized car, "We should be at a police station and here you are changing your plugs! If you were doing that three months ago instead of screwing around, we wouldn't be in this mess. I hope you know what you can do with those plugs when you get 'em out!" When Williams barges into their home, A-M bops him with a flashlight, then engages him in conversation that turns him against Glover. "Motherfucker busts in your house," grunts Williams, "you always serve him drinks?"

Once he's gone, Scheider comments on the Decay of Modern Life: "One damn move and these animals rush in." Don't miss the big porn party where Glover films bare-breasted women while Williams stalks him as if he had watched *I Walked With a Zombie* too often. Anyway, Glover swipes A-M and shoots her up with heroin, but vengeance is Scheider's when he traps Glover in his Jag to the strains of a flag-waving march! Luckily, the producers are less active in the business than they once were or they'd probably shoot this one a third time with, oh, say, Steven Seagal, Kelly LeBrock, and Danny Aiello.

Produced by Menahem Golan and Yoram Globus, directed by John Frankenheimer. Screenplay by Leonard and John Steppling, from Leonard's novel. C, 114 m., V, L

Hanover Street (1979) ❤

It's not immediately apparent whether this is actually a Bad Movie We Love or just a plain old Bad Movie patched together with John Barry's theme, the likes of which—either for insistent romanticism or for constant repetition—hasn't been heard since the year in which the film is set, 1943. However, one hour into *Hanover Street*, we're treated to what is arguably the zaniest plot twist in Bad Movie history, and it becomes clear why fans claim this is indeed a Bad Movie To Really Love.

Till then, the flick boasts two seemingly unrelated, utterly improbable, giggle-inducing storylines. One is the World War II saga of flyman Harrison Ford's achingly overwritten love affair with married Brit nurse Lesley-Anne Down, who bleats, "I never knew it could be like this," while Ford pants, "I don't even know your last name." The other is the tale of Down's stiff-upper-lip intelligence-officer husband, Christopher Plummer, who's having a devil of a time training would-be spies to stand up under the strain of passing as Nazi soldiers when they cross onto German-occupied territory. A very bad voice-double is used to convince us that Plummer can issue torrents of verbal abuse in German to trainees, making it seem as if Plummer has been possessed.

Then out of the blue, and with no explanation whatsoever, Ford is recruited to fly a special mission to drop a spy instead of the usual bombs, and yes, at the very last second, Plummer substitutes himself for the scheduled spy (for, as he has demonstrated in many Bad Movies We Love, he's as destructive as any bomb). When the plane's shot down, Plummer (in full Nazi drag) and Ford (in standard U.S. warwear) team up together, neither of them knowing they love the same woman (who, by the way, has no idea where either fellow is). The movie suddenly tries to become a thriller, as if there could possibly be any doubt about the outcome: Plummer has been a stalwart enemy of Nazis as far back as *The Sound of Music* and Ford is, well, *Indiana Jones*. They're caught, and about to be shot, by a French milkmaid resistance member when Harrison blurts, "Betty Grable, Hershey bar, Yankee Stadium, hello Joe." Guess her name must be Joe, for this ruse works and she helps them escape. It's only the beginning of the utter lunacy, for among the highlights of the delirium that follows are Ford being passed off as a mute Nazi, Plummer advising Ford about his love life ("When we get back, go to her, hold her, and never let her go. That's what I'm going to do"), and later still, when Plummer is hanging off a broken suspension bridge, his begging Ford: "Back in London, please look up my wife."

With Patsy Kensit (as Down's precocious daughter), Richard Masur, Michael Sacks, Alec McCowen. Produced by Paul N. Lazarus III, directed by Peter Hyams. Screenplay by Hyams. C, 109 m., V, L

Jet Pilot (1957) ❤ ❤

For reasons known only to him, bosom-obsessed movie meddler Howard Hughes spent seven years and countless zillions to tinker and re-tinker with Josef von Sternberg's supremely warped *Ninotchka*esque howler. Intended as a sexy airborne spectacle to rival *Hell's Angels*, it instead ranks as the most haywire film ever made (at least, in part) by a great director.

The Cold War–era hilarity erupts when American pilots intercept a Russian jet bound from Siberia, out of which pops spectacular Janet Leigh, who, when she removes her helmet and tosses back her hair, evokes these cries from three pilots: "A woman!" "A lady!" "A dame!" With Commie-basher John Wayne on hand to interrogate her, Leigh—who speaks perfect, unaccented English—offers no resistance when Wayne insists on searching her, zippering-off her flight suit until she displays her incomparable charms in a turtleneck, and jets on the soundtrack shriek a wolf-whistle.

"I'm a jet man, not a gigolo," Wayne barks when General Jay

C. Flippen orders him to romance Leigh for state secrets. But, soon, after the two have flown their separate jets in very close formation (suggesting an airborne Fred and Ginger dance number), Wayne calls her his "silly Siberian cupcake," and kisses her, which prompts her cool response, "I believe in looking at merchandise before I buy it."

They fly to Palm Springs, where he takes her to a bra and swimsuit shop and observes, "That's one thing we have in common with the Soviets: we both believe in uplifting the masses," dropping his jaw and half-closing his eyes to signal what a cool breeze he thinks he is. Later, Leigh says, "One minute, I want to kill you, next minute, I want to kiss you and kiss you and kiss you," and, after a night of dancing and cocktails, things grow serious when she learns she's to be deported. So Wayne—believe it or not!—marries her. "Looks like fifteen years in the penitentiary," Wayne barks, "the way they're tightening up on you Commies."

The pair escape to Russia, where Leigh is exposed as a treacherous turncoat leading a double life. ("I always think of you as two girls," muses Wayne. "Anna, the lovely kid I thought was a refugee, and Olga, a Soviet Tootsie-Roll that made a chump out of me.") There's more mirthful melodrama when Wayne is to be injected with a deadly drug of which Russian baddie Hans Conried says, "In thirty-six hours, he'll be a complete idiot," a fate that provokes Leigh to renounce her ideology for love—and further trips to Palm Springs where the action ends with a shot of our lovebirds chomping juicy steaks. Umm-mmm, good!

Produced by Jules Furthman and Howard Hughes, directed by Josef von Sternberg (and, among many others, Furthman and Robert Stevenson). Screenplay by Furthman. C, 112 m., TV

King Kong Lives (1986) ❤

It's going out on a limb to call any one flick the most unnecessary sequel in movies, but we're not afraid: this is it. It starts with a premise so bonkers you're sure it's all a skit on "In Living Color"—but no, they're not kidding: Kong didn't die in the 1976 *King Kong*; he's spent the past ten years waiting for a new seven-million-dollar heart, plus another big ape blood donor.

As (our) luck would have it, Brian Kerwin happens upon a female Kong, so she's raced to America to assist Kong in his hour of need. Mouths agape, we watch the blood pumping from one gorilla to the other in big clear plastic tubes, knowing it's going to get crazier—and boy, does it ever. As massive operating instruments the size of props from an *Incredible Shrinking Man* movie are wheeled on, a gigantic claw (like a nightmare version of the arcade game where one maneuvers to pick up toys before time runs out) dives in and heaves Kong's bloody heart up out of his chest. It's an all-time high point of black comedy, but there's more: by the time a spanking clean, humongous plastic heart (roughly the size of, oh, the space pod in *2001*) is lowered into place, it's the audience who are in need of medical help.

Despite iron shackles and "enough Thorazine to kill a whale," you can't keep a smitten Kong down. Once he picks up Lady Kong's scent, he wants her, and he wants her now. Those pesky humans try to stop Kong—by running tractors into his shins— but he sweeps Lady Kong up into his arms and they head for "Honeymoon Ridge" (as a helpful sign tells us), with Kerwin, Linda Hamilton, and the entire U.S. Army in hot pursuit.

Ever wondered what humans in ape suits, sitting on a landscape from a toy train set, look like as they bill and coo? This is the movie for you. While camping out nearby, Hamilton unzips her sleeping bag, gives Kerwin a come-hither look, and utters a come-on that's never failed anyone: "We're primates, too."

Lady Kong gets captured, Kong escapes, and though we're told that the Army has searched for him "everywhere," they apparently failed to check out all the soundstages, for he's hiding out in a tacky swamp set, feasting on rubber alligators. When he rampages back into society, determined to set Lady Kong free, he gobbles down any extra that gets in his way, spitting out the occasional hunting hat. A '70s sort of Dad, Kong wants Lady Kong to give birth out in the country, in a barn (well, actually, she lays down *on* a barn). Just then, Kong's ticker gives out, leaving Lady Kong a single mother—a very contemporary ending.

With Peter Elliot as King Kong and George Yiasomi as Lady Kong. Produced by Martha Schumacher, directed by John Guil-

lermin. Screenplay by Ronald Shusett and Steven Pressfield.
C, 105 m., V, L

The Liberation of L. B. Jones (1970) ❤

"Cohabitation between white and colored is dynamite!" thunders
corrupt Southern lawyer Lee J. Cobb. Guess the studio that made
this incendiary trashfest sure hoped so, but it did one of the all-
time fast fades into box office oblivion—providing a disgraceful
finale to the career of once-peerless director William Wyler.

Cobb's happiness that nephew Lee Majors has returned home
with bride Barbara Hershey sours when Majors wants to handle
the divorce case of the town's black undertaker, Roscoe Lee
Browne. Since Browne's adulterous wife, Lola Falana, is cheating
with white cop Anthony Zerbe, Cobb predicts that the ensuing
scandal will be ruinous for everyone—or as he puts it, "See what
comes from practicing nigger law?" Majors sneers, "You wouldn't
mind if I called you a racist?" and Cobb launches into a reverie
about how years ago he fell in love with a black servant girl.
"After some time," Cobb blathers, "I began to see her as a real
person." Majors murmurs, "I'm glad you saw one Negro as a
human being."

But the entrance into the movie of Falana—stark naked, shaking her bare booty at Browne, and boasting that her lover is
"twice a man"—very nearly begs the question. Her hothouse
vixen, replete with see-through babydolls trimmed in fur, is not
human, it's 100 percent pure starlet—equal parts Ann-Margret
and Joey Heatherton. When Zerbe pulls a gun on her, Falana
leaves her white counterparts in the dust and speeds into ground-
breaking new "bad girl" territory. "Beating up women, that's yer
style," she taunts. "I don't quite feature you for no trigger man.
Beating up women, yeah, I knowed that with the first whiff of
yer hair tonic." She's right: When she reveals she's carrying
Zerbe's baby, he beats her to a pulp.

In a shanty dive, Browne hasn't dowsed the torch he carries
for his faithless wife: Brenda Sykes dances before him, but he
keeps seeing Falana. Zerbe and partner Arch Johnson blow off
steam by, first, raping a black woman in their squad car and

then—as if Wyler thought we needed more provocation to hate
these goons—they shoot a blind man's Seeing Eye dog!

It gets loonier: When the cops kill Browne, too, they pistol-
whip Falana into taking the rap, only they don't use a pistol, they
use "a cattle prod," then demonstrate how this electric torture
device works by zapping cop Chill Wills in the butt. Yaphet Kotto,
who's been waiting the whole movie to kill Johnson, catches the
farming officer on his day off, atop his hay-bailing machine, and
instead of just shooting him, Kotto pushes him into the grinder.
(Wyler shies away from showing us the resulting bundle—it's the
only nanosecond of decorum in the movie.) Rent this politically
incorrect stinker at your own risk.

Produced by Ronald Lubin, directed by Wyler. Screenplay by
Stirling Silliphant and Jesse Ford Hill, from Hill's novel. C, I02
m., V

No Mercy (1986) ❤

The "new Hollywood" is largely comprised of actors who are just
plain bad, but then there's that other, august group of ineffably
bad, supremely self-enchanted thespians, Bad Actors We Love.

This neo-*noir* thrill-less thriller is about a Chicago undercover
cop who goes to New Orleans to avenge his partner's death.
(When Jeroen Krabbe, decked out in a Eurotrash Steven Seagal
ponytail, shows up with his goon squad and wastes Richard Gere's
partner, Gere escapes by scuttling under the hooves of stockyard
cattle.) We know Gere and Kim Basinger are going to deliver
bigtime from the moment they meet: After he insults her, she
slaps his face and he slaps her back.

"You cross me," warns a New Orleans cop when Gere turns
up in the Big Easy seeking justice, "and I'll personally grease the
pole that slides you into a tub of dirt." But the only tub of dirt
Gere has his pole poised to slide into is Basinger, whom he tracks
down in a disco and handcuffs; then, after stealing a car, with
Krabbe and his boys in hot pursuit, he crashes the car into the
river.

They're still handcuffed, mind you, but they not only swim to
the surface, swipe a canoe, and elude Krabbe's army, but also

find themselves slogging through the blue bayou and swapping insults like Charlton Heston and Jennifer Jones in *Ruby Gentry*. The forced intimacy grates on Kim who throws one hell of a hissy fit, screaming, "I can't stand it anymore! I've got to get away from you!" sending them both floundering in the water until Gere bellows, finally, "WILL YOU JUST SHUT UP!!??"

Lovers of Bad Movies know, of course, that Kim will soon reveal her sad, touching past and, sho' nuff, she tells Gere how Krabbe paid her mother for her in cash when she was thirteen. "Every hooker's got a hard-luck story," Gere snarls. "That's a real prize-winner." Soon, they break into a deserted shanty where she teaches him how to eat crawfish. "You take 'em and you break the head off and you suck the juice out of it," she explains, remembering in midsentence that she's supposed to be playing a Cajun.

They hole up in a French Quarter hotel, and after they make love, you get to savor their tender, existential gumbo. She: "What are you thinking?" He: "How fast things fade, finally." She: "Do they? Or do you just learn to live with them?" Hollywood has certainly learned to live with this peerless pair of players—after *No Mercy* did a fast fade at the box office, who'd have dreamed the duo would be reteamed for 1992's *Final Analysis*?

Produced by D. Constantine Conte, directed by Richard Pearce. Screenplay by Jim Carabatsos. C, 105 m., V, L

Orca (1977) ❤ ❤

The mega-success of *Jaws* left in its wake many toothless imitators, from *Tentacles* and *Alligator* to *Jaws 2, 3*, and *4*. None is quite as loopy and lovably bad as producer Dino De Laurentiis's overproduced whopper about Orca, the killer whale out to avenge the death of his mate and baby at the hammy hands of overactor supreme Richard Harris.

"We know very little about the nature of the killer whale's intelligence," we're told by dour whaleologist Charlotte Rampling, "except that it exists, it's powerful, and in some respects may even be superior to man's." Rampling doesn't note the obvious—that killer whales are not so intelligent that they hire top-flight agents to advise them to swim clear of movies like this one, presumably because neither did she. "What we call language," Rampling continues, "whales might call unnecessary, redundant, or retarded."

Well, they certainly would if they read this script. In one of the most outrageously funny plot parallels in Bad Movie history, Harris too has lost his wife and child: "I understand what that whale is feeling, 'cause the same thing happened to me," he says. Harris's confession prompts Rampling to respond, "I thought you were an insensitive boor. You're a sensitive boor." The saga of two grieving widowers, *Orca* is, of all things, Melville with a '70s "sensitive male" spin.

When Harris decides he must go it alone against the whale, Rampling wishes him "Lots of bad luck," but that's hardly necessary—no one's career survives monumental bombs like this one. Just ask Keenan Wynn or Robert Carradine, who get picked off by Orca, leaving Will Sampson to live on (and on), as he intones mumbo-jumbo about Man vs. Nature: "She speaks you the truth. She knows it from the university. I know it from my ancestors." Oh, how you'll root for Orca to zero in on him, too.

It's unfathomable why Orca didn't land his own TV series after this, for he's so playful when he's mad: he sinks boats, eats extras, torches the sets, uses Harris as a human pinball between huge foam rubber icebergs, and (apparently fed up with all the bad acting on shore) bites Bo Derek in two. Was "Flipper" ever this much fun?

Produced by Luciano Vincenzoni, directed by Michael Anderson. Screenplay by Vincenzoni and Sergio Donati. C, 92 m., V, L

Perfect (1985) ❤ ❤

Just the idea of John Travolta portraying an "investigative journalist" is more than enough to start most Bad Movie buffs tittering, but get set for some serious guffawing when you learn that he's cast here as *Rolling Stone*'s top reporter, hot on the trail of an important story: "Health clubs are turning into the singles bars of the '80s," Travolta says, "inflated bodies, airheads . . ." Of course, he should talk since, two years before this movie was made, Travolta helped define the term "airhead" by flaunting his near-naked, newly "inflated body"—shaved to the skin and oiled to a sheen—to promote *Staying Alive* on the pages of (yes, that's right) *Rolling Stone*.

The magazine's real editor/owner, Jann Wenner, inexplicably agreed to essentially play himself in this flick, the jerk who's certain Travolta is proposing a major cover story: "Hot tubs, alfalfa sprouts," Wenner practically cackles, "we haven't done L.A. in a long time." No parodists need apply to "do" Wenner for, unintentionally, he offers up a definitively hilarious character assassination on himself, whether he's telling us, "Rough night! Mikey Douglas was in town," or being "just folks" while cooking up pasta with Lauren Hutton, or noisily barking over the phone to Travolta, "Eat shit and die."

What saved Wenner from having to kill himself after this movie came out (and died) is the fact that the rest of the cast is every bit as embarrassing (talk about ensemble acting). Travolta, working "undercover" at West Hollywood's Sports Connection club, calls it the "Sports Erection," tells aerobics whiz Jamie Lee Curtis, "I think we've come full circle, almost back to Emersonian America," and reveals his reporter's trade secret: "Always treat a famous person as if they're not, a person that's not famous as if they were, and think of your interview as a seduction."

Does it work? Curtis types onto Travolta's computer the immortal entry, "Wanna fuck?" When Laraine Newman, playing "the most used piece of equipment in the gym," fails to score Travolta, she gets off an unforgettable aside, "I'm gonna go see if I can scare up a gang bang." When Curtis's scandalous past is regurgitated in print, Travolta calls to apologize from Morocco (played none-too-authentically by the L.A. restaurant Dar Magreb) but the unforgiving Curtis rages, "You're a sphincter muscle!" Travolta then wins the biggest laugh in the movie by remarking to a passing waiter, "When Mr. Bowles comes, tell him I had to go back to the States."

Happily, return he does, in time for the "We-don't-believe-our-eyes" finale when the whole cast (the chubby Wenner included) dons form-fitting sweats for an aerobics workout.

With Marilu Henner, Anne De Salvo, Mathew Reed (as a tough pretty boy who snarls at Travolta, "Just don't call me a male stripper—I'm an exotic dancer, and don't ever forget it"). Produced and directed by James Bridges. Screenplay by Aaron Latham and Bridges, based on Latham's articles for *Rolling Stone*. C, 120 m., V, L

Players (1979) ❤

Although celebrities from Liv Ullmann and Peter Ustinov to future *Can't Stop the Music* co-stars Bruce Jenner and Steve Guttenberg watch Dean-Paul Martin play Guillermo Vilas at a Wimbledon match, Martin can't stop thinking about Ali MacGraw. We flash back to how these lovers met: In Mexico, after he's saved her from a burning car, MacGraw says, "You're very pretty but I'm too old, and . . ." "Married?" Martin guesses. "Not exactly," she replies, hoping that her flared nostrils will come off as somehow mysterious.

Martin injures his hand when his pal Guttenberg—who's given to saying things like "Speako Spanisho?"—gets roughed up for pulling a tennis scam (don't ask), so MacGraw takes Martin to recuperate at her home. "What's it like to be a hustler?" she asks. "Is there some skill involved?" Martin says, "It's kinda like fishing" and though it's transparently clear why MacGraw wants to talk about hustling, Martin never guesses—not even when MacGraw gets a phone call from zillionaire tycoon Maximilian Schell and drops everything for a Riviera jaunt on his yacht.

On her return, she tells Martin, "I want you for a month," starting a romance that's equal parts *True Confessions* (MacGraw on her background: "Greenwich, Vassar, the Arts Students League, innumerable parties, senators, stockbrokers, young lions, young tycoons") and Grand Ol' Opry (Martin treats us to his self-indulgent rendition of some Willie Nelson tune, pure second-generation show-biz "talent" that makes him MacGraw's filmic soulmate).

The honeymoon's over when Martin steals her cash. "Creep!" she snarls, "I think you wanted to let me know your services were worth . . ." "$1,557.23," sneers Martin, "is that what you think I'm worth?" He threatens her with his tennis racket and lobs this one over the net: "You're a real pussy!"

He stalks off to become a tennis great and, oh, a year later, she shows up to resume their affair. "When I die and go to heaven," MacGraw says, "I hope it turns out to be this." (What, dying on-screen in a desperate bid for a big movie comeback? Why then, you're in heaven now, Ali.)

There are hours of tennis games (keep that "FAST-FORWARD" button nearby), then Schell summons MacGraw again, furious that she's making headlines as Martin's gal. "Even the sailors on my boat are laughing at me!" says Schell, which suggests at least he's prepared for the reviews. He's sent a henchman to tell Martin the truth about MacGraw. "You never told him about Shirley, the little girl who was a cashier in a theater on Broadway," says Schell. "If you love someone, you don't tell lies." Will MacGraw fill her empty seat at Wimbledon before Martin finishes his game? *Players* is well worth a look, say, after you've seen every other film in this book.

Produced by Robert Evans, directed by Anthony Harvey. Screenplay by Arnold Schulman. "Miss MacGraw's wardrobe by Calvin Klein." C, 120 m., V

Reflections in a Golden Eye (1967) ♥♥♥

Now, here's one John Huston corker that separates the Bad Movie diehards from the dilettantes.

On an army camp in peacetime Georgia, Major Marlon Brando lusts after enlisted man Robert Forster, who rides stallions in the nude, while Elizabeth Taylor, Brando's wife, taunts her poor hubby by calling him "Prissy" and sticking out her butt at him. "You look like a slattern goin' around the house this way," Brando mumbles, sounding as if his mouth were filled with peanut butter, so Taylor strips naked while, outside, Forster watches. "I swear I'll kill you," Brando screams (at least, that's what we think he says because that's one Methody mumble he's packing), to which Taylor retorts, "Have you ever been collared and dragged out into the street and thrashed by a naked woman?"

Alas, Taylor doesn't make good on this threat, perhaps because she's too busy getting it on with neighbor army brassman Brian Keith whose wife, Julie Harris, is recuperating after having cut off her nipples with a pair of garden shears. Soon, Forster is sneaking nightly into Taylor's bedroom, where, unseen by her, he fondles and sniffs her personal items.

Bouncy, vulgar Taylor can't understand why fragile, neurotic Harris doesn't just, well, snap out of her funk, counseling cheerily, "Whenever I'm sick or tired, I get on the back of a horse and ride myself better!" Brando, out riding Taylor's prized stallion, spies Forster sunbathing in the buff, and goes gaga, savagely beating the horse. Taylor learns of the atrocity during a huge party and horsewhips Brando in full view of their astonished guests. Not only does Brando not flinch but, after the incident, Taylor tells Keith, "He's a changed boy. He's even polite to me when we're alone."

Meanwhile, when Harris decides to leave Keith, he ships her off to a classy asylum. "Alcoholics, senility, paresis, my God, what a choice crew," Harris snaps, observing her fellow inmates—or does she mean her co-workers?—before expiring, probably from utter humiliation. Keith doesn't even get a chance to ham up this loss before Brando's back with an astonishing monologue that has him waxing nostalgic on life among enlisted men in the army, where "they eat and they train and they shower and they play jokes and go to a brothel together. They sleep side by side . . ." Listening to this, Taylor's eyes bug. Whose wouldn't?

Tragically for Forster, it all ends up not in Brando's bedroom, but in Taylor's, where shots ring out, and in one of the most hilariously inept stabs at "hipness" by an old master director, Huston whips the camera endlessly between Taylor screaming and Brando, uhmm, Brandoing. The studio was reportedly so angered by this expensive dud, it's a wonder someone didn't take a pair of garden shears to the negative.

Produced by Ray Stark, directed by John Huston. Screenplay by Chapman Mortimer and Gladys Hill, based on Carson McCullers's novella. C, 108 m., V

Revolution (1985) ❤

It's 1776 and Al Pacino is a Continental Army–conscripted soldier who mutters incomprehensibly on the soundtrack as the camera shows insurrection-gripped Brooklyn, "We was bringin' furs down the riv-ah. You could hear the city a mile off. New Yawk was goin' crazy."

He soon meets Nastassia Kinski, the daughter of an Irish Tory, who mutters incomprehensibly throughout the entire movie and scandalizes her family, including mother Joan Plowright, by supporting the rebel colonists. Pacino then encounters Donald Sutherland, who mutters incomprehensibly in a British accent, playing the general who absconds with Pacino's son to make him a drummer boy against his will.

Singer Annie Lennox plays a revolutionary colonist who mutters incomprehensibly in a bad wig while painting walls with graffiti: "Piss on all British!" Zillions of dollars were wasted on miscast actors, a horrendous script, and staggeringly inane direction by Hugh (*Chariots of Fire*) Hudson so Pacino could make such pronouncements as "We're goin' home—it's ovah fuh us." (The audience—what little there was of it—felt exactly the same way.)

At one point, Pacino gets abused by a pack of elite Brits, who hire him and a burly extra to drag an effigy of George Washington while a pack of hounds pursue them. A fey, effeminate officer wagers a small fortune that only Pacino will stay the course, practically licking his lips as he says, "It's the little man you have to watch out for." (Not *this* little man; Pacino was off the screen, presumably licking his wounds, for a long, lonnng time afterwards.)

Later, sneaking into the enemy camp, Pacino finds his boy left for dead, carries him off, then, in a scene that defies all previously known limits of self-indulgent acting and directing, mumbles for hours into his ear while mystic Indians balm his wounds. Eventually, through years of battles and separations meant to be reminiscent of *Gone With the Wind*, Pacino and Kinski manage to vow their love and, when the war is over—before you can utter, "How Vietnamlike!"—Pacino is embittered to find that he and thousands of other vets have been bilked out of the money and acreage promised to them when the fight began. The once meek Pacino bellows at the officer dispensing postwar cash, and when he's told to watch his mouth, he screams one of the greatest of all the many unforgettable lines in Bad Movie history: *"My mouth belongs where I put it!"* Career suicide for all concerned, this one's a Hollywood history lesson all its own.

Produced by Irwin Winkler, directed by Hudson. Screenplay by Robert Dillon. C, 123 m., V, L

Road House (1989) ❤❤

You're Patrick Swayze, the movies' sinewy Neanderthalish dish, and you cause a sensation playing a hip-grinding dance instructor in *Dirty Dancing*. What to do next? Well, being not only a martial arts buff but also a spiritual guy who some consider a major blue-collar babe, how about playing a martial arts/spiritual guy/major blue collar babe–type bouncer, hired to clean up a sex-, drugs-, and violence-ridden bar in some Neanderthal's reworking of *High Noon*? (Nearly every man who meets Swayze sizes him up, head to toe, and says, "I thought you'd be bigger.")

Fans of Swayze's babe-osity will be in hog heaven as their star stares in soulful disrespect at the booze-swilling, knife-wielding, brawling denizens of the Double Deuce bar—and of course, their hot mamas, who live to expose their busts and bump 'n' grind for rednecks. Between loopy scenes of Swayze getting out of bed (nude), practicing T'ai Chi (shirtless), and not flinching as he stitches up a knife wound on his own shoulder (shirtless again), he enrages the whole town by firing most of the staff. Finding one of the bouncers screwing a bimbo in the storeroom doggy-style, Swayze axes him although the fellow protests, "I'm on my break."

Then Swayze fires the thieving bartender, who happens to be the nephew of venal millionaire Ben Gazzara. In retaliation, Gazzara's goon squad stages a bar brawl that lands our hero in the hands of Kelly Lynch, the local emergency room doc, who sizes up Swayze and observes, "With that line of work, I thought you'd be bigger." She's so turned on—not only when Swayze refuses anesthesia ("Pain don't hurt") but also when he imparts the sum total of his N.Y.U. philosophy degree ("Man's search for faith, that sort of shit")—that she's soon shirtless with him, yanking at his zipper.

But once Lynch's old boyfriend—Gazzara!—gets wise, all hell

breaks loose, and from then on, it's a Bruce Lee movie with more fistfights, karate chops, and penis references than you can, well, shake a stick at. "Ya wanna fight, dickless?" growls one of Gazzara's thugs at Sam Elliott, to which Swayze's grizzled guru grunts, "Well, I sure ain't going to show you my dick." During a martial arts showdown between Swayze and Kevin Tighe, Tighe gets off the zinger that guarantees this film a place in Bad Movie history: "I used to fuck guys like you in prison."

The grand finale has Swayze conquering an army of foes with every trick in his arsenal—including that old standby, toppling a stuffed polar bear on one of them.

Produced by Joel Silver, directed by Rowdy Herrington. Screenplay by Herrington. C, 109 m., V, L

Siesta (1987) ❤ ❤

"She's gonna be on every Cracker Jack box in America; we're gonna be doin' Tampax ads, Fruit-of-the-Loom, Gatorade, you name it," drawls Martin Sheen, in a *very* broad Southern accent, about wife Ellen Barkin, who plans to freefall from a plane and land, 25,000 feet later, on a fake Mt. St. Helen's. No dummy, Barkin instead high-tails it to Spain to see her ex-lover, Gabriel Byrne, and then, for the rest of the movie, mumbles such insignificant yet significant things as "Somewhere, I don't know where, I turned a corner and there was no turning back; somewhere, I made a mistake," walks a tightrope, gets raped by a cabbie with metal fangs for teeth, and cops artsy attitudes with such Euro-trash as Julian Sands, Grace Jones, and Jodie Foster.

Foster, doing a hooty Joan Greenwood–type Brit accent, turns up in a women's bathroom, and seeing Barkin sheltering there, out of nowhere shares this astonishing reminiscence: "We're all spoiled for choice, aren't we, darling? I knew after the first three days and nights that I'd blown it. I married for love instead of money. I came home and I found him sleeping in my garter belt. So, I left him and I married a Mexican who owned an ocean liner and two hundred acres of Acapulco and after about a week, I knew that I'd really blown it. Here I am in the bathroom, utterly pissed, alone on my birthday—without love, without money—

asking myself, 'What else is there?' " Barkin's equally astonishing reply? "Ambition and a half-hour of prime-time TV." Indeed, since—after this one—it's hard to believe this duo wasn't sent to TV sitcom Siberia forever.

Barkin's mind unravels (no, not from doing this movie) when she learns that Byrne, a circus highwire artiste, has married rich Isabella Rossellini. So she pals around with Foster and insufferably self-enamored photographer Sands, who quotes Corinthians ("Oh, grave, where is thy victory?") when not asking such questions as, "Would you like to put your hands inside my pants?" Finally, the three play out a bed scene, and later, Foster plants a memorable kiss on Barkin.

While Barkin grows battier, the movie plays *Last Year at Marienbad*-type games with flashbacks and flashforwards—all accompanied by moody Miles Davis riffs—in hopes of camouflaging how little is actually going on. Barkin collapses in an elevator, wailing (not surprisingly), "I can't go on," then Foster explains, "I think you're coming off a bad trip" and spirits her to the mansion of Grace Jones, who dresses and acts like Maria Montez in *Cobra Woman*. Barkin, overhearing Foster tell Sands, "For her own good, she's got to be committed," hurtles out a window and lands atop a bus which she rides all over Spain. Cinema of the self-deluded of the highest order.

Produced by Gary Kurfirst, directed by Mary Lambert. Screenplay by Patricia Louisiana Knop. C, 100 m., V, L

Just What the Doctor Ordered

We've always believed that laughing at Bad Movies We Love is good for anything that ails you. When Hollywood tackles the heartrending but hooty stories of the lives, loves, and foibles of those noble, self-sacrificing men and women in white, that goes double. Take our word for it: Watching any of these movies will make you think twice before getting sick.

The Bramble Bush (1960) ❤ ❤

"This view makes our stinking little town seem almost attractive," sneers dying Tom Drake, staring out from his hospital bed at a New England seacoast village while childhood pal Dr. Richard Burton looks on, helplessly. And you'll be helpless, too, with glee, watching everyone involved in this movie (taken from a steamy Charles Mergendahl novel) sweat bullets to convince you that it's about a Big Issue—Burton's mercy killing of Drake by morphine injection—when it's actually just another small-town sex-and-scandal potboiler.

No sooner does Burton return to his hometown from studying medicine in Boston than he's called to minister to fire victims at a hot-sheet motel where he discovers his co-worker, sultry nurse Angie Dickinson, shacked up with oily attorney Jack Carson. "You think I'm a tramp?" Dickinson simmers. "Maybe I *am* a tramp—I don't love him." Burton counsels, "You know, if people had to be in love, Saturday night would be the dullest night of the week." Delighted he's not going to blow the whistle, Dickinson assures Burton, "One thing I am is a damned good nurse!"

Meanwhile, Drake begs Doc Burton to put him out of his misery and urges him to take his devoted wife Barbara Rush sailing. When Burton asks Rush whether she's eaten that day she replies, "Yes, one red pill, one green pill, and two yellow ones." Soon, they're meeting in secret and Rush suggests that lurking beneath her well-tailored exterior is a tigress. (The screen fades to black, but we're certain the earth moved.)

Dickinson longs to burn the sheets with Burton too, confessing, "I think about it all the time." He tells her he doesn't love her but she grabs his leg, pleading, "Then, lie to me! Oh, tell me you love me!" Dickinson gets into trouble again when she lets local newspaper editor Henry Jones blackmail her into a nude photo session. Carson beats the tar out of Jones, but Burton covers the scandal, assuring Dickinson, "Everybody has his own skeleton in his closet."

Soon, there's a tiny skeleton rattling in Burton's: "I'm carrying your baby," Rush reveals. "Did I love you that night or was I just an animal?" (Not just an animal—a tigress!) Burton assures the comatose Drake, "It's not your baby, but that doesn't mean she's stopped loving you," administers the killing morphine, then dimly leaves the syringe and empty medicine bottle lying around for practically the entire hospital staff to find.

Carson blackmails Burton into letting him act as his attorney in the showy murder trial and though Burton's acquitted, everyone in the cast is, well, sadder but wiser. Rush bids Burton goodbye and Dickinson spurns Carson, who screams after her, "You'll wind up a shrivelled-up old maid or a motel tramp!" (Or maybe just a TV policewoman.)

Produced by Milton Sperling, directed by Donald Petrie. Screenplay by Sperling and Philip Yordan, based on Mergendahl's novel. C, 105 m., TV

The Caretakers (1963) ❤ ❤ ❤

"You've seen these women—disturbed, psychotic, miserable," Dr. Robert Stack tells starlet nurses about the patients in Borderline, his controversial group therapy experiment. We can't agree that they're mentally ill, for these aren't Borderline Bad Actresses—they're the Long Since Gone Over the Distant Horizon players.

Meet the gals: Finger-snappin' Sharon Hugueny coos, "Free like a daisy, a lazy daisy" and ex-hooker Janis Paige snarls, "Play it, kid: 'I Was a Teenage Lunatic' "; mute Barbara Barrie demonstrates that no dialogue's required to fit in with this crowd; Ana St. Clair (whose screen credit reads, "courtesy DeMedici Productions of Argentina") has such a terminal case of Needing to Be Photographed Through Lots of Vaseline Over the Lens that when she's shot in closeup she's out of focus. When Stack adds to the mix Polly Bergen—who freaked out in a movie theater during a newsreel by putting her hands over her ears in imitation of Joan Crawford, only to later growl at Stack, "Tie me up, I'm out of my head, what am I doing loose, Doctor?" (bucking for an Oscar, we'd guess)—the place goes, well, bonkers.

Paige, spotting that Bergen's game of "Polly Wanna Go Crackers?" is stealing the show, yanks her hair when Bergen bitches, "You're the filth of the world!" News of the catfight reaches head nurse—yes, it's Joan Crawford—who tells Stack that Bergen once tried to kill a nurse. "Have you ever been attacked by a patient?" Crawford asks. "I have. It can only be handled by the intelligent use of force." How? Crawford runs a judo class for her nurses, demonstrating attack chops on her devoted, equally mannish aide Constance Ford. Trying, hilariously, to give Crawford some—any—feminine touch, designer Moss Mabry adds to her black leotards and tights a black chiffon scarf.

We're not the only ones who find Crawford a tad butch—she does herself. When Stack says, "I want to talk to you, man to . . . ," Crawford smiles knowingly and finishes the sentence, "man to man?" Bergen, as promised, does try to kill Ford, the night that Paige, tipsy on her own "home brew," sets free St. Clair's bird. Barrie retrieves it, strikes a Christ-on-the-cross pose, and squeezes the bird to death, that's right, in closeup. (Producer-director Hall Bartlett returned to these thematic issues in his 1973 *Jonathan Livingston Seagull*.)

We haven't yet mentioned the patients' picnic where—in a

touch Freud would've loved—Stack barbecues hot dogs for his lady loonies. Bergen wanders into the wrong ward, gets gang-raped, but is assured by Stack, "Nothing's happened." (Guess it depends on what you call nothing, Doc!) When Barrie torches the ward, it's not Stack who talks her down, it's Bergen—and Barrie speaks for the very first time: "So-o-o-o-o good." It sure is.

With Diane McBain, Van Williams, Susan Oliver, Robert Vaughn, Herbert Marshall, Ellen Corby. Produced and directed by Bartlett. Screenplay by Henry Greenberg; screen story by Bartlett and Jerry Paris, from the Dariel Telfer book. B&W. 97 m., TV

Doctors' Wives (1970) ❤ ❤ ❤

"I want to know about the length of it," sex-mad Dyan Cannon chirps lasciviously in the opening line of this riotously sex-mad movie from Frank G. Slaughter's sex-mad novel. And, if you love wallowing in glossy, overproduced absurdities, you'll be howling through the length of it.

Mirth explodes when Cannon, during a game of bridge, judges her rich, pampered fellow doctors' wives to be suffering from "sexual malnutrition." Announcing that she intends to diagnose her pals' shortcomings by bedding each of their spouses, then prescribing treatment, she coos: "Darlings, I'm not bluffing; matter of fact, I've covered fifty percent of the territory already." As funny as this lame-brained premise is (renowned surgeon shoots promiscuous wife, implicates his illustrious colleagues in a sex scandal, is forced to perform experimental brain surgery on a little black boy), it's even more fun to savor the mad subplots, madder performances, and maddest dialogue.

The murder of Cannon, the movie's one lively character, leads Daniel Taradash's way-out-there screenplay to offer us instead terribly prim Marian McCargo—wife of George Gaynes, the doc caught in the hay with Cannon—who is shacking up with a studly young intern. "I don't mean to be insulting, babe," her lover tells her in bed, "but I've had more action in a rocking chair." Then there's medical student Kristina Holland who, years before *sex*, *lies and videotape*, tapes all her sexual encounters ("Erogenous zones responding," she murmurs into her tape recorder in the middle of heavy petting, ". . . sublingual glands secreting").

Next up is Janice Rule (wife of philandering Doc Richard Crenna) who secretly shoots morphine, does a slow shimmy to *Zorba the Greek*–type music, and seduces Crenna away from his mistress by doing it on the floor, "like people," she explains helpfully, "in paperbacks." But is Crenna appreciative? "After sixteen years of marriage," he observes, "cool Amy Hughes, who liked it in the dark, always pretended it was rape, finally pulls her pants down."

Also caught with her pants down is boozy, delightfully scenery-gulping Cara Williams, ex-wife of urologist Carroll O'Connor, who philosophizes about their murdered friend Cannon: "The truth is, we're all tramps. Only she was an honest tramp."

Ripest of all is dykey golf pro Rachel Roberts, who confesses to hubby Gene Hackman that *she* shared a one-night stand with the sexually voracious Cannon that started when a cinder flew into her eye: "I remember she said, 'Some people are stagestruck. Some are clothes-struck. And I'm sex-struck.' The way she touched me . . . it was a hot night and I wore a thin blouse and no bra . . . she kissed me. It was wonderful, Dave!" Wonderful is right. See *Doctors' Wives* and you, too, will be sex-struck.

With Ralph Bellamy, Diana Sands (as Crenna's head nurse and mistress). Produced by M. J. Frankovich, directed by George ("Winner of Eight Emmy Awards") Schaefer. Screenplay by Daniel Taradash (see *The Other Side of Midnight* in chapter 19), from the novel by Slaughter. Theme song, "The Costume Ball," by Marilyn and Alan Bergman, sung by Mama Cass Elliott. C, 100 m., V

Flatliners (1990) ❤ ❤

From Columbia, the studio that gave us both *The Interns* and *The New Interns*, comes this gaga thriller that should have been called "The New Age Interns." Kiefer Sutherland is the mad scientist who convinces his med school pals to accompany him when he checks out whether there's life after death. "I don't wanna die," he explains. "I wanna come back with the answers to death." Needless to say, no one ever thinks to ask him, "What was the question?" Instead, his cronies (Julia Roberts, Kevin Bacon, William Baldwin, Oliver Platt) are more interested in whether their heart-stopping experiments will get them profiled on "60 Minutes." Sutherland insists that, yes, "Fame is inevitable" (which, come to think of it, does explain his career) though Bacon warns everyone, "Die and be a hero someday, but don't die to be a celebrity." Of course, Bacon could afford to talk this way since—having survived the crash-and-burn of earlier movies like *Quicksilver*—he'd already come back from the dead.

So what happens when each star dies, then returns? Well, first the good news: Death's kinda like an MTV video—albeit without the accompanying hit pop tune—but even so, it's comforting to know that in the afterlife, we'll each have our own personal cinematographer (though only stars with famous relatives seem to rate aerial photography from a helicopter).

On the down side, extras follow you back into the here and now. Why? (Glad you asked.) "We've experienced death and somehow we've brought our sins back," Sutherland says, "and they're pissed." Uh-huh. As if this could explain why Roberts is haunted by the ghost of her dead dad (maybe she's guilty of her movie father's suicide?), or why Sutherland is stalked by a small tyke wearing a red hood (maybe he's guilty of his real father's movie career?—this menace first turned up terrorizing Donald Sutherland back in 1973's *Don't Look Now*). As if anything could explain why Baldwin's seeing the specter of comely babes in black and white who murmur, "We can stop whenever you want," "Of course I'll still respect you," and "We don't have to do anything, we can just lie together in our underwear." (Our guess is that he must be guilty of insulting the art director who made the TV commercials hawking Calvin Klein's Obsession.)

In the up-to-the-minute psychobabble of the day, the movie urges us to "Face your fears." So we did just that: We decided to watch this movie all the way to the end. (Only one mystery lingers when *Flatliners* is over: Why did Julia Roberts ever want to work with director Joel Schumacher again? They reteamed the following year for *Dying Young* but they died here first.)

Produced by Michael Douglas and Rick Bieber, directed by Schumacher. Screenplay by Peter Filardi. C, III m., V, L

The Harrad Experiment (1973) ❤❤

In this oh-so-daring movie version of Robert H. Rimmer's dreary novel ("Over 2½ million paperbacks sold!" screamed the publicity), sexologist Tippi Hedren strips down to her bra and panties on the lawn of the college she runs with hubby James Whitmore, the better to confront campus stud Don Johnson (who, in real life, became her son-in-law by marrying—twice!—Hedren's daughter Melanie Griffith), and seethes: "Why not run off with the swinging wife of the swinging director and knock off a piece? Lovemaking to you is like a stallion mounting a mare. Real people make love with their minds and their understanding, not just with their bodies!"

The very topic—a school where students are encouraged to have sex with their opposite sex roommates—promises big laughs the moment that nice girl Laurie Walters (who gets an "Introducing" credit here and vanished afterward into obscurity) wanders onto the woodsy campus hugging trees as an Anne Murray–soundalike warbles, "I'm just the total of what I've become."

Meanwhile, shaggy-haired Johnson, Walters's roommate-to-be, checks in at a greasy spoon for directions to the school. "It probably takes a pretty stiff requirement to get in," says the cook, insinuatingly. "Well, I understand," shoots back Johnson, "that they're planning on some courses in adult extension." Nerdy Bruno Kirby—who survived this to later do *When Harry Met Sally . . .* and *City Slickers*—gets paired with Victoria Thompson, who's already naked in bed, expectant, so he's forced to explain: "Guess I'm just not the type of guy who goes around laying every girl he sees."

Mercifully, the nude yoga scene ("Push all the toxins down into the earth," counsels the instructor) helps prepare one for a later sequence in which Hedren lectures on fidelity ("Should the approach be a string of affairs? Conventional marriage? Group marriage?") followed by Whitmore proposing an improv exercise to show the kids how nonliberated they are. "Don't expect much, we're not really actors," Walters says—needlessly.

Walters finally comes through, shedding her inhibitions along with her clothes, in a scene ripped off from *The Last Picture Show*, by stripping down at the campus pool ("You're an absolute miracle," Johnson gushes) and her in-the-buff plunge is followed by the entire young cast doing the same (including an unbilled Gregory Harrison). Once they finally "do it," Johnson bares his soul to Walters with a line he's probably still using: "I'd like to meet the kid that I was when I was five years old because I think he's the only person on the planet who knows who I really am."

Produced by Dennis F. Stevens, directed by Ted Post. Screenplay by Michael Werner and Ted (Lurch on "The Addams Family") Cassidy, from Rimmer's novel. C, 97 m., V

The Interns (1962) ❤

This movie opens with the following Emergency Room exchange: "What is your church preference?" an admitting nurse asks an elderly woman, who replies, "Oh, I guess I like red brick." So much for the film's *intentional* guffaws—from here on in, it's all utterly unintentional hilarity.

From the scene where Dr. Nick Adams uses his stethoscope on a Thanksgiving turkey to the sequence where Dr. Michael Callan goes insane because he's suspected of a "mercy killing," everything about *The Interns* calls to mind the title of another '60s medico pic: *Doctor, You've Got to Be Kidding!* Take, for starters, Dr. Cliff Robertson's encounter with fashion model Suzy Parker. When Robertson notes that her eyelashes are "false," Parker says, "Dear, everything else is real." When he calls her "fresh," she volleys, "What do you do with a fresh girl like me, doctor? Wash her mouth out with formaldehyde?" When he asks for "a date," she asks for "an abortion"!

Back at the hospital, the head nurse warns her student nurses, "Rule number one, girls: Never talk to the interns. They're all sex maniacs," yet it's new nurse Stephanie Powers who's sporting a hickey on her neck (or, in the hepcat jive of this flick, "a little passion berry"). One of the interns asks, "Who put it there, ducky-poo?" but Powers won't tell; certainly it wasn't her beau, goody two-shoes Dr. James MacArthur.

They attend the interns' New Year's Eve bash, a "you-gotta-see-it-to-believe-it" wild party where the booze is served via IVs, doctors dance with skeletons, nurses strip to their underthings, and an extra we've never seen before waves a cigarette holder as she utters her only line of dialogue, "It's all sort of Mondrian, Klee, Kabuki-like, don't you think?" We sure do.

Robertson, swearing his devotion to Parker ("I won't let you go to one of those back-alley butchers!"), gets caught stealing drugs to help her lose the baby and is tossed out of the hospital. Callan, meanwhile, is using two different women to get ahead and so takes drugs to keep up the, uh, pace. We're meant to agree when head of the hospital Buddy Ebsen asks chief surgeon Telly Savalas, "How do you suppose it looks for you to be throwing scalpels at the interns?" but the fact is, we just wish his aim were a little more accurate. MacArthur ponders big questions like "Who are we to play God?" but the real question is "Who are they to play doctors?"

With Haya Harareet, Anne Helm. Produced by Robert Cohn, directed by David Swift. Screenplay by Swift and Walter Newman, from the alleged best-seller by Richard Frede. B&W, 120 m., V, L

Magnificent Obsession (1954) ❤ ❤ ❤

When producer Ross Hunter remade the 1935 tearjerker about a playboy who widows, then blinds a woman he then falls in love with (that remedies the first problem), then becomes a brilliant neurosurgeon (which fixes the second dilemma), no expense was spared: countless violins throb and heavenly choirs sing—sure, you'll laugh, but just try not crying when the sentimentality's laid on this thick.

After reckless rich guy Rock Hudson has accidentally killed the saintly doctor wed to Jane Wyman, he offers to pay for the damages. "Get in a mess with a showgirl, write a check!" rages Wyman, "when a man dies, write a check to his widow!" He leaves, and Wyman rather prophetically remarks, "I'll never have to see him again."

Hudson then accidentally causes the incident that blinds Wyman, and her stepdaughter Barbara Rush growls, "She'll never see again. Write a check for that." Hudson, contrite, longs to follow in the footsteps of Wyman's late hubby, who belonged to a cultish spiritual group. A believer imparts mumbo-jumbo about realizing your own potential, but warns, "This is dangerous stuff. One of the first men that used it went to the cross at the age of thirty-three." (Ah, that's what happened to Christ—he got in touch with his feelings.)

"Here comes a high, fast one," Hudson says later, and he's not kidding: He's befriended Wyman using a false name (so she won't know he's her bad luck charm boy), he's anonymously paying for treatment by European specialists, and he's entering med school. Wyman's disappointed, again and again, by every doc she consults. If that doesn't get your tear ducts going, director Douglas Sirk launches an all-out assault: "The night time is the worst time," Wyman wails, "knowing that when I wake up, there won't be any dawn." Distraught, she stumbles out onto the balcony of her hotel room, and she's about to jump . . . when, just then, Hudson bursts in, gushing, "Let me be your eyes." "I can't believe it," exults Wyman, and neither can we.

They go out on the town, dance the night away, he proposes marriage, and they vow, "Starting tomorrow, we'll never be apart." But in the morning, Wyman has vanished, leaving only a note that says, "If you love me, don't try to find me." Hudson returns to the States, becomes a surgeon who's spiritually correct and generous to a fault—in short, he becomes the very man whose life he took—and eventually he gets word that Wyman is in a coma in New Mexico. Will Hudson rush to her side? Will he be the only doctor qualified to operate? Will Wyman pull through? Will they again vow, "Starting tomorrow, we'll never be apart"? We wouldn't want to ruin the ending for you—but have some Kleenex handy.

With Agnes Moorehead. Produced by Hunter, directed by Sirk. Screenplay by Robert Blees; adaptation by Wells Roor, based on the screenplay by Sarah Y. Mason and Victor Herman, from Lloyd C. Douglas's novel. C, 108 m., V

Not as a Stranger (1955) ❤

From the opening line, it's clear this is a Stanley Kramer special: Never state anything that isn't already apparent and, if possible, overstate the obvious. A dead body is wheeled into an operating theater, surgeon Broderick Crawford looks up at his interns, pauses, then looks down and says, "Gentlemen, this is a corpse." Robert Mitchum gets the second laugh when he—one of the movies' most notorious womanizers—tells fellow med student Frank Sinatra that he'll pass on his offer to set up a blind date: "I'm saving myself till the right girl comes along."

Since Mitchum is flat broke, his dream gal is a Swedish nurse who has prudently saved a bundle. This is, of all people, matronly Olivia de Havilland, sporting a hilarious platinum blonde 'do and an even funnier accent. "Vat you vant vit me?" she lilts at Mitchum. He proposes marriage. "Have you flipped your lid?" rants Sinatra. "This is not the kind of dame you marry!" We expect him to point out that she's beyond childbearing years, but Sinatra explains, "She oughtta marry a farmer."

Realizing Mitchum's game, Sinatra tells him (again and again), "You're taking advantage of a poor square that's afraid of being an old maid—you're letting yourself be kept!" After very nearly killing Sinatra for that remark, Mitchum mumbles, "And I was gonna ask you to be best man."

There are hours of hospital procedure, endless operations, and such true-to-life details as patients who smoke cigars in bed to try to divert us from the fact that this is just an overproduced soap opera about one ambitious doctor's love life, but even the smoke screen of a typhoid epidemic can't fool us. When Mitchum and de Havilland want to move to what Crawford terms "Hicksville," Crawford tells Mitchum, "Stop living your life like a Greek tragedy, or you'll muff it."

In the small town, trouble turns up in the form of hard-drinking widow Gloria Grahame, who breeds prize-winning horses and knows a show pony trick or two herself. Hang on for the sequence when Mitchum stands outside her stables, watching a blue-ribbon stud whinnying up a storm and getting all the mares jumping up and down with excitement. Grahame appears, and Mitchum kisses her, hard, as if to say, "That horse ain't the only stud on this farm." A heel, Mitchum stays out all night, and while de Havilland knows what that means, what Mitchum doesn't know is that she's carrying his foal, er, baby.

Don't miss de Havilland's big—if tasteful, polite, ladylike, *Svedish*—mad scene, where she tears all the infant clothes she'd been hiding to shreds. Yet another operating room emergency at the finale provides our favorite aside in any hospital flick: "O'Dell!" a nurse bellows out a door, "more blood!"

With Charles Bickford, Lon Chaney, Lee Marvin. Produced and directed by Kramer. Screenplay by Edna and Edward Anhalt, from Morton Thompson's novel. B&W, 135 m., TV

Possessed (1947) ❤ ❤ ❤

It's just another day in the local Psychopathic Ward: "One manic, three seniles, six alcoholics, and ten schizos," an intern counts— before they examine civilization's latest casualty, Joan Crawford, who lies before them, catatonic. Given Crawford's bent for steam roller–style acting, you pray she'll stay catatonic, but no, the docs shoot her up with that movie drug that makes any patient talk, propelling her into flashback memories of engineer Van Heflin playing Schumann on the piano at his lakeside cabin while she tidies herself up after they've been (ahem!) "swimming." She yaks about wanting "a monopoly" on him and to put her off, Heflin yaks about symmetry, parabolas, and girders. Crawford gushes, "Why don't you love me like that? I'm much nicer than a girder and a lot more interesting."

That, of course, is debatable but anyway, he dumps her, leaving Crawford to don full nurse drag and return to caring for wealthy Raymond Massey's invalid, unstable wife, who's soon a corpse on the bottom of the lake. Geraldine Brooks, the corpse's snooty coed daughter, accuses Massey of loving Crawford, at whom she rages, "She killed herself because of you. So long as you're in my father's house, I'd rather be somewhere else!" We would too, doll, but it's her movie.

Meanwhile, Heflin turns up to visit Massey, and Crawford says when they're alone, "Go ahead and kiss me. You don't have to mean it." When he does and she can't help but notice he doesn't mean it, Heflin explains, "You watch temperatures go down and then go up again. In love, there are no relapses."

Luckily for Crawford, Massey proposes marriage and she accepts. "Something happens to a woman when she isn't wanted, something dreadful," throbs Crawford, who certainly knew, having just bounced back, with *Mildred Pierce* and then *Humoresque*, from near box-office oblivion. When Heflin and Brooks start making moves on each other, Crawford storms out of a concert hall—where the soloist plays the Schumann piece Heflin played for her—back to her bedroom, where she grimaces, rolls those eyes, and stops just short of chewing the drapes. Our star becomes so unhinged she hallucinates up a swell, moody sequence with deafening ticking noises, pounding heartsounds, buzzers that call her name—even Brooks hissing, "You killed my mother!" to which Crawford admits, "Yes! Yes, it's true!"

Solicitous Massey ships Crawford off to the best specialists, to one of whom she emotes, "You're describing schizophrenia, aren't you . . . I knew there was something wrong with me. I had no idea it was—insanity!" Now that she knows, well, she kills again. A distraught Massey tracks her to the psycho ward where, with the drug now worn off and no co-star left to upstage, she sleeps it off, dreaming, no doubt, of what to wear on Oscar night.

Produced by Jerry Wald, directed by Curtis Bernhardt. Screenplay by Silvia Richards and Ranald MacDougall, based on Rita Weiman's novel *One Man's Secret*. B&W, 108 m., V, L

Bad Movies
à Go-Go

Back when tie-dyes, love-ins, sit-ins, be-ins and freak-outs were the happening thing, corporate Hollywood blew its mind. An entire industry's obsessive frenzy to be considered hip, with-it, and *now* produced some of the most out-there movies in Hollywood history. We're guessing that, just like us, you'll flip your love beads when you get a load of these trippy, hysterically uncool flashbacks from the Woodstock years.

The Grasshopper (1969) ❤ ❤ ❤

This deeply important Bad Movie find, conceived, oh, ten seconds after its makers saw Julie Christie in *Darling*, follows Jacqueline Bisset on the road to ruin, '60s-style.

Bisset gets picked up by horny comic Corbett Monica, who takes her to a swinging Vegas party. Hoping for a mercy hump, Monica tells her, "I know—I have a pixie quality. When's the last time you saw a pixie get laid?" Deciding to become a showgirl, Bisset chirps, when a nightclub boss asks if she's had any show biz experience, "I did *Little Women* in school." He replies, "Did you do it nude?" for he's not convinced she's got big enough "tickets." Bisset says, "In my hometown, I was considered one of the overdeveloped girls," as she whips off her blouse. No sooner has she landed the job than another showgirl—whom the head dancer calls "the Welcome Wagon"—smacks Bisset's butt and says, "If you need anything, just ask me."

Out clubbing to check out a hot rock band with one of the gay male chorus boys, Bisset spots at the foot of the stage respected director-to-be and sister of the producer-screenwriter, Penny Marshall (billed here as one of the "Plaster Casters"), ogling a band member's crotch and flicking out a tape measure. Bisset takes up with Jim Brown, whose crotch in golfing shorts she studies while he stands, legs apart, before her.

In voice-over, Bisset goes existential, telling us, "I know what I want. No, I don't. Yes, I do. I don't know," and "No matter what I'm doing and how much fun I'm having, somewhere way back in my head, I'm thinking: somebody, somewhere else is having more fun than I am." Surely not as much fun as we're having, watching when a boozy minister's wife—eyeing marrieds-to-be Bisset and Brown, plus their two witnesses lope in—tells her husband: "It's serious, Jed. A white girl, a Negro, a Jap, and a sissy."

When Bisset is widowed, she stops the funeral to ask hippies, "Are you holding? Do you have any shit? Hash? Downers? Anything?" Bisset becomes a call girl in a montage that's overlaid by a tiresome song, then becomes the mistress of ancient, rich Joseph Cotten. "I'd propose on both knees," he tells her, "but I'm afraid I'd never get up."

She then takes up with old boyfriend Christopher Stone, who sells her in cheap motels. It's the "only thing you were ever any good at," he snarls, "balling!" The grand finale? Bisset, high, skywriting "Fuck it!" Why? "Why not?" Bisset growls, then, when the cop who arrests her asks her age, she rasps, all tough and used-up: "Twenty-two!" Girls, beware!

Produced by Jerry Belson and Garry Marshall, directed by Jerry Paris. Screen story and screenplay by Belson and Marshall, from the novel *The Passing of Evil* by Mark MacShane. C, 98 m., V

The Happening (1967) ❤

This go-go, go-go, gone flick opens the morning after the unlikeliest "love-in" of all time: extras wearing bathing suits are draped, unconscious, over tree branches, in bushes, standing on their heads! The cops arrive, and four youngsters (we're using that word very loosely indeed) escape in a boat. Meet college coed Faye Dunaway ("I'm hungry—I hate my friends"), James Dean–imitator Michael Parks ("They call me 'Sureshot' 'cause I never miss"), nerdy Robert Walker, Jr. ("Hey, what goes?"), and far-from-young, heavily madeup hustler George Maharis ("I never took a nickel off a broad I didn't like").

Dunaway sighs, "Another day, nothing's going to happen" but she's full of suggestions. "Let's rob a house," she says, "so maybe I'd feel something." Or "let's kidnap the bear from the zoo." Walker chirps, "The zoo isn't open yet," and Dunaway replies, with existential angst, "The—zoo—is—never—open."

Instead, they "accidentally" kidnap former Mafia honcho Anthony Quinn, who's insulted to be "kidnapped by a beach party!" When Quinn isn't intimidated by Maharis's gun, Parks and Dunaway start growling at him like animals, which cowers him into submission. "What are you kids?" Quinn asks. "You're out in space or something." Parks responds, "That's right, and just when you get with it, baby, we change the rules."

The movie's bizarre view of hippies as sociopaths-in-the-making reflects the studios' anxiety about how to reach, or even depict, a new generation—so much so that another studio was shooting the exact same O. Henryish story at the exact same time. (See *The Biggest Bundle of Them All* in our next volume, coming soon to a bookstore near you.)

The plot kicks in when—just as in the later *Ruthless People* —it develops that no one wants Quinn back. Quinn grabs the gun and announces, "I'm taking this thing over" and—seeking revenge on his wife, his partner, his Don, his mother—he teaches them how to pull an elaborate sting. (To judge from Maharis's performance, which gets worse, Quinn was giving acting tips on the side, too.) Quinn and company descend on his house, while his missus, Martha Hyer, is there.

When Quinn tears her favorite fur coat in half, Maharis says, "Bam, etcetera!" and the kids go wild, destroying the whole mansion. Then, even Hyer joins in this frenzy—this tearing down of the established order—why, it's . . . a happening! "Easy come, easy go!" hollers Maharis (certainly true of his career) and Parks cries, "Today, Miami—tomorrow, the world!" (actually, dinner theater would be more like it).

Later, things get tense when they've scored big bucks, and Maharis shoots . . . the cash. How meaningful, how significant, how very 1967. Director Elliot Silverstein, trying hard for an American version of the French "New Wave" flicks, didn't know the wave had passed. Until the reviews came out, that is.

With Milton Berle. Produced by Sam Spiegel, directed by Silverstein. Screenplay by Frank Pierson, and James Buchanan and Ronald Austin, from a story by Buchanan and Austin. C, 101 m., TV

R.P.M. (1970) ❤ ❤

When college students stage a sit-in and demand that the university president resign, he does, which is just the beginning of this desperate attempt to be with-it, '60s-style, from aging, out-of-it auteur Stanley Kramer.

The kids will only accept one of the following as the new president: "Che Guevera, Eldridge Cleaver, Paco Perez." Since Che was dead and Eldridge presumably wanted too much money, it's a lucky thing that Anthony Quinn was available to play the fictional Paco who, conveniently, is already a motorcycle-riding, free-thinking professor on campus.

"Man, you really are a fake," bitches Quinn's live-in lover Ann-Margret (who's supposed to be a grad student but looks to be the president of Starlet U). "The second he gets a call from the Dean, the big nonconformist hops lickety-split over to his office!" Quinn asks, "Lickety-split? Where the hell do you get your vocabulary?" "It's really curious how fast you went for power and glory," she says of his agreement to become acting president (though *overacting* would seem the more apt job description). "You're a fifty-year-old fanny picker who's about to discover that the one thing better than sex is power. I see you without your pajamas—I'm your link to reality." Quinn's response? "That's not reality, honey, that's flab." Hang on for A-M's sage comeback: "Flab is reality."

When Quinn remembers to drop by the "sit-in," hilariously run by the mild-mannered Gary Lockwood and Paul Winfield, students crack about Quinn, "Look what the revolution dragged in." (Another rebel extra wonders, "Why is the good ass never radical, and the radical ass never good?") Quinn also meets with the feisty old trustees and hallucinates how they "really are": they're wearing clown hats, Renaissance headgear, halos and wings, and one is sporting a Borgia ring—the better to poison Quinn.

He hurries home for another terrible meal prepared by A-M. "What's eating you?" she asks. "What I'm eating is what's eating me," Quinn explains. "So, next year," she suggests, "hump a Home Economics major." Quinn replies, "I tried. The food is good, but the talk is lousy"—as if he's with curvy pinup A-M for their conversations! Like, perhaps, her next remark? "I'm writing my 131 term paper," she says, " 'Technological Pressures on Personality Development.' " Quinn tells her, "The whole campus calls you 'Paco's Pillow.' "

This duo's endless chatter reaches a zany apex when, after one of the rebels has taunted him, Quinn asks Ann-Margret, "Did you ever say I was a lousy lay?" She says, "I might have known it, but I never said it." Miraculously, the movie ends with a foreshadowing of what thousands of critics said: after cops have beaten and arrested the students, Quinn leaves the police station to find thousands of extras yelling "Boo!"

Produced and directed by Kramer. Screenplay by Erich Segal. C, 97 m., V

Secret Ceremony (1969) ❤ ❤

Pay attention now, because this flick gets crazed in ways that were only possible in the drug-addled '60s. Aging Elizabeth Taylor, a whore in a blonde Mia Farrow-circa-*Peyton Place* wig, becomes the obsession of schizoid Mia herself, who wears a Liz Taylor-circa-*Cleopatra* wig. Casting together screendom's most legendary home-wrecker with the newly scandalous Farrow (consort of André Previn and Frank Sinatra before Woody Allen) seemed guaranteed to set tongues wagging, but even if the studio had bused in all the actresses' hubbys and lovers past and future, no one could have turned this Joseph Losey howler into a hit.

Taylor lives in a dingy London flat, mourning her drowned daughter whom Farrow resembles; Farrow rattles around in an Art Nouveau mansion, mourning her dead mother whom Taylor resembles. Taylor moves in, and before you can say "half-baked Harold Pinter," the two are playing out kinky master-and-servant games. They're a perfect sadist-masochist couple—screaming at each other, bathing together with a rubber ducky, stomping on each other's lines, and crawling together into a big bed. "You used to say . . . remember?" says Farrow in that fey British accent she borrowed from her own mother, Maureen O'Sullivan, " 'All one needs is a great big bed with all the people one loves in it?' " Replies the much-married Taylor, in joyful self-parody, "When you're older, you'll appreciate the advantages of sleeping alone."

Farrow later tells Taylor, "We can't have you looking like a whore," and stuffs her into a dizzying array of furs and frocks. "That's too drab for a spring day," Taylor remarks about one costume, "that should be worn on a day when it rains like piss." Staring at herself in the mirror and beating us to the punch, Taylor explodes, "I am getting so fat!"

Robert Mitchum (wearing, as Mia's randy stepfather, the phoniest beard in screen history) starts lurking outside their windows. "Was daddy Albert a great lover? Was he gentle and also brutal? Did he make you give out a sound?" Farrow asks, after which both actresses favor us with simulated imitations of orgasms. Mitchum has shown up to seduce his stepdaughter. "The first time I saw you, you were eleven and you came sliding down the banister in blue jeans," he says in his best Humbert Humbert imitation, adding, "I thought: that's for me."

Farrow gets "pregnant" by stuffing things under her dress, then Liz takes her to a glamorous beach resort, and Mitchum follows. "You don't look like my ex-wife at all," he tells Taylor when they're alone. "She was well-bred and rather frail, except for her famous mammalia . . . You look more like a cow than my late wife. Oh, no offense. I'm very fond of cows. Moooooo!" The whole weird farrago ends with Taylor shooting Mitchum dead over the coffin of Farrow, who expired, presumably, from terminal embarrassment.

Produced by Paul M. Heller, John Heyman, and Norman Priggen, directed by Losey. Screenplay by George Tabori, based on Marco Denevi's story. Taylor's hilariously bad hairstyles by Alexandre of Paris. C, 109 m., V

Skidoo (1968) ❤

Ever long to see Jackie Gleason dropping acid? Or Groucho Marx disrobing a blonde starlet while reading lines off cue cards? Or John Phillip Law in hippy drag describing utopia as a world with organic supermarkets? Then, look no further than director Otto Preminger's big-budget, all-star freakout, an old warhorse's attempt to groove with the '60s deepest terror: the young, restless, and unwashed will bury us. (Instead, this movie—made in response to that fear—is what buried Preminger.)

The plot line—and to call it that bends the definition beyond recognizability—has to do with mob boss Marx having retired hitman Gleason kidnapped into prison by henchmen Cesar Romero and Frankie Avalon so that Gleason can rub out an archenemy. His fellow prisoners include Frank Gorshin, on hand to do a Burt Lancaster imitation without moving his lips. No worse, really, than what Gleason has to contend with back home: wife Carol Channing, with whom he "duels" with separate TV remote control units for the family console, and daughter Alexandra Hay, who's *studying* to be a hippy. (This entire movie plays as if you're on heavy medication which, under the circumstances, might be advisable.)

Anyway, when Gleason mysteriously disappears, Hay—who fulfilled her destiny by appearing in *The Love Machine*—does the only logical thing: packs her parents' house with protest song–singing, pot-smoking, body-painting flower children led by Law—who fulfilled his destiny by starring as *The Love Machine*—who philosophizes: "You know what I want to be? Nothin', you dig? If you can't dig nothin', you can't dig anything, you dig?"

We're sure you'll want to fire up your Bic and wave it over

your head as Harry Nilsson sings pseudo Woodstockian songs of peace and love, all indescribably inane.

The generation-gap laughs turn grotesque when embalmed Broadway legend Channing tarts herself up in a tear-away mini-skirt to discover Gleason's whereabouts by seducing former teen idol Avalon. "I'll bet you're a good—dancer," she gurgles. Avalon responds, "I'm a good everything," and when Channing vamps, "Prove it," we're thinking, we don't know if we can handle this as she strips and leaps into his bed but—mercifully—Avalon jams a control button that lowers her into the floor and seals her over.

You may want to miss Gleason's acid trip, but how else could you possibly believe us when we tell you that his swirling psychedelic "visions" include Peter Lawford as a Fed badgering racketeers, Mickey Rooney doing a song and dance, Gorshin in halo and wings, and Gleason himself bellowing to Channing, "I don't care how many guys you've slept with!"? But do not—repeat, do not!—miss the psychedelic musical number with dancing garbage cans. We can't swear Preminger slipped his entire cast, crew and studio a massive hit of LSD, but what other possible explanation could there be?

Produced and directed by Preminger. Screenplay by Doran William Cannon. C, 98 m., TV

The Swinger (1966) ❤ ❤

It's hard not to love *The Swinger*, since it's proof positive that Elvis Presley didn't star in the worst movies in Hollywood history—Ann-Margret did. In fact, *The Swinger* just might be the all-time tackiest major studio movie: the opening voice-over features a narrator who belches not once but three times.

"I'm not a nudie, I'm a writer!" squeals nice girl A-M when *Girl-Lure* magazine editor Tony Franciosa advises that, though her stories are "too innocent," she'd make a great naked center-fold. Determined to publish or perish, A-M longs to prove she's no "innocent," and invites Tony to an orgy at which she becomes a human paintbrush that is rolled across a canvas by burly strangers wearing only trousers and hoods. Though he has an office with push buttons that hide a rollaway bar and bed, Tony is shocked by the orgy. Instinctively knowing that he must do the right thing, he decides to kidnap A-M in order to reform her before it's too late.

A-M sees parallels to, of all things, *Pygmalion* (in her words, the story of "That Higgins cat, the stuffy john who made a lady out of a piece of garbage"), and since she just loved *My Fair Lady*, she goes along with the gag, pretending to be a hard-hearted, alcoholic, nymphomaniac party girl who needs to be saved. (A-M later did a respectable turn as Blanche DuBois in *A Streetcar Named Desire*, proving you can triumph over a past that includes *The Swinger*, but hey, admit it: Who doesn't prefer A-M as a quasi–Eliza Doolitle in heels and bikini?)

The Swinger boasts unforgettable scenes like the one in which A-M tells Tony that she craves liquor ("It's the monkey on my back") before promptly going into a seductive musical number, replete with chiffon scarf and wind machine. (Just like most alcoholics we know.)

Suspecting that perhaps he's been put on, Tony forces A-M to pose for compromising photos, then puts the make on her with a leering line of seduction you'll surely want to try soon: "Even a person on a diet can go off once in a while." Now it's A-M's turn to be shocked—she runs home to her parents and confesses: "I was in an orgy, I was a stripper, I was a streetwalker, then in a motel a man tried to forcibly seduce me." Her mother comforts her thus: "There, there, dear. If you think these things are bad, wait till your children grow up."

Riding her motorcycle back home, A-M crashes head-on into Tony, who's driving a stolen police car (don't ask), and both die. But, this being Hollywood, the film goes literally into reverse, rewinds, and a different ending is played out: A-M and Tony pull off the road and kiss, leaving her intact to sing the inane title song over the end credits.

With Robert Coote. Produced and directed by George Sidney. Screenplay by Lawrence Roman. C, 81 m., TV

The Thomas Crown Affair (1968) ❤ ❤ ❤

"It's not the money," business tycoon Steve McQueen drawls soulfully, "it's me and the system. The system." Oh, so that '60s catchall phrase explains why the ineffably cool McQueen—who plays polo, drives a Rolls, pilots his own glider plane and dune buggy, and lives in a killer Back Bay Boston mansion—masterminds multimillion-dollar bank robberies on the side. And that further explains why he romances haute couture–wrapped insurance investigator Faye Dunaway, even when she announces on meeting him that she's going to bust him. "What a funny, dirty little mind," he observes, underplaying to the teeth, to which she replies, daring him to out-cool her, "It's a funny, dirty little job, so shoot me in the leg."

Everything's so terribly, laughably with-it in Norman Jewison's chi-chi epic—even McQueen's and Dunaway's hair colors match—that you could bliss out with glee from all the faux hip dialogue, multiple-screen images, the *Vertigo*–ripoff 360-degree turn that surrounds McQueen and Dunaway after their infamous *Tom Jones*–inspired chess game, and the Lovers' Montages set to the Oscar-winning tune "The Windmills of Your Mind."

Dunaway, all teeth and legs, and blissfully unaware of how disastrously dated she's gonna look in these Theodora Van Runkel costumes, works alongside Paul Burke, setting a trap to catch a thief, McQueen. Working on the theory, as she breathily tells Burke, that "Every crime has a personality," she marvels over McQueen's criminal artistry, "What a mind . . . what a man." "Who do you work for? *Bazaar*? *Vogue*?" McQueen asks when they just happen to meet at an art auction. Later, Burke rails at her for bedding her target. Dunaway, a child of the times, flares, "All right, I'm immoral—so is the world" and "I know what I am. Don't put your labels on me!" Hell, no, any more labels on her and Dunaway would be a walking edition of *Women's Wear Daily*, the bible of the day.

A sharp cookie like McQueen knows when he's cornered, so he offers to cut a deal with this relentless duo. When Burke refuses, here's McQueen's gee-I-wish-I'd-said-that comeback to Dunaway: "Samba. Sugar Loaf. Jungle. Piranha. Don't you see, there's no way out? You've done too good a job, Vicky. I'm all hung up."

With Jack Weston, Yaphet Kotto, "and introducing Astrid Heeren." Produced and directed by Jewison. Screenplay by Alan R. Trustman. C, 102 m., V, L

Wild in the Streets (1968) ❤ ❤

With his bedroom eyes, killer cheekbones, and perpetual pout, Christopher Jones had all of Hollywood—from his father-in-law, Lee Strasberg, and director David Lean to cheapo maestro Samuel Arkoff, who tried to force-feed him to '60s teens—convinced he'd be the "new" Dean, the "next" Clift. When they realized that he couldn't act and—far worse—inspired no cult following, Jones disappeared pronto. But while he had his minute, movies were custom-designed for him, of which this is the most haywire.

Jones plays a twenty-two-year-old multimillionaire rock star ("more famous than Jesus") whose entourage includes Richard Pryor ("drummer, anthropologist, author of *The Aborigine Cookbook*"), Kevin Coughlin ("at fifteen, the youngest graduate in Yale's history"), and Jones's "latest creature comfort," Diane Varsi ("ex-child star, mystic, vegetarian, acidhead").

When aspiring politician Hal Holbrook woos Jones to perform on live TV as part of his campaign, Jones tells America that he wants the voting age lowered to fourteen in the goofball song "Fourteen or Fight."

Jones—with his impassioned plea "We outnumber the fuzz. We got more cats than little ol' Mahatma Gandhi had"—gets Varsi elected to the Senate where, sporting a leather miniskirt, a tattoo, and a Napoleon chapeau, she bangs her tambourine before saying, "Mr. Speaker, America's greatest lesson has been teaching the world that getting old is such a drag!" Old-time Senator Ed Begley snaps, "Filthy rabble—appalling!" but what's really appalling is Shelley Winters as Jones's mother, who tries to keep up with the times by donning a long wig, smoking marijuana, and going "under the care of an LSD therapist."

When Jones wants to run for President, he gleans his political strategy from watching Senator Varsi, stoned on acid in his pool,

alternately weeping and mewing "Meow"—yeah, that's it, put
LSD into the Washington water supply! It works and President
Jones declares, "We're going to make thirty a mandatory retire-
ment age, and set up mercy camps" where the oldsters will be
forcibly fed LSD.

But some of the over-30s hide away in attics—among them,
Holbrook's wife Millie Perkins and Winters (who once costarred
together in another attic for *The Diary of Anne Frank* and, even
more bizarrely, who both later played Elvis Presley's mother on
TV)—but even when caught and drugged, nothing can tame Winters, who runs amok hollering, "I'm being presented at the court
of St. James! The Queen is receiving me! I want feathers!" Essential viewing, especially for '90s teens who are heavily into
"retro" fashion and say they're sorry they missed the '60s.

With Bert Freed, Larry Bishop, Dick Clark, Army Archerd,
Pamela Mason. Produced by Arkoff and James H. Nicholson,
directed by Barry Shear. Screenplay by Robert Thom. C, 97 m.,
V, L

X, Y, and Zee (1972) ♥ ♥ ♥

Liz Taylor nearly kissed off her stunning *Who's Afraid of Virginia
Woolf?* comeback with an almost unbroken string of howl fests
—and this is one of the best of the worst. Wildly painted and
bursting out of '60s psychedelic frocks in her à-go-go gone-amok
phase, Taylor plays the sadistic, horny, wealthy, foul-mouthed
wife of masochistic, horny, wealthy, foul-mouthed London architect Michael Caine.

The action starts when Caine, at a party, flashes his eyes at
achingly sensitive boutique owner Susannah York. "You know,
she told me she's prone to weeping if anything nice happens to
her," hostess Margaret Leighton tells Liz of widow Susannah.
Taylor bugs her eyes and gags: "Yuck! YUCK!" Precisely.

Taylor turns into a woman run mad—she's forever blaring bad
rock music at home and rattling trash cans under the windows of
York's flat yelling, "Is my husband in your chickenlike arms?"
(You can tell that Caine likes York better because, in his scenes
with her, his hair is washed.) After Liz barges in on the couple

during a tête à tête, things start to get really weird: York mentions she's the mother of twins, and Taylor asks whether she breast-fed them, then relates, "I sat next to a man at dinner one night who said you haven't lived until you've seen a woman breast-feed twins. Evidently his wife would lie sprawled on the bed, a tit in either direction, and it was just fantastic."

York warns Caine, "Your wife—she's possessed!" but all the sparring seems to get the married couple hot and bothered: Caine is soon back home tying up Taylor in bed while she bellows, "You woman-hater! You Jew-hater! You fascist swine!" But, when he moves to release her, she says "No! No! Don't untie me. I want it that way."

Inevitably, Caine finds Taylor with her wrists slashed in a tubful of blood and when she doesn't die, Taylor turns up the performing dial to "MAXIMUM," acting as if she's playing Martha in *Virginia Woolf* all over again (blissfully ignoring such details as the fact that this time she didn't have Mike Nichols—or anyone else, apparently—directing her in an Edward Albee prize-winning play).

Taylor elicits from York, who is at her hospital bedside, a rollicking confession of a Youthful Lesbian Incident. With a nun, yet. "You know," vamps Taylor, "I could get used to having you as my personal slave." While Caine gets it on with his mousy secretary, York and Taylor (mercifully, mostly, off-camera) play slave and mistress games, only to be discovered by Caine. The love-'em-and-leave-'em Taylor leaves York a snivelling mass, Caine doubly cuckolded, declaring about York, "She sees beauty in everything—especially shit!" We couldn't put it better.

Produced by Elliot Kastner, Jay Kanter, and Alan Ladd, Jr., directed by Brian Hutton. Screenplay by Edna O'Brien, from her novel. Theme song, "Going in Circles," sung by Three Dog Night. C, 109 m., V

Soap Gets in Your Eyes

Hungry for heartbreak? Misfortune? Anguish? Noble self-sacrifice? Acting that knows no top to go over? Do you like your melodrama set to the accompaniment of throbbing violins, big lacquered coiffures, sparkly jewels, and gowns by Jean Louis? Then get set for a wild, nonstop ride to Tragedy Town, land of incurable, photogenic diseases, impossible (and impossibly chic) marriages, and more loony plot twists than a pretzel. Critics scoffed at them, audiences sniffled, but most of the moviemakers responsible for these epics cried all the way to the bank. If you're anything like us, you'll be howling with laughter through your tears.

Ada (1961) ❤ ❤

Dean Martin plays a dim-witted populist politician with a show biz background who doesn't want to be bothered with the day-to-day details of public office. His fearfully ambitious wife, Susan Hayward, is razor-tongued, grudge-bearing, and the power behind the throne. Sound like any scary Mr. and Mrs. President we once knew? (Part of the kick one gets from this enjoyably tawdry little number is how weirdly life can imitate art.) But even staunch Republicans might chuckle over seeing how a formidable gang of political sharks promotes bucolic, guitar-picking Martin into the governor's mansion despite the fact that he's saddled with a former hooker for a wife.

"Do they make governors different from other men?" asks good time gal Hayward when she's set up for the first time with Martin. Hayward quizzes Martin on his political views, a line of questioning she continues to pursue in vain once they get to his hotel room. He's simple, see, much more interested in personal stuff like how our white trash heroine got her name. "My daddy had a workhorse named Ada," she snaps. "Maybe he thought some of it would wear off on me." Next day, Martin's so in love ("Stop lookin' at me that way," Hayward drawls. "I'm not on the menu this morning") he wants to marry her. And does.

That might put a crimp in his gubernatorial candidacy, but Hayward handles reporters, backstabbers, and political cronies like the seasoned pro she is. Vicious, high-ranking politician Wilfrid Hyde-White takes to Hayward at once. "If you want to grow a beautiful rose," he says, "there's nothin' like a touch of manure." That, this movie's got.

Martin aces the election—with a boost from Hyde-White, who makes sure that the wife of the rival candidate is booked on a narcotics charge—but storm clouds brew. While Martin blunders his way around the governor's mansion, Hayward tries bulldozing her way into the tea parties of high society ("What are we," she bellows, "trash?").

The pot boils over when Hayward, frustrated by Martin's do-nothingness, engineers herself into the lieutenant governor's seat; soon after, Martin barely escapes death when his car is rigged to explode. "Once in a back room of a saloon, somebody gave me a broad as a present," he says, insulting Hayward from his hospital bed. "I never once thought she'd turn on me or try to kill me."

When Hayward starts cleaning up the crooked politicians, Hyde-White entraps her by taping her in a blackmail attempt by her former madam. But Martin redeems himself—and Hayward's reputation—in a grandstanding speech finale that's almost as off-key as his voice when he sings (twice!) his campaign song, "May the Lord Bless You Real Good."

Produced by Lawrence Weingarten, directed by Delbert Mann (who in palmier days won an Oscar for *Marty*). Screenplay by Arthur Sheekman and William Driskill, from the novel *Ada Dallas* by Wirt Williams. C, 109 m., TV

All That Heaven Allows (1955) ❤ ❤ ❤ ❤

Producer Ross Hunter and director Douglas Sirk recycled their *Magnificent Obsession* stars and proved that box office lightning can be made to strike twice. The result is Bad Movie manna.

Jane Wyman is a well-off widow who always seems to be getting put off by her country club friends, like Agnes Moorehead, or her kids, snooty Princeton son William Reynolds and daughter Gloria Talbott, a psychobabble-spouting social work student who lectures boyfriend David Janssen on "sex attraction." Since Wyman's no spring chicken, the best offer she gets is from leering, married Charles Drake, who suggests, "Why don't we meet in New York? I know a place."

Then Wyman starts noticing young gardener Rock Hudson, who's always more than willing to trim her bushes. He hustles her to the picturesque old mill left him by his late father and Wyman, frightened by a bird, falls into his arms. Romance hangs heavy in the air, so Wyman tries changing the subject by suggesting Hudson fix up the place for some "nice girl" he'll one day marry. "I've met plenty of girls—nice and otherwise," he says, and kisses her.

Soon, Wyman is turning down Moorehead's invitations because she'd rather party with Hudson's bohemian, colorful pals, including a lobster fishermen and a primitive painter. To Wyman's delight—and our hilarity—Hudson, one of the most constricted actors in screen history, here sings, plays the piano, dances, tosses back his head in a terrifying impersonation of a "regular Joe" free spirit. Wyman falls, hard, and Hudson counsels her not to ignore what her friends will say about her being involved with a poor, young buck. Don't miss the scene in which she asks Hudson whether fearlessness was something he taught one of his friends, who has dropped out of the Madison Avenue rat race. Hudson replies, "You can't learn that from anybody . . . Mick discovered that for himself. That he had to make his own decisions. That he had to be a man." Wyman says, "And you want me to be a man?" Hudson's reply? "Only in one way."

Wyman's kids and friends go apoplectic at the news that the lovebirds plan to be wed. A busybody at one of Moorehead's parties marvels to Wyman about Hudson's gorgeous tan from working outdoors, adding, "Of course, I'm sure he's handy indoors, too." Wyman can't stand the heat, so she breaks off with Hudson, and succumbs to migraines. Her doctor advises her to marry Hudson, chiding, "Let's face it. You were ready for a love affair, but not for love."

Soon after, Hudson topples down a mountain and Wyman, in a reversal of their *Magnificent Obsession* roles, comes to his aid as composer Frank Skinner's violins nudge us to tears. You'll shed tears, all right, but not exactly the kind that the moviemakers intended.

With Virginia Grey. Produced by Hunter, directed by Sirk. Screenplay by Peg Fenwick. C, 89 m., V

Ash Wednesday (1973) ❤

How's this for a premise? Fading middle-aged beauty undergoes excruciating surgery in hopes of regaining her youth and rekindling her wandering husband's passion. Just about the time that middle-aged beauty Elizabeth Taylor dove head first into this vat of whipped cream, she was undergoing one of her many cosmetic surgeries in hopes of regaining *her* youth and winning back wandering husband Richard Burton's passion. Sure, the script claims she's playing a lawyer's wife from Grosse Pointe, Michigan, but when Taylor's star shone brightest, moviemakers made sure no one knew how to tell her real life from her reel life. This one must have struck Taylor followers as practically a documentary—what with foreign-accented plastic surgeons marking up Taylor's features for slicing!

Wandering around the European clinic in *Invisible Man*-type bandages, Taylor overhears such patient chit-chat as "Darling, I thought you were the fifth most famous fashion photographer in the world," and moviegoers clucked knowingly—this is the price that Liz pays to be our Liz. When, rather improbably, Taylor says she'll never submit to such torture again, even the other characters in the film don't believe her. Fellow patient Keith Baxter says, "You'll forget—we all do, once we've tasted at the Fountain of Youth." (Audiences then, as now, surely erupted into gales of laughter when Taylor's doctor says she must eat simply, and quit both smoking and drinking.)

Her treatment complete, Liz jets to Cortina to rendezvous with hubby Henry Fonda. When he doesn't show, she wanders around sporting various Alexandre of Paris hair creations, searching in vain for a storyline. At dinner, she spots kept boy Helmut Berger being slapped by his latest female companion. Spotting his next meal ticket, he flits to Taylor's table and asks if he may join her. "You'll have to give me a minute or two to think about it," she says, waiting, like, two seconds, then deciding, "Yes."

In no time flat, Taylor and Berger are lovers, till Fonda finally arrives. Looking totally unprepared (did he agree to do this movie because he was nearby shooting another flick?), Fonda takes one gander at Liz, and mutters, "My god, . . . you're beautiful." Not beautiful enough, however, to make him give up his young mistress—a hamfisted warning to women in the audience willing to trade places with La Liz, no?

Outraged, Taylor brays in her best *Virginia Woolf* fishwife voice, "Look at the stitches, Mark. Look at them! Count them! Every one of them was for you, so you could open your eyes again when you took me to bed. Look at these breasts. Aren't they beautiful? What more do you need?" Well, what more does anyone need than late-period Liz—working without a script, director, or co-star—to keep us in stitches?

Produced by Dominick Dunne, directed by Larry Peerce. Screenplay by Jean Claude Tramont. C, 99 m., V

The Betsy (1977) ❤ ❤

Laurence Olivier screws, swindles, and schticks his way through this all-star howler in which he plays not only an octogenarian Henry Fordish auto magnate but also, in flashback scenes—with tons of makeup and hair dye—his younger self.

The elder Olivier proposes to race car driver Tommy Lee Jones that they develop together a cheap, pollution-free car that'll revolutionize the ailing auto industry. When Jones expresses amazement at his plans, Olivier barks, "Did you think I was just an old man jerkin' off?" No, we thought you were an old ham in need of a fast buck. Forgotten starlet Kathleen Beller (Olivier's great-granddaughter Betsy, for whom he names his new car) makes sure Jones sees her skinny-dip in the pool, and this whiff of passion flips Olivier into 1930s Flashbackland where he recalls bedding a housemaid, while his daughter-in-law Katharine Ross watched—during the wedding reception for Ross and Olivier's son, mind you.

In the present, Jones encounters Olivier's steely grandson, Robert Duvall, who, since he's unhappily wed to Jane Alexander, is carrying on a hot affair with interior decorator Lesley-Anne Down. At a dinner soiree, Jones and Down exchange ripe looks and riper banter. "He was good," Jones says of the driving prowess of Down's late husband. "Unfortunately," she quips, "not quite good enough," to which Jones says, "Who is?" Well, certainly neither of them, which makes it all the more fun to watch the unfolding of their affair. "There is no bigger fool in this world than a calculating woman who miscalculates," says Down after the obligatory love scene. No, we want to correct her, there's no bigger fool in the world than a road company Joan Collins who suffers delusions that she might have been the next Ava Gardner.

All hell breaks loose when Duvall tries every dirty trick in the book to keep the Betsy off the market (someone should have done the same for its namesake film), resulting in a confrontation with Olivier, who intones, "Over my dead body!" Duvall's response? "Any way you want, grandfather." Meanwhile, back in the infidelity-riddled past, Olivier—ever on the alert for nookie opportunities—watches Ross breast-feed her son (who grows up to be Duvall), and beds her. (Having seen him rut the maid, she has "wanted it ever since.") Sure.

In the present, Down shocks Duvall by unexpectedly turning up at Beller's birthday bash, then bitching, within earshot of Alexander, "Just because she chooses to hang on to the pretense of a marriage, I'm supposed to remain in some permanent social limbo?" Beller receives a memorable present from Jones: a quick hump in a candlelit gazebo. Duvall, who'll stop at nothing to stop Olivier, swears, "I'll give him a taste of what he gave his own son: humiliation, despair, defeat!" making us wonder why America ever fretted about a gas shortage with this cast in this script.

Produced by Robert R. Weston, directed by Daniel Petrie. Screenplay by William Bast and Walter Bernstein, from Harold Robbins's novel. C, 125 m., V

Diamond Head (1962) ❤❤

Hot winds stir the second Yvette Mimieux returns home to tell her highly possessive widower/landowner/brother Charlton Heston that she wants to marry fellow college grad James Darren, cast as—of all things—a native Hawaiian. Heston, a supposed liberal with senatorial aspirations, makes "Guess Who's Coming to Luau?"–like noises. Though their family has "been on the islands over a hundred years, we've never mixed our blood." Darren's hot-blooded, half-breed brother, George Chakiris, reminds Heston of his alleged open door policy toward minorities. "I don't mean all doors," Heston growls, "not the door to my sister's bedroom." Chakiris—like the rest of the movie—aims straight below the belt, telling Heston, "You don't want the door to her bedroom open to anybody." Meaning anybody *else*, that is.

Heston, natch, is secretly keeping island beauty France Nuyen as his back-hut mistress. In their love nest, he relives for her, in a hilariously deadpan monologue, how his wife and son were swept away by a tidal wave. When Nuyen confesses to Heston that she's pregnant with his child, he says they're through. Nuyen's brother Richard Loo decides to blackmail Heston: "You go shake the cradle, and I'll go shake the money tree."

Meanwhile, even Chakiris isn't sure Yvette and Darren should tie the knot, recalling how she once stripped naked and beckoned him to join her behind a waterfall. "You bring out the spitting witch in me," Yvette hisses at Chakiris. "One of us must be an awful person." Just one? At the engagement luau—where Heston rages as he watches Yvette and Darren dance a hot hula—Heston, uh, *accidentally* stabs Darren dead. "I don't feel anything, just a blank," confesses comely Yvette, most convincingly, and soon, she's boozing it up in bars. "I don't know how to love," she sobs (or, we might add, how to act).

As Heston's empire crumbles (his sister spurns him, his mistress dumps him, his senatorial bid goes sour), Yvette passes out and gets rescued by Chakiris, who slips her into his dead brother's bed, where she wakes up in sweats from a dream sequence in which she gets naked near a waterfall and beckons Chakiris—then Darren—to, umm, swim with her. Chakiris comforts her, one thing leads to another, and the morning after, they're at each other's throats. "Still the spitting witch even in Paul's bed," he snarls. "Last night you didn't care whose bed it was, did you?" she volleys.

He tells her, still harping on her incestuous feelings for her big brother, "There's a war going on in your head. As for me, I wouldn't sleep well three in a bed." Yvette returns home to brother Heston and they clutch hands in Significant Closeup. When Nuyen dies in childbirth, Yvette is shocked by Heston's indifference, and runs off with Chakiris—and Heston's love child. Now, this is what we call paradise, Hawaiian-style.

Produced by Jerry Bresler, directed by Guy Green. Screenplay by Marguerite Roberts, from the novel by Peter Gilman. C, 107 m., V, L

Dying Young (1991) ❤

. . . and *slowly*. Are you hankering to wring your Kleenex over another *Dark Victory*, that old Bette Davis workhorse later redone as *Stolen Hours* with Susan Hayward, and later still, with a tweak or two, as *Love Story*? Then make tracks to your video emporium to learn the mind-bending reason rich leukemia patient Campbell Scott jeopardizes his survival by terminating chemotherapy after he has shacked up with pretty caretaker Julia Roberts.

Before we learn the awful truth, we first must watch as blue-collar Roberts and blue-blood Scott get to know one another. Sure, Julia spews the *F* word at every possible opportunity, and sure, Campbell (unlike such earlier dying swans of the cinema as Ali MacGraw) vomits and sweats bullets on camera, but most of the movie screams 1930s, replete with a wisecracking butler and cute dialogue. "So, why'd you pick me?" Roberts wonders when

Scott hires her, adding, "I had the shortest skirt, huh?" He replies, "No, actually, there was one with a shorter skirt, but he was never a candy striper."

Being driven in his limo to a chemo session, Scott lectures Roberts on various San Francisco landmarks, telling her the names of their architects and construction dates. Roberts looks out the car window and identifies one on her own: "Ronald McDonald, 1986." Her Home Shopping Club–addicted mother, Ellen Burstyn (who must have honed this turn at the Shelley Winters School of Dramaturgy), advises Roberts to knock off feeding Scott macrobiotic health food: "Make him a ham. I mean, it's hot—it sticks to the ribs."

The smell of ham certainly lingers in the air when Scott woos Roberts at a chic restaurant where he says, over nouvelle cuisine, "My mother always said, 'You don't have to like everything, but you have to try everything.' " Roberts volleys back, "My mother always said, 'Pass the Velveeta.' " When they start having sex (which, in this movie, means falling madly in love), Roberts becomes antsy about taking any more money from him. "Well, then," says Scott—about to launch into a line that would have clutched throats even when "women's movies" were a dime a dozen—"I only have one thing to give you: my heart."

When Roberts finally catches wise that Scott, rapidly worsening, must have lied to her about having completed his chemo, she calls his father, David Selby, who asks—at last—the crucial question: Why? And Scott's answer? "I wanted her to see me with hair," he replies, which would be reward enough for any Bad Movie fan, even without Selby's response, which is: "So why didn't you tell me that? You think I wouldn't understand?" Scott and Roberts shed so many tears there's no need for anyone else to. Pass the Velveeta, for sure.

With Colleen Dewhurst (Scott's real mother), Vincent D'Onofrio. Produced by Sally Field and Kevin McCormick, directed by Joel Schumacher. Screenplay by Robert Friedenberg, from the novel by Marti Leimbach. C, 105 m., V, L

Last Rites (1988) ❤ ❤ ❤

Sexy priest Tom Berenger gets hot under the clerical collar for a Latina, Daphne Zuniga, the playmate of his Mafia brother-in-law who was shot dead ("Once in the head and once in the dick," says a cop) for cheating on Berenger's sister, hit woman Anne Twomey. Dining with pal Chick Vennera, Berenger insists, "I haven't broken my vows—I don't intend to start now," though just then a blonde interrupts to remind Berenger that they'd once "made love. Don't you remember? After the polo match? We were looking for a bottle of Dom Perignon? The champagne was to celebrate our engagement."

The shock of his brother-in-law's murder forces Berenger to re-examine his inner conflicts, which he does by hearing confessions—like the one from a tyke who seeks forgiveness for having used her sister's toothbrush to clean the toilet—and another, in which Zuniga practically seeks forgiveness for being "a dancer—*West Side Story* at the moment." (That tips us off where she picked up her laughably *theeeeeck* Hispanic accent, but nothing could explain Berenger's fascination for her.)

Twomey and Berenger's Mafia Don father, Dane Clark, decide to have Zuniga rubbed out. Dodging bullets, Berenger takes a hit in the arm; gushing blood, he thoughtfully reassures a cab driver, "Looks worse than it really is. Hot shower, it'll be just fine, thank you." A cold shower is what's needed, for Berenger shelters Zuniga but can't help gazing at her as she sleeps. She awakens, crosses the room to him, removes his collar, they have wild sex, then—uh-oh!—her face dissolves and becomes his sister's. (It's a dream, see?) Anyone can see that Berenger is overcome with lust. At his brother-in-law's funeral, he's reminded, "You were born to do more than just sprinkle water."

Meanwhile, stuttering priest Paul Dooley, who has one of the funniest monologues in the movie ("When I'm shocked, I don't stutter for a couple of hours. Nobody knows why. I never stuttered in 'Nam"), dresses Zuniga up in priest drag, and Berenger (apparently the only priest hearing confessions in all New York) learns from sis Twomey that she killed his brother-in-law.

Rushing out of the booth, Berenger enumerates her late husband's many sexual dalliances. "Why is it I only lose control when I'm with you?" Twomey asks sultrily, and when he warns her she will burn in hell, she murmurs meaningfully, "We've both known that since you were fifteen." When Clark asks how Berenger and Zuniga possibly became lovers, Twomey should answer, "Because the script insisted on it," but instead answers, "He was ordained, papa, not castrated." (Well, she ought to know!)

Raging hormones lead our forbidden lovers to Mexico for the bloody finale where Zuniga—who has actually worked again since—meets her maker when Berenger, pledging his love, opens the door to her hotel room and lets Twomey shoot her dead. If there really were a God, Twomey would have plugged Berenger, too.

Co-produced (with Patrick McCormick) and directed by Donald P. Bellisario. Screenplay by Bellisario. C, 103 m., V, L

The Last Time I Saw Paris (1954) ❤❤

Embittered expatriate novelist Van Johnson—who surely would have been *our* choice to play a surrogate for embittered, self-tortured expatriate F. Scott Fitzgerald—wanders scenic postwar Parisian locales mourning dead Elizabeth Taylor. Wherever he roams, someone is warbling the title song, *their* song.

Wandering into a bistro, *their* bistro, Johnson encounters all-purpose ethnic barman Kurt Kaszner, who reminds Johnson of those glorious wartime days and nights. "Maybe we had too many laughs, Maurice," reminisces Johnson (and so may you) when he then tumbles into Flashbackland, where, among throngs of celebrants as World War II ends, he meets Donna Reed—who looks him straight in the eye and toasts, "To men!" She invites Johnson to a gala party hosted by her rakish, ne'er do well father, Walter Pidgeon, and gorgeous sister, Taylor, who kisses him and asks, "Do you think someday soon you might be rich?" Reed, accustomed to losing beaux to Liz, instead weds George Dolenz, leaving Liz and Van to tie the knot and birth a daughter who grows up to be the sort of *cher enfante* who speaks breathy Franglais and scampers around in toe-shoes.

Johnson plugs away writing novels that publishers reject, so at a Beaux Arts ball, Pidgeon counsels, clearly hip to the secret of movies like this, "Would you like to know the secret of success? Mediocrity, my boy. To be a rich writer, you've got to remember your three R's: riches, ruffians, and rape."

Things go sour when Liz takes up with tennis pro Roger Moore in retaliation for Johnson's taking up with the much-married Eva Gabor who, on meeting him at a bar for an interview, announces, "I haven't picked out my next husband yet—might be the bartender—at least he has talent." Taylor asks hubby Johnson about paramour Moore, "How do you like him? Don't you think he makes me look years drunker?"

Liz and Van grow more beautiful and dissolute—he can't write a word, see, he's too busy driving racecars in Monte Carlo—until she pleads that he return with her to America. "Let's go back before we crack up!" she says throbbingly, and you'll crack up right along with them as the stars sweat in vain to convey the sense of loss, pain, and anguish of the Fitzgerald tome on which the movie is based. But damned if you'll be able to control your tear ducts when Taylor, dying of pneumonia, whispers to Johnson about their daughter, "Take care of Vickie. Don't let Vickie make the same mistakes. I'll always love you." Fitzgerald it ain't, but we'll take our swoony swill where we can get it.

Produced by Jack Cummings, directed by Richard Brooks. Screenplay by Julius J. and Philip G. Epstein and Brooks, from Fitzgerald's *Babylon Revisited*. C, 116 m., V

Love Story (1970) ❤ ❤

Three box-office words explain why Paramount made this silly tearjerker—*Romeo and Juliet*, on which they had just made a fortune. "What can you say about a twenty-five-year-old girl who died?" asks Ryan O'Neal, sitting in the snowy bleachers of a field in Cambridge. The answer, of course, is plenty, though it would take somebody with talent to make us care about her, plus a talented writer and director to build a story around her.

Anyway, our doomed lovebirds "meet cute" when Radcliffe librarian Ali MacGraw—who doesn't look like she's seen twenty-five anytime recently—blocks O'Neal from borrowing books because, she says, "You look stupid and rich." No, he only looks stupid, but the script insists that he's loaded. Though she's forever calling him "preppy" and he's calling her "bitch," she's soon making calf eyes at him while he sits in the penalty box for playing dirty on the hockey rink.

"Would you ever total me?" she asks, so irritatingly that, if O'Neal won't oblige, thousands of others would. O'Neal's face gets creamed at one hockey game, attended by his pop, Ray Milland, who observes, "You probably want a steak, son," to which O'Neal replies—thinking Milland means a steak for his bruised face— "Thank you, father, but the doctor took care of it." (Well, MacGraw warned us he was stupid.)

The womanizing O'Neal baffles his roomies, including Tommy Lee Jones, by suddenly knuckling down to his law studies; O'Neal marvels to MacGraw, "It's amazing. I'm really studying." Amazing, indeed, but not as amazing as O'Neal's proposing marriage. Damned if we aren't as puzzled as she is. "You're a preppy millionaire," she whines, "and I'm a social zero."

Though meeting the folks goes badly, they marry anyway and move to New York when he gets appointed to a swank law firm. True love runs smooth until—uh-oh!—O'Neal learns that he's going to lose MacGraw to one of those Unspecified Terminal Diseases so beloved by Bad Moviemakers. The sight of flesh wasting away? Hair falling out in chunks? Nausea? No, Ali just grows a tad pale and asks O'Neal to take her to the hospital where, her hair spread out decoratively on the pillow, she assures him there's no pain, explaining, "It's like falling off a cliff in slow motion, you know? Only, after a while, you wish you'd hit the ground already." (We feel the same way.)

O'Neal sits on the bleachers near the playing field and waxes nostalgic ("She loved Mozart and Bach, the Beatles, and me") while the snow falls. This howler made so much money, it actually got nominated for six Oscars and spawned a sequel, *Oliver's Story*, but, hey, Trash means never having to say you're sorry.

Produced by Howard G. Minsky, directed by Arthur Hiller. Screenplay by Erich Segal, from his book. C, 100 m., V, L

Monsignor (1982) ❤ ❤

A huge procession of cardinals pays homage to the pope in St. Peter's in the Vatican. Seated among the holy men is cardinal Christopher Reeve, the movies' *Superman*, apparently figuring that one crimson cape is as good as another, when—uh-oh!— among the holy sisters filing into the cathedral is nun-to-be Genevieve Bujold, with whom he's just been burning up the sheets. She thought he was just a soldier, see, and now knowing his true vocation, she stops before him, thunderstruck, causing one hell of a bottleneck.

Later, the forbidden lovers meet in secret and Bujold seethes, "I was free with you and let you into my life, and you betrayed me! . . . It's not love you betrayed—it's me: Clara! God can't forgive you, only I can forgive you. And I never will. Never!" (And you've never heard anyone, anywhere pronounce "Clara" the way vinegary, smart Bujold does.) Peeling off her lingerie and nylons while shallow, glassy-eyed Reeve watches, Bujold explains, "God gave me a strange gift. He made me attract love affairs that quickly become disasters. That's why I decided to become a nun. But, here I am, ready for another disaster." Tossing back her head, our *Earthquake* survivor growls, "I'll have some champagne."

Well, disaster Bujold gets, in spades, so who can fault her for looking at Reeve as if she's choosing a capon at the poulterer? Sure, this epic from the filmmaking team that brought us *Mommie Dearest* aspires to *Godfather*-like pronouncements on the Vatican's ties with the Mafia, but in its dirty little heart, *Monsignor* is just the ever-hilarious old potboiler about the sexy priest—see *Rain, Miss Sadie Thompson, The Sandpiper, Last Rites*—who gets hot under the collar for forbidden fruit. Reeve feels just guilty enough to gush, confession-style, to a priest, "Father . . . I'm a priest. And I think I love her!" Later, Bujold tells Reeve, after he's kissed her, "I taste guilt there," a line that would have made a silent movie queen choke. You'll be jamming your "FAST FORWARD" and "REWIND" buttons to savor such laugh-out-loud stuff as Mafia creep Jason Miller growling, when he finds father Reeve and his Black Market pal Joe Cortese hung over from an orgy and surrounded by whores, "You think you're king of the shithouse!" This is topped by holy eminence Fernando Rey responding to Reeve's disclosure of his sins by counseling, "That happens." No expense was spared, but nothing short of a miracle could have saved this holy mess, which permanently parked the career build-up Reeve had been getting at the time, but as Bujold asks in one of our favorite lines, "You think God was planning to waste a miracle on us?"

Produced by Kurt Neumann, directed by Frank Perry. Screenplay by Abraham Polonsky and Wendell Mayes, from Jack Alain Leger's novel. C, 121 m., V

The Other Side of Midnight (1977) ❤❤❤

"If you don't love me, Larry, don't lay me," says virginal Susan Sarandon to the smarmy bounder who's after her in *The Other Side of Midnight*. Then, when the cad professes his true love, Susan sighs, "I guess it's time to retire the trophy." And that's just the subplot of this vintage gem based on the Sidney Sheldon trash masterpiece.

The main story features the doomed love affair of a pathological liar and a sociopathic movie star, both of whom will be executed at the finale for a murder they didn't commit (which, by film's end, seems like justice). At the beginning of World War II, French innocent Marie-France Pisier is picked up in a hotel lobby by American flying ace John Beck. "I'm not a whore," she says, and he replies, "You're kidding." A standard happy-in-love montage, complete with the lovers running through Paris in the rain, is thankfully intercut with steamy sex scenes to help keep you awake until the plot gets rolling.

When Beck abandons her, Pisier aborts their love child with a wire hanger, and—what's a nice girl to do?—gets revenge by sleeping her way to the top of the film industry. (Don't laugh, this is precisely how many top stars got their start.) Pisier auditions for a famous filmmaker (played by Christian Marquand, the director of *Candy*, another Bad Movie We Love), only to be told that yes, he liked her reading, but, "Now we must see if you have talent." If you guessed that the next scene shows the two of them naked atop a bearskin rug in front of a roaring fire, then maybe you won't be surprised to learn that Pisier brings him to climax with strategically placed ice cubes—and gets the role. (Acting hopefuls, take note.)

It all ends, as overwrought and overproduced nonsense like this must, during a hurricane in which Sarandon is washed away in a boat moored on the Greek island where Pisier has become the bejeweled mistress of an Onassis-like Greek tycoon played by Raf Vallone, probably because Anthony Quinn was busy elsewhere. (In the '70s these two hams were a virtual cottage industry, overacting as Onassis knockoffs, and together they turned up the very next year as Onassis-like brothers in *The Greek Tycoon*—but that's another Bad Movie We Love.)

With Clu Gulager. Produced by Frank Yablans and Martin Ransohoff, directed by Charles Jarrott. Screenplay by Herman Raucher and Daniel Taradash, from the Sheldon novel. C, 165 m., V

The Tarnished Angels (1957) ❤❤❤❤

Set in New Orleans at an aerial stunt show during Mardi Gras, this gem from schmaltz king Douglas Sirk features some of Hollywood's most cockeyed, mock-poetic dialogue, situations, and performances.

"Those flying gypsies look like you and me, but they're not human beings," mutters cynical newspaperman Rock Hudson, referring to the stunt pilots he's trailing for a big story. "Burn them and they don't even holler. Scratch one and it's not even blood they bleed. They're a strange race of people, without any blood in their veins at all. Just crankcase oil."

Hudson's reporting leads him to meet and fall for sad, sexy, badly married Dorothy Malone. Billed as that "Beautiful Distaff Daredevil," Malone's aerial specialty number has her climb, in a billowy white dress and matching gloves, from the plane piloted by her surly husband, Robert Stack, and dangle from a rope. The crowd roars, but Malone is wise to them. "The boys," she says, shrugging, "were hoping the wind would tear my dress off."

Hudson is horrified when, after Stack survives the flame-out of his plane, Stack sends Malone to kiss up to the richest, most disgusting man in town—a guy who's been hot for her for years. "I need this plane like an alcoholic needs his drink," Stack pleads. "Roger's thoughts never come down to earth," Malone confides to Hudson about her husband. Snaps Hudson: "They go down to the gutter."

After Malone confesses how much she loathes having to sell herself for a plane, Hudson (has he been guzzling crankcase oil himself?) knows what he must do. . . . Later, he finds Malone in her seedy hotel room and tells her he's seen the rich guy and gotten the plane on Stack's behalf. When she wants to know how, Hudson grins suggestively and says, "Just used my natural talents."

Sirk lards on the pseudo-surreal (closeups of blind organists, extras wearing bizarre Mardi Gras masks) to liven things up while Hudson learns that Stack thinks he's on a mission to redeem himself and his marriage. Stack tells Malone he wants to use the prize money to start a new life for them, but then his new plane crashes, just as his colleagues are throwing a farewell dinner for him. "The food has been cooked, the wines chilled—" says Hudson, to which Malone adds, "—and the guest of honor's on the bottom of the lake." He offers to take Malone away from all this mess, but she refuses; before she and her young son take off for a better life, she observes, "I hate airports. Too many airplanes."

With Robert Middleton, Christopher Olsen (the annoying little kidnap victim in Alfred Hitchcock's 1956 version of *The Man Who Knew Too Much*), Troy Donahue (as a doomed pilot!). Produced by Albert Zugsmith, directed by Sirk. Screenplay by George Zuckerman, from (*very* distantly) William Faulkner's novel *Pylon*. B&W, 91 m., TV

CHAPTER 20

Slay It
With Music

Remember the lighter-than-air grace of the dancing Fred Astaire and Ginger Rogers? The knock-'em-dead show biz exuberance of Judy Garland and Gene Kelly? The biting brilliance of *Cabaret*? Get a grip—those days are kaput! We keep hearing that big-budget musical bonanzas will stage a glittering comeback, but instead Hollywood has been making this glittering array of gems: Crooned by the tone-deaf, danced by the spastic, scripted and directed by the rhythm-free, these are Bad Musicals We Love.

Great Balls of Fire! (1989) ❤ ❤

Certain actors weren't so much born to play real-life show biz legends as to become possessed by them. Faye Dunaway *is* Joan Crawford, for instance, and less cataclysmically, Sissy Spacek is Loretta Lynn, Beverly D'Angelo is Patsy Cline, and Gary Busey is Buddy Holly. Ads for this awesomely off-key musical bio pic claimed "Dennis Quaid *is* Jerry Lee Lewis" but he sho 'nuff isn't, though the good-in-other-movies actor waggles his pencil-laden brows, flicks his bleached and permed locks, smacks his lips, slacks his jaw, blows Bazooka bubbles, and trashes pianos while lip-synching badly to Lewis's tracks.

It all begins in Memphis with a kid playing Lewis as a tyke, sneaking off to hear "the Devil's music," sung and danced by black extras directed and choreographed like a road company of *Ain't Misbehavin'*. Grown up, Quaid sits tickling the ivories, blissfully rearranging the lyrics to the hymn "How Great Thou Art" to "How Great I Am!" when in strolls his thirteen-year-old, gum-popping jailbait cousin, Winona Ryder, with whose father, John Doe, Quaid plans to start a band. "I'm goin' to be the main attraction, of course. I've got a ferocious, God-given talent on me," Quaid tells Ryder, who eyes him the way a vegetarian eyes a platter of sugar-cured ham. This is the kind of movie in which, whenever Quaid goes for a spin in his convertible, hordes of badly choreographed, "Happy Days"–type high schoolers, car hops, and jocks bop and rock to his tunes; it's the '50s familiar to us all from those "Rock's Greatest Hits" commercials.

While Quaid is making Popeye faces, Ryder is stealing his movie, though Alec Baldwin, as Quaid's Bible-thumping preacher cousin Jimmy Swaggart, tries to steal it from her by bellowing "God will not be mocked!" Meanwhile, Quaid rockets to the top wailing on "The Steve Allen Show" (watch for a bizarre cameo by the bewigged Allen, playing himself thirty years earlier). Idolized by fans like the doll who leaps into his limo and growls, "I want you to play me like you play that piano, hot stuff," Quaid instead weds Ryder, who looks like his daughter.

When the hatchet-wielding British press, led by Peter Cook, discovers that Quaid and Ryder are kin and that Quaid isn't even divorced from his second wife, they deport him. "England can kiss my ass!" Quaid shouts, but, from there on in, our star goes into overdrive in a Self-Destructive Montage making us hope for that standard rock bio movie finale—a nice, tragic, violent death. No such luck, for a title turns up to remind us that the real Jerry Lee "is playing his heart out somewhere in America tonight," while Quaid, presumably, is out there somewhere trying to live this one down.

With Joe Bob Briggs, Lisa Blount. Produced by Adam Fields, directed by Jim McBride. Screenplay by Jack Baran and McBride, from the book by Myra Lewis with Murray Silver. C, 107 m., V, L

Lost Horizon (1973) ❤ ❤ ❤

Hungry for memorably, side-splittingly Bad? Here's 143 minutes' worth, dished up faux Asian style by producer Ross Hunter, who was already richer than Croesus from producing such gems as *Imitation of Life* and *Magnificent Obsession* when he spent zillions to remake Frank Capra's classic movie fantasy about Shangri-La into a Burt Bacharach/Hal David musical, all of it starring nonsinging, nondancing nonactors.

The hilarity begins with a planeload of cardboard characters: diplomat Peter Finch, his surly brother Michael York, engineer George Kennedy, entertainer Bobby Van, and Sally Kellerman as a suicidal *Newsweek* photographer who, at the first sign of air turbulence, starts popping pills. Hyperventilating, Kellerman swoons, "I feel we're heading for outer space."

No such luck: Instead of a snowy death, our heroes' plane crash dumps them in a smiley utopia apparently inspired by a Liberace theme park. Resident guru, ancient John Gielgud (picture a mummy on Prozac), brings Finch to confer with the even more ancient High Lama Charles Boyer (picture a mummy beyond Prozac), who suggests that Finch linger forever. He doesn't need much convincing; he's already fallen for schoolmarm Liv Ullmann. "Is there some delicious drug in our food?" Finch asks, "or is this all a mirage?" Drugs are the only possible explanation; in any case, only drugs can help get you past the sight of Ullmann swinging her hands, bugging her eyes, thrashing in fields, and lip-synching "The World Is a Circle"—it's enough to make one appreciate Cybill Shepherd in *At Long Last Love*.

No sooner is Kellerman talked down from leaping off a ledge (did she foresee the reviews?) than she, too, is bleating in song. Then steel yourself for the "Festival of the Family" number, in which James Shigeta and scads of arrythmic extras dance a two-step, singing about family values.

Everybody's soooo bloody happy except York, who plots his escape with dewy (if obviously pregnant) librarian Olivia Hussey. Gielgud grumbles that Hussey's youthful facade will shatter if she leaves this magical land—it's only Shangri-La that keeps her from growing ancient, you see—but York eventually persuades

Finch to escape with them. Just as Gielgud predicted, Hussey ages to, oh, about Gielgud's age, and York tumbles to his death down a mountainside. Lucky them.

Finch, sadder but wiser, returns to his paradise "with its feet rooted in the good earth of this fertile valley while its head explores the eternal." We can't vouch for where anybody's head was at in making this movie, but we can hazard a guess. Essential, if life-shortening, viewing.

Produced by Hunter, directed by Charles Jarrott. Screenplay by Larry Kramer, from James Hilton's novel. C, 143 m., V, L

Purple Rain (1984) ❤

It's not easy being purple, the trademark color of Prince, who made his screen debut playing a narcissistic rocker (sound like anyone whose records we don't buy?) in this unforgettably awful vanity production about a singer grappling with interpersonal problems while trying to do his Art.

That's it for the plot, so there's plenty of time to revel in the utter, well, purpleness of it all. Like the purple cone, out of which peeks a hand puppet with which Prince shares a scene (and gets upstaged), as the puppet mimes, "You don't need these girls or their stupid music. All you need is me." Then, there's the purple eye shadow the star applies by the ton, the better to jazz up endless closeups of him batting his lashes, and peering over the rims of his Jackie Onassis–like sunglasses.

Women in the real world would take one look at Prince and decide: "Deadly competition for the bathroom mirror," but every babe in this movie positively purples with lust just at the sight of him. Apollonia Kotero, playing an ambitious kid out to Make It Big, straps herself onto his purple motorcycle for a ride to the lakeshore where Prince challenges her to pass his "initiation." What, we shudder, would that entail, Gerri Curl and Maybelline at thirty paces? "You have to purify yourself," he explains, "in the waters of Lake Minitanta," at which point Apollonia peels and hurls herself into the freezing water. "That ain't Lake Minitanta," Prince smirks, then roars off on his cycle.

We get hipped to how Prince came by his winning ways with

women when, after his father—played by former "Mod Squad" idol Clarence Williams III—nearly beats his mother, Olga Karlatos, to a bloody pulp, she mumbles, "I'm just trapped here. You don't let me have any fun."

Above all, there's the Godawful purpleness of the star's snits, like the one in which he madly stomps about his dressing room, Joan Crawford–like, when a club promoter snarls, "Nobody digs your music but yourself." (But even Crawford never wore anything quite like Prince's purple velveteen high-heeled boots.)

In a giddy high point, Prince shocks Apollonia to tears when he does pelvic thrusts while singing about a girl he met "in a hotel lobby masturbating in a magazine." (Excuse us, but isn't this the same Apollonia who shed her clothes at the drop of a hat?) For a big finish, Prince knocks the crowd dead with a dirgelike rendition of the title song that makes Barbra Streisand's self-indulgent finale in *A Star Is Born* seem like an act of self-effacement.

How can a movie make a fortune at the box office and at the same time squash a movie career? Watch this one if you dare—but remember, dress purple.

Produced by Robert Cavallo, Joseph Ruffalo, and Steven Fargnoli, directed by Albert Magnoli. Screenplay by Magnoli and William Blinn. C, III m., V, L

Satisfaction (1988) ❤

Proof that the New Hollywood can not only make Bad Movies We Love the way they did in the old days, they can make 'em even worse, *Satisfaction* is a brainless reworking of *Where the Boys Are*. The four coeds are updated as four rock 'n' roller starlets who are described thus: "The lead guitar's a junkie, the drummer's a gangster, and the bass player—on good days—is a slut."

What about the lead singer, you ask? Well, she's class valedictorian Justine Bateman, and the laughs start at her high school graduation. "We can make the kind of noise that's going to wake the world from its stagnant slumber," declares Bateman, "or we can bloat ourselves like those who have gone before us on the synthetic pap sucked from the techno tit of those who will lead us to the tyrannical bullshit our apathetic asses sometimes deserve." (While the entire class is giving her a standing ovation, you'll probably recall those words of wisdom handed down through the ages: People who star in "synthetic pap" shouldn't throw stones.)

Bateman's guitarist says she's heard that "rock 'n' roll is the Devil's music, and people who play it are working for the Devil" which makes us wonder, then who are actors who play rock 'n' rollers working for? (According to the credits, it's Aaron Spelling.)

The "slut" bassist is none other than Julia Roberts, who has all the movie's loopiest lines: "I like to spend my time curled up with a good book—I just finished *Thin Thighs in Thirty Days*." Before a party, she tells her pals: "Anybody who doesn't act elegant is a douche bag"; then, when the host jumps her, Roberts offers up this date-rape bon mot: "Do you want me to just lay here and be quiet while you ball me?" (The answer, of course, is "yes.")

When the girls break into the beachfront pad of club owner Liam Neeson, and his deadly Doberman stops snarling as soon as he hears the band sing "Amazing Grace"—just another born again attack hound—Neeson complains, "You broke my dog." As terrible as Bateman is, Neeson is worse—because he, after all, could be acting if he'd felt like it. Taught, as a stage-trained performer, that the true test of acting is listening, clearly no one ever warned Neeson about having to listen to Bateman sing "Dedicated to the One I Love."

Here's what Roberts's old flame tells her about their act: "You girls are nothing but meat up there. My girl don't tease pud for no money." Who wouldn't swoon for such sweet talk like this? He and Roberts bed down for twenty-four hours in the group's van—and as it sways to and fro, over and over again, that's as close to rock 'n' roll as *Satisfaction* ever gets.

With Scott Coffey, Trini Alvarado, Britta Phillips, Debbie Harry. Produced by Spelling and Alan Greisman, directed by Joan Freeman. Screenplay by Charles Purpura. C, 92 m., V, L

Shout (1991) ❤

"In the tradition of *Flashdance*," it says on the video box as if that were a recommendation. The back-handed hurrahs continue: "Directed by Jeffrey Hornaday, the acclaimed choreographer of *Dick Tracy* and *Flashdance*." Never mind that there's no mention of the magic he also brought to the movie of *A Chorus Line*, let's just say . . . there's acclaim and then there's *acclaim*.

Happily, *Shout* really does live down to these promises, right from the opening where '50s troublemaker James Walters is taken to a boys' farm for JDs—which, in a movie like this, can only mean James Dean knockoffs. The school is run by straitlaced Richard Jordan, whose daughter Heather Graham arrives home for the summer at the same time that the new music teacher shows up —John Travolta, sporting Elvis sideburns, talkin' jive like "Loosen up, man," and on the lam for killing a white man who was hasslin' a black man—we mean, he be one cool dude, bro'.

Though his pupils have no musical skills whatsoever (when Travolta says to Walters, "Pick with your right," he sticks his finger up his nose) Travolta lets them hear rock 'n' roll and, natch, then they can play. How come? Let one of the characters in the screenplay by Joe Gayton explain it: Rock 'n' roll, well, "gave me a boner." The only student slow to get it is piano man Scott Coffey, so Travolta gives him after-class tutoring. The sight of Travolta demonstrating that what's needed is for Coffey to learn to walk, squawk, and flap like a chicken must be seen to be believed— and, while both are making like poultry, Walters, watching from afar, mutters, "What a dick!" (We don't know which actor he means, but—does it matter?) Hilariously, Coffey can then— *voilà!*—wail on piano!

It gets even crazier when the underage reform school lads bust out one night and make the scene at a local blues joint where, in the back room, forbidden rock 'n' roll is played (accurately, for the period, by blacks). Swigging a beer, Professor Travolta suggests that Walters get up on stage and play. When he does, he's a sensation—a real rockin' rebel—so then Travolta joins in on harmonica, and they're maybe the coolest white guys alive. This is topped when the joint's hot black mamas just can't wait to get that white jailbait out on the dance floor.

The whole notion of this deranged movie—that blue-collar teen trash can be reformed into something useful like, say, a back alley outlaw band—is a Bad Movie first. Stick around for the finale where Travolta's hauled off to jail as his ragtag troupe entertains the town with music so hot that fireworks go off in the sky. Nothing can stop them now! Except the reviews.

With Linda Fiorentino, Glenn Quinn, Frank Von Zerneck, Michael Bacall, Sam Hennings, Gwyneth Paltrow. Produced by Robert Simmonds, directed by Hornaday. Screenplay by Gayton. C, 89 m., V, L

Staying Alive (1983) ❤❤❤

Before the title of this film bursts on screen, the three credits that precede it—"A Robert Stigwood Production," "A Sylvester Stallone Film," and "John Travolta"—tip us off that we're in for one unforgettable Bad Musical We Love, for back in 1983 no one in show biz had been associated with worse recent films than this creative trio: *Moment by Moment*, *Sgt. Pepper's Lonely Hearts Club Band*, *Grease 2*, *Nighthawks*, and *Victory*, just for starters.

The title sequence establishes that Travolta (reprising his *Saturday Night Fever* character, thick lug Tony Manero) is a rebel Broadway dancer, too much of an original to just do the steps a choreographer requires, though the only thing that's original about Travolta is that he's sporting an entirely new body, pumped up (and up, and up) under the guidance of director/mentor Stallone. Despite the new pecs, Travolta's nowhere near as musclebound as Stallone's screenplay, which features such lowbrow high points as Travolta's unintentionally hilarious flirting with stage star Finola Hughes: "I do have this singing lesson I'll have to cancel," she teases about running off with him; he volleys, "I have to cancel my brain operation"; and she asks, "Do you think that's a good idea?"

Everyone in this film seems to be suffering from brain damage, for what else could explain Travolta throwing over sincere chorine Cynthia Rhodes for the impossible-to-like Hughes (caught on film here midway on her slide from the height of fame in *Cats*, to TV soap stardom, to a walk-on in *Soapdish*)? What else could explain the casting of Stallone's brother Frank as a rock star? (Unless, of course, it's to demonstrate that Sly's not the only no-talent in the family.)

When Travolta gets cast in Hughes's new show, mama Julie Bovasso begs, "Tony, keep your clothes on!" No such luck; the movie bends over backwards to get Travolta out of his shirt, stripped down for love scenes, and—here's a new one—washing himself and his undies in the shower.

Opening night of the show, which is called *Satan's Alley*, is what guarantees *Staying Alive* deserved immortality: An impossibly funny series of overproduced production numbers, it's high-tech camp heaven as Travolta, clad only in Bob Mackie's barely there Centurion outfit, struts and leaps around a set filled with moaning chorus girls in cages, laser beams, and all the dry ice in America. (Out in the audience, Bovasso crosses herself, but it's too late: Travolta's movie career has definitely gone straight to Hell.) Travolta then spontaneously breaks into a dance of his own creation—doing a ooooh-baby, Chippendale's stripper shimmy while being whipped by muscled chorus boys—which, naturally, brings the first-nighters to a screaming, stomping, standing ovation.

Produced by Stigwood and Stallone, directed by Stallone. Screenplay by Stallone and Norman Wexler, based on Nik Cohn's characters. C, 96 m., V, L

Stepping Out (1991) ❤

Since audiences steered clear of the film version of *A Chorus Line*, that paean to the heartaches of professional dancers, who'd have guessed that Paramount execs would believe the world was waiting for a tribute to the heartaches of amateur dancers? To play the failed Broadway chorus girl reduced to teaching tap in Buffalo, who better than a star whom Hollywood failed, Liza Minnelli? Though she always resisted portraying her mother, Judy Garland, here Minnelli's remaking one of her mom's 1940s "Let's-put-on-a-show-in-the-barn" pictures, fifty years and several pounds too late.

When Nora Dunn gives Minnelli's ungainly tap class a chance

to appear in a local charity benefit, Minnelli enthuses, "Look, you already know a lot of steps, we just put 'em together and show 'em what we can do!" To keep us awake, Minnelli calls up her own career too, in a reverie about her days as a Broadway hoofer: "I even auditioned for Bob Fosse once," she recalls shamelessly. "I didn't get the job, but I got to touch his sleeve." What she doesn't say is that Fosse—in real life, the director of her Oscar-winning triumph, *Cabaret*—is now dead; what she doesn't need to say is that—since she's starring in self-exploitative trash like this—she's dead, too.

Shelley Winters plays Minnelli's senior citizen pianist, who sits around reading magazine articles called "What Do Women Want Now?" (Not movies like this, to judge from its box office belly flop.) The divas square off in the ladies room so Winters can launch into her big monologue, "I don't have to do this, I have my social security and my pension," she begins, while Minnelli (like us) can't help sneaking a glance at her wristwatch. One by one, each tap student reveals the riotous sorrow of their drab little lives— Ellen Greene says of her son, "One minute he's in a rock group, the next minute he's in a coma"; Sheila McCarthy says that when she cooks for the homeless, she tries "to make every meal nutritious, well-balanced, yet fun"; so unmarried Minnelli gets into the act and drops a secret of her own: "I'm pregnant—and I don't want to be!"

If you doubt the ruffian troupe's the hit of the gala, perhaps you've never seen a movie before. Greene gushes to Minnelli, "You've taught us about finding out how to be us." The movie insists that self-esteem is more important than talent, which may be true in real life but, judging from the evidence here, sure isn't true in movie musicals. (Minnelli's class, which includes Julie Walters, Andrea Martin, and Bill Irwin, is more convincing as the toast of Buffalo than could possibly have been intended.) *Stepping Out* says that we all need to find our inner child, then buy it tap shoes.

With Jane Krakowski, Carol Woods, Robyn Stevan. Produced and directed by Lewis Gilbert. Screenplay by Richard Harris, based on his play. C, 113 m., V, L

Xanadu (1980) ❤ ❤ ❤

The musical that would've reunited the stars of *Grease* if Olivia Newton-John had had her way (but John Travolta, apparently holding out for an even worse script, waited for the 1983 *Two of a Kind*), *Xanadu* broke new Bad Movie ground by grafting '40s whimsy together with late '70s muzak to pioneer discokitsch. From the opening scene—when a wall mural of nine babes comes alive so that chorus girls dressed in Bobbi Mannix's peasant-chic garb can run, hop, and rollerskate—it's clear that this is the inevitable companion to *Can't Stop the Music*. Delightfully dreadful on their own, viewed together back-to-back they are unassailable as the worst movie musicals ever.

Acting exactly as if she were still a painting on a wall, Newton-John has come to earth to "inspire" down-on-his luck artist Michael Beck, hoping this movie will do for her what *Down to Earth* did for Rita Hayworth and *One Touch of Venus* did for Ava Gardner. "Inspire" him to do what, you ask? Why, to open a roller-disco nightclub, natch, with the backing of rich, lonely Gene Kelly. (Some favor she's doing them, for such skating palaces faded faster than Pet Rocks.)

After giving Beck only her first name, Newton-John aptly sums up her cinematic appeal when she says, "Listen, you know enough about me already—any more, and you're going to get a headache." Meanwhile, Kelly looks in a mirror and says exactly what we're thinking: "You're getting old." Indeed, his presence effectively makes Newton-John look, well, youngish.

The movie's tacky highlight occurs when Beck and Kelly literally conjure up their visions of their club-to-be, combining the worst of faux '40s musicals with shallow '70s rock, and the two clash together on screen in an electric-orange-jumpsuits-meet-striped-zoot-suits production number that punishes both the eye and the ear—while tickling the funny bone. "I love it," enthuses Kelly, "I may be crazy." (*May be?*)

The madness escalates when Beck and Newton-John take Kelly shopping at Fiorucci—the Eurotrash emporium of the day—which they correctly call "a franchise glitz dealer." Kelly's musical fashion show is one for the ages—he must've been desperate for a comeback to agree to dance as a giant pinball across a pinball game set (because the only other explanation is senility). "We've been painted by Michelangelo, Shakespeare's written sonnets for us, Beethoven's played music for us," Newton-John muses to Beck (never mentioning that now Electric Light Orchestra has wailed for them). "Let's skate!" cries Kelly on the club's opening night, so jugglers, mimes, waiters, and what appear to be Tomorrowland employees all skate in circles, hollering "Ho!" (Someone should have guessed that audiences would be pealing, "Ho, ho, ho!")

With Sandahl Bergman, Matt Lattanzi, and the voices of Wilfrid Hyde-White and Coral Browne. Produced by Larry Gordon, directed by Robert Greenwald. Screenplay by Richard Christian Danus and Marc Reid Rubel. Animation (don't ask) by Don Bluth. C, 88 m., V, L

CHAPTER 21

The Hall
of Shame

This is it. These are them. Not just unintentionally amusing, miscast, overacted, overdirected—overeverything—these are the biggest, the baddest, the side-splittingest of them all: where everything went so deliriously haywire that they're in the Pantheon of Bad Moviedom. Here are the ones that, if they don't get you giggling, you'd better check your pulse. Not only is this final collection supremely, ineffably, gloriously, life-changingly bad, they're also the Bad Movies some of us live by.

So have a ball. But please, exercise caution. We can't predict the long-term consequences of watching more than one in too short a time. Who knows? You, too, might be driven to write a book like this. Or worse, make a Bad Movie of your own.

Beyond the Forest (1949) ❤ ❤ ❤ ❤

"Evil is headstrong—is puffed up," note the titles that preface this fleapit classic, arguably *the* definitive high camp hootenanny. Legend goes that mighty Jack Warner hauled out the tackiest script in his story files and forced it on Bette Davis, double-daring her to walk out again on her studio contract. Well, Hollywood didn't nickname the star Mother Goddamn for nothing, and Davis called Warner's bluff. It's hard to say who came out ahead, except for dyed-in-the-wool fans of Bad Movies We Love.

Riotously miscast as trashy mantrap Rosa Moline, a milltown Emma Bovary, Davis runs rampant, tweezing her brows, toying with her Morticia Addams wig, undulating her hips and breasts, shotgunning porcupines ("I don't like 'em," she snarls), and spitting out what would become her signature phrase, "What a dump!" as she surveys the home she shares with mealymouthed doctor Joseph Cotten. Leaving no co-star or piece of scenery unchewed, Davis murders a witness to her torrid affair with Chicago millionaire playboy David Brian, gets pregnant, and gulps poison.

It doesn't kill her, however—it seems nothing can because she's driven to one day make it to the Big City and Live It Up. "If I don't get out of here, I'll die," Davis says, in chest-heaving closeup, then adds, "If I don't get out of here, I hope I'll die." Take it from a character in Lenore Coffee's "I-can't-believe-I'm-hearing-this!" screenplay: "It's tough on a girl like Rosa living in a town like this." Shoots back another: "It's tough on the town." Ain't it the truth, girls.

Finally, frustrated Davis whips herself into such a frenzy, she dumps her hubby and sashays to Chicago—the locale Max Steiner's loco music evokes whenever wanderlust overtakes Davis—where her rich beau jilts her, largely, one suspects, because of such crimes of fashion as grisly makeup and godawful frocks.

Back to helltown she slumps, but we'll be damned if by the time that Davis, dying—of lust fever or something—drags herself one final time to the railroad tracks, where she expires, she hasn't grabbed you by the throat with full-throttle star power. "You're somethin' for the birds," says a character of Rosa Moline, to which Davis spits back, "And you're something to make the corn grow tall." Exactly.

With Ruth Roman, Dona Drake, Regis Toomey. Produced by Henry Blanke, directed by King Vidor. Screenplay by Coffee, from the novel by Stuart Engstrandt. B&W, 96 m., V

Can't Stop the Music (1980) ♥ ♥ ♥

Steve Guttenberg plays a composer who decides that if he can't make it in show biz, it's "back to dental school" (which is, in real life, where Guttenberg came from). Valerie Perrine, portraying "the Garbo of models," offers to wander around Manhattan to round up singers who can do justice to Guttenberg's songs, and starts her search by "going for a Baskin-Robbins rush"—thus blaming sugar for her selection of the Village People as this movie's stars of tomorrow (the only other guilty party besides sugar might be producer Allan Carr).

This late '70s disco group made up of chorus boy types had only one gimmick: They decked themselves out in fantasy "macho" regalia—one as a cop, another as a cowboy, plus a construction worker, a G.I., a leather-wrapped bad boy, and yes, an Indian. Model agency magnate Tammy Grimes puts it succinctly when she growls, "There's really no accounting for taste."

With a basso profundo voice that makes her sound like a drag queen, Grimes acts like one when she eyes Bruce Jenner: "Fruit-of-the-Loom is doing a big ad campaign, and something tells me you could really fit into a pair of jockey shorts." (He's soon stripped to his boxers, with both Perrine and Guttenberg on their knees in front of him—you don't want to know why.)

How lads look in and out of their underwear is the movie's recurring motif, an obsession that swells to epic proportions in the production number "Y.M.C.A.": The Village People prance around a health club singing as male wrestlers pin each other to the mat in geometric patterns (like chorines in a Busby Berkeley musical), Speedo-clad boy bathing beauties dive into a pool (like chorines in an Esther Williams musical), and naked dudes lather up one another in the shower (like nothing you've ever seen before).

Answering the question "Whatever Happened to Baby June?" Gypsy Rose Lee's kid sis, June Havoc, turns up to observe that the Village People are "just like Judy Garland at Carnegie Hall" (actually, they're just like Garland's audience) and to tell her son, Guttenberg, "It's your music that's bringing all these boys together—they ought to get down on their knees!" Such double entendres run in the family, for when Perrine needs courage, Guttenberg assures her that "anybody who could swallow two Sno-Balls and a Ding-Dong shouldn't have any trouble with pride!"

It's Perrine who gets the most telling line of all: "This is the '80s! You're going to see a lot of things you've never seen before." Well, yes, but little did she realize that she, Jenner, the Village

People, and Allan Carr musicals weren't going to be among them. Nobody saw this movie, which might have been more aptly titled "Can't Stand the Music."

With Paul Sand, Leigh Taylor-Young, Selma Archerd. Produced by Carr, Jacques Morali and Henri Belolo. Directed by Nancy Walker (any guesses why she never directed another feature?). Screenplay by Bronte Woodard and Carr. C, 117 m., V

The Cobweb (1955) ❤ ❤ ❤ ❤

"There it is—the house of Usher!" announces angst-ridden artiste John Kerr as Gloria Grahame drives him up to the mental clinic where he's under doctors' care. Kerr remarks that the staff "is getting ready to hang new drapes in the library. One look, and all the patients will hang themselves. Everybody's tilted here— you can't tell the patients from the doctors." "I can," says Grahame, who's married to Richard Widmark, head of the clinic. "The patients get better." A snappy retort, to be sure, but dead wrong—we can't tell the patients or the doctors from the moviemakers, who were clearly mad to tackle this saga of the deep psychological crises sparked by . . . new drapes.

Grahame phones a pal in Chicago, even though "they shouldn't allow me within a hundred miles of material when there's a budget involved," and impulsively orders costly drapes from her swatch of "Chippendale rose on antique satin." Meanwhile, at the patients' "self-government" meeting, Widmark learns that they want, long, need to design and silk-screen the new drapes themselves, based on Kerr's childlike paintings for, as Oscar Levant notes, he's "the Cezanne of psychos."

Grahame tells her plan to ancient administrator Lillian Gish, who snaps that she'd prefer "a few swatches of money" from Grahame's friend, and when reminded that the pal "has been chairman of the board for five years," Gish says, dismissively, "Sprung up like a toadstool overnight!" then—yes—orders cheapo drapes.

Widmark tells his paramour, art therapist Lauren Bacall, "if we can make this work," perhaps Kerr will view them as "good parents." Bacall tries explaining this to Gish, who calls her "a cat's-paw" and snarls, "Muslin cartoons, indeed!"

Out on the town, Grahame and lonely married psychiatrist Charles Boyer both finger her swatch of fabric, and he murmurs, "Either we starve or we look for it outside." When Widmark worries, "We'll have so many drapes you could wrap the clinic up in them!" Grahame rages, "I don't care if they never go up," but wishes he'd pay more attention to her and their kids: "Yesterday in school they asked Rosie what she wanted to be when she grew up. Like to know what she answered? 'A patient'!" Then Grahame goes wild and hangs up her drapes, causing Kerr to run away and the patients to go loco, throwing a drunken party (a "wake," we're told, to "mourn" their drapes)!

Sure, you've guessed that Widmark tears down the fancy drapes, but who'd ever guess that when Kerr stumbles in, half dead, that Grahame would make up a bed for him on the sofa, using those drapes as sheets? *Warning*: You'll never look at your Levolors the same way again. Not yet available on videocassette, this movie is reason enough to purchase a laserdisc player.

With Susan Strasberg, Tommy Rettig, Fay Wray. Produced by John Houseman, directed by Vincente Minnelli. Screenplay by John Paxton; from William Gibson's novel; additional dialogue by Gibson. C, 124 m., L

The Fountainhead (1949) ❤ ❤ ❤

When headstrong rich girl Patricia Neal, flicking a riding crop, gets a gander at visionary architect-turned-manual laborer Gary Cooper ramming his long, thick drill into her daddy's hard granite quarry, she flips into Bad Girl, Bad Movie heaven. You know the symptoms: an overpowering compulsion to heave the bosom, tear wildly at one's lustrous hair with manicured fingers, flare nostrils, chomp scenery.

Why, in her very first moments in this rococo classic, Neal swishes to her penthouse window and feverishly hurls out—no, let's hear her explain it: "I had a statue which I found in Europe—a statue of a god. I was in love with it. But I broke it.

I threw it down the airshaft so that I wouldn't have to love it." Got that? You ain't heard nothin' yet for, every time we're sure Neal's head has hit the top, damned if she just doesn't raise the ceiling.

Things really steam up when Neal, who's being wooed by fabulously corrupt magnate Raymond Massey, again encounters fabulously incorruptible Cooper at a party celebrating Cooper's daring new skyscraper. "I wish I'd never seen your . . . building," she tells Cooper. Apparently still thinking of his long drill, she adds, "It's the things that we admire or want that enslave us. And I'm not easy to bring into submission." (Not to judge from this performance, anyway.)

Though Neal warns Cooper how the mediocre masses will make him suffer for his genius ("They hate you for the greatness of your achievement!" she booms, rolling her eyes like the next Bette Davis—thinking again about that big drill), Cooper rebuffs her, so she weds Massey, despite having admitted, after their first kiss, "You see, I suppose I'm one of those freaks you hear about. A woman completely incapable of feeling." Massey hires—who else?—Cooper to design a tribute to Neal on five hundred Connecticut acres: "a temple to Dominique Wynand." (Five hundred thousand acres wouldn't begin to be a large enough plot of land to do justice to Neal's bravura badness here.)

When Cooper's designs for an urban housing project are altered, and the result is a compromised monstrosity, Neal helps him dynamite it to rubble—a scandal that nearly topples both Cooper and Massey. It all ends when Massey shoots himself, clearing the way for our lovers to come together in what is, even for a movie packed with out-there Freudian symbolism, an eye-popping finish. Neal rides up a long, long, long construction elevator to the top of the city's tallest skyscraper where Cooper, legs astride, stands waiting. Michael Cimino has talked about remaking this. Soon, Michael, soon, before Oliver Stone gets the idea.

Produced by Henry Blanke, directed by excess-meister King Vidor (*Duel in the Sun, Ruby Gentry, Beyond the Forest*). Screenplay by Ayn Rand, whose novels are considered unfilmable, and this movie proves it. Based on her novel. B&W, 114 m., V, L

The Greatest Show on Earth (1952) ❤❤❤❤

Hurry, hurry, hurry, folks, step right up to your video store counter and rent the all-time weirdest, screwiest, funniest Best Picture Oscar-winner. Ancient hambone Cecil B. DeMille scored big with this sawdust saga of . . . well, let the maestro himself speak his hilarious narration: "Men and beast, through flood and mud and heat and storm and adversity! Fourteen hundred souls! Each sure the season will bring his heart's desire!"

A three-ring hootfest awaits in the hot rivalry on the flying trapeze between scenery-guzzling Betty Hutton and beefy Cornel Wilde, plus the hot rivalry between Hutton and sultry elephant girl Gloria Grahame for wooden-Indian circus boss Charlton Heston, all of it interspersed with circus acts, a song warbled on a trampoline by Hutton, another in a Hawaiian pageant featuring former sarong gal Dorothy Lamour (with cameos by her *Road* movie co-stars Bob Hope and Bing Crosby!), and yes, James Stewart as a clown who harbors a Terrible Secret.

Ordered by his backers to economize, Heston barks, "You can't put fourteen hundred people out of work because the world has a stomachache!" The solution? Hire crowd-pleasing aerialist Wilde, which makes Hutton flare, "The audiences are going to be looking at me!" They stage such death-defying competitions ("They're workin' without nets!" gasps Grahame) you expect them to sing "Anything You Can Do, I Can Do Better" from Hutton's recent hit *Annie Get Your Gun*.

Anxious to swing with Wilde after the show, Hutton exults, "We're not people up there, we're like two streaks of light with wings!" Meanwhile, Grahame's elephant man, Lyle Bettger, figuring Grahame's got the hots for Wilde, seethes, "Your hair is too red, your legs are too thin, you have lips like a cat," then thumping his heart, adds, "but you make a fire, here!" Hutton upstages Wilde with a one-armed rope swing that lasts, like, years till Heston—knowing the rope is (oh no!) frayed!—lowers her down.

Hutton is fighting mad but later she melts when Wilde says, in a Maurice Chevalier–style French accent, "Some women are like sweet Sauterne, some are warm like Burgundy . . ." leaving out that some are just, well, the supremely overconfident, unbelievably grating Betty Hutton. Then Wilde takes a near-fatal plunge and is reduced to selling popcorn because, as Hutton puts it, "He's tied to a dead arm for the rest of his life. A claw hand!"

The fun peaks when Grahame's guy causes a supposedly spectacular wreck of what's obviously a model circus train. You'll be hoping the animals leap from their cages to devour the cast, but instead Stewart sacrifices himself to the police by revealing his Terrible Secret (he's actually a doctor who murdered the woman he loved) so he can treat Heston, who is bleeding to death. Rare blood-type donor Wilde boasts, "If he should make love well after this, it will be me!" Tons o' fun.

Produced and directed by DeMille. Screenplay by Fredric M. Frank, Barre Lyndon, Theodore St. John; story by Frank, St. John and Frank Cavett. C, 151 m., V, L

Kitten With a Whip (1964) ❤❤❤

Long before Ann-Margret proved she could act, she proved that she couldn't—and this little-known "dangerous youth" gem demonstrates just how completely the studios failed to find quality scripts for the promising young wildcat. Instead, she was handed films that could have hurtled her into Starlet Hell, stuff that gave her no chance to show what she could do. (It all worked out surprisingly well, since flicks like this gave A-M something really bad to come back from.)

We can hardly hope to sum up *Kitten With a Whip* any better than its original advertising copy ("This is the story of Jody . . . the kicks she digs . . . the swingers she runs with . . . and the special kind of hell she can make for a man!!!") but, nevertheless, we're gonna try. This laugh-out-loud yarn warns you to beware of befriending pouty teen temptresses (who only exist in crazed Hollywood movies like this one in the first place), lest you wind up being held prisoner in your own suburban home. (Would the tabloids cry out, "I WAS HELD CAPTIVE BY A KITTEN WITH A WHIP"?)

That's exactly the fearful fate that befalls trusting married man John Forsythe when his wife is away for the weekend, and he can't help being nice to sometimes-schizo runaway A-M, who has broken into his home after escaping a juvenile hall straight out of *Caged*. We're told on a TV newscast, "She stabbed the matron after setting fire to the girls' detention quarters." As a bad girl who wants to be good (but can't seem to help herself), when A-M's not smearing lipstick over a framed photo of Forsythe's wife, she's bumpin' and grindin' and growling out such camp classic dialogue as "Why do you think you're such a smoky something when you're just nothing painted blue?"

When her bad-news pretty-boy pals Peter Brown and Skip Ward show up, the party kicks into high gear, and A-M behaves as if what she'd been studying in reform school was Go-Go Dancer Poses and Pouts 101. Working without a script, a director, or a net, A-M has more costume changes than facial expressions (and she doesn't have many costume changes). It all ends, as hothouse soap operas like this must, with Tragedy in Tijuana. Now *here's* a movie begging to be remade.

With Patricia Barry, Richard Anderson, Ann Doran, Audrey Dalton. Produced by Harry Keller, directed by Douglas Heyes. Screenplay by Heyes, from the novel by Wade Miller (if you find a copy, please send it to us). B&W, 83 m., TV

Moment by Moment (1979) ❤ ❤ ❤ ❤

At the height of their popularity, Lily Tomlin and John Travolta combined their considerable clout—and lookalike shag hairdos—to bring their careers to a halt with this screamingly funny melodrama about a Beverly Hills matron's fling with a studly young gigolo. Written and directed by Tomlin's longtime collaborator Jane Wagner, the movie commits two fatal errors: This ripe-for-parody trash is (inexplicably) played straight-faced, and Travolta's character is (even more inexplicably) named "Strip." Every time Tomlin speaks his name, she seems to be asking him to peel—even when he's already naked, as in the hot tub scene that made audiences cry with laughter. Travolta: "I love you. Do you love me?" Tomlin: "Strip . . ." Travolta: "You don't love me?" Tomlin: "Oh, Strip . . ." Travolta: "I'm not good enough for you, is that it?" Tomlin: "Strip! This is ridiculous. Oh, Strip!" Travolta: "When you're ready to admit you love me, you can have me, but not until." Tomlin: "Strip!"

Names are not, however, the only problem. Tomlin's meant-to-be-heartbreaking (but-we're-afraid-they're-side-splitting!) telephone conversations with her estranged husband go thus: "Trish," says the husband's voice, "we've got to talk . . . What about the pool filter?" Tomlin replies, sadly, "What about it?" "What do you want me to do?" he asks. "You decide," she says, before collapsing in tears.

As embarrassing as all this is, Tomlin never stoops to Travolta's level. He agreed to be photographed from the waist down while tugging off his pants so the camera can lovingly stare at his, uh, bathing suit as he bumps 'n' grinds his way down into the sea. (And what was he thinking of when he agreed to call Tomlin such catchy nicknames as "Miss Ultra-Frost" and "Miss Fabu-Lash"?)

What was anyone thinking of when they decided not to cut out the howler scene in which Travolta says, "I've had it with cheap sex, it leaves me feeling cheap," and Tomlin replies, "I've never had cheap sex before—I was sort of looking forward to it."? Then there's the foot fetish show at an art gallery, where Tomlin informs Travolta, "I don't like to see you drink so much at your age," and he responds, "I'm not so young as I used to be—and this party's going to turn me gray overnight." (It's amazing that the movie's reviews didn't do just that.)

After they fight, Travolta says, "I'm splitting. Pretty soon you'll be old enough to be my grandmother." "Where will you go?" Tomlin asks. Travolta runs through his options: "Maybe Vegas. A rich lady asked me to go to St. Tropez," then adds, in the film's only believable moment, "I got offered a porno movie." When he's gone, Trish runs through the house, calling "Strip, Strip, Strip, Strip!" then, embarks, wide-eyed, on a drive through Trailer Park America to find the hustler she loves. Want to sign our petition to get it released on video?

With Andra Akers. Produced by Robert Stigwood, directed by Wagner. Screenplay by Wagner. C, 105 m., TV

Mommie Dearest (1981) ❤❤❤❤

Here's one that separates the fainthearted from the strong. Faye Dunaway, in the role she was born to play, is deeply, deeply scary as Joan Crawford who, according to daughter Christina's best-selling book, tyrannized her kids almost beyond belief. The moviemakers surely expected to be rolling in dough and acclaim for this posh version of a red-hot literary property, so imagine their surprise when audiences rolled in the aisles. Why? Dunaway. So over-the-top, so out-there, so, well, *Faye*, she instantly installed herself as the all-time Contessa of Camp.

The fun begins when Dunaway, as aging MGM star Crawford, realizes that her career's skidding, so everyone around her catches hell. Wailing at her maid as she shoves aside a huge potted plant, Dunaway cleans the floor herself, saying, "You have to move the tree! I'm not mad at you. I'm mad at the dirt."

Mad is right: Figuring that, since she can't have children, she'll reap fabulous publicity by adopting one, enter orphan Christina, who isn't the cooperative dream child Dunaway envisioned. When the kid gets sassy, Dunaway locks her up. Out of work, Dunaway gets battier, cursing her studio boss while she jogs: "The biggest female star he's got—ever had—and he's burying me alive. Survive! Survive!" and demonically chopping off Christina's hair when she finds the kid mimicking her, snarling, "I'd rather you go bald to school than looking like a tramp!" She lays into lover-lawyer Steve Forrest, so when he starts to walk out, she pleads with him to stay, crying, "I'm not acting!" while doing nothing but.

When MGM drops her, brace yourself for full frontal Faye as she rampages in the middle of the night, cutting the blooms off her prize roses, then bellowing "Tina—bring me the axe!" Don't miss the scene where Dunaway, her face covered in a cold-cream Kabuki mask, trashes her daughter's clothes closet, shrieking "No wire hangers!" then showers the bathroom floor with Dutch Cleanser, ordering Christina to clean up the mess. This is capped with the most bizarre closeup in movie history, as Dunaway s-l-o-w-l-y turns her head away while staring out cross-eyed into space. (It's anybody's call whether Crawford's supposed to be insane, or whether Dunaway perhaps just went bonkers playing her.)

Dunaway clashes with grownup Christina too, nearly strangling her child in full view of a horrified magazine reporter. Widowed by a Pepsi magnate, Dunaway stuns a board meeting of executives who try to shove her out of the picture by uttering, "Don't fuck with me, fellas, this ain't my first time at the rodeo."

In the end, Crawford cuts both kids out of her will. "As usual, she has the last word," says grownup Christopher. "Does she?" asks Christina. No, we do, and we declare *Mommie Dearest* about as high in the Bad Movie pantheon as it is possible to go.

With Diana Scarwid, Mara Hobel. Produced by Frank Yablans, directed by Frank Perry. Screenplay by Yablans, Perry, Tracy Hotchner, and Robert Getchell based on Christina Crawford's book. C, 139 m., V, L

The Oscar (1966) ❤❤❤❤

Bad Movie nirvana beckons in this foot-stompingly funny movie about a louse who stomps all over other louses to reach the top of the Hollywood dung heap.

We fade in at an Oscar ceremony where, since Bob Hope is positively slaying the celebrity audience, we know it's a period fantasy. Personal manager Tony Bennett (making his movie debut—and farewell) stares bitterly at Best Actor nominee Stephen Boyd, while musing, "Here you sit on top of a glass mountain called success." Cue in the flashback in which, years before, Boyd, Bennett, and stripper Jill St. John are stiffed out of their earnings by a shady club owner. They blow town for New York, where Boyd is invited to a "swinging party in the Village," and encounters Elke Sommer posing like a Chanel model. "You a tourist or a native?" he asks. Her response? "Take one from Column A and two from Column B—you get an eggroll either way." Boyd speaks for us all when he quips, "You make my head hurt with all that poetry."

He ditches St. John—who doesn't tell him that she's carrying his child—when super talent scout Eleanor Parker spots that certain something in Boyd. She and superagent Milton Berle pitch

Boyd to studio mogul Joseph Cotten, who seems to know what that certain something is: "Once in a while, you bring me meat like this. It all has different names: prime rib of Gloria, shoulder cut of Johnny. Meat!"

Cotten signs Boyd while Bennett, in voice-over, explains Boyd's meteoric rise: "He wanted to swallow Hollywood like a cat with a canary."

Making movies by day, at night Boyd services the voracious Parker, who bellows from her bed, "I'm not some sort of garbage pail you can slide a lid on and walk away from!" For no apparent reason, Boyd marries Sommer, but soon, he's back to tomcatting around. "He used them like Kleenex," Bennett tells us, "once and threw 'em away."

When Boyd's movies bomb, we're treated to a dream sequence that ranks high in the Bad Movie annals—whirling smoke and bad actors mouthing bad dialogue from Boyd's past. Boyd lands an unexpected Oscar nomination, so he hatches his master plan to win the sympathy vote by paying slimy detective Ernest Borgnine to leak the story of how Boyd had once been accused of a morals charge. (Boyd believes the voters will think one of the other nominees leaked the story.) "You most be suffering from oxygen starvation," Bennett says, disapprovingly. "You lie down with pigs, you come up smellin' like garbage."

During the final Oscar ceremony, Boyd gets a hooty come-uppance we wouldn't dream of spoiling for you. Essential, hallucinatory viewing before you ever watch another Academy Awards ceremony.

With Ed Begley, Edie Adams, Walter Brennan, Hedda Hopper, Peter Lawford, Merle Oberon. "Presented by Joseph E. Levine." Produced and directed by Russel Rouse. Screenplay by Harlan Ellison, Rouse, and Clarence Greene, from Richard Sale's novel. C, 118 m., V

Sudden Fear (1952) ❤ ❤ ❤ ❤

In this irresistible potboiler, Joan Crawford is Manhattan's greatest playwright and San Francisco's wealthiest heiress, wooed by younger Jack Palance—an actor she once fired. Cue up would-be suspense music, and prepare to laugh.

Tripping, carefree, down stone steps to the bay, Crawford shrugs off Palance's warning that a railing is needed. "Remember what Nietschze said," she chirps, " 'Live dangerously.' " Palance replies, "He's dead." Palance's fellow con artist and lover, Gloria Grahame, turns up to help plot Crawford's demise, even as Crawford is rejecting her lawyer's plea to leave Palance little in her will. "I'm not going to hang onto any man from the grave," she insists.

That night, Grahame and Palance talk privately in Crawford's study. Come morning, Crawford slips into the room to use her futuristic, ultrasophisticated recording device to dictate changes in her will—leaving everything to Palance—but finds she'd absent-mindedly left the machine on. Prepare for your jaw to drop as Crawford dives headlong into a bravura display of Bad Acting, listening in mounting shock, horror, and unrelieved hamminess to the record of Palance's conversation with Grahame.

For seven l-o-n-g minutes, listening to pithy remarks like Palance's "Sometimes when I'm with her, it's all I can do to keep from saying, 'Wise up. Love you? I never loved you, never for one second,' " Crawford goes where no one's ever gone before, gasping, crying, furrowing her brow, shutting her eyes, widening her eyes, darting her eyes from side to side, clamping her hands over her ears.

And that's *before* she hears them plot to kill her. "It'll have to look like an accident," says Palance. "We'll work something out," replies Grahame. "I know a way." The record starts skipping, so Grahame's voice repeats, "I know a way," over and over, thirty-two times while Crawford acts and acts and acts.

What next? She picks up the record and—accidentally breaks it. In bed, Crawford has crazed nightmares of being pushed from a building, her car going off a cliff, Palance smothering her only to wake up and find that she's holding a pillow over her own face!

Delightfully, the fun has just begun, for Crawford—our greatest playwright, remember?—schemes a plan of her own. Suffice to say that it involves several key cast members having personalized stationery, duplicate keys, a bottle labelled "POISON," a hidden gun, Crawford's natural flare for forging signatures, a fall down a staircase, a toy windup dog, a truly crazed "mad scene" into a mirror, and—oh yes—*the random occurrence* that Crawford and Grahame will, *by chance*, wear *exactly* the same color dress, coat, gloves, and scarves.

Funniest of all is that Crawford and Palace got Oscar nominations!

Produced by Joseph Kaufman, directed by David Miller. Screenplay by Lenore Coffee and Robert Smith, based on Edna Sherry's story. B&W, 111 m. Not yet available on video, *Sudden Fear* is reason enough to scour the pages of *TV Guide* and subscribe to cable TV.

Valley of the Dolls (1967) ❤ ❤ ❤ ❤

"You've got to climb Mount Everest to reach the Valley of the Dolls," whispers a voice at the start of *Valley of the Dolls*, which is the Mount Everest of Bad Movies About Show Biz. Hollywood filmmakers forget what little they ever knew about scripts, acting, and taste when they "tell all" in exposés of the entertainment industry and the ruthless machinations of people who are—well, just like them!

It's extremely unusual for a box office smash to not help the careers of its three stars, but perhaps the clue to why that happened to the trio of hopefuls here is contained within the dialogue. Barbara Parkins: "I'm not an actress." Sharon Tate: "I don't have any talent." Patty Duke: "You call this acting?" (No, Patty, we call it Bad Acting, of the very highest order.) In a typical exchange with her put-upon Hollywood husband, Martin Milner, who nags, "You're spending a lot more time than necessary with that fag Ted Casablanca," Duke bellows back, "Ted Casablanca is not a fag, and I'm the dame who can prove it!"

Duke was already an Academy Award–winning star when she hurled herself off this cliff—hopelessly miscast as the booze-swilling, pill-popping, Judy Garlandesque screen queen "Neely O'Hara"—and since both her singing and her dancing are dubbed in, it's too bad Duke didn't have someone phone in her acting too. Susan Hayward, who actually replaced the real Judy Garland to play an Ethel Merman–type Broadway monster, is another Oscar-winner slumming here, and she's no slouch in the scenery-chewing department herself. So when Hayward and Duke square off for a wig-pulling cat fight in the ladies' room, *Valley of the Dolls* soars into Bad Movie Heaven.

Confined to a mental ward after a nervous breakdown, Duke sings a duet with another star who's wasting away from a terminal disease. (The other mental patients then break into applause—and you will, too.) Duke eventually descends to drunkenly rolling around in the alley outside the very theater where she was once a great star.

Preposterous claptrap, you say? Two decades after making *Dolls*, Duke was co-anchoring L.A.'s live TV coverage outside the 1986 Academy Awards (quite a comedown for any one-time Oscar winner—outside looking in) when, in a moment as crazed as anything ever dreamed by the "writers" who pen trashy bestsellers about Hollywood, then-current Oscar nominee Anne Bancroft stopped by to chat. The two had, of course, both won Oscars for their teamwork in *The Miracle Worker* twenty-four years before. We were devastatedly disappointed when Duke "forgot" to include this scene in the TV movie of her own not-quite-tell-all autobiography, *Call Me Anna*.

With Tony Scotti, Lee Grant, Paul Burke. Produced by David Weisbart, directed by Mark Robson. Screenplay by Helen Deutsch and Dorothy Kingsley, from Jacqueline Susann's novel. C, 123 m., V, L

Zandalee (1991) ❤❤❤

It's quite a while before it sinks in fully that this movie isn't an *Airplane* or *Hot Shots*–style send-up of such trash classics as *9½ Weeks* and *Wild Orchid*, but just utterly deadpan, unintentionally funny moviemaking. The plot's the ol' eternal triangle between impotent businessman Judge Reinhold, studly TV repairman Nicolas Cage, and owner of a boutique for cross-dressers Erika Anderson.

As Anderson's hubby, Reinhold is given faux–Tennessee Williams speeches that not even a talented actor could manage: When they're both in the buff and he has failed to perform, Reinhold tells Anderson, "I'm just paralyzed—a paraplegic of the soul." Cage sizes up Anderson as a good Catholic and says to her, "Without creativity, without life, then you are truly unable to go straight up the Devil's ass, look him right in the face, smile, and survive." Needless to say, Anderson is repulsed yet somehow attracted (because there's no movie if she's not—but then, there's no movie anyway).

When they meet on the street, Cage whispers a come-on line worth memorizing: "We're inevitable. I want to shake you naked and eat you alive, Zandalee!" She drops her panties in response, then goes to his loft where he fingerpaints her naked torso blue. (This movie should do for blue fingerpaint sales what *9½ Weeks* did for the sale of ice cube trays.) In a scene that is like a parody of every hot sex scene of the past decade, *Zandalee* tops the lovemaking-in-the-kitchen-sink sequence from *Fatal Attraction* with Anderson and Cage doin' it atop a rumblin' clothes dryer, with this added fillip: Reinhold, friends, and family are awaiting dessert in the dining room just outside!

Another day, Cage confronts Anderson on the street, demanding, "Why'd you marry him?" When Anderson says, "He was a poet," Cage sticks his paw down her jogging shorts and heads south, asking, "Isn't this poetry?" Back in his loft, she draws herself up off Cage and claims, "I can't be what you want me to be." "Yes, you can," he assures her. "Roll over on your stomach." While your eyes are popping out of your head, Cage then mixes together olive oil and cocaine and, uh, applies it topically to Anderson's nether regions, while pondering, "Where else can you express this need?" (This movie should do for olive oil sales what this movie should do for blue fingerpaint sales.)

Now here's the kicker: Everything described above happens in the movie's first hour. We haven't told you about the second hour, in which Reinhold and Cage slow dance (each fighting to lead); and in which Cage tells Anderson, "When I go in my kitchen and I make toast, I smell your skin"; and in which Cage seduces Anderson in her Catholic church, taking her by force—from behind—inside the confession booth (when he's finished, Cage rolls his eyes heavenward and rasps, "Thank you, Father!"). Our sentiments exactly.

With Joe Pantoliano, Viveca Lindfors, Zach Galligan. Produced by William Blaylock and Eyal Rimmon, directed by Sam Pillsbury. Screenplay by Mari Kornhauser. C, 100 m., V

Selected Bibliography

Agee, James. *Agee on Film*. New York: Perigee, 1960.

Anger, Kenneth. *Hollywood Babylon*. New York: Dell, 1981.

Cameron, Ian and Elisabeth. *Broads*. London: Movie Magazine Limited, 1969.

Consumer Guide. Best, Worst and Most Unusual: Hollywood Musicals. New York: Beekman House, 1983.

Core, Phillip. *Camp—The Lie That Tells the Truth*. New York: Delilah, 1984.

Dmytryk, Edward. *It's a Hell of a Life but Not a Bad Living*. New York Times Books, 1978.

Fane, Frankie. *Hollywood Is a Four-Letter Word (as told to Hymie Kelly)*. Madrid: Cartegena, 1970.

Finler, Joel. *The Hollywood Story*. New York: Crown, 1988.

Halliwell, Leslie. Edited by John Walker. *Halliwell's Film Guide* (7th ed.). London: HarperCollins, 1991.

———. *Halliwell's Filmgoer's and Video Viewer's Companion* (10th ed.). New York: Perennial Library, 1990.

Hamblett, Charles. *The Hollywood Cage*. New York: Hart, 1969.

Harvey, Stephen. *Directed by Vincente Minnelli*. New York: Museum of Modern Art, Harper & Row, 1989.

Kael, Pauline. *5001 Nights at the Movies*. New York: Holt Rinehart and Winston, 1982.

Lawson, Helen. *My Broadway, My Way*. New York: Diva, 1974.

Maltin, Leonard. *Leonard Maltin's Movie and Video Guide 1993*. New York: Signet, 1992.

McClelland, Doug. *Hollywood Talks Turkey—The Screen's Greatest Flops*. Boston: Faber and Faber, 1989.

Morden, Ethan. *Movie Star: The Women Who Made Hollywood*. New York: St. Martin's, 1983.

———. *The Hollywood Studios*. New York: Knopf, 1988.

———. *Medium Cool*. New York: Knopf, 1990.

Negulesco, Jean. *Things I Did and Things I Think I Did*. New York: Simon and Schuster, 1984.

O'Hara, Neely. *Riches to Rehab to Reno to Recovery*. Center City, MN: Hazeldon, 1979.

Peary, Danny. *Cult Movies*. New York: Dell, 1981.

———. *Cult Movies 1*. New York: Dell, 1983.

———. *Cult Movies 2*. New York: Simon and Schuster, 1988.

———. *Cult Movie Stars 3*. New York: Simon and Schuster, 1991.

Peters, Neal, and David Smith. *Ann-Margret—A Photo Extravaganza and Memoir*. New York: Delilah, 1981.

Pilar, Miriam. *The True Story Behind "Valley of the Dolls."* Los Angeles: Rhino, 1970.

Quinlan, David. *Quinlan's Illustrated Registry of Film Stars*. New York: Holt, 1991.

Scagnetti, Jack. *Movie Stars in Bathtubs*. New York: Jonathan David, 1975.

Schatz, Thomas. *The Genius of the System*. New York: Pantheon, 1988.

Shipman, David. *The Great Movie Stars—The Golden Years*. New York: Hill and Wang, 1970.

———. *The Great Movie Stars—The International Years*. New York: Hill and Wang, 1972.

Stallings, Penny. *Flesh and Fantasy*. New York: Harper and Row, 1978.

Weldon, Michael. *The Psychotronic Encyclopedia of Film*. New York: Ballantine, 1983.

Index

Abdul, Paula, 136
Adams, Catlin, 64
Adams, Edie, 289
Adams, India, 132
Adams, Maud, 16–17
Adams, Nick, 229
Aherne, Brian, 84
Ajaye, Franklyn, 64
Akers, Andra, 286
Akins, Claude, 144
Albee, Edward, 247
Albert, Edward, 60, 193, 194
Albert, Edward, Jr., 163
Albert, Katherine, 30
Albertson, Jack, 190
Alda, Alan, 151
Alda, Robert, 23
Aldrich, Robert, 72, 122, 123
Alexander, Jane, 253
Alexander, Ronald, 51
Alexandre of Paris, 241, 252
Algren, Nelson, 153
Allen, Corey, 184
Allen, Elizabeth, 108
Allen, Irwin, 177, 178, 185,
    190, 191, 192, 193, 194,
    195, 201

Allen, Lewis, 142
Allen, Peter, 144
Allen, Sheila, 193, 194. *See
    also* Sheila Mathews
Allen, Steve, 266
Alvarado, Trini, 67–68, 270
Amber, Toni, 127
Ambrose, David, 140
Ames, Leon, 49, 107
Anderson, Erika, 292–294
Anderson, James, 52
Anderson, Kevin, 15
Anderson, Michael, 213
Anderson, Richard, 45, 285
Andersson, Bibi, 186
Andress, Ursula, 168
Andrews, Dana, 115, 180
Andrews, Edward, 154
Anhalt, Edna, 233
Anhalt, Edward, 233
Ann-Margret, 85, 86, 204–205,
    210, 238, 239, 242–243,
    284–285
Anthony, Tony, 39
Archer, Anne, 2
Archerd, Army, 246
Archerd, Selma, 280

Arkoff, Samuel, 245, 246
Arlen, Harold, 115
Arnaz, Lucie, 63, 64
Arthur, Beatrice, 65
Arthur, Maureen, 126
Ashley, Elizabeth, 159
Asner, Edward, 85
Asquith, Anthony, 32
Astaire, Fred, 193
Astin, Patty Duke, 191. See also Patty Duke
Astor, Mary, 50, 154
Atkins, Christopher, 174–175
Aumont, Jean-Pierre, 127
Austin, Pamela, 96
Austin, Ronald, 238
Avalon, Frankie, 241–242
Averback, Hy, 91
Avery, Phyllis, 52
Avildsen, John G., 175
Ayres, Lew, 72–73
Aznavour, Charles, 156

Bacall, Lauren, 21–22, 166–167, 280–281
Bacall, Michael, 272
Bacharach, Burt, 267
Bacon, Kevin, 227
Baddeley, Hermione, 11
Baker, Carroll, 115–116, 121–122, 158–159, 188
Baker, Diane, 83
Baker, Herbert, 64
Baldwin, Alec, 266
Baldwin, Daniel, 36
Baldwin, William, 227
Balin, Ina, 107–108
Ball, Lucille, 57, 64
Ballard, Jack, 127

Balsam, Martin, 187
Bancroft, Anne, 173, 292
Bane, Lisa, 146
Bannen, Ian, 147
Baran, Jack, 266
Bardot, Brigitte, 57, 62
Barkin, Ellen, 220–221
Barrie, Barbara, 224, 225
Barry, John, 206
Barry, Patricia, 285
Barrymore, Diana, 30–31
Barrymore, Drew, 18, 100, 111–112
Barrymore, John, 30
Barrymore, Lionel, 106
Bartlett, Hall, 224, 225
Bartlett, Sy, 120
Basehart, Richard, 27
Basinger, Kim, 36–37, 211, 212
Bass, Ronald, 16
Bass, Saul, 152
Bast, William, 254
Bateman, Justine, 269–270
Bauer, Belinda, 172
Baxley, Craig R., 136
Baxter, Anne, 152
Baxter, Keith, 251
Beals, Jennifer, 171–172, 198–199
Beatty, Ned, 201
Beatty, Warren, 54, 94
Beck, John, 262
Beck, Michael, 275–276
Begley, Ed, 245, 289
Behr, Edward, 111
Bel Geddes, Barbara, 41
Bell, James, 145
Bellamy, Ralph, 226

Beller, Kathleen, 253
Belli, Agnostino, 196–197
Bellisario, Donald P., 258
Bellwood, Pamela, 182
Belolo, Henri, 280
Belson, Jerry, 236
Bennett, Belle, 67
Bennett, Charles, 177
Bennett, Constance, 25, 26
Bennett, Tony, 288, 289
Bensen, Greg, 169
Bercovici, Eric, 85
Berenger, Tom, 203, 204, 257–258
Bergen, Candice, 156
Bergen, Polly, 224, 225
Berger, Helmut, 252
Berggren, Thommy, 156
Bergin, Patrick, 8–9, 14–15
Bergman, Alan, 226
Bergman, Marilyn, 226
Bergman, Sandahl, 276
Berle, Milton, 238, 288–289
Berman, Pandro S., 21
Bernard, Joseph, 52
Bernhardt, Curtis, 234
Bernstein, Walter, 254
Besch, Bibi, 124
Bettger, Lyle, 283
Beymer, Richard, 54–55
Bianchi, Edward, 22
Bickford, Charles, 106, 233
Bieber, Rick, 228
Biehn, Michael, 21–22
Bigelow, Kathryn, 14
Billingsley, Jennifer, 79
Bishop, Joey, 187, 188
Bishop, Larry, 245
Bisset, Jacqueline, 38, 151, 162–163, 179, 193, 194, 235–236
Bisson, Alexandre, 26
Black, Karen, 6, 143, 180
Blair, Linda, 180, 200, 201
Blakely, Susan, 186, 193
Blanke, Henry, 31, 278, 282
Blaylock, William, 294
Blees, Robert, 72, 231
Blinn, William, 269
Bloom, Claire, 42–43
Blore, Eric, 113
Blount, Lisa, 266
Bluth, Don, 276
Blyth, Ann, 130–131
Bochner, Lloyd, 116, 124
Boehm, Sidney, 116
Boetticher, Bud, 117
Bond, Ward, 78
Bondi, Beulah, 97
Boone, Richard, 158
Boorman, John, 201, 202
Booth, James, 182
Borchers, Donald, 56
Borden, Lizzie, 9
Borgnine, Ernest, 78, 109, 156, 190, 193, 289
Bovasso, Julie, 273
Bowman, Lee, 154
Boyar, Sully, 64
Boyd, Stephen, 83, 288–289
Boyer, Charles, 267, 281
Bradford, Richard, 199
Brady, Scott, 77
Brando, Marlon, 157, 199–200, 216, 217
Brauner, Asher, 91
Braunstein, George G., 58

Brazzi, Rossano, 88, 89, 95, 156, 204
Brennan, Eileen, 67
Brennan, Walter, 289
Brent, George, 101
Bresler, Jerry, 25, 255
Brian, David, 75, 278
Bridges, James, 215
Bridges, Lloyd, 161, 162
Briggs, Joe Bob, 266
Bronson, Charles, 28
Brooks, Bob, 17
Brooks, Geraldine, 233, 234
Brooks, Louise, 141
Brooks, Richard, 259
Brown, Bryan, 145, 146
Brown, Clancy, 198
Brown, Jim, 236
Brown, Peter, 285
Browne, Coral, 123, 276
Browne, Roscoe Lee, 210, 211
Bruce, Eve, 125
Bruce, Virginia, 53
Bruckheimer, Jerry, 172
Buchanan, James, 238
Bujold, Genevieve, 188, 261, 262
Buñuel, Joyce, 17
Buñuel, Luis, 17
Burke, Paul, 244, 292
Burkhart, Jeff, 91
Burns, Mark, 114
Burstyn, Ellen, 201, 204, 256
Burton, Richard, 27–28, 32, 196–197, 200–201, 222– 223, 251
Busch, Niven, 107
Busey, Gary, 13

Butler, Hugo, 123
Buttons, Red, 122, 190, 193
Byrne, Gabriel, 220, 221
Byrum, John, 127

Caan, James, 79
Caesar, Sid, 180
Cage, Nicolas, 292, 293–294
Cain, James M., 59, 60
Caine, Michael, 110, 191–192, 246–247
Caldwell, Erskine, 144, 145
Cali, Joseph, 124
Callan, Michael, 229, 230
Calley, John, 28
Campos, Rafael, 79
Cannon, Dyan, 125, 126, 225, 226
Capra, Frank, 267
Capucine, 152
Carabatsos, Jim, 212
Cardin, Pierre, 152
Carey, Harry, 107
Carey, Phillip, 74
Carlson, Joel, 60
Carpenter, John, 203
Carr, Allan, 91, 279, 280
Carradine, John, 78, 129, 213
Carrera, Barbara, 194
Carson, Jack, 222, 223
Carter, Jimmy, 13
Cassavetes, John, 3, 4
Cassidy, Ted, 229
Catto, Max, 134
Cattrall, Kim, 10
Cau, Jean, 63
Cavallo, Robert, 269
Cavett, Frank, 284

Chakiris, George, 254, 255
Chamales, Tom T., 109
Chamberlain, Richard, 137, 191, 193
Chandler, George, 74
Chandler, Jeff, 50, 51, 76, 77
Chanel, Coco, 143
Chaney, Lon, 233
Channing, Carol, 241, 242
Chanslor, Roy, 78
Chapman, Priscilla, 22
Charisse, Cyd, 132
Charo, 185
Chayevsky, Paddy, 161, 162
Chong, Rae Dawn, 203
Cimber, Matt, 60
Cimino, Michael, 33, 34, 35, 282
Clapton, Eric, 61
Clark, Dane, 257, 258
Clark, Dick, 246
Clark, Susan, 180
Clemenson, Christian, 19
Cline, Patsy, 265
Close, Glenn, 1, 2, 12
Cobb, Lee J., 210
Coburn, James, 7, 8
Coby, Michael, 103–104
Cochran, Steve, 130, 131
Cochrane, Ian, 169
Coe, Barry, 49
Coffee, Lenore, 142, 278, 291
Coffey, Scott, 270, 271
Cohen, Rob, 127
Cohn, Nik, 273
Cohn, Robert, 230
Colbert, Claudette, 94
Colbert, Robert, 145

Collins, Gary, 179
Collins, Jackie, 104, 114
Collins, Joan, 103–104, 114, 196
Collins, Stephen, 67, 68
Colton, John, 113
Connell, Jane, 65
Connelly, Joe, 85
Connery, Sean, 141, 142
Connors, Mike, 165–166
Conrad, Robert, 92–93
Conried, Hans, 208
Conte, D. Constantine, 212
Convy, Bert, 98, 99
Cook, Carole, 176
Cook, Donald, 101
Cook, Peter, 266
Cook, Roderick, 37
Cooper, Ben, 78
Cooper, Gary, 281, 282
Cooper, Jackie, 125
Cooper, Wyatt, 43
Coote, Robert, 243
Copeland, Joan, 161
Corby, Ellen, 105, 225
Corey, Jeff, 79
Corman, Roger, 36, 182, 184
Cort, Robert W., 146
Cortesa, Valentina, 194
Cortese, Joe, 261–262
Cosmatos, George Pan, 185
Costner, Kevin, 65–66
Cotten, Joseph, 106, 182, 236, 278, 289
Coughlin, Kevin, 245
Cousins, Margaret, 47
Cox, Ronnie, 138
Cozzens, James Gould, 41

Craig, H. A. L., 182
Craig, Yvonne, 41
Crawford, Broderick, 232
Crawford, Christina, 81, 287, 288
Crawford, Joan, 24, 69, 71–72, 73, 74–78, 80–81, 83–84, 131–132, 224, 233–234, 265, 269, 287–288, 289–291
Crenna, Richard, 226
Cresson, James, 65
Crichton, Michael, 8
Crisp, Quentin, 198
Cromwell, John, 105, 162
Crosby, Bing, 283
Crouse, Lindsay, 34, 60, 61
Cruise, Tom, 145–146, 170
Cukor, George, 42, 43
Cummings, Constance, 148
Cummings, Irving, Jr., 177
Cummings, Jack, 259
Cummings, Robert, 159
Cunningham, E. V., 116
Curtis, Bruce Cohn, 204
Curtis, Jamie Lee, 214
Curtis, Tony, 133, 134
Curtiz, Michael, 75

D'Abo, Olivia, 169
Dallesandro, Joe, 117
Dalton, Audrey, 285
Dalton, Timothy, 143
Daltrey, Roger, 63
Daly, Robert, 13
Damon, Mark, 39
D'Angelo, Beverly, 265
Danning, Sybil, 104, 186, 196
Danton, Ray, 31, 43

Danus, Richard Christian, 276
Darren, James, 254, 255
Darwell, Jane, 105
Daves, Delmer, xix, 94, 95, 96, 97, 99, 153, 154
David, Hal, 267
Davidson, John, 186
Davis, Bette, 29, 30, 69–70, 73–74, 78, 165, 166, 255, 277–278
Davis, Luther, 80
Davison, Bruce, 65
Day, Doris, 5–6, 10–11
Dearden, James, 3
De Blasio, Edward, 123
De Concino, Ennio, 197
Dee, Sandra, 23, 27, 97
De Felitta, Frank, 139
De Grunwald, Anatole, 32
De Havilland, Olivia, 69, 72, 73, 79–80, 156, 182, 191, 232–233
Dehner, John, 43
Delaney, Dana, 10, 22
De Laurentiis, Dino, 35, 150, 212
Delay, Claude, 144
Delon, Alain, 186
Delon, Nathalie, 196
De Mille, Cecil B., 283, 284
De Mornay, Rebecca, 4, 5, 58
Deneuve, Catherine, 62
Dennis, John, 41
Dennis, Patrick, 65
DePalma, Brian, 4
Depp, Johnny, 92
Derek, Bo, 168–169, 213
Derek, John, 168, 169
Dern, Bruce, 16

De Salvo, Anne, 214
Deutsch, Armand, 131
Deutsch, Helen, 292
De Vol, Frank, 123
De Vorzon, Barry, 8, 16
Dewhurst, Colleen, 256
Dey, Susan, 7, 8
Diamond, Neil, 63–64
Dickinson, Angie, 95, 96, 199, 222–223
Dillon, Robert, 219
DiMaggio, Joe, 161
Divine, 104
Dmytryk, Edward, 152–153, 159, 166, 196, 197
Doe, John, 266
Doel, Frances, 184
Dolenz, George, 258
Domergue, Faith, 176–177
Donahue, Troy, 23, 92–99, 153, 264
Donaldson, Roger, 146
Donati, Sergio, 213
D'Onofrio, Vincent, 256
Dooley, Paul, 257
Doran, Ann, 285
Douglas, Gordon, 116, 122, 145
Douglas, Kirk, 3, 4, 52–54, 157–158, 163–164
Douglas, Lloyd C., 231
Douglas, MacGregor, 56
Douglas, Michael, 1–2, 228
Dourif, Brad, 203
Down, Lesley-Anne, 206, 253
Downey, Robert, Jr., 8
Drai, Victor, 199
Drake, Charles, 250
Drake, Dona, 278

Drake, Tom, 222, 223
Dru, Joanne, 115
Duggan, Andrew, 43
Duke, Patty, 161, 291–292. See also Patty Duke Astin
Dullea, Keir, 26
Dumbrille, Douglass, 100
Dunaway, Faye, 81, 157–158, 192, 193, 202–203, 237, 244, 265, 287–288
Dunn, Nora, 273–274
Dunne, Dominick, 252
Dunne, Griffin, 22
Dunnock, Mildred, 21, 49–50
Durning, Charles, 3
Duvall, Robert, 199, 253

Eastwood, Clint, 12–13, 116–117
Ebsen, Buddy, 230
Eden, Barbara, 108
Egan, Richard, 96–97
Eisenman, Rafael, 118
Electric Light Orchestra, 276
Elias, Alix, 174
Elizondo, Hector, 22
Elliot, Jane, 85
Elliot, Mama Cass, 226
Elliot, Peter, 209
Elliott, Sam, 220
Ellis, Perry, 61
Ellison, Harlan, 289
Elwes, Cary, 198
Emerson, Hope, 104–105
Engstrandt, Stuart, 278
Epstein, Julius J., 165, 259
Epstein, Philip G., 259
Erickson, Leif, 158

Erman, John, 68
Ertz, Susan, 149
Estrada, Erik, 180
Eszterhas, Joe, 172
Eunson, Dale, 30
Evans, Bob, 83
Evans, Linda, 168, 196
Evans, Robert, 216
Evelyn, Judith, 76
Everett, Chad, 43, 96, 144

Falana, Lola, 210–211
Falk, Rosella, 123
Fancher, Hampton, 95, 96
Fante, John, 153
Fargnoli, Steven, 269
Farrell, Sharon, 126
Farrow, John, 177
Farrow, Mia, 182–183, 239–241
Fassbinder, Rainer Werner, 187
Faulkner, William, 44, 45, 264
Fawcett, Farrah, 129
Fehmiu, Bekim, 156
Feldman, Charles K., 152
Fell, Norman, 180
Fenn, Sherilyn, 55–56
Fenwick, Peg, 251
Ferrara, Abel, 204
Ferrer, José, 51, 191
Ferrer, Miguel, 66
Ferris, John, 4
Field, Betty, 21, 49
Field, Chelsea, 36
Field, Sally, 256
Field, Ted, 146
Fields, Adam, 266
Fields, Freddie, 172–173

Filardi, Peter, 228
Finch, Peter, 122, 123, 148–149, 267, 268
Fine, Mort, 163
Fineman, Irving, 96
Finney, Albert, 7, 8
Fiorentino, Linda, 272
Fisher, Eddie, 20
Fiskin, Jeffrey, 66
Fitzgerald, F. Scott, 119, 120, 258, 259
Fitz-Richard, Arthur, 52
Flack, Roberta, 13
Flannery, Susan, 193
Fleischer, Richard, 64, 150
Fletcher, Louise, 55, 200–201
Flippen, Jay C., 207–208
Fluegel, Darlanne, 202
Flynn, Errol, 30, 31
Foch, Nina, 127
Fonda, Henry, 191, 252
Fonda, Jane, 42, 43, 61–62, 94, 148–149, 152, 199, 200
Fontaine, Joan, 72
Foote, Horton, 200
Forbes, Bryan, 87
Ford, Constance, 96, 144, 224
Ford, Harrison, 206, 207
Foreman, Carl, 195
Foreman, Stephen H., 64
Forrest, Steve, 287
Forster, Robert, 183, 187, 216, 217
Forsythe, John, 25, 26, 285
Fosse, Bob, 274
Fossey, Brigette, 143
Foster, Jodie, 220, 221
Fox, George, 189
Fox, James, 200

Foxworth, Robert, 182
Franciosa, Anthony, 45, 85, 108–109, 242–243
Francis, Connie, 89
Franciscus, James, 59, 153, 162, 193, 194
Frank, Fredric M., 284
Frank, Gerold, 120
Frank, Harriet, 45
Frank, Laurie, 9
Franken, Steve, 183
Frankenheimer, John, 140, 206
Franklin, Sidney, Jr., 132
Frankovich, M. J., 126, 226
Fraser, Brent, 118
Frechtman, Bernard, 63
Frede, Richard, 230
Frederick, Vicki, 138
Freed, Bert, 246
Freeman, Everett, 128
Freeman, Joan, 270
Freeman, Leonard, 145
Frey, Leonard, 16
Friedenberg, Robert, 256
Friedlob, Bert, 30
Frye, William, 181, 182
Fryer, Robert, 65, 130
Furlong, Kirby, 65
Furth, George, 182
Furthman, Jules, 113, 208

Gabor, Eva, 153, 259
Gallagher, Helen, 54
Gallagher, Peter, 175–176
Gallico, Paul, 191
Galligan, Zach, 294
Galloway, Don, 56
Gammon, James, 66

Garcia, Andy, 175
Gardner, Ava, 184, 188, 189, 275
Garland, Beverly, 181
Garland, Judy, 148, 273, 291
Garner, James, 22
Garrett, Oliver H. P., 107
Gary, Lorraine, 185
Gavin, John, 11, 22, 23, 102, 103
Gaynes, George, 225
Gaynor, Mitzi, 29
Gayton, Joe, 271, 272
Gazzara, Ben, 219
Gazzo, Michael V., 203, 204
George, Gladys, 75
George, Susan, 150
Gepova, Sergio Soldan, 197
Gerard, Danny, 35
Gerard, Gil, 181
Gere, Richard, 211, 212
Gershen, Gina, 146
Gertz, Jami, 171
Getchell, Robert, 68, 288
Getz, John, 16
Gibson, William, 281
Gielgud, John, 267–268
Gilbert, Lewis, 156, 157, 274
Gilbert, Paul, 115–116
Gilbert, Sara, 111–112
Giler, David, 130
Gilman, Peter, 255
Gish, Lillian, 106, 280, 281
Givney, Kathryn, 89
Gleason, Jackie, 241, 242
Gless, Sharon, 181
Globus, Yoram, 206
Glover, John, 10, 205
Goetz, William, 72

Goff, Ivan, 12, 27
Goff, John, 60
Golan, Menahem, 138, 188, 206
Goldberg, Leonard, 16
Goldman, William, 87
Goldsmith, Jerry, 137
Goldstone, James, 195
Goldwyn, Samuel, Jr., 68
Golino, Valeria, 139
Golonka, Arlene, 182
Goodhart, William, 202
Goodman, David Zelag, 203
Goodman, John, 67
Gordon, Larry, 276
Gordon, Michael, 27
Gordy, Berry, 127
Gorshin, Frank, 89, 241, 242
Gortner, Marjoe, 189
Gould, Heywood, 146
Grade, Lew, 185
Graham, Heather, 271
Graham, Sheilah, 119, 120
Graham, William, 85
Grahame, Gloria, 232–233, 280, 281, 283, 284, 290, 291
Grant, Lee, 181–182, 191, 292
Grauman, Walter, 80
Green, Alfred E., 101
Green, Guy, 165, 255
Green, Janet, 12
Greenberg, Henry, 225
Greene, Clarence, 289
Greene, Ellen, 274
Greene, Lorne, 71, 188
Greene, Shecky, 126
Greenstreet, Sidney, 75
Greenwald, Robert, 276

Greenwood, Bruce, 39
Greer, Dabbs, 56
Greisman, Alan, 270
Grey, Virginia, 25, 26, 27, 251
Grieco, Richard, 92
Griffi, Giuseppe Patroni, 148
Griffin, Eleanore, 23, 103
Griffith, Melanie, 203–204, 228
Grimes, Tammy, 279
Grizzard, George, 108
Guest, Val, 70
Guillermin, John, 193, 209–210
Gulager, Clu, 263
Guttenberg, Steve, 215, 278–279

Hackman, Gene, 160, 189–190, 226
Hagen, Jean, 74
Haggard, H. Rider, 136, 138
Haigh, Kenneth, 104
Hailey, Arthur, 179, 180, 181, 182, 186
Hale, Barbara, 179
Haley, Jack, Jr., 126
Halsey, Brett, 50
Hamady, Ron, 58
Hamel, Veronica, 193
Hamilton, George, 40, 41, 89–90, 91, 165
Hamilton, Linda, 209
Hamlisch, Marvin, 22
Hamner, Earl, Jr., 93
Hannah, Daryl, 3, 175–176
Hanson, Curtis, 5, 20
Harareet, Haya, 230
Hardin, Ty, 42, 92, 93
Harewood, Dorian, 7

Harlow, Jean, 121
Harris, Julie, 216–217
Harris, Richard (actor), 184, 185, 212, 213
Harris, Richard (author), 274
Harrison, Gregory, 229
Harrison, Jim, 66
Harrison, Rex, 11
Harry, Debbie, 270
Hart, Dolores, 89, 90
Hartman, Don, 44
Hartman, Lisa, 91
Hartwell, John, 22
Harvey, Anthony, 216
Harvey, Laurence, 21, 152
Hastings, Michael, 157
Hauer, Rutger, 143, 160, 161
Havoc, June, 279
Hawkins, Screamin' Jay, 56
Hawks, Howard, 58
Hay, Alexandra, 126, 241
Hayden, Sterling, 29–30, 77, 78
Hayes, Helen, 178, 179, 183, 184
Hayes, John Michael, 20, 21, 50, 121, 122, 133, 159, 166
Hayes, Joseph, 35
Hayward, Susan, 102–103, 165–166, 248–249, 255, 291–292
Hayworth, Rita, 32, 275
Head, Edith, 25, 46, 47, 121
Heatherton, Joey, 166, 196–197, 210
Hedley, Tom, 172
Hedren, Tippi, 228
Heeren, Astrid, 245
Heflin, Van, 178–179, 233–234

Heims, Jo, 13
Heisler, Stuart, 30
Heller, Paul M., 241
Hellman, Lillian, 199, 200
Hellstrom, Gunnar, 51
Helm, Anne, 230
Helmore, Tom, 47
Hemingway, Margaux, 172–173
Hemingway, Mariel, 173
Hemmings, David, 126
Henner, Marilu, 214
Hennings, Sam, 272
Henreid, Paul, 74, 200
Henshaw, Jere, 36
Hepburn, Audrey, 10
Herczeg, Geza, 113
Herman, Jerry, 64
Herman, Victor, 231
Herrington, Rowdy, 220
Hershey, Barbara, 210
Hervey, Irene, 12–13
Herzog, Arthur, 192
Heston, Charlton, 46, 47, 51–52, 180, 188, 254–255, 283
Hewitt, Martin, 55, 170–171
Heyes, Douglas, 285
Heyman, John, 241
Hill, Arthur, 148
Hill, Gladys, 217
Hill, James, 134
Hill, Jesse Ford, 211
Hill, Robert, 77
Hill, Steven, 162
Hiller, Arthur, 260
Hilton, James, 268
Hingle, Pat, 47
Hirt, Al, 96
Hitchcock, Alfred, 1, 5, 264

Hobel, Mara, 288
Holbrook, Hal, 245
Holden, William, 193, 194
Holland, Anthony, 124
Holland, Betty Lou, 162
Holland, Erik, 10
Holland, Kristina, 225–226
Holloway, Jean, 26
Holly, Buddy, 265
Holman, Libby, 166
Hooks, Robert, 182
Hope, Bob, 283, 288
Hopkins, Anthony, 34
Hopkins, Miriam, 199, 200
Hopper, Hedda, 289
Hornaday, Jeffrey, 271, 272
Houseman, John, 149, 281
Hudson, Ernie, 4
Hudson, Hugh, 218
Hudson, Rock, 166, 167, 182–
    183, 204, 230–231, 250–
    251, 263–264
Hughes, Finola, 272
Hughes, Howard, 176, 207,
    208
Hughes, Wendy, 117–118
Hugueny, Sharon, 94, 95, 224
Hull, Henry, 199
Hume, Doris, 99
Humphries, Dave, 115
Hunter, Evan, 54
Hunter, Jeffrey, 47, 48
Hunter, Ross, 11, 23, 26, 27,
    103, 179, 230, 231, 250,
    251, 267, 268
Hurst, Fannie, 23, 102, 103
Husmann, Ron, 25
Hussey, Olivia, 267–268

Huston, John, 66, 129, 130,
    216, 217
Huston, Virginia, 75
Huston, Walter, 106, 112, 113
Hutchins, Will, 144
Hutton, Betty, 283–284
Hutton, Brian, 247
Hutton, Jim, 89
Hyams, Peter, 207
Hyde, Johnny, 161
Hyde-White, Wilfrid, 249, 276
Hyer, Martha, 84, 159, 199,
    200, 237–238
Hyland, Diana, 199

Illiff, W. Peter, 14
Ingalls, Don, 181
Inge, William, 54, 55
Ireland, John, 81
Irving, Amy, 3–4
Irwin, Bill, 274
Isaacs, Anthony Rufus, 37
Ives, Burl, 43, 44, 56

Jackson, Mahalia, 23
Jackson, Michael, 135
Jacobs, Emma, 114
Jaffe, Rona, 82, 84
Jaffe, Stanley R., 3
Jagger, Dean, 95
James, Rian, 74
Jameson, Jerry, 182
Janis, Conrad, 180
Janssen, David, 164, 165, 250
Jarre, Maurice, 199
Jarrott, Charles, 263, 268
Jeffrey, Howard, 8
Jenner, Bruce, 215, 279

Jennings, Claudia, 126
Jevne, Jack, 72
Jewison, Norman, 244, 245
Johns, Glynis, 42, 142
Johnson, Arch, 210
Johnson, Ben, 191
Johnson, Bruce, 204
Johnson, Don, 35, 45, 228, 229
Johnson, Lamont, 173
Johnson, Lyndon, 13
Johnson, Lynn-Holly, 91
Johnson, Nunnally, 73
Johnson, Van, 130, 131, 258–
    259
Jones, Carolyn, 127–128
Jones, Christopher, 245
Jones, Grace, 220, 221
Jones, Henry, 223
Jones, James Earl, 201
Jones, Jennifer, 51, 52, 106,
    193
Jones, Tommy Lee, 202–203,
    252–253, 260
Jordan, Richard, 271
Joseph, John, 85
Jourdan, Louis, 6, 7, 32, 83,
    88, 89
Julia, Raul, 203
Jurgens, Curt, 151

Kabilju, Alfi, 139
Kaczender, George, 144
Kahn, Madeline, 65
Kallianiotes, Helena, 160
Kanter, Jay, 247
Kass, Ronald S., 114
Kastner, Elliot, 247
Kaszner, Kurt, 258

Kaufman, Joseph, 291
Kazan, Elia, 157, 158
Kazan, Lainie, 187
Keach, Stacy, 59, 60
Keith, Brian, 85, 216, 217
Keith, Robert, 167
Kellaway, Cecil, 76
Keller, Harry, 285
Kellerman, Sally, 267
Kellin, Mike, 64
Kellogg, Virginia, 105
Kelly, Gene, 127, 128, 275–
    276
Kelly, Jack, 7
Kelly, Orry, 148
Kennedy, Arthur, 49, 96, 145
Kennedy, George, 169, 178–
    179, 181, 182, 186, 187,
    189, 267
Kennedy, Jacqueline, 162
Kensit, Patsy, 207
Kernochan, Sarah, 37
Kerr, Deborah, 71, 119–120,
    157, 158
Kerr, John, 280–281
Kershner, Irwin, 202, 203
Kerwin, Brian, 209
Kiley, Richard, 171
King, Harry, 173
King, Henry, 120
King, Perry, 149, 150, 173
King, Zalman, 33, 37, 38, 39,
    55, 56, 117, 118
Kingsley, Dorothy, 292
Kinsey, Dr., 42
Kinski, Nastassia, 218
Kirby, Bruno, 228
Kirkland, Jack, 150

Kirkland, Sally, 66
Kirkwood, Gene, 175
Klein, Calvin, 216
Kleiser, Randall, 175, 176
Knight, Shirley, 170, 171
Knop, Patricia Louisiana, 37,
    39, 221
Koch, Howard W., 165
Koch, Howard W., Jr., 175
Koepp, David, 20
Kohner, Susan, 23, 41
Kolker, Henry, 101
Korngold, Erich, 137
Kornhauser, Mari, 294
Koteas, Elias, 35
Kotero, Apollonia, 268, 269
Kotto, Yaphet, 211, 245
Kovack, Nancy, 54, 115
Kovacs, Ernie, 53
Krabbe, Jeroen, 211
Krakowski, Jane, 274
Kramer, Larry, 268
Kramer, Stanley, 232, 233,
    238, 239
Krieger, Stu, 91
Kristel, Sylvia, 186
Kruger, Otto, 107
Kuenstle, Charles, 182
Kurfirst, Gary, 221

La Capria, Raffaele, 148
Ladd, Alan, 158, 159
Ladd, Alan, Jr., 247
Ladd, Cheryl, 111
Lambert, Mary, 221
Lamour, Dorothy, 283
Lancaster, Burt, 71, 133–134,
    178, 179, 184
Landau, Ely, 163

Landis, Jessie Royce, 179
Lang, Jennings, 185, 186
Lange, Hope, 49, 83–84
Langella, Frank, 58
Langlais, Rudy, 9
Lansbury, Angela, 45, 121,
    148–149, 188
Lansing, Sherry, 3
Lapotaire, Jane, 160
Latham, Aaron, 215
Lattanzi, Matt, 276
Lauria, Dan, 37
Law, John Phillip, 125–126,
    185, 241
Lawford, Peter, 74, 115, 116,
    121, 242, 289
Lawrence, André, 85
Lawrence, Elizabeth, 15
Lawrence, Jerome, 65
Lazarus, Paul N., III, 207
Leachman, Cloris, 43
Lean, David, 245
Lederer, Richard, 202
Lee, Christopher, 181
Lee, Edna, 81
Lee, Gypsy Rose, 54
Lee, James, 85
Lee, Robert E., 65
Lee, Ruta, 128
Leger, Jack Alain, 262
Le Gros, James, 14
Lehman, Ernest, 108
Leigh, Janet, 207–208
Leighton, Margaret, 246
Leimbach, Marti, 256
Leisen, Mitchell, 58
Leitch, Donovan, 58
Lemmon, Jack, 181
Lennox, Annie, 218

Leonard, Elmore, 204, 206
Leonard of London, 199
Levant, Oscar, 280
Levin, Don, 139
Levin, Henry, 90
Levin, Ira, 87
Levine, Joseph E., 17, 115,
116, 121, 122, 159, 166,
289
Levy, Michael I., 10
Levy, Robert, 14
Lewis, Fiona, 4
Lewis, Jerry Lee, 265, 266
Lewis, Monica, 182, 185–186,
189
Lewis, Myra, 266
Lindfors, Viveca, 115, 294
Liotta, Ray, 123
Lisi, Virna, 196, 197
Lloyd, Sue, 103, 104, 114
Lockhart, June, 60
Lockwood, Gary, 239
Logan, Joshua, 93–94
Logan, Robert, 145, 174–175
Lollobrigida, Gina, 108–109,
133
Long, Richard, 72
Loo, Richard, 254
Loren, Sophia, 43, 44, 184
Losch, Tilly, 107
Losey, Joseph, 240, 241
Louis, Jean, 23, 27, 53, 102,
248
Louise, Tina, 86, 87
Lovejoy, Frank, 7
Lovell, Dyson, 171
Lowe, Rob, 9–10, 18–19
Lowry, Hunt, 66
Loy, Myrna, 11, 107, 180, 181

Lubin, Ronald, 211
Ludwig, William, 103
Luft, Lorna, 91
Lustig, Jan, 133
Lynch, Kelly, 33–34, 146, 219
Lyndon, Barre, 284
Lyne, Adrian, 2–3, 37, 172
Lynley, Carol, xx, 50–51, 54,
85, 86, 190
Lynn, Jeffrey, 21
Lynn, Loretta, 265

Mabry, Moss, 125, 224
MacArthur, James, 230
McBain, Diane, 94, 144–145,
225
McBride, Jim, 266
McCambridge, Mercedes, 77–
78, 123, 185
McCargo, Marian, 225
McCarthy, Andrew, 139–140
McCarthy, Sheila, 274
McClure, Doug, 205
McCormick, Kevin, 256
McCormick, Patrick, 258
McCowen, Alec, 207
McCoy, Matt, 4, 5
McCullers, Carson, 217
McDonald, Christopher, 91,
118
McDonald, Daniel, 91
MacDougall, Ranald, xix, 81,
109, 234
McDowall, Roddy, 11, 190
McEnery, Peter, 62
McGavin, Darren, 181
McGillin, Howard, 91
McGiver, John, 65

MacGraw, Ali, 215–216, 255, 259–260
McGuire, Dorothy, 88, 96–97, 98
McKay, Gardner, 85
Mackie, Bob, 59, 273
MacLaine, Shirley, 20, 116–117
McMahon, Ed, 60
MacMurray, Fred, 191
McNair, Barbara, 84
McNamara, Maggie, 88
McNichol, Kristy, 56
McPartland, John, 48
McQueen, Steve, 192, 193, 244–245
Macready, George, 74
Madden, Ben, 152
Madden, David, 5
Madonna, 63
Magnoli, Albert, 269
Maharis, George, 115, 116, 237, 238
Mahin, John Lee, 47
Majors, Lee, 210
Malden, Karl, 51, 52, 74, 94
Malone, Dorothy, 30, 31, 167, 263–264
Maltz, Albert, 117
Mamet, David, 60
Mankiewicz, Don M., 43
Mankiewicz, Tom, 185
Mann, Delbert, 21, 44, 249
Mann, Stanley, 142
Mannix, Bobbi, 275
Mansfield, Jayne, 59
Marcovicci, Andrea, 186
Markey, Gene, 101
Markham, Monte, 182

Marlow, Lucy, 80, 81
Marquand, Christian, 262
Marquand, Tina, 62
Marsh, Mae, 7
Marshall, E. G., 199
Marshall, Garry, 236
Marshall, Herbert, 11, 106, 225
Marshall, Penny, 236
Martin, Andrea, 274
Martin, Dean, 178, 179, 248–249
Martin, Dean-Paul, 215
Martin, Jared, 124
Martin, Pamela Sue, 190
Martin, Quinn, 152
Martinelli, Elsa, 32
Marvin, Lee, 187, 233
Marx, Groucho, 241
Mason, James, 149–150
Mason, Marsha, 67
Mason, Morgan, 28
Mason, Pamela, 246
Massey, Raymond, 233–234, 282
Masters, Quentin, 114
Masterson, Mary Stuart, 87
Masterson, Peter, 86–87
Masur, Richard, 207
Mathews, Sheila, 185, 193. See also Sheila Allen
Matthau, Walter, 53–54, 188–189
Mature, Victor, 113
Maugham, Somerset, 27
Mayersberg, Paul, 161
Mayes, Wendell, 191, 262
Mazurski, Mike, 113
Medford, Kay, 21

Melcher, Martin, 7, 11–12
Mell, Marisa, 127
Meltzer, Lewis, 72
Mercouri, Melina, 44, 164
Meredith, Burgess, 26, 193, 194
Mergendahl, Charles, 222, 223
Merrill, Dina, 21
Merrill, Gary, 69–70
Metalious, Grace, 48, 50, 51, 153
Mewshaw, Michael, 140
Meyer, Russ, 56
Middleton, Robert, 264
Midler, Bette, 67–68
Miles, Vera, 71, 102–103
Milford, Penelope, 171
Milian, Tomas, 66
Milius, John, 13
Milla, 56
Milland, Ray, 260
Millard, Oscar, 74
Miller, Arthur, 161
Miller, David, 12, 103, 291
Miller, Jason, 261
Miller, Wade, 285
Miller, Winston, 47
Mills, Donna, 12, 13
Milner, Martin, 30, 31, 291
Mimieux, Yvette, 89–90, 254–255
Minnelli, Liza, 273–274
Minnelli, Vincente, 28, 281
Minsky, Howard G., 260
Mirisch, Walter, 41
Mitchell, Cameron, 47, 48
Mitchell, Thomas, 41, 72, 73
Mitchum, Robert, 176–177, 204, 232–233, 240

Monica, Corbett, 235
Monroe, Marilyn, 54, 55, 161
Montalban, Ricardo, 25
Moore, Joanna, 152
Moore, Juanita, 22–23, 56
Moore, Roger, 259
Moore, Terry, 49
Moorehead, Agnes, 104–105, 231, 250–251
Mora, Phillipe, 61
Morali, Jacques, 280
More, Julian, 144
Morgan, Henry, 132
Morita, Pat, 194
Morris, Edmund, 153
Morris, Richard, 85
Morse, David, 35
Mortimer, Chapman, 217
Moses, Rick, 183
Movieline magazine, xix, xx
Moyle, Allan, 9
Munson, Ona, 112, 113
Murcell, George, 139
Murray, Anne, 228
Murray, Barbara, 70
Murray, Don, 170, 171
Murray, Jan, 203

Napoleon, Art, 31
Napoleon, Jo, 31
Neal, Patricia, 281–282
Neame, Ronald, 190
Neeson, Liam, 270
Negulesco, Jean, 58, 82, 84, 85, 86, 89
Nelson, Barry, 179
Nelson, Craig T., 135, 136
Nelson, David, 49
Nelson, Ed, 181

Nesbitt, Cathleen, 89
Nettleton, Lois, 59
Neumann, Kurt, 262
Newman, Laraine, 214
Newman, Nanette, 87
Newman, Paul, 45, 107, 108, 192, 193, 194
Newman, Walter, 230
Newton, Helmut, 203
Newton-John, Olivia, 275, 276
Nicholas, Paul, 64
Nichols, Barbara, 90
Nichols, Mike, 247
Nicholson, James H., 246
Nielsen, Leslie, 121, 190
Nilsson, Harry, 242
Nixon, Cynthia, 16
Nixon, Richard, 13
Nolan, Jeanette, 182–183
Nolan, Lloyd, 26, 49, 98, 179
Norris, Chuck, 187
North, Edmund H., 76
North, Sheree, 47
Norton, Ken, 150
Nouri, Michael, 171, 172
Novak, Kim, 52–54, 122–123
Nuyen, France, 254, 255
Nye, Louis, 54

Oberon, Merle, 289
Obregon, Ana, 168, 169
O'Brian, Hugh, 24
O'Brien, Edna, 247
O'Brien, Liam, 134
Occipinti, Andrea, 169
O'Connor, Carroll, 226
O'Hara, Gerry, 104
O'Hara, John, 20, 21, 108
O'Herlihy, Dan, 23

Oliver, Susan, 20, 225
Olivier, Laurence, 63–64, 252–253
Onassis, Aristotle, 162, 263
O'Neal, Griffin, 152
O'Neal, Patrick, 87, 107
O'Neal, Ryan, 259–260
O'Neal, Tatum, 152
O'Neill, Eugene, 43, 44
Onstott, Kyle, 150
Oscar (Academy Award) nominations, 2, 5, 49, 179, 249, 283, 291–292
O'Sullivan, Maureen, 176, 240
Otis, Carré, 38
Ouspenskaya, Maria, 113
Overton, Frank, 43
Owens, Patricia, 47–48

Pacino, Al, 217–219
Page, Genevieve, 153–154
Page, Geraldine, 198
Paige, Janis, 224
Palance, Jack, 289–291
Palmer, Betsy, 80
Paltrow, Gwyneth, 272
Paluzzi, Luciana, 50
Pankow, John, 139
Pantoliano, Joe, 294
Paris, Jerry, 225, 236
Parker, Corey, 37
Parker, Eleanor, 50–51, 104, 105, 288–289
Parker, Sachi, 20
Parker, Suzy, 83, 229, 230
Parkins, Barbara, 151, 291
Parks, Michael, 237, 238
Parrish, Robert, 47
Parry, Natasha, 11

Pasternak, Joe, 90
Patrick, Dorothy, 132
Patrick, John, 89
Patrick, Lee, 105
Patten, Luana, 109
Paul, Don Michael, 36
Paxton, John, 281
Pearce, Richard, 212
Peck, Gregory, 106, 120
Peerce, Larry, 252
Penn, Arthur, 199, 200
Peppard, George, 158, 159
Perkins, Anthony, 43, 44, 127
Perkins, Millie, 56, 246
Perlman, Milton, 162
Perrine, Valerie, 278–280
Perry, Frank, 262, 288
Perry, Luke, 92
Pesci, Joe, 160
Peters, Jean, 88
Peters, Jon, 202, 203
Petrie, Daniel, 254
Petrie, Donald, 223
Petty, Lori, 14
Pevney, Joseph, 77
Phillips, Britta, 270
Phillips, Lee, 49
Phillips, Michelle, 138
Piccoli, Michel, 61–62
Pidgeon, Walter, 258
Pierson, Frank, 238
Pillsbury, Sam, 294
Pine, William H., 47
Pisier, Marie-France, 142–
    144, 262–263
Platt, Oliver, 227
Pleshette, Suzanne, 95–96,
    153
Plowright, Joan, 218

Plummer, Christopher, 206–
    207
Pointer Sisters, 136
Polaire, Hal W., 139
Poll, Martin H., 116
Polonsky, Abraham, 262
Ponti, Carlo, 185
Porter, Don, 154
Posner, Vladimir, 73
Post, Ted, 229
Powers, Stephanie, 24, 92, 93,
    229–230
Preminger, Otto, 241, 242
Prentiss, Paula, 86, 87, 89
Presley, Elvis, 84, 145, 242,
    246
Pressburger, Arnold, 113
Pressfield, Steven, 210
Pressman, Edward, 111, 140
Preston, Kelly, 205
Preston, Robert, 65
Previn, André, 240
Price, Nancy, 16
Priggen, Norman, 241
Prince, 136, 268–269
Principal, Victoria, 189
Prouty, Olive Higgins, 67, 68
Pryor, Richard, 245
Puzo, Mario, 189

Quaid, Dennis, 265–266
Quennessen, Valerie, 175, 176
Quested, John, 104
Quick, Ben, 45
Quine, Richard, 54
Quinlan, Kathleen, 182
Quinn, Anthony, 26–27, 65,
    66, 162–163, 237–239, 263
Quintano, Gene, 138

Racklin, Martin, 117
Raffin, Deborah, 164–165
Railsback, Steve, 138
Rainey, Ford, 145
Rains, Claude, 177
Raksin, David, 115
Rambeau, Marjorie, 131, 132
Rampling, Charlotte, 212–213
Rand, Ayn, 282
Randall, Bob, 22
Randall, Shawn, 125
Randall, Tony, 47, 48
Ransohoff, Martin, 263
Rappaport, David, 198–199
Rapper, Irving, 70, 128
Rascoe, Judith, 171
Rattigan, Terence, 32
Raucher, Herman, 263
Ravetch, Irving, 45
Ray, Aldo, 115
Ray, Nicholas, 78
Raye, Martha, 185
Rayfiel, David, 173
Reagan, Ronald, 13
Reddy, Helen, 180
Redford, Robert, 86, 199, 200
Reed, Carol, 134
Reed, Donna, 258
Reed, Rex, 129
Reeve, Christopher, 261–262
Reeves, Keanu, 13, 14
Reinhold, Judge, 292–293
Reisner, Dean, 13
Remick, Lee, 45
Reneau, Robert, 136
Rettig, Tommy, 281
Rey, Fernando, 156, 262
Reynolds, Debbie, 20

Reynolds, William, 250
Rhodes, Cynthia, 172, 272
Rhys-Davies, John, 137
Rice, Tim, 22
Rich, David Lowell, 186
Richards, Beah, 127
Richards, Silvia, 52, 234
Richardson, Tony, 127
Riklis, Meshulam, 59
Rimmer, Robert H., 228, 229
Rimmon, Eyal, 294
Ritt, Martin, 45, 48
Ritter, Thelma, 46
Robards, Jason, Jr., 40–41
Robbins, Harold, 123, 125,
    155, 157, 158, 159, 165,
    166, 254
Roberts, Ben, 12, 27
Roberts, Julia, 14–15, 227,
    255–256, 270
Roberts, Marguerite, 25, 255
Roberts, Meade, 55, 149
Roberts, Pernell, 43–44
Roberts, Rachel, 226
Robertson, Cliff, 24, 71–72,
    229, 230
Robson, Mark, 50, 108, 189,
    292
Roddam, Franc, 199
Roeg, Nicolas, 159, 160, 161
Rogers, Mimi, 34
Roman, Lawrence, 243
Roman, Ruth, 24, 278
Romero, Cesar, 241
Rooney, Mickey, 242
Rose, Helen, 108
Rosenberg, Aaron, 109
Rosenthal, Mark, 35

Ross, Diana, 126–127
Ross, Katharine, 86–87, 191, 253
Rossellini, Franco, 148
Rossellini, Isabella, 221
Rossovich, Tim, 7
Rosten, Leo, 177
Roth, Eric, 186
Roundtree, Richard, 189
Rourke, Mickey, 2, 33–39, 56, 160
Rouse, Russel, 289
Rubel, Marc Reid, 276
Ruben, Andy, 112
Ruben, Joseph, 16
Rubin, Mann, 84
Rubin, Stanley, 66
Ruffalo, Joseph, 269
Rule, Janice, 199–200, 226
Rush, Barbara, 47, 48, 53–54, 176, 223, 231
Rush, Deborah, 174
Russell, Theresa, 160–161
Rutherford, Margaret, 32
Ryan, Robert, 125
Ryder, Winona, 266

Sacks, Michael, 207
Saint, Eva Marie, 28
St. Clair, Ana, 224
St. John, Frank, 284
St. John, Howard, 89
St. John, Jill, 288
St. John, Nicholas, 204
Saks, Gene, 65
Sale, Richard, 289
Salkind, Alexander, 197
Sampson, Will, 213

Sand, Paul, 280
Sands, Diana, 226
Sands, Julian, 220, 221
Sarandon, Chris, 172, 173
Sarandon, Susan, 262, 263
Sarne, Michael, 129, 130
Savage, Mildred, 95
Savalas, Telly, 230
Savant, Doug, 10
Sawyer, Mary, 130–131
Saxon, John, 27
Scalia, Jack, 203
Scarwid, Diana, 288
Scavullo, Francesco, 172
Schaal, Wendy, 90–91
Schaefer, George, 226
Schaefer, Natalie, 76
Schaffner, Franklin, 55
Scheff, Michael, 182
Scheider, Roy, 204–205
Schell, Maximilian, 215, 216
Scherick, Edgar J., 87
Schnee, Charles, 21
Schoenfeld, Bernard, 105
Schubert, Karin, 197
Schulman, Arnold, 216
Schulman, Irving R., 121
Schumacher, Joel, 227, 228, 256
Schumacher, Martha, 209
Schweitzer, S. S. "Paddy," 85
Schygulla, Hannah, 187
Sciorra, Anabella, 4, 5
Scola, Kathryn, 101
Scott, Allan, 23
Scott, Campbell, 255–256
Scott, Martha, 180
Scott, Tony, 66

Scott, Zachary, 75
Scotti, Tony, 292
Seagal, Steven, 211
Seal, Charles, 79
Seaton, George, 179
Seberg, Jean, 178–179
Secondari, John, 86, 89
Sedaka, Neil, 89, 91
Segal, Erich, 239, 260
Selby, David, 256
Selleck, Tom, 130
Selzer, Milton, 122
Selznick, David, 105–107
Selznick, Joyce, 139
Serna, Assumpta, 39
Shaw, Irwin, 44
Shea, Katt, 112
Shear, Barry, 246
Sheen, Martin, 184
Sheinberg, Sidney, 185
Sheldon, Sidney, 262, 263
Shepherd, Cybill, 45, 267
Sherwood, Madeleine, 95
Shields, Brooke, 170–171
Shields, Teri, 171
Shigeta, James, 267
Shore, Roberta, 54
Shue, Elisabeth, 146
Shusett, Ronald, 210
Sidney, George, 243
Siegel, Don, 12, 116, 117
Siegel, Sol C., 86, 89
Siemaszko, Nina, 117–118
Silke, James R., 138
Silliphant, Stirling, 191, 192,
    193, 195, 211
Silver, Amanda, 5
Silver, Joel, 136, 220
Silver, Murray, 266

Silverstein, Elliot, 238
Simmonds, Robert, 272
Simmons, Richard Alan, 77
Simon, Paul, 63
Simpson, Don, 172
Simpson, O. J., 184, 193
Sinatra, Frank, 88, 232, 240
Singer, Alexander, 25
Siodmak, Robert, 73
Sirk, Douglas, 23, 167, 231,
    250, 251, 263, 264
Skala, Lilia, 172
Skerritt, Tom, 111–112, 117
Skinner, Frank, 251
Slaughter, Frank G., 225, 226
Sloane, Everett, 41
Smith, Alexis, 164
Smith, David Lowell, 26
Smith, Jaclyn, 156
Smith, Kent, 54
Smith, Maggie, 32
Smith, Robert, 291
Smith, Shawnee, 35
Snodgress, Carrie, 3, 174
Sommer, Edith, 84, 86
Sommer, Elke, 288, 289
Sorel, Louise, 91
Sothern, Ann, 79, 115
Spacek, Sissy, 265
Spader, James, 19, 170
Spangler, Larry G., 144
Spano, Vincent, 58
Spark, Muriel, 148
Sparv, Camilla, 163
Spector, David, 182
Spelling, Aaron, 270
Spencer, Scott, 171
Sperling, Milton, 128, 223
Spiegel, Sam, 200, 238

Stack, Robert, 166–167, 223–225, 263–264
Stallone, Sylvester, 272, 273
Stanley, Kim, 161
Stanwyck, Barbara, 67, 68, 100–101, 152
Stapleton, Maureen, 21–22, 178
Stark, Ray, 217
Steel, Anthony, 70
Steiner, Max, 97, 278
Steppling, John, 206
Sterling, Jan, 76, 105
Sterling, Robert, 51
Stern, Richard Martin, 193
Sternhagen, Frances, 61
Stevan, Robyn, 274
Stevens, Andrew, 3–4
Stevens, Connie, 92–93, 94, 97–99
Stevens, Dennis F., 229
Stevens, Robert, 149
Stevens, Stella, 190
Stevens, Warren, 26
Stevenson, Robert, 208
Stewart, Alana, 91
Stewart, Fred Mustard, 152
Stewart, James, 182, 283, 284
Stigwood, Robert, 22, 272, 273, 286
Stiller, Jerry, 180
Sting, 198, 199
Stockwell, Guy, 181
Stone, Andrew, 7
Stone, Harold, 43
Stone, Oliver, 282
Stone, Sharon, 135–140
Storch, Larry, 181
Stowe, Madeleine, 65, 66

Straight, Beatrice, 170
Strasberg, Lee, 184, 185, 245
Strasberg, Susan, 187, 281
Streisand, Barbra, 202, 269
Strieber, Whitley, 60, 61
Sturges, John, 41
Sullivan, Barry, 7, 80, 142
Sullivan, Tom, 182
Susann, Jacqueline, 125, 126, 163, 165, 292
Sutherland, Donald, 218, 227
Sutherland, Kiefer, 226–227
Svenson, Bo, 187
Swaim, Bob, 10, 111
Swalha, Karim Nadim, 110
Swanson, Gloria, 64, 180, 181
Swarthout, Glendon, 90, 91
Swayze, Patrick, 14, 219, 220
Swift, David, 230
Sykes, Brenda, 150, 210

Tabori, George, 241
Talbott, Gloria, 250
Taradash, Daniel, 225, 226, 263
Tate, Sharon, 291
Taurog, Norman, 93
Taylor, Elizabeth, 18, 20–21, 27–28, 32, 108, 116, 146–147, 216–217, 239–241, 246–247, 251–252, 258–259
Taylor, Lisa, 202
Taylor, Rod, 32
Taylor, Samuel, 126
Taylor-Young, Leigh, 7, 156, 280
Terrio, Denny, 174
Tetzel, Joan, 107

Tewkesbury, Joan, 174, 175
Theroux, Paul, 111
Thinnes, Roy, 180
Thom, Robert, 123, 246
Thomas, Gordon, 195
Thomas, Jeremy, 161
Thomas, William C., 47
Thompson, Hilary, 3
Thompson, J. Lee, 137, 138, 163
Thompson, Morton, 233
Thompson, Victoria, 228
Three Dog Night, 247
Thulin, Ingrid, 185
Tierney, Gene, 86, 100, 112– 113, 115
Tiffin, Pamela, 85, 86
Tighe, Kevin, 220
Tilly, Meg, 9–10
Tinti, Gabrielle, 123
Tisch, Steve, 20
Tobias, Oliver, 113–114
Todd, Russell, 91
Tolo, Marilu, 162, 163, 196
Tomlin, Lily, 285–286
Toomey, Regis, 85, 278
Tramont, Jean Claude, 252
Travolta, John, 213–215, 271– 273, 275, 285–286
Trevor, Claire, 46, 54, 127– 128
Trumbo, Dalton, 28
Turkel, Ann, 184
Turner, Cheryl, 23, 165
Turner, Lana, xx, 18–19, 22– 27, 40–41, 48–49, 141– 142, 165
Twomey, Anne, 257–258

Tyson, Cicely, 185
Tyson, Richard, 55–56

Ullmann, Liv, 215, 267
Ustinov, Peter, 215

Vaccaro, Brenda, 164, 181–182
Vadim, Roger, 57–58, 61–63
Valli, Alida, 185
Vallone, Raf, 121, 163, 263
Van, Bobby, 267
Van Dyke, Jerry, 92, 93
Vanity, 135, 136, 205
Van Patten, Joyce, 65
Van Runkle, Theodora, 244
Varsi, Diane, 48–49, 245–246
Vaughn, Robert, 187, 193, 225
Vennera, Chick, 257
Vidal, Gore, 129, 130
Vidor, King, 51, 52, 107, 278, 282
Vidov, Oleg, 39
Vilas, Guillermo, 215
Village People, 279–280
Villechaize, Herve, 56
Von Sternberg, Josef, 112, 113, 207, 208
Von Sydow, Max, 200
Von Zerneck, Frank, 272

Wagner, Jane, 285, 286
Wagner, Robert, 186, 193
Wald, Jerry, 45, 47, 48, 50, 51, 55, 75, 81, 84, 105, 120, 234
Walken, Christopher, 60–61
Walker, Arnetia, 8
Walker, Jimmie, 186

Walker, Nancy, 280
Walker, Robert, Jr., 237
Wallace, Dee, 87
Wallace, Irving, 43
Walston, Ray, 27
Walter, Jessica, 12, 13
Walters, Charles, 132–133
Walters, James, 271
Walters, Julie, 274
Walters, Laurie, 228, 229
Ward, Skip, 285
Warhol, Andy, 117, 147
Warner, David, 186
Warner, Jack, 93–94, 277
Warren, Lesley Ann, 174–175
Warwick, Dionne, 125
Washbourne, Mona, 148
Waters, John, 48, 99
Wayne, John, 101, 207–208
Weathers, Carl, 135, 136
Weaver, Sigourney, 100, 109–110
Webb, Clifton, 88–89
Webb, David, 102
Webb, James R., 134
Webber, Robert, 28, 54, 55
Weidman, Jerome, 131
Weingarten, Lawrence, 249
Weisbart, David, 292
Welch, Raquel, 129–130, 196, 197
Weld, Tuesday, 50–51
Welles, Orson, 31, 32, 44–45, 59–60, 182
Wells, George, 90
Wendkos, Paul, 152
Wenner, Jann, 214
Werner, Michael, 229

West, Mae, 18, 129, 130
Weston, Jack, 245
Weston, Robert, 125, 254
Wexler, Jodi, 125
Wexler, Norman, 150, 273
White, Vanna, 8
Whitman, Stuart, 60
Whitmore, James, 228–229
Whitney, Brad, 13
Whitton, Margaret, 36, 37
Widmark, Richard, 192, 280, 281
Wight, Peter, 103
Wilde, Cornel, 283, 284
Wilder, Robert, 75–76
Wilding, Michael, 132
Wilhoite, Kathleen, 20
Williams, Billy Dee, 126, 127, 203, 204
Williams, Cara, 226
Williams, Clarence, III, 205, 269
Williams, Emlyn, 70
Williams, Grant, 97, 98, 167
Williams, John, 11
Williams, Paul, 199
Williams, Van, 225
Williams, Vanessa, 36
Wills, Chill, 90, 211
Wilson, Michael, 28
Wilson, Sloan, 97
Wincer, Simon, 36
Winfield, Paul, 239
Winkler, Irwin, 219
Winn, Kitty, 201
Winters, Shelley, 42, 187, 189–190, 245, 246, 274

Winwood, Estelle, 74
Wolf, Dick, 10
Wong, Anna May, 27
Wood, James, 8
Wood, Natalie, 29,
    127–128
Woodard, Bronte, 280
Woods, Carol, 274
Woodward, Joanne, 44–45,
    47, 48, 54–55,
    107–108
Worth, Howard, 39
Wouk, Herman, 128, 153,
    154
Wray, Fay, 281
Wright, William H., 74
Wyler, William, 210,
    211
Wylie, I. A. R., 133
Wyman, Jane, 46–47, 230–
    231, 250–251
Wynn, Ed, 127–128
Wynn, Keenan, 213

Wynn, Ned, 131
Wynter, Dana, 179

Yablans, Frank, 4, 263, 288
Yates, Herbert J., 78
Yordan, Philip, 48, 78, 223
York, Michael, 267–268
York, Susannah, 246–247
Young, Gig, 132
Young, Sean, 8–9

Zadora, Pia, 59–60, 123–125
Zane, Lisa, 19
Zanuck, Darryl F., 42, 43, 101
Zanuck, Richard, 42, 43
Zeffirelli, Franco, 170, 171
Zerbe, Anthony, 210–211
Zimbalist, Efrem, Jr., 30–31,
    40–41, 42, 43, 180
Zola, Émile, 61, 62–63
Zuckerman, George, 167, 264
Zugsmith, Albert, 77, 167, 264
Zuniga, Daphne, 257, 258

Index of Movie Titles

Action Jackson, 135–136

Ada, 248–249

Adventurers, The, 155–157

Agnes of God, 10

Airport, 27, 178–179, 191

Airport 1975, xix, 6, 41, 180–181

Airport '77, 181–182, 185

All About Eve, 69

Allan Quatermain and the Lost City of Gold, 137

All That Heaven Allows, 250–251

Ambassador, The, 204

And God Created Woman (remake 1987), xix, 57–58

Another Man's Poison, 69–70

Another Time, Another Place, 141–142

Arrangement, The, 157–158

Ash Wednesday, 251–252

At Long Last Love, 267

Autumn Leaves, 71–72

Avalanche, 182–183

Baby Face, 100–101

Back Street, 102–103

Bad Influence, 18–20

Ball of Fire, 58

Basic Instinct, 135, 138

Beloved Infidel, 119–120

Best of Everything, The, xix, 82–84, 85

Betsy, The, 252–254

Beyond the Forest, xix, 51, 107, 277–278, 282

Beyond the Poseidon Adventure, 94

Big Cube, The, xx

Big Wednesday, 13

Bluebeard, 152, 196–197

Blue Lagoon, The, 174, 175

Body Heat, 33

Bolero, 168–169

Born on the Fourth of July, 145

Bramble Bush, The, 222–223

Bride, The, 198–199

Bus Stop, 55, 161

Butch Cassidy and the Sundance Kid, 192

Butterfield 8, xx, 20–21

Butterfly, 59–60

By Love Possessed, xx, 40–41

Cabaret, 274

Caged, 104–105

Candy, 262

Can't Stop the Music, xx, 275, 278–280

Caretakers, The, xx, 223–225

Carpetbaggers, The, 20, 121, 152, 158–159

Cassandra Crossing, The, 184–185

Cat Women of the Moon, xvii

Chanel Solitaire, 142–144

Change of Habit, xx, 84–85

Chapman Report, The, xx, 42–43

Chase, The, 152, 199–200

Children of Paradise, 112

Chorus Line, A, 273

Claudelle Inglish, xx, 144–145

Cleopatra, 27, 32

Cobweb, The, xx, 280–281

Cocktail, xviii, 145–146

Collector, The, 16

Come Fly With Me, 82, 94

Communion, 60–61

Concorde—Airport '79, The, 185–186

Conversation, The, 1

Crowded Sky, The, 180

Dark Mirror, The, 72–73

Dark Victory, 255

Days of Thunder, xviii

Dead Ringer, xx, 73–74, 94

Delta Force, 186–188

Desire Under the Elms, 43–44

Desperate Hours, 33–35, 61

Dial M for Murder, 11

Diamond Head, 254–255

Diary of Anne Frank, The, 56, 246

Diner, 33

Doctors' Wives, 225–226

Down to Earth, 275

Driver's Seat, 146–148

Duel in the Sun, xviii, xx, 51, 52, 105–107, 282

Dying Young, 255–256

Earthquake, 188–189

Endless Love, 170–171

Eureka, 159–161

Exorcist, 201

Exorcist II: The Heretic, 200–202

Eyes of Laura Mars, 202–203

Fan, The, 21–22

Fatal Attraction, xviii, 1–3, 4, 12, 293

Fear City, 203–204

Female on the Beach, xx, 76–77

52 Pick-Up, 204–206

Flamingo Road, 74–76

Flashdance, 171–172

Flatliners, xviii, 226–228

Follow the Boys, 89

Fountainhead, The, 51, 281–282

From Here to Eternity, 71

From the Terrace, 107–108

Fury, 3–4

Game Is Over, The, 61–63

Goddess, The, xx, 161–162

Go Naked in the World, xx, **108–109**

Grasshopper, The, **235–236**

Grease, 175

Grease 2, 272

Great Balls of Fire, **265–266**

Greatest Show on Earth, The, xviii, **283–284**

Great Waltz, The (1972 re-make), 7

Greek Tycoon, The, **162–163**, 263

Half Moon Street, **109–111**

Hand That Rocks the Cradle, xviii, **4–5**

Hanover Street, **206–207**

Happening, The, xx, **237–238**

Harley Davidson and the Marlboro Man, **35–36**

Harlow, xx, 20, **121–122**, 152

Harrad Experiment, The, **228–229**

Heaven's Gate, xviii

Hotel, 94

Howard the Duck, xviii

How to Marry a Millionaire, 85

Hudson Hawk, xvii, 136

Hurricane, 182

Hurry Sundown, 152

Imitation of Life, xviii, **22–23**, 27, 267

Interns, The, **229–230**

In the Cool of the Day, **148–149**

Ishtar, xvii

Jagged Edge, 2

Jaws, 185

Jazz Singer, The (1980), xx, **63–64**

Jet Pilot, **207–208**

Johnny Guitar, **77–78**

Jonathan Livingston Seagull, 64, 224

Julie, **5–7**

Killer Fish, 173

King Kong Lives, **208–210**

King Solomon's Mines, **136–138**

Kitten With a Whip, xix, **284–285**

Klute, 1, 12

Lady From Shanghai, The, 32

Lady in a Cage, **78–80**

Last Rites, **257–258**

Last Time I Saw Paris, The, **258–259**

Laura, 115

Lawrence of Arabia, **37–38**

Legend of Lylah Clare, The, **122–123**

Liberation of L. B. Jones, **210–211**

Lipstick, **172–173**

Lonely Lady, The, **123–125**

Long, Hot Summer, The (1958), **44–45**

Long, Hot Summer, The (1985), 45

Looker, **7–8**

Looking for Love, 89

Lost Horizon (remake 1973), 27, **267–268**

Love Crimes, 8–9
Love Has Many Faces, 24–25
Love Machine, The, 125–126,
    241
Love Story, 255, 259–260
Lucy Gallant, 46–47

Madame X (1966 remake),
    25–26
Magnificent Obsession, 230–
    231, 251, 267
Mahogany, xix, 126–127
Mame, xix, 64–65
Mandingo, 149–150
Man Who Knew Too Much,
    The, (1956), 264
Marjorie Morningstar, 127–
    128, 153
Masquerade, 9–10
Masquerade in Mexico, 58
Mephisto Waltz, The, 150–152
Meteor, 94
Midnight, 58
Midnight Lace, 10–12
Miracle Worker, The, 292
Moment by Moment, 272,
    285–286
Mommie Dearest, 287–288
Monsignor, 261–262
Morgan, 186
Myra Breckinridge, 129–130

Nanny, The, 4
Nighthawks, 272
Night in Heaven, A, 174–175
9½ Weeks, 2, 15, 36–37, 55,
    292
No Down Payment, 47–48
No Mercy, 211–212

North by Northwest, 1
Not as a Stranger, 232–233
Now, Voyager, 74
Oliver's Story, 260
Once Is Not Enough, 163–165
One Touch of Venus, 275
Orca, xix, 212–213
Oscar, The, 288–289
Other Side of Midnight, The,
    142–143, 226, 262–263

Palm Springs Weekend, 92–
    93
Parrish, xx, 93–95
Perfect, 213–215
Peyton Place, 20, 47, 48–50,
    50, 108
Plan 9 From Outer Space,
    xvii
Players, 215–216
Play Misty for Me, 12–13
Pleasure Seekers, The, xx, 58,
    85–86
Point Break, 13–14
Poison Ivy, 111–112
Portrait in Black, xx, 26–27
Poseidon Adventure, The,
    185, 189–191
Possessed, 233–234
Psycho, 1, 2, 13, 16
Purple Rain, 268–269

Queen Bee, 80–81

Rain, 27
Raise the Titanic!, 182
Rear Window, 1
Rebecca, 4

Reflections in a Golden Eye, 216–217

Return to Peyton Place, 50–51, 153

Revenge, 65–66

Revolution, 217–219

Risky Business, 145

Road House, 219–220

Rome Adventure, xx, 95–96

R.P.M., xx, 238–239

Ruby Gentry, 51–52, 282

Sanctuary, 44

Sandpiper, The, xviii, xx, 27–28

Satisfaction, xx, 269–270

Saturday Night Fever, 272

Scissors, 138–139

Secret Ceremony, 239–241

Sgt. Pepper's Lonely Hearts Club Band, 272

sex, lies, and videotape, 28, 176, 225–226

Shanghai Gesture, The, 112–113

Shout, 271–272

Siesta, 220–221

Silence of the Lambs, 1

Skidoo, xx, 241–242

Slander, 130–131

Sleeping With the Enemy, xviii, 14–16

Slugger's Wife, The, 58

Song Is Born, A, 58

Spartacus, 38

Splash, 176

Star, The, 29–30

Star Is Born, A (1954), 38

Staying Alive, 272–273

Stella, 67–68

Stepford Wives, The, 86–87

Stepping Out, 273–274

Sting II, The, 94

Stolen Hours, 255

Story of Temple Drake, The, 44

Strangers When We Meet, 52–54

Streetcar Named Desire, A, 243

Stripper, 54–55

Stud, The, 103, 104, 113–115

Sudden Fear, 289–291

Summer Lovers, 175–176

Summer Place, A, xx, 96–97

Sunset Boulevard, 64, 112

Susan Slade, 97–99

Swarm, The, 191–192

Swinger, The, xx, 242–243

Sylvia, 115–116

Taming of the Shrew, The, 28

Tarnished Angels, The, 44, 263–264

Tattoo, 16–17

Taxi Driver, 16

Thomas Crown Affair, The, 244–245

Three Coins in the Fountain, xx, 58, 82, 85, 88–89

Three Faces of Eve, The, 54

Tom Jones, 7

Too Much, Too Soon, 30–31

Top Gun, 145

Torch Song, 20, 131–133

Towering Inferno, The, 185, 192–193

Trapeze, 133–134

Two-Moon Junction, 55–56

Two Mules for Sister Sara, 116–117
Two of a Kind, 275

Valley of the Dolls, The, xx, 108, 191, **291–292**
Vertigo, 122
Victory, 272
V.I.P.s, The, 31–32

Walk on the Wild Side, xx, **152–153**
When Time Ran Out . . ., 185, **193–195**
Where Danger Lives, **176–177**
Where Love Has Gone, 23, 152, **165–166**
Where the Boys Are (1960), **89–90**
Where the Boys Are '84, 90–91

Who's Afraid of Virginia Woolf?, 28, 246
Wild Angels, The, 36
Wild in the Streets, xx, **245–246**
Wild Orchid, xx, 15, **37–39**, 55
Wild Orchid 2: Two Shades of Blue, 111, **117–118**
Woman in the Dunes, 16
Written on the Wind, **166–167**

Xanadu, 275–276
X, Y, and Zee, **246–247**

Year of the Dragon, 33
Year of the Gun, **139–140**
Youngblood Hawke, **153–154**

Zandalee, xx, **292–294**
Zero Hour, 180